New essays by an international team of scholars in Latin literature and ancient philosophy explore the understanding of emotions (or 'passions') in Roman thought and literature. Building on recent work on Hellenistic theories of emotion and on philosophy as therapy, they look closely at the interface between ancient philosophy (especially Stoic and Epicurean), rhetorical theory, conventional Roman thinking and literary portrayal. There are fresh, searching studies of the emotional thought-world of a range of writers: Catullus, Cicero, Virgil, Seneca, Statius, Tacitus and Juvenal. Issues of current debate such as the ethical colour of Aeneas' angry killing of Turnus at the end of the *Aeneid* are placed in a broader and illuminating perspective. Written in clear and non-technical language, with Greek and Latin translated, the volume opens up a fascinating area on the borders of philosophy and literature.

THE PASSIONS IN ROMAN THOUGHT
AND LITERATURE

9

45 pos quote

214	STOIC/ARISTOTELIAN
215	ENERGY
222	"
223	FAILURE TO CONTROL

THE PASSIONS
IN ROMAN THOUGHT
AND LITERATURE

EDITED BY

SUSANNA MORTON BRAUND

Professor of Latin, Royal Holloway, University of London

AND

CHRISTOPHER GILL

Reader in Ancient Thought, University of Exeter

CAMBRIDGE
UNIVERSITY PRESS

CAMBRIDGE UNIVERSITY PRESS
Cambridge, New York, Melbourne, Madrid, Cape Town, Singapore, São Paulo

Cambridge University Press
The Edinburgh Building, Cambridge CB2 2RU, UK

Published in the United States of America by Cambridge University Press, New York

www.cambridge.org
Information on this title: www.cambridge.org/9780521473910

First published 1997
This digitally printed first paperback version 2006

A catalogue record for this publication is available from the British Library

Library of Congress Cataloguing in Publication data
The passions in Roman thought and literature / edited by Susanna Morton Braund
and Christopher Gill
p.   cm.
Based on a conference held at the University of Exeter in July 1992.
Includes bibliographical references and indexes.
ISBN 0 521 47391 8 (hardback)
1. Latin literature – History and criticism.   2. Emotions in literature.
3. Philosophy, Ancient.   4. Rome – In literature.
I. Braund, Susanna Morton.   II. Gill, Christopher.
PA6029.E56P37   1997
870.9′353–dc21   96–47371   CIP

ISBN-13 978-0-521-47391-0 hardback
ISBN-10 0-521-47391-8 hardback

ISBN-13 978-0-521-03090-8 paperback
ISBN-10 0-521-03090-0 paperback

Contents

Preface

This volume of new essays is based on a conference on 'Understanding the Passions in Roman Literature and Thought' held at the University of Exeter in July 1992. Eight of the chapters are based on papers given at the conference; three were written specifically for the volume. We would like to thank the British Academy, the Classical Association, the Society for the Promotion of Roman Studies, and the University of Exeter for financial assistance to the conference and to the costs of preparing this book. We are grateful to all those who participated in this conference, as well as to those contributing to the volume; also to Pauline Hire at the Cambridge University Press for her guidance and support, and to the two readers for the Press. Special thanks are due to Kerensa Pearson for her characteristically meticulous secretarial work in preparing the volume for publication.

SMB and CG

Conventions

The abbreviations used for ancient authors and works are normally those given in H. G. Liddell, R. Scott, H. S. Jones, *A Greek–English Lexicon*, 9th edn (Oxford, 1940) (=LSJ) and P. Glare, ed., *Oxford Latin Dictionary* (Oxford, 1982) (=*OLD*). In quoting Latin words, we follow current practice (e.g. that of *OLD*) in using *u* instead of *v* in all words (e.g. *uirtus*, 'virtue') except personal names. All quotations in Latin, Greek and other foreign languages are translated. References within the volume are usually given in this form: 'see Fowler, Ch. 1, Sect. [=Section] 1, text to nn. 3–4'. All modern scholarly works cited (by name and date) are listed in the Bibliography, with the exception of the works listed below, which are cited in abbreviated form:

DK   H. Diels, *Die Fragmente der Vorsokratiker*, rev. W. Kranz, 2 vols., 10th edn (Berlin, 1961)

LS   A. A. Long and D. N. Sedley, *The Hellenistic Philosophers*, 2 vols. (Cambridge, 1987). References are to sections and passages (not pages), unless otherwise indicated

LSJ   Liddell–Scott–Jones (as above)

OLD   *Oxford Latin Dictionary* (as above)

RE   *Real-Encyclopädie der classischen Altertumswissenschaft* (Stuttgart, 1893–)

SVF   H. von Arnim, *Stoicorum Veterum Fragmenta* 3 vols. (Leipzig, 1903–24)

Note also Galen *PHP* (=*De Placitis Hippocratis et Platonis*) (abbreviation not in LSJ), references to books, chapters and paragraphs in De Lacy (1978–84)

Introduction

I About this volume

Susanna Morton Braund and Christopher Gill

This volume of new essays explores the Roman understanding of emotions. Central to our focus are the intense, problematic emotions which are often called 'passions', a term standardly used in connection with the Stoic theory of the emotions.[1] We examine the presentation of these in Roman thought, particularly in philosophy, and in Roman literature. We are especially concerned with the relationship between Roman thought and literature. A central question is whether the most elaborate and famous theory of emotion in the Roman period, the Stoic theory of the passions, is as influential on Roman literature as is sometimes claimed. A special feature of the book is that this question is raised not just in connection with Roman writers who are obviously influenced by philosophy, such as Cicero and Seneca, but also in a range of authors, including Catullus, Virgil, Statius, Tacitus and Juvenal, about whose psychological assumptions there is more room for debate.[2] One of our aims is to develop communication and shared enquiry on this topic between specialists in ancient philosophy and in Latin literature.

In recent years, the subject of Hellenistic theories of emotion and desire has moved increasingly close to the centre of scholarly interest in three interrelated ways.[3] First, the subject has formed part of the

---

[1] Although 'passion' was used in seventeenth–eighteenth-century English as a synonym for 'emotion' (or 'desire'), it is mostly used in modern English to denote an overpowering emotion to which one is, or feels oneself to be, subject or 'passive', and which is to this degree problematic; see *Oxford English Dictionary*, 2nd edn (Oxford, 1989), sense III, 6a. The Stoic theory presents *all* emotions as being of this type, and so is normally described as a theory about 'passions'. On the theory of emotions in general, and on the question whether the analysis and classification of emotions is culture-specific or universal, see Fowler, Ch. 1, Sect. 1; on ancient and modern ways of conceiving 'passions', see K. Cameron (1996).

[2] We do not, of course, attempt to deal, in one medium-sized volume, with *all* the Roman authors who could be considered: on the scope and limits of our project, see further text to nn. 42–4 below.

[3] There is a distinguished tradition of Continental scholarship on this type of subject, including Rabbow (1914), (1954); I. Hadot (1969); P. Hadot (1981); Voelke (1993). But it has only

current upsurge of research on Hellenistic and Roman philosophy. This has produced a number of excellent studies which can help scholars and students make sense of the Stoic and Epicurean theories of emotion and explore the issues that they raise. Long and Sedley (1987) provide a useful collection of sources on the Stoic theory of the passions, and scholars such as Julia Annas, Michael Frede and Brad Inwood have made important contributions.[4] Martha Nussbaum's *Therapy of Desire* (1994) offers a vivid and personal survey of the whole subject. A second important development is the readiness of some scholars to treat the surviving Hellenistic and Roman essays on ethical philosophy as intellectual and literary works in their own right and not just as source material for earlier theories. There is a growing view that it is only if we take into account the distinctive intellectual objectives and literary character of these works that we can gauge properly what they tell us about the earlier Greek theories.[5] A third relevant feature of current scholarship is the interest in exploring the significance of philosophical debate in the Roman period for the interpretation of Latin literature; this interest has been most marked in connection with the interpretation of Aeneas' killing of Turnus at the close of Virgil's *Aeneid*.[6]

This volume makes some contribution to all three of these lines of current scholarly enquiry, but is especially focused on the third.[7] It is organised in a way that enables the reader progressively to explore the question of the relationship between the Hellenistic theories of the emotions or passions and the presentation of certain key passions in different areas of Roman prose and poetry. The book opens with a re-examination (and critique) of the Epicurean conception of anger by D. P. Fowler, analysed in part by contrast with the Stoic view of anger as a passion that should be removed or 'extirpated' completely.

---

recently become a major subject of Anglo-American research, which is now more closely linked with Continental work on this; see e.g. Brunschwig and Nussbaum (1993), Engberg-Pedersen and Sihvola (forthcoming).

[4] See Long and Sedley (1987) = (LS) 65. See also Inwood (1985), ch. 5; Frede (1986); Annas (1989), (1992), chs. 5 and 9; Brennan (forthcoming). Important relevant editions include De Lacy (1978–84); Indelli (1988).

[5] See e.g. Nussbaum (1990*b*); Inwood (1993), esp. 150–61; also Colish (1985), 1–5; Griffin and Atkins (1991), xxi–xxvii.

[6] See refs. and discussion in Fowler, Ch. 1, Sect. IV; Wright, Ch. 9, text to nn. 1, 24–6; Gill, Ch. 11, Sect. V.

[7] Broadly speaking, Ch. 1, on Epicurean theories of anger, contributes to the first line of enquiry; Chs. 2–3, on Cicero and Seneca's philosophical prose, and Ch. 6, on the treatment of emotions in rhetoric, contribute to the second; and the remaining chapters contribute to the third.

Fowler also considers the possibility that the (rather more moderate) Epicurean position on anger can usefully be drawn into the scholarly debate about Aeneas' anger at the end of the *Aeneid*. The two following chapters focus on two treatments of what is (for the Stoics) another passion to be extirpated, namely grief: Andrew Erskine discusses Cicero and Marcus Wilson discusses Seneca, both in connection with the philosophico-literary form of the 'consolation'. Both scholars suggest, in different ways, that the Roman thinkers' treatment of this Stoic theme is shaped (and partly qualified) by some distinctively personal, or distinctively Roman, preoccupations. Susanna Morton Braund brings out the importance of reading Juvenal *Satire* 13 against the background of Greco-Roman philosophical thinking about consolation. She maintains that, although Juvenal's poem does not have a consistent philosophical position, we need to recognise that he plays off against the intellectual background to make his satiric point; his ironic *consolatio* substitutes fraud for death and anger for grief.

The next three chapters, though examining three different topics, have in common a focus on the arousal of emotions by artistic or rhetorical means. Alessandro Schiesaro takes a sceptical look at the usual view that Seneca's tragedies can plausibly be read as (cautionary) vehicles for Stoic teaching about the extirpation of the passions. He argues that Seneca's dramatic practice (and some of his theory) implies a different message: that divine, 'irrational' possession is a prerequisite for the most profound kind of human understanding. Ruth Webb highlights the significance of a particular strand in Greco-Roman thinking about the production of emotions in an audience: namely the arousal of feeling by vivid illustration (*enargeia*) or visualisation (*phantasia*) in both rhetoric and other literary genres. D. S. Levene suggests that, if any ancient theory is relevant to understanding the presentation of emotions in the Roman historians, it is Aristotle's rhetorical teaching about producing emotions by promoting the appropriate kind of ethical reactions, as mediated by the Roman rhetorical tradition. This suggestion forms the starting-point for Levene's analysis of the presentation of fear, and the arousal of pity, in Tacitus' portrait of Vitellius, an analysis couched in terms of the contrast between 'analytic' (ethical) and 'audience-based' (emotional) reactions.

The remaining four chapters all scrutinise the relevance of the contemporary intellectual background, especially the Stoic theory of the passions, to the interpretation of the portrayal of intense emotions in various aspects of Roman poetry. Joan Booth reviews features of Catullus' literary and intellectual background that help us to understand the sense in which he describes his persistent (and reluctant) passion for Lesbia as a 'sickness' (*morbus*) in Poem 67. M. R. Wright, starting from recent scholarly controversy about the end of the *Aeneid*, locates the presentation of anger in the poem in the context of the contrast between Aristotelian and Stoic attitudes to anger, which is an important theme in philosophical debate in Virgil's time. She argues that an Aristotelian attitude is more pervasive in the poem than a Stoic one, and that, by Aristotelian standards, Aeneas' anger is presented no more favourably than Turnus'. Elaine Fantham is also sceptical of the idea sometimes proposed, that the representation of emotions in Statius' *Thebaid* reflects a specifically Stoic perspective. Focusing on the presentation of hatred as a type of contagious madness, she suggests that this expresses a distinctive response to his Greco-Roman literary background rather than a theoretically based portrayal. Christopher Gill examines more generally the phenomenon in Roman poetry which Fantham highlights in the *Thebaid*, the presentation of intense passion as a kind of madness. He gives special attention to cases in Seneca and Virgil where this is seen as the outcome of 'akratic' (weak-willed) self-surrender. He sees this mode of portrayal as significantly different from Greek poetic presentation of akratic surrender and as a feature that is best explained as a fusion of Stoic psychology and Roman ethics.

Several contributors argue against assimilating the literary representation of emotions too closely to the standpoint of any one theory (in particular, the Stoic one); indeed, they sometimes question how far that standpoint is fully expressed even in works, such as Cicero's and Seneca's, which officially adopt a doctrinal position. However, their discussion also brings out the importance of placing the presentation of emotions in Roman literature against its contemporary philosophical background, as a key part of forming a culturally relevant framework of interpretation. The volume thus shows that the interplay between intellectual and literary modes of characterising the emotions forms an important strand in the larger nexus of discourse on this subject in Roman culture. In this respect, the volume can usefully be juxtaposed with work on the Roman discourses of sexuality and immorality, as initiated by Michel

Foucault and developed by, for instance, Paul Veyne, Amy Richlin and Catharine Edwards.[8]

II The emotions in Greco-Roman philosophy

Christopher Gill

For the most part, our contributors provide as much information about the Greco-Roman philosophical context as is needed to make sense of their arguments. However, there is a general feature of that philosophical context which is worth underlining here, since it bears on the claims made in many of the chapters. Also, it is possible, by reference to that feature, to underline certain ways in which the contributors' arguments have implications for each other as well as for the overall project of the volume.

This feature is the contrast (sometimes drawn by Roman thinkers themselves) between the Aristotelian approach to the emotions and the Stoic,[9] the latter being shared (to some extent) by other Hellenistic schools, notably the Epicurean. The key point is that, in an Aristotelian approach, emotions as such are not regarded as bad; they are graded as good or bad according to their appropriateness to the situation. For the Stoic approach, *all* emotions (as normally understood) are bad; they are all 'passions', in the sense of being affective states which overwhelm and disrupt human rationality.[10] This difference is related to a second one, concerning the type of context in which emotions are properly formed and judged. To put it very broadly, the Aristotelian approach sees emotions as shaped and evaluated primarily by the ordinary modes of interpersonal and communal discourse. The Stoic (and Epicurean) approach stresses, rather, the idea that philosophical discourse plays a crucial, 'therapeutic' role in counteracting the emotions typically validated and promoted by ordinary contexts of discourse.

[8] See Foucault (1986), (1988); also Veyne (1983); Richlin (1992); Edwards (1993).

[9] See e.g. Cic. *Tusc.* 3.71–6; 4.37–47; Sen. *De ira* 1.9–10, 17; 3.3.

[10] On this sense of 'passion', see n. 1 above, and on the Stoic theory, text to nn. 21–4 below. The Stoics use the same term for passion as Aristotle does for emotion, namely *pathos*, sometimes contrasted with the limited number of 'good emotions' (*eupatheiai*) that are compatible with normative rationality or 'wisdom' (LS 65 F). On the question how to translate the Stoic concept of 'passion' into Latin, see Cic. *Tusc.* 3.7–11, 23.

To clarify these points, we need to distinguish, more sharply than is usually done, between three versions of the 'Aristotelian' approach.[11] One is the kind of approach that we find in the surviving school texts based on Aristotle's own lectures. In the ethical works, for instance, we find the idea that virtue is expressed in hitting the 'mean' (*meson*) in emotions as well as in actions. Hitting the 'mean' signifies having the kind, and level, of emotion that is ethically appropriate to the situation; as Aristotle puts it, such emotions are 'as reason directs' (meaning that they are 'right' or 'reasonable', given the context). This general theory is applied, for instance, though without special emphasis, to the emotion of anger. The good-tempered person (*praos*) 'tends to be angry in the manner, at the things, and for the length of time that reason dictates'.[12] Analogously, in the *Rhetoric*, the discussion of the production of emotions (*pathē*) in Book 2 presupposes that these are normal affective responses to ethical judgements about how people have acted. For instance: 'Anger may be defined as a desire accompanied by pain for a conspicuous revenge for a conspicuous slight at the hands of men who have no call to slight oneself or one's friends.'[13] Similarly, Aristotle's famous analysis of the best type of tragic plot in *Poetics* 13 assumes that the audience's emotional reactions (crucially, those of pity and fear) are normally closely aligned with the ethical judgements that are made on the actions and characters represented in the plays.[14]

This Aristotelian approach to emotions is well recognised and much analysed; a second one is much less so, though some scholars are beginning to explore the idea that this constitutes a distinct approach. Although Aristotle's school, the Lyceum or Peripatos, continued and had some influence, especially in rhetoric, the school texts based on his lectures were, apparently, not widely available from the third to the first century BC.[15] The 'Aristotelian' or

---

[11] See also Gill (1995*b*), reviewing Nussbaum (1994), for whom the contrast between Aristotelian and therapeutic (e.g. Stoic) approaches is a central one.

[12] Arist. *NE* 4.5, 1125b35–1126a1; on the idea of the 'mean' in actions and emotions, 2.6, 1106b16–28; see also *EE* 2.3; 3.3.

[13] Arist. *Rh.* 2.2, 1378a30–2, trans. Barnes (1984). See also the comparable definition of the 'dialectical' account of anger in *de An.* 403a29–b3.

[14] Arist. *Po.* 1452b20–1453a12. See further, regarding Aristotle on emotion in general, Fortenbaugh (1975); in Aristotle's ethical thinking, Annas (1993), 53–61; in *Po.*, Halliwell (1986), 216–26; Nehamas (1992); Nussbaum (1992).

[15] According to Strabo 13.1.54, Plutarch *Sulla* 26, Aristotle's school texts were lost between Theophrastus' death (*c.* 287 BC) and their publication by Andronicus, around the time of

'Peripatetic' position on the ethical status of emotions, as characterised in later Hellenistic and Roman ethical texts, is, arguably, rather different from that of the school texts, at least in presentation and emphasis. 'Aristotle' is said to advocate 'moderate emotions' (*metriopatheiai*), rather than maintaining that emotions (whether weak or strong) should be ethically appropriate to the specific situation. Relatedly, 'moderating' emotions, rather than 'extirpating' them, is presented as being Aristotle's approach to the question of the proper 'therapy' of the emotions (whereas the idea of philosophy as therapy is not prominent in Aristotle's surviving school texts). The unemphatic inclusion of 'good temper' among the virtues in the school texts reappears in Roman writers as the stronger claim that anger is a necessary emotional stimulus to virtue.[16] In essence, what seems to have happened is that the Aristotelian approach has been reshaped, or at least re-presented, in the light of the altered preoccupations of Hellenistic philosophy, and, especially, in response to the influential Stoic theory of the passions.[17]

The third approach is an analogue of the Aristotelian approach, rather than being based, directly or indirectly, on this. It can be characterised as a conventional or 'vernacular' equivalent of this approach. The core feature, as in the Aristotelian school texts (text to nn. 12–14 above), is the idea that emotions constitute a valid type of response, provided that they are ethically justified by the situation. Several contributors to this volume point out that this feature of Aristotle's thinking represents a theorised version of the standard view of emotions in Greek society, one also expressed in the major serious genres of Greek poetry, epic and tragedy. Relatedly, contributors also point out that we can find a comparable view of emotions in Roman poetic and prose texts, whether or not these texts are directly influenced, in this regard, by the Aristotelian ethical and

---

Cicero (but not mentioned by him). On the history of the Lyceum in general, see Lynch (1972); on the post-Aristotelian tradition in rhetoric, see G. Kennedy (1972), 114–16; Bonner (1977), 79–83; Fortenbaugh and Mirhady (1993). The importance of this discontinuity in the availability of Aristotle's school texts for our study of Stoic philosophy is stressed by Sandbach (1985).

[16] See e.g. Cic. *Tusc.* 3.22, 74; 4.39–46, esp. 43; Sen. *De ira* 1.7; 8.4–5; 9; 10.4; 11.1; 12.1–3; 14.1; 17.1. See further Dillon (1983); also Annas (1993), 60–1, who, however, lays less emphasis than is done here on the difference between the school texts and the later Peripatetic view.

[17] On the contrast between the ethical approach of the Aristotelian school texts (though without discussion of whether this approach was subsequently reshaped) and the 'therapeutic' approach of the Hellenistic schools, see Nussbaum (1994), chs. 2–3.

rhetorical tradition. In later Hellenistic and Roman culture the position is rather more complex than in earlier Greek culture. In the later period, it is at least conceivable (and sometimes evident) that 'conventional' thought has also been influenced by, or is compatible with, the contrasting ('therapeutic') approach to emotions promoted by the Stoics and Epicureans.[18] Indeed, much of the complexity of our subject in this volume derives from the fact that the presentation of emotion in Roman literature expresses both types of approach; and that it is not easy (and is a subject of scholarly debate) to determine which approach is dominant in any one work or passage.[19]

In the case of the Hellenistic theories, it is also possible (though rarely straightforward) to draw distinctions between (1) the Hellenistic theories as originally formulated in the third century BC and (2) later Hellenistic and Roman modifications of these.[20] However, what is more important in the present context is to outline the main features of Stoic and Epicurean thinking on emotions, and to contrast their shared ('therapeutic') approach to the three versions of the Aristotelian approach.

In Stoic theory, the initial paradox to be confronted is the claim that passions are both 'rational' and 'irrational'. They are rational in that, like all adult human psychological processes, they involve beliefs and reasoning. In terms of Stoic psychology, it is only when someone 'assents' to a 'rational' (verbal) 'impression' that he or she has the impulse to action (*hormē*) that constitutes an emotion. More precisely, the assent is to certain kinds of impression, those involving the thought 'that *x* is good or bad, and that it is right to react accordingly'.[21] However, *pathē* are irrational, or contrary to right (normative) reason, in the sense that they involve assent to *false* beliefs about what is good or bad and about how it is right to react. They are also irrational, and 'unnatural', in the different (though

---

[18] See further on the points made in this paragraph text to nn. 33–41 below.

[19] See e.g. the debate about the end of the *Aeneid* (refs in n. 6 above); and the interplay between Stoic and non-Stoic attitudes highlighted (in writers influenced by Stoicism) by Erskine, Ch. 2; Wilson, Ch. 3; Schiesaro, Ch. 5.

[20] Drawing such distinctions is not straightforward since the evidence for Hellenistic theories, both in their original and in their modified forms, is late and indirect; see further text to nn. 23–4, 26 below.

[21] In seeing emotions as a response to a value-laden belief, the Stoic theory is comparable with Aristotle's; anger, as characterised in Arist. *Rh.* (text to n. 13 above) involves the belief 'that it is right to react' in a given way. On similarities between the two psychological models, see Lloyd (1978); Inwood (1985), chs. 1, 5.

related) sense that they are intense psychophysical reactions which disrupt normal human functioning. They are 'fresh' (vivid) beliefs, and associated with reactions such as 'shrinking' at something supposed to be bad and 'swelling' at something supposed to be good. This 'excessive' impulse is sometimes compared to running, rather than walking, legs: starting to run involves (rational) agency, but, when the movement gets going, it cannot be controlled in the way that walking can.[22]

The account of passion just given is that ascribed to Chrysippus (c. 280–206 BC), the main systematiser of Stoic thought, by Galen (c. AD 129–99), an important but hostile source. According to Galen, Posidonius (c. 135–50 BC) modified Chrysippus' theory, admitting the possibility of affective states which are not fully 'rational' in the way that Chrysippus supposed, thus explaining 'akratic' inner conflict more effectively.[23] In a perhaps related development, we find, in Seneca and elsewhere, the idea of 'pre-emotions' (*propatheiai*), involuntary or instinctive reactions of fright or impatience that anyone can feel. It is only when someone assents to these pre-emotions (with the thought that 'it is right to react' in this way) that one has a fully-fledged, 'rational' passion; and this state is then strong enough to overwhelm any remaining correct judgements to the contrary.[24]

The psychology of the Epicurean theory of emotions is not so fully elaborated, at least in surviving sources. But this theory also contains the idea that emotions, like desires, are shaped by value-laden beliefs, and that it is therefore appropriate to distinguish between 'natural' and 'empty' emotions as well as desires. Roughly speaking, the distinction is between emotions which are and are not consistent with the stable ('pleasant') psychophysical state that Epicureans regard as the supreme fulfilment of human nature. As D. P. Fowler

---

[22] See Gal. *PHP* 4.1.14–2.44, De Lacy (1978–84), vol. 1 238–47; LS 65 A–F; also Gill (1983a); Inwood (1985), ch. 5; Frede (1986); Engberg-Pederson (1990), ch. 8; Annas (1992), ch. 5; Nussbaum (1994), ch. 10; Brennan (forthcoming).

[23] LS 65 K, M–R; Gal. *PHP* 4.5.19–7.46, De Lacy (1978–84), vol. 1 262–91; see Kidd (1971). For the claim that Galen exaggerates the differences between Chrysippus and Posidonius, and that the latter's innovation may consist simply in introducing the idea of 'affective motions' alongside (rational) *pathē*, see Fillion-Lahille (1984), 121–62; Cooper (forthcoming); Gill (forthcominga). See further Gill, Ch. 11, Sect. III, text to nn. 43–5.

[24] Sen., *De ira* 2.2.5–4.2; see also LS 65 X–Y. The latter feature, pursuing the object of passion 'at all costs' (*utique*), i.e. whether right or wrong (2.4.1), may be taken either as marking a distinct, third stage, or as expressing in different language Chrysippus' idea that a passion involves the 'rejection' of reason, LS 65 J. See also Gill, Ch. 11, Sect. III, text to nn. 46–9. For the view that Seneca's account presents a personal elaboration of Chrysippus' theory, not a modified version of it, see Inwood (1993), 164–83.

brings out in this volume, this enables the Epicurean Philodemus to reject as empty (and as potentially painful) the intense kind of anger that is based on the false belief that retaliation is worthwhile. But it also enables him to retain scope (though of a kind that cannot be easily defined) for the relatively mild, 'natural' anger that is compatible with Epicurean wisdom and absence of emotional disturbance (*ataraxia*).[25]

In the Epicurean, as well as the Stoic and Aristotelian, theories it is possible, though not uncomplicated, to consider whether later Epicureans, such as Lucretius, make significant modifications to the original Epicurean theory of emotions.[26] But what is more important, here, is to define the general difference between the Aristotelian and the Stoic or Epicurean ('therapeutic') approaches as regards emotions and the social context. Broadly speaking, both the Stoic and Epicurean theories present intense, violent emotions as a product of misguided beliefs about the proper goals of a human life. For the Stoics, the error lies in the failure to see that virtue is the only real good and that the other so-called goods (such as health, wealth, power) are 'matters of indifference' (LS 58). For the Epicureans, the error is the failure to see that the only real good is pleasure, understood as freedom from pain in the body and distress in the mind; and that what are normally pursued as goods (including, again, wealth and power, though not health) do not yield happiness (LS 21). In so far as conventional societies propagate these false beliefs about what is valuable, and thus generate misguided and violent emotions, such societies are, for both schools, 'sick' and in need of 'therapy'. The Epicurean Diogenes of Oenoanda says that 'most people are sick all together ... of false opinion' and that 'because of their reciprocal emulation, they get the disease from each other'. For this reason, Diogenes uses the public form of an inscribed stoa to 'put out in public for all the drugs that will save their lives'.[27] Analogously, Chrysippus sees as one of the two main sources of human corruption 'the oral instruction [or conversation, *katēchēsis*] of

---

[25] See Annas (1989), (1992), ch. 9; also LS 21 on Epicurean thinking on pleasure and desire; Fowler, Ch. 1, esp. Sect. III, pursues the question whether the Epicurean account of anger is a coherent one.

[26] For some suggestions about possible Lucretian modifications regarding desires and emotions, see Nussbaum (1994), chs. 5–7. The question could also be raised, in principle, in connection with Philodemus (first century BC); but, given the paucity of evidence for Epicurus' own view of emotion, this would be a more difficult line of enquiry to sustain.

[27] Diogenes of Oenoanda frs. III–IV, Chilton (1971), cited from Nussbaum (1994), 137.

the majority of people'. He also offers philosophy as the 'medicine of the psyche', seeking to get 'inside' the sufferings that affect the psyche, with the aim of 'extirpating' the false action-guiding beliefs that generate intense, 'diseased' passions.[28]

There is an obvious contrast between this type of view and the Aristotelian type outlined earlier, according to which conventional societies are seen as the context in which people properly shape their ethical beliefs and emotional patterns.[29] However, there are certain relevant variations both between and within the two schools. The Epicureans generally stress the idea that it is only in communities in which people help each other to live fully Epicurean lives (such as Epicurus' own Garden) that people can acquire a proper understanding of what the virtues involve and the correlated patterns of emotion and desire.[30] There is, however, evidence that some Roman Epicureans (though not Lucretius) de-emphasised the difference between Epicurean and conventional ethics, or claimed, controversially, that one could be a good Epicurean and, for instance, fight for a good cause.[31] Within Stoicism, we can find a wide spectrum of positions, ranging from the quasi-Cynic rejection of conventional ethics ascribed to Zeno to the synthesis of Stoic and Roman ethics in Cicero's *De officiis*. The fundamental Stoic position on this is, perhaps, the claim that one can develop towards virtue in conventional societies, and should participate fully in the life of such societies, but if and only if this kind of development and participation is compatible with objective standards of virtue.[32] These features of Epicurean and Stoic thinking qualify, without negating, the contrast drawn earlier between the 'Aristotelian' and 'therapeutic' approaches, and have significant implications for understanding the

[28] Galen, *PHP* 5.5.14, De Lacy (1978–84), vol. 1 318–21; 5.2.22–4, vol. 1 298–9. See further Nussbaum (1994), chs. 9–10, esp. 316–17, 328–9, 388.

[29] To put the contrast less starkly, the Hellenistic schools accentuate the role given by Aristotle (e.g. in *NE* 10.7–8) to philosophy in modifying the patterns of belief and desire promoted by one's upbringing and society; see further Gill (1995a), ch. III, sect. 2, and (1996c), ch. 4, sect. 6, and ch. 5, sects. 6–7.

[30] That Epicureanism provides an ethic for interpersonal and group life (and not just for leading a life as an individual) is underlined by Long (1986a); Nussbaum (1994), 115–37.

[31] The difference between Epicurean and conventional ethics is not stressed in Torquatus' account of the virtues in Cic. *Fin.* 1.42–54. In Cic. *Fam.* 15.19, Cassius claims that Epicureanism is compatible with fighting a worthwhile war (on the issue, see also *Fam.* 7.12; 15.17); I am grateful to M. T. Griffin for drawing my attention to these passages. Contrast Lucretius' claim, in effect, that Epicurus has revised radically the meaning of the virtues: 1.69–101; 5.13–54, 1194–203.

[32] See further Schofield (1991), esp. ch. 1 and App. D; and Vander Waerdt (1994a); also LS 67; on Cic. *de Off.* see Gill (1988).

range of responses, in Roman thought, to the Hellenistic theories of the emotions.

This contrast between Aristotelian and therapeutic approaches to emotions (in their various versions) forms an important part of the background for the volume as a whole. It is one whose relevance for the claims of some of the chapters can be highlighted here. For instance, both Ruth Webb and D. S. Levene underline features of Greco-Roman thought which reflect the Aristotelian approach to rhetoric. Webb emphasises that the prevalent assumption in Hellenistic and Roman rhetorical treatises is that the effectiveness of oratorical (and poetic) visualisation *depends* on the fact that the orator invites a response which is 'normal', considered in relation to the audience's social and ethical assumptions. Visualisation, like other aspects of oratory, involves an appeal to 'plausibility', and 'plausibility' presupposes a nexus of normative assumptions which limit the scope of the orator's visualisation as well as that of the audience's response.[33] Webb's discussion has possible implications for one of the points made in Alessandro Schiesaro's critique of the idea that Senecan tragedy is best interpreted as a cautionary exemplification of the Stoic passions. Schiesaro denies that Stoic theory validates the idea that an author can guarantee that the audience gives, or withholds, its 'assent' to an 'impression' in a way that is consistent with Stoic standards of rationality (Ch. 5, Sect. III). The implication of Webb's discussion is that Seneca presupposes in his audience (or readership) a higher measure of ethical and emotional predictability than Schiesaro allows. However, for this point to make a substantive difference to this issue, we need also to supply the idea that Seneca sees his audience as disposed to respond in line with *Stoic*, and not merely conventional, ethical assumptions, and this further assumption can, of course, be questioned.[34]

Webb's concern is with the influence of the Aristotelian approach, as propagated through Peripatetic and Roman rhetorical treatises; Levene's interest is, rather, in what I have called the 'vernacular' equivalent of the Aristotelian approach (text to n. 18 above). He argues that the arousal of fear and pity by the Roman historians needs to be understood by reference to the 'Aristotelian' (and

---

[33] Webb, Ch. 6, summarised in her Sect. 1 and concluding paragraph; see also text to n. 13 above on Arist. *Rh.*

[34] The question whether Stoic tragedy can be regarded as ethically effective even for a Stoic audience (whether of sages or those 'making progress') is raised in Schiesaro, Ch. 5, Sect. IV.

conventional Roman) assumption that such responses can count as justified responses to certain types of ethical situations, rather than by reference to Stoic or Epicurean norms for emotions (Ch. 7, Sect. 1). However, Levene takes this approach further, by suggesting that Tacitus' account of Vitellius' fall (for instance) is best analysed by highlighting the interplay between 'analytic' (roughly, ethical) and 'audience-based' (roughly, emotional) modes of representation. Although the audience-based appeal to emotions sometimes reinforces the ethical judgements made, it sometimes works independently, thus suggesting that imaginative sympathy with a historical figure can outweigh the ethical judgements we should otherwise make (Sect. III).

As noted earlier (text to n. 18 above), the Aristotelian approach to emotions, as stated in the school texts, can be seen as a theorised version of the view found in Greek culture (for instance in Homer and tragedy) that emotions are ethically justifiable responses to specific situations. In this volume, M. R. Wright and Elaine Fantham make this suggestion;[35] Wright also argues that we can find in Virgil's *Aeneid* a 'vernacular' equivalent for the Aristotelian view. She sees in Virgil's presentation of anger the combination of a cognitive (and psychophysical) model of mind with a focus on the social context of anger which is characteristic of the Aristotelian view. She locates the idea of 'justified anger' in this Aristotelian framework, by contrast with those scholars who read the poem as presenting anger and other emotions, in a Stoicising way, as destructive and irrational 'passions'.[36] Fantham, on the other hand, contrasts the 'Aristotelian' view of emotions in Greek tragedy with the tendency of Roman tragic and epic poetry (for instance, Virgil, Seneca, Statius) to see emotions such as hatred as a product of a contagious, self-destructive madness or frenzy (*furor*), rather than as an intelligible response to interpersonal grounds for emotion. Although these passionate emotions are, typically, linked with divine forces, they are also explained psychologically, at both the divine and the human level.[37] Is this mode of representing emotions influenced by Stoicism? Fantham

[35] Ch. 9, Sect. II; Ch. 10, text to nn. 3–6.

[36] Wright's claim is that Virgil, drawing on the Greek poetic tradition which also embodies this view, and which is encapsulated in Aristotle's theoretical writings, evolves a Roman poetic equivalent for this view; she does not claim that Virgil was influenced directly by the Peripatetic tradition. On scholarly debate about whether the *Aeneid* should be read in a Stoic or Aristotelian way, see refs. in n. 6 above.

[37] See Ch. 10, esp. text to nn. 19–23, 31–6, 39–48.

sees this mode as, in Seneca at least, compatible with Stoic thought; but in Statius, she is inclined to see, instead, the expression of a bleak, personal vision, without the sense of moral absolutes, at the human and cosmic level, that should inform a Stoic-influenced world-view.[38]

The implication of the volume, as so far summarised, might seem to be that Roman conventional, non-philosophical, thought about emotions consists largely of a vernacular equivalent of the Aristotelian view, and that the alternative, 'therapeutic' view is confined to certain philosophical circles.[39] However, other features of the volume point to a different conclusion. Although Erskine and Wilson accentuate ways in which Cicero and Seneca (who are major Roman politicians as well as intellectuals) colour or qualify the Stoic approach to emotions, their chapters also bring out the power of this approach for them, and its importance for their real-life problems as well as for theory. Even more striking is Braund's demonstration of the way in which the impact of Juvenal *Satire* 13 depends on the familiarity of Stoic and Epicurean use of the *consolatio* as a vehicle for therapy of the emotions and of the related ethical beliefs.[40] Gill, exploring the sources of the idea of passion as madness in Roman poetry (to which Fantham draws attention), points to analogues in Roman popular or ideological thought for the Stoic contrast between virtue-wisdom and 'madness', and for the Stoic idea that virtue consists in 'passionless' adherence to duty. Just as Wilson finds in Seneca's mode of consolation a telling fusion of distinctively Roman attitudes and Stoic therapy, so Gill sees a similar fusion underlying Virgil's presentation of 'akratic' self-surrender as a kind of madness.[41]

[38] See Ch. 10, esp. text to nn. 2, 23–4, 68–9. Fantham's view raises a more general question: to what extent can a Stoic (rather than an Aristotelian) psychological model shape the representation of emotions in a literary work unless that work is also shaped by a Stoic conception of morality and the cosmos? Booth, Ch. 8, Sect. III, text to nn. 33–43, also raises this issue: Catullus may not be a good Stoic, but does this mean that his analysis of his 'sickness' is not informed by Stoic thought-patterns?

[39] This view is stated in a strong form by Wright, Ch. 9, text to nn. 2–3, 23–4, suggesting, in effect, that only the Aristotelian (rather than Stoic) framework has the kind of psychological and ethical complexity and credibility that a conventional or vernacular thought-world also requires.

[40] Ch. 4, esp. Sect. I and final paragraph. The fact that Juvenal deploys philosophical ideas from an intellectually disengaged standpoint (for satiric effect) only serves to reinforce Braund's point about the extent to which such ideas have become part of 'vernacular' Roman thought.

[41] Wilson, Ch. 3, Sects. IV–V; Gill, Ch. 11, Sect. IV.

This volume has not attempted to provide comprehensive coverage of the rich and complex subject of the emotions in Roman thought and literature. Among intellectual approaches, we offer no discussion of, for instance, the Sceptics, or, more relevant to literature, the Cynics.[42] Of Roman authors not considered here, Horace (especially in his *Satires* and *Epistles*) and Lucretius are, perhaps, the most obvious examples.[43] Another question that could be taken much further is that of the relationship between the social and political structures of Roman life and the presentation of emotion in literature and philosophy. We have seen our project as that of contributing to a stimulating area of current debate by pursuing *some*, and by no means all, of the possible lines of enquiry. But we think that our volume makes a special contribution in widening the circle of Roman authors who are usually brought into this debate, and, in connection with these authors, in pressing the question of the relationship between philosophical categories and literary topoi and modes of representation. As already highlighted, this volume provides the opportunity for following through, in a sustained way, the question of the relationship between 'Aristotelian' (in several senses) and therapeutic (especially Stoic) views of emotion, as this bears on the interpretation of Roman thought and literature.[44]

[42] On Sceptics, see e.g. Sextus *PH* 1.25–6, 28–9, taken with Annas (1993), 209–10, and ch. 17. On Cynicism, see Dudley (1967); Goulet-Cazé and Branham (1993).

[43] See e.g. on Hor. *Ep.* 1 McGann (1969), Macleod (1979), and (on Cynicism in Horace) Moles (1986); on Lucretius, see Segal (1990); Nussbaum (1994), chs. 5–7.

[44] As noted in n. 11 above, this relationship is also a main theme in Nussbaum (1994), though treated there with a different range of subject-matter and a rather different conceptual approach.

CHAPTER I

Epicurean anger

D. P. Fowler

I

The passion of anger is beset by ambivalence.[1] One aspect of this
was noted already by Aristotle, in his famous remark at the beginning
of *De anima* that the physicist and the dialectician would define anger
differently: the latter would call it something like the desire for
retribution, the former a boiling of the blood and heat around the
heart:

> Hence a physicist would define an affection of soul differently
> from a dialectician: the latter would define e.g. anger as the
> appetite for returning pain, or something like that, while the
> former would define it as a boiling of the blood or warm substance
> surrounding the heart. The one assigns the material conditions,
> the other the form or account; for what he states is the account of
> the fact, though for its actual existence there must be embodiment
> of it in a material such as is described by the other ... Which,
> then, amongst these is entitled to be registered as the genuine
> physicist? The one who restricts himself to the material, or the
> one who restricts himself to the account alone? Is it not rather the
> one who combines both?[2]

This dual physiological and cognitive aspect of the passion remains
in modern discussions. There is undoubtedly a physiology of anger,
which was for long the focus of interest for psychologists: in the

---

[1] I am especially indebted for help with this chapter to my psychology colleague Mansur
Lalljee, though I doubt that he would feel anything other than horror at its amateur
treatment of his subject. Amongst the mass of material on anger and the emotions in general,
I have found Averill (1979) and (1982) most helpful. There is a sketch of some thirty theories
of emotion in Strongman (1987). Useful volumes of readings are M. B. Arnold (1968) and
(1970), and Plutchik and Kellerman (1980): see also Plutchik (1980). Note also the *International
Review of Studies on Emotion* = Strongman (1991). For an anthropological perspective, see Lutz
and Abu-Lughod (1990): note also Kovecses (1986).
[2] Aristotle *De anima*, 1.1, 403a26–b9 trans. J. A. Smith. See Rorty (1992), 8.

celebrated James–Lange view of the emotions (see Cannon (1927)), the physiological effects were made the causes of the psychological manifestations. My blood does not boil because I want to get back at my enemy, but I am angry because my blood boils. A physiological focus of this kind eventually leads to the wilder shores of sociobiology, and to statements such as that of C. E. Izard in his book *Emotions*, that 'in human beings the expression of anger and the experiential phenomenon of anger are innate, pancultural, universal phenomena'.[3] But I take it we are all constructionists now. At the most, the physiological effects of anger, as graphically described by ancient moralists, form a *complex syndrome*, as Averill (1979, 5) terms it, in which 'no single response, or subset of responses, is essential'. After a famous experiment with injections of epinephrine, Stanley Schachter even concluded that there was really only one emotion, from a physiological point of view: that 'the same state of physiological arousal could be interpreted by the subject as joy or anger, or any other emotional state, depending upon the situational context'.[4] The experiment was flawed, and different emotions can be distinguished at a physiological level, but only as loose bundles of responses. There is no physiological essence of anger. Anger is therefore very far from being a cultural universal, even if the only people who are said to have nothing that could be called anger at all are the Utku of Canada (it is not surprising that they do not get angry with each other, since there are only 20–35 of them in 35,000 square miles).

Anger cannot be separated from the discourse of anger, as though one were 'reality' and the other 'cultural expression'; rather, anger is constituted by that discourse. In this discourse, the representation of anger in art has a peculiarly central role: books, plays and films play a central part in learning how to be angry, as in learning how to love.[5] It is, of course, the very existence of the Western tradition of anger that tempts modern interpreters towards a sense of common humanity: it is a commonplace that the literature of Europe begins with the word *mēnin*, 'wrath'. The role of that tradition in the construction of modern anger has played an interesting minor role in the debates over the value of 'Western civilisation' in general. Allan

---

[3] Izard (1977), criticised in Averill (1979), 71.
[4] See Lazarus, Opton and Averill (1970), 208. The same volume contains Schachter's own account of his experiments.
[5] See Myerowitz (1985); D. Kennedy (1993), esp. 24–45.

Bloom claimed that modern American feminists were emasculating the male youth of America by denying them access to the spunky 'spirit' of antiquity and to a positive evaluation of aggression. In reply, Martha Nussbaum pointed out that most ancient writing on anger aimed to encourage its elimination.[6] The theme of gender has been central to the modern discussion of anger; not only in criticism of the role that anger plays in the making of a man, but also, more positively, in response to the bind that has traditionally denied women access to anger, except in limited roles like that of the 'woman scorned'.

Philosophers try to reduce the complex inheritance that is Western anger to some sort of order. The more the construction of anger in discourse is stressed, the more philosophers may hope that it can be brought within the sphere of reason. Yet, if we stress too much the cognitive side of anger, as Chrysippus allegedly did,[7] we are in danger of missing the sense that we have of anger as a 'passion', in the sense of something which takes hold of people, and carries them away. It is, of course, possible to try to account for this view of anger in functionalist terms. J. R. Averill, for instance, defines anger as:

a socially constituted response which helps to regulate interpersonal relations through the threat of retaliation for perceived wrongs, and which is interpreted as a passion rather than as an action so as not to violate the general cultural proscription against deliberately harming another.[8]

But, however explicable from an evolutionary perspective, this view of anger as a *passion* leads to its own paradoxes, as Averill himself remarks (1979, 10): 'being something which happens to a person, a passion is in a sense alien to the self. Yet states such as anger, fear, love, hope, and sorrow are generally considered among the truest reflections of the self.' In Platonic terms, we feel both that our real self is the little person (reason) within the psyche, and that a human being is, necessarily, the whole monstrous compound of the psyche.

---

[6] Bloom (1987), reviewed by Nussbaum (1987a).

[7] See Nussbaum (1987b), esp. 137: 'if judgements are *all* that the passions are, if there is no part of them that lies outside the rational faculty, then a rational art that sufficiently modifies judgements, seeking out the correct ones and installing them in place of the false, will actually be sufficient for curing human beings of the ills that are caused by the passions'.

[8] Averill (1979), 71. See his later definition, Averill (1982), 317 (his italics):
Accordingly, anger may be defined as a *conflictive* emotion that, on the biological level, *is related to aggressive systems and, even more important, to the capacities for cooperative social living, symbolization, and reflective self-awareness*; that, on the psychological level *is aimed at the correction of some appraised wrong*; and that, on the sociocultural level, *functions to uphold accepted standards of conduct*.

Philosophy has to be optimistic that this ambivalence can be resolved, and that there is a rational solution to the problem of anger. What is not clear is how this optimism can be grounded.

This ambivalence has traditionally been expressed in terms of debate over the *evaluation* of anger. Is it a good thing to get angry? Or should we keep our cool? Can we eliminate anger? Or is it something we need to integrate into our sense of the self? Do we want to be little Peripatetics or little Stoics? Or do we want to come down somewhere in the middle? As Averill again remarks, perhaps a little blandly (1982, 340):

In sum, it is easy to condemn anger because of its excesses. It is also easy to praise anger, to 'let it all hang out' in the name of some self-righteous adventure. It is much more difficult to maintain a balanced perspective, to understand anger in both its positive and negative aspects, and to behave accordingly.

That is, perhaps, do we really want to be little Epicureans? Notoriously, the Epicureans were opposed both to Aristotle and to the Stoa: can we find in their views a coherent middle ground? Has Epicureanism something to offer to the philosophers' quest for a solution to the problem of anger? As will be seen, my answer is that, unfortunately, it does not; but the insinuation will be that it could not help to solve the problem, because philosophy is doomed to failure.

II

Apart from some brief aphorisms, our main sources for the Epicurean view of anger are: *De rerum natura* (*DRN*) 3.258–322, Seneca *De ira* 2.1–17, and the treatise of Philodemus *On Anger* contained in PHerc. (*Papyri Herculanei*) 182. None of these is straightforward as a source of philosophical doctrine, if anything ever is. The Lucretian passage is part of a Latin hexameter poem with its own network of concerns; the Senecan passage does not name Epicurus as its target, and, very probably, attacks some non-Epicurean positions as well as Epicurean ones; and the Philodeman treatise is incomplete and at times fragmentary, as well as being written in Philodemus' usual compressed and jargony 'professional philosopher's' Greek. It is, moreover, clear from Philodemus' treatise that there were differing views within the school on the positions of the Epicurean masters and the proper interpretation of these. But, as always, I make these methodological cautions only to ignore them:

we can only ever tell the best story we can on the basis of what we have got.

I begin with Lucretius. In *DRN* 3.258–322, he is concerned with the way in which the four parts of the soul relate to each other. In Epicurean theory, the soul is a mixture of air, wind, heat and a nameless 'fourth element' (*quarta natura*) which plays a central role in perception and cognition. These elements form a true mixture, but the proportion of each is not constant; and it is variation in the proportion of the elements which determines mood (288–93) and temperament (294–306). When we are angry, our personality (*animus*) has more heat in it; and those who easily boil over into anger have generally a greater proportion of heat in their souls. This also explains the temperamental differences between lions, deer and oxen. There is a problem here for Epicureanism, however, which, in general, has strong rationalist, Socratic tendencies: once one has seen the light, the whole tempest of the soul is supposed to be dispersed. The physiological account, on the other hand, might lead one to think that, if one is born with a constitutionally disturbed soul, there is not going to be much that reason can do to alter one's psychic state. Lucretius, therefore, takes pains to stress that, while there are ineradicable original traces (*uestigia prima*) of particular natures left in the soul after Epicurean instruction, they are so small that nothing prevents us from leading a life worthy of the gods.

In 310, we are told that these temperamental tendencies are 'bad' (*mala*): they cannot be 'plucked out root and all' (*radicitus euelli*), but they can clearly be very much reduced. This suggests an obvious line for an Epicurean to take on anger: it is a true passion, in that reason cannot completely control it, but its effects can be very much minimised. This is in line with a number of other Epicurean pronouncements which stress that reason cannot completely transform an individual's constitution (*sustasis*). It is even allowed, for instance, that someone with a particular bent for glory may need to take part in political life because of the nature of her/his constitution.[9] That example, however, shows the problem for Epicureans: if reason can modify one's *sustasis* to a certain extent, why not suppose that it can totally remove anger or a desire for glory by restoring the balance of elements in the soul? And, if the answer is merely that there are limits built into the nature of the soul as a physical mixture,

---

[9] See Fowler (1989), 126–7.

the objection may be made that those limits might be set much higher. If reason is unable to modify the balance in the soul completely, why suppose that it can modify the balance at all? Clearly, we may be able to try to answer some of these problems if we switch to talking of anger at the cognitive level; but it is, of course, the Epicureans themselves who are so keen on referring everything back to physiology.

But this is not the whole story. It is not only excessive anger which is 'bad' (*malum*) here, but excessive placidity: the ox-person is criticised as well as the lion-person. It is also a fault, we are told, if one accepts things 'more mildly than one should' (*clementius aequo*, 313), like the ox whose 'vital constitution has a greater proportion of calm air' (*placido magis aere uiuit*, 302). One might expect that an Epicurean, for whom it is better 'to live a quiet life as a subject' (*parere quietum*) than 'to hold rule with authority' (*regere imperio res*, 5.1129–30), could not be said to accept things 'more mildly than one should'. But, as we shall see, this is not just a piece of casual Peripatetic contamination: the Epicureans are committed to a more positive view of anger.

I now turn to Seneca, *De ira* 2.1–17. The people against whom Seneca argues here are, as I say, anonymous, but J. Fillion-Lahille (1970, 1984) has, I think, rightly identified the main target as the Epicureans, though I suspect that the arguments are drawn more widely towards the end of the section. The main ground for seeing the enemy here as Epicurean is a similarity to arguments in Philodemus' treatise, to be discussed shortly. But Seneca also counters the point which is implicit in Lucretius' account, that anger cannot be wholly eradicated because of human nature. At 2.12.3 he considers the objection but simply denies that this is so: the mind is sovereign over all:

> 'But it is not possible,' you say, 'to banish anger altogether from the heart, nor does human nature permit it.' Yet nothing is so hard and difficult that it cannot be conquered by the human intellect and be brought through persistent study into intimate acquaintance, and there are no passions so fierce and self-willed that they cannot be subjugated by discipline. Whatever command the mind gives to itself holds its ground ... (trans. J. W. Basore)

> 'non potest' inquis 'omnis ex animo ira tolli, nec hoc hominis natura patitur.' atqui nihil est tam difficile et arduum quod non humana mens uincat et in familiaritatem perducat adsidua

meditatio, nullique sunt tam feri et sui iuris adfectus ut non
disciplina perdomentur. quodcumque sibi imperauit animus
optinuit ...

The Stoic and Epicurean positions, however, may be less far apart
than they seem at first. Seneca had begun Book 2 by asking how
anger begins (2.1.1):

> Now we must come to narrower matters; for the question is
> whether anger originates from choice or from impulse, that is,
> whether it is aroused of its own accord, or whether, like much else
> that goes on within us, it does not arise without our knowledge.
> (trans. Basore)

> nunc ad exiliora ueniendum est; quaerimus enim ira utrum
> iudicio an impetu incipiat, id est utrum sua sponte moueatur an
> quemadmodum pleraque quae intra nos <non> insciis nobis
> oriuntur.

In reply, Seneca had given the standard Stoic answer that anger
involves assent to an impression, not merely the impression itself.
Anger is not like shivering when cold or getting dizzy when on a
precipice, but something that can be routed by precepts. It is a
'weakness of the mind that is subject to the will' (*uoluntarium animi
uitium*, 2.2.2):

> But anger may be routed by precepts; for it is a weakness of the
> mind that is subject to the will, not one of those things that result
> from some condition of the general lot of man and therefore
> befall even the wisest, among which must be placed foremost that
> mental shock which affects us after we have formed the impression
> of a wrong committed. (trans. Basore)

> ira praeceptis fugatur; est enim uoluntarium animi uitium, non ex
> his quae condicione quadam humanae sortis eueniunt ideoque
> etiam sapientissimis accidunt, inter quae et primus ille ictus animi
> ponendus est qui nos post opinionem iniuriae mouet.

Amongst this latter class of shocks which happen even to the wise
are the vicarious emotions of literary experience, as, for instance,
when we hear of Cicero's treatment at the hands of Clodius or
Antony. These are not real passions: they are 'emotions of a mind
that would prefer not to be so affected ... not passions, but the
beginnings that are preliminary to passions' (*motus ... animorum moueri
nolentium, nec adfectus sed principia proludentia adfectibus*, 2.2.5). That is,
they are prokatarchic causes, in Stoic terminology, or preliminary
stimuli. The mind does not assent to them. In an earlier passage

(1.16.7), Seneca has called such a reaction a 'slight and superficial emotion' (*leuem quendam tenuemque motum*), not really passion but 'certain suggestions and shadows of passion' (*suspiciones quasdam et umbras adfectuum*):

> 'What then?' you say; 'when the wise man shall have something of this sort to deal with (i.e. wickedness), shall not his mind be affected by it, will it not be moved from its usual calm?' I admit that it will; it will experience some slight and superficial emotion. For as Zeno says: 'Even the wise man's mind will keep its scar long after the wound has healed.' He will experience, therefore, certain suggestions and shadows of passion, but from passion itself he will be free. (trans. Basore)

> 'quid ergo? non, cum eiusmodi aliquid sapiens habebit in manibus, tangetur animus eius eritque solito commotior?' fateor: sentiet leuem quendam tenuemque motum; nam, ut dicit Zeno, in sapientis quoque animo, etiam cum uulnus sanatum est, cicatrix manet. sentiet itaque suspiciones quasdam et umbras adfectuum, ipsis quidem carebit.

An Epicurean might well agree with this phenomenology, but simply choose to call these 'beginnings that are preliminary to passions' (*principia proludentia adfectibus*) 'passions' after all. This is a very plausible candidate for the category of 'natural anger' to which the Epicureans seem to feel committed, on the basis of their physiology. A passage in *Epistle* 85 of Seneca makes a similar point. Although most of the argument in the letter is directed at the Peripatetics, in section 14 he switches to attacking 'some men' who are, again, plausibly taken as the Epicureans: they believe that the wise person is tranquil 'as regards the attitude and habit of his mind', but not 'as regards the outcome':

> Some men have made a distinction as follows, saying: 'If a man has self-control and wisdom, he is indeed at peace as regards the attitude and habit of his mind, but not as regards the outcome. For, as far as his habit of mind is concerned, he is not perturbed, or saddened, or afraid: but there are many extraneous causes which strike him and bring perturbation upon him.' What these men mean to say is this: 'So-and-so is indeed not a man of an angry disposition, but still he sometimes gets angry.' (trans. R. M. Gunmere)

> quidam ita distinxerunt, ut dicerent: ‘temperans ac prudens positione quidem mentis et habitu tranquillus est, euentu non est. nam, quantum ad habitum mentis suae, non perturbatur, nec

contristatur nec timet, sed multae extrinsecus causae incidunt,
quae illi perturbationem adferant.' tale est quod uolunt dicere:
iracundum quidem illum non esse, irasci tamen aliquando.

Seneca's reply to this is that these perturbations, once admitted, will
inevitably alter the constitution. In effect, however, the Stoics and
Epicureans do not seem to be very far apart: in each case there is an
immediate involuntary reaction which is straightaway repressed by
the wise person.

III

But the Epicureans did not just argue that anger was inescapable;
they also argued that it was, on occasions, beneficial, a view which
Seneca takes pains to counter. But, before considering his counter-
arguments, it is necessary to turn to Philodemus' *De ira*. This is
among the better preserved of the Herculaneum papyri, and is
available in a good modern edition by Giovanni Indelli (1988), which
includes a translation and extensive notes. We also have lucid and
philosophically aware discussions of the treatise by Julia Annas and
John Procopé.[10] Despite this, I find the work a difficult one: as with
many of Philodemus' polemical works, one has a constant sense of
somehow missing the point of the argument.

The work is, clearly, in two parts: in the first part (columns I–XXXIV)
the evil effects of anger are outlined (I–XXXI), and the Peripatetics are
explicitly attacked for defending it (XXXI–XXXIV). This 'diatribal'
section has many points of contact with the treatises against anger of
Seneca and Plutarch,[11] and is relatively straightforward. Philodemus
is at pains, however, to justify this description of symptoms against the
attacks of one Timasagoras, who seems to have thought this sort of
therapy pointless, since there is no arguing with people in the grip of
anger. The philosophical position of Timasagoras is not clear.
F. Longo Auricchio and A. Tepedino Guerra argued that he was a
dissident Epicurean;[12] and, indeed, this must be true if he is the same
as the 'Timagoras' mentioned by Cicero and Aetius. But, even if this
is accepted, we still would like to know why he took up this position.
One possibility is that he saw anger solely as a natural reaction that

---

[10] Annas (1989), (1992), 189–99; Procopé (1993). See also Erler (1992a), 116–22.
[11] See the notes and introduction in Indelli (1988), together with Fillion-Lahille (1984).
[12] Longo Auricchio and Tepedino Guerra (1979). See also Procopé (1993), 378–81, and 385 on
Nicasicrates.

was inescapable, without a cognitive element of any kind: the wise person will be subject to this in a minor way, but will not be affected beyond the initial 'slight emotion' *(leuis motus)*. The wise person, therefore, cannot be affected by a discourse on the evils of anger; and there is no point trying to moderate the passions of a non-Epicurean, since there is no real salvation outside the Garden.

Philodemus, however, holds that such diatribal therapy is useful because there is a strong cognitive element: the passions in the soul occur 'because of our false belief' (διὰ τὴν ἡμετέραν ψευδοδοξίαν), as he remarks in column VI. The second half of the treatise, columns XXXIV to the end, attempts to set out his view of Epicurean orthodoxy. A number of distinctions are basic to his position. First, he distinguishes between 'natural' anger and anger which is 'empty' *(kenē orgē)*. Julia Annas saw this opposition as similar to the distinction between necessary, natural and empty desires, which she analysed exclusively in cognitive terms. An empty desire is one based on a false belief that an object of desire is irreplaceable – as, for instance, when I long for lobster and 'have the empty belief that there is something about lobster worth caring about in its own right and not just as a means of nourishment' (1989, 152). I think her analysis of desires is mistaken because it neglects the physiological basis of the Epicurean analysis. 'Necessary' desires are for objects which bring about katastematic pleasure; 'natural' desires are for objects of sensual or kinetic pleasure; and 'empty' desires are so called precisely because they cannot issue in any bodily effect at all, and therefore can never be satisfied.[13] I see nothing un-Epicurean, therefore, in the scholion on Aristotle that constitutes fr. 456 in Usener's collection:

> Epicurus and his followers make the following distinction: of the desires, some are necessary, some natural but not necessary, and some neither necessary nor natural but occurring in accordance with empty belief. The desire for food and clothing is necessary;[14] the desire for sex is natural, but not necessary; but the desire for a certain kind of food or a certain kind of clothing or a certain kind of sex is neither natural nor necessary.

---

[13] I follow here again (see Fowler (1989), 141) the account of Epicurean desires and pleasures in Diano (1974); see Rist (1972), 101–11 and Appendix D, and, for some criticisms, Gosling and Taylor (1982) and Giannantoni (1984). See also Procopé (1993), 371–7.

[14] The reference is to clothing needed for survival against cold: cold is always mentioned alongside hunger and thirst as basic pains to be avoided which lead to death if they are not countered (see e.g. Vat. 33 with Arrighetti). Hence, Annas' point (152 n. 16) that 'we have as plausible a need for sex as for clothing' is invalid: you do not feel pain or die without sex.

The desire for food is necessary (without it we lack katastematic pleasure, that is, we feel pain and, ultimately, die); that for nice-tasting food is natural (the sense organs are stimulated or 'varied'), but that for lobsters, as such, is neither necessary nor natural, but empty, a perversion of the mind such as wanting sex with a particular person.[15] Therefore, if we wish to draw an analogy between the desires and anger, physiology ought to be more important than it is in Annas' analysis. This does not necessarily invalidate her analysis at the cognitive level. But we hit an immediate and obvious problem: anger at the cognitive level is not merely analogous to a desire, it involves a desire, for retaliation or whatever. How can such a desire *ever* be other than an empty desire, in Epicurean terms, since it cannot issue in any sort of pleasure that they would recognise? And if one stresses, as Procopé does, that anger may produce the good of security by deterring aggression, one risks again compromising Epicurean invulnerability.[16]

This brings me to another distinction. The wise person will get angry, but not *very* angry: she will be subject to anger in a small way (*orgē*), but not to the much more violent passion (*thumos*).[17] Indeed, Philodemus claims that even *orgē*, as conventionally understood, is not a very exact description of the passion of the wise person, and that this has resulted in the misinterpretation of some statements of the Epicurean masters Epicurus, Hermarchus and Metrodorus, by those who did not appreciate that sometimes they spoke of anger in the usual sense and sometimes of the special Epicurean version. The Stoics saw here an opening for attack. If the wise person gets angry in a small way at stimuli of a certain kind, why should she not get more angry at an increased stimulus? After all, as Seneca says in a passage of diatribal social criticism, the wise person will have far more to get annoyed at than normal people just by what she sees when walking through the forum (*De ira* 2.9). And if one discards the notion of the strength of anger being proportional to the strength of the stimulus, will this not be unfair? The Epicurean wise person is thus faced with a dilemma (2.6.3–4):

[15] See, of course, the end of *De rerum natura* 4, taken with R. Brown (1987) and Nussbaum (1989), though I do not agree with all the latter's conclusions.

[16] Procopé (1993), 371–7; see Averill (1979), 71, quoted above. 'Tit for tat' is a very useful social tactic, but as the computer model of it shows, it does not require any emotional correlate (see Axelrod (1984)).

[17] On this distinction, see Indelli on xii 26, with Manuli (1988); see also Procopé (1993), 375–7; Nussbaum (1994), 250.

Besides, if it is the part of a wise man to be angry at wrong-doings, the greater they are the more angry will he be, and he will be angry often; it follows that the wise man will not only become angry, but will be prone to anger. But if we believe that neither great anger nor frequent anger has a place in the mind of a wise man, is there any reason why we should not free him from his passion altogether? No limit, surely, can be set if the degree of his anger is to be determined by each man's deed. For either he will be unjust if he has equal anger toward unequal delinquencies, or he will be habitually angry if he blazes up every time crimes give him warrant. (trans. Basore, modified)

et si sapientis est peccatis irasci, magis irascetur maioribus et saepe irascetur: sequitur ut non tantum iratus sit sapiens sed iracundus. atqui si nec magnam iram nec frequentem in animo sapientis locum habere credimus, quid est quare non ex toto illum hoc adfectu liberemus? modus enim esse non potest, si pro facto cuiusque irascendum est; nam aut iniquus erit, si aequaliter irascetur delictis inaequalibus, aut iracundissimus, si totiens excanduerit quotiens iram scelera meruerint.

The Epicurean answer that Philodemus gives to this is that the wise person will not get very angry because there cannot be anything to get very angry about. As he remarks in column XLI, 'external goods or evils' (*ta exothen*) are simply not very important. If the wise person will not be disturbed even in the presence of great pains, *a fortiori* she will not get very angry at any damage done to her by another. Annas (1989, 158 n. 27) sees what she calls the 'internalization of Epicurean good' as a sign of influence from developments subsequent to Epicurus himself; but there is nothing about this concept which is un-Epicurean. The Epicurean wise person had always been able to be happy, even in the brazen bull of Phalaris. What is strange about Philodemus' answer is that one would expect 'externals' (*ta exothen*) to be completely *unimportant*, not just of slight importance. Again, it looks as if the admission of anger makes too many concessions to vulnerability: what phenomenon in the external world could ever irritate a true Epicurean?[18]

---

[18] I am taking here a hard line on the Epicurean attachment to invulnerability (cf. Fowler (1989), 127 n. 34): for more sophisticated and nuanced approaches see especially Mitsis (1988) and Nussbaum (1994), esp. 234–79. The emotions which move a Lucretius or a Diogenes of Oenoanda (cf. fr. 3 Smith) to urge their fellow men towards Epicureanism are obviously relevant here, but I cannot see how they are compatible with Epicurean self-sufficiency *(autarkeia)*.

There is one more distinction of importance that Philodemus makes in the *De ira*. In the evaluation of anger, he argues in xxxvii–xxxviii that all anger, even natural anger, is an evil, 'considered in itself' (κατὰ διάληψιν), because it is painful: but it may even be a good 'in connection with the constitution of the mind' (κατὰ τὴν συμπλοκὴν τῇ διαθέσει). In itself, that is, even natural anger is painful, but it is good because it is an affection of a person with a good constitution. By contrast, empty anger proceeds from a bad constitution (*diathesis*) and brings with it many troubles. But what does it mean to say that anger is a good if we consider it 'in connection with' the constitution of the wise man? Philodemus explains that, in such a case, the anger 'arises from the perception of how the nature of things is, and from having no false opinions in the measurement of damages and the punishment of people doing us harm' (xxxvii 32–9). This looks like an explanation of why the natural anger of the wise person will not be excessive or violent. The language recalls *Letter to Menoeceus* 130 where Epicurus says that we must measure pains and pleasures against each other and sometimes treat an evil as good, or vice versa. The wise person will put the apparent damage done to her in a proper perspective, and not dwell on it; in particular, as Annas argues, she will know that any pleasure in revenge will be outweighed by pain. But none of this explains why anger in such a person is actually a good, rather than merely less of a bad than it is for a person who is unphilosophical (*mataios*). Why should not an appropriate constitution remove anger entirely?

There are other arguments in Philodemus' treatise for a positive valuation of anger. He refers, at one point, to the treatise *On Freedom of Speech* (*peri parrhēsias*), which is concerned with reproof of error within the Epicurean community; and it has been suggested that the two treatises should be seen as linked. The wise person will naturally get angry at the mistakes of the neophytes, though not, of course, to the point of suffering the violent passion of *thumos*. This role of anger in philosophical reproof may help us to understand a puzzling feature of Lucretius' philosophical stance. Although, in writing the *De rerum natura*, he should, as an Epicurean, preserve calm during the 'peaceful nights' (*noctes ... serenas*) of composition, he often falls naturally into the stance of the philosopher angry at the waste inherent in 'normal' human life. Like Nature in Book 3, Lucretius angrily upbraids contemporary Roman society. In doing so, he takes on a role that was standard in didactic writing and satire;[19] but the Epicurean background may also be relevant. This point may provide an explanatory context for the defence of anger in Philodemus; but it does not really help his argument. Philodemus himself criticises the Peripatetic claim that judges and soldiers need anger to act; and it is hard to see why the same should not be true of encounter-group leaders. Indeed, early in the second part of the treatise, Philodemus, puzzlingly, talks of the Epicurean wise person, who is not angry or irascible (*aorgētos*), not as becoming angry but as giving the appearance, *phantasia*, of the irascible person; even Epicurus 'gave some people such an impression' (ἀπέδωκεν ἔνιοις τοιοῦτου φαντασίαν). This may merely mean, again, that, as Annas remarks (1992, 196 n. 27),'the behaviour may appear the same, but its causes are so different that we do not really have the same emotion'; but to open up a gap of this kind between action and emotion is to allow the Stoic arguments about judges to go through. There might be an occasion for an Epicurean to speak sharply to an unruly Virgil or Horace misbehaving at the back of the lecture room: but not to get angry. At all.

I have tried in this exposition of Philodemus not to reconstruct his views sympathetically but to expose the problems that they reveal – a much easier task than Julia Annas set herself. The Epicureans' views on anger clearly excited a great deal of philosophical discussion. Within the *De ira*, Philodemus criticises the views of one Nicasicrates, who seems to have opposed any clear distinction between natural and empty anger: he held that even the former leads to the behaviour characteristic of the violent passion of *thumos*. Nicasicrates' position is, again, a matter of controversy: he has been held to be a Stoic or Peripatetic, or, indeed, as Asmis suggests, cutting the Gordian knot, an Academic; but it seems very possible that he was another dissident Epicurean.[20] His position could be read as that of a rigorist opposed to anger, but, if he really took it to be inevitable, he may be associated with the group that Philodemus is combating at the end of the treatise. They held that the wise man should get not just a little angry, but very angry; and they backed up their arguments with detailed reference to the sayings of Epicurus and the other masters.

---

[19] For anger in the satiric tradition, see especially Braund (1988). I hope to examine some aspects of the stance of didactic in a volume of essays on didactic that I am editing with Alessandro Schiesaro.

[20] See Longo Auricchio and Tepedino Guerra (1981); Asmis (1990), 2395–9.

These again seem to be dissident Epicureans. If they are, it is remarkable that the doctrine should have excited such divergent views within the school; and, of course, we should not necessarily assume that it is Philodemus who represents orthodoxy in this.

This was clearly a difficult area for Epicureanism; and one can see why. They join with the Stoics in extirpating the passion of love – which for them is a non-natural and non-necessary empty desire for a particular kind of sex. Why not go the same way and extirpate anger, rather than accommodating it? It too could be defined cognitively as an empty desire for vengeance. Philosophies which defend anger often do so because they also wish to defend attachment to people and things; and it is argued that one cannot really be attached to something and not feel anger if it is harmed. But Epicureanism stresses self-sufficiency (*autarkeia*) as strongly as the Stoics: the Epicurean wise person is invulnerable. One can, of course, play the cultural historian, and suppose that the ancient positive evaluation of anger was too strong for the Epicureans to renounce it, but this is implausible. Philodemus himself argues (in column XXXI) that it is right to defy the establishment of parents, philosophers, orators and poets who urge one towards anger, the whole rag-bag (*grumea*) of conventional education. These are the people who tell us to 'live a quiet life as a subject' (*parere quietum*, Lucr. 5.1129); they are not afraid of standing out against convention.

Well, maybe Epicurus himself was an irascible guru who could not give up the pleasures of his temper. But that is the sort of story that one wants to tell only as a last resort. I should prefer to see in this implausible Epicurean vacillation a sign of how deeply ingrained is the ambivalence towards anger with which I began.

IV

I have said scarcely anything up to now about literature, because I do not think that there is any sign of the direct influence of Epicurean views. The area in which most effort has been expended is the anger of Aeneas in Virgil's *Aeneid*, especially with regard to the final act of the epic, in which Aeneas first contemplates sparing the wounded Turnus but then, when he sees the sword-belt of the boy Pallas whom Turnus had killed, becomes 'inflamed by fury [or the Furies] and terrible in his anger' (*furiis accensus et ira* | *terribilis*, 12.946–7) and slays his prostrate enemy. Those who wish to distinguish this from the rage of a Mezentius or a Turnus have often turned to Peripatetic notions of the right measure of anger[21] but more recently there have also been attempts to use Epicurean theory, notably by G. Karl Galinsky and Michael Erler.[22] The case against has been well stated by Michael Putnam (1990), but the debate raises some important issues about the ways in which we approach the passions in ancient literature, and I want to offer a few remarks of my own.

Galinsky employs a familiar opposition between the subjectivism of those who find Aeneas' anger disturbing and the scientific objectivity of those who do not, because they ground their interpretation in the original context of production and reception. (Some) modern sensibilities may be disturbed; (all?) ancient ones would not be. There is an equally familiar two-pronged objection to the attempt to resolve literary disputes in this way by an appeal to context and the original horizon of expectations: that the interpreter's point of view must inevitably enter into the hermeneutic act both in the delineation of context and in the analysis of its relationship to the text. What is the philosophical context of the *Aeneid*? Should one read it against a background of Stoic views? Or Peripatetic views? Or Epicurean views? Galinsky (1988, 339) indeed had claimed that 'so far from finding Aeneas' anger repugnant, most of the ancient ethical tradition would find it entirely appropriate and even praiseworthy'. But he acknowledges (1994, 6) that there is no such unity of view: 'there was no monolithic dogma about anger in the Hellenistic ethical philosophers taken as a whole'. Philodemus himself shows that even within one school there could be significantly differing views, and one might take anger as a paradigm case of how implausible it is to talk of 'What the Ancients Thought'. To try to fit the *Aeneid* to one school is a heroic act that few interpreters attempt, and most prefer an eclectic approach. This only exacerbates the problem, however, since which bits are selected will depend on the interpreter. Erler and Galinsky both stress the utility in relation to Aeneas' act of the Epicurean notion of proportionality in anger, given the heinous nature of Turnus' offence; but, as we have seen Seneca arguing above, that is in conflict with the requirement that the wise person should not get very angry. Why is one part of the doctrine part of the 'context' but not another?

---

[21] E.g. Thornton (1976), 159–63; E. Henry (1989), 169–71; Cairns (1989), 82–4. For bibliography on anger in the *Aeneid* see especially Erler (1992a), 105; Rieks (1989), 175–95.

[22] Galinsky (1988), (1994); Erler (1992a) with (1992b).

The arbitrary nature of the restriction of context is clearest with Erler, who explicitly sets out to find a context in Philodemus which will fit an apologetic approach to the anger of Aeneas: thus, the criterion for delineating the context for the poem is an interpretation of it. There is nothing wrong with this version of the hermeneutic circle, but we obviously cannot then claim for context the role of an objective foundation for interpretation. Galinsky (1994, 2) is prepared to accept that the context provides more than one possible way of reading the *Aeneid*,[23] but he still sees this as merely an intermediate stage through which the reader passes on the way to certainty:

> Vergil knows that there are different viewpoints on anger, and readers may respond differently, but he does not leave things diffuse or ambiguous in the sense of an aporia. Instead, this so-called ambiguity is really a means to have the reader work through a multiplicity, an authorially intended multiplicity, of alternatives and nuances, so that the poet's intentions may be understood all the better.

Again, however, the 'control' here is exercised by (a reading of) the text, not by the context: the context in itself does not provide a secure position outside interpretation from which meaning can be determined.

This raises more acutely the question of the relationship between text and context. Eclectic readings of Aeneas' anger allow both similarities to, and differences from, a particular school position to be significant, and the interpreter's subjectivity inevitably enters into the question of whether one stresses similarity or difference in a particular case. The problem can be seen clearly in relation to the intertextuality of the *Aeneid* not with philosophical texts but with its most central (and most discussed) models, the *Iliad* and the *Odyssey*.[24] The acceptance of these as a context for the *Aeneid* patently does not settle the question of the poem's interpretation. Is the end of the *Aeneid* more like *Iliad* 22 or *Odyssey* 22?[25] Do we stress resemblance to, or difference from, *Odyssey* 24 and *Iliad* 24? More generally, do we oppose the romance-like attempt to return to paternal origins in the *Odyssey* and *Aeneid* 1–6 to the progress of the *Iliad* and *Aeneid* 7–12 (as does Quint, 1993), or see the tragic stasis of the *Iliad* and the

[23] For Galinsky's 'discovery' of polysemy, see also Galinsky (1992a).

[24] See Galinsky (1988), 348, on 'intertextuality with the Homeric poems' as a companion tool to 'the Greco-Roman tradition of moral philosophy and ethics' in the contextualisation of the *Aeneid*.

[25] See Cairns (1989), 177–214.

teleological theodicy of the *Odyssey* everywhere in tension? Agreeing on the context does not here lead automatically to agreement on interpretation. A similar point has been made by R. O. A. M. Lyne (1994, 193–4) about the *Aeneid*'s relationship to Lucretius. Anchises enjoins the Roman in 6.851 to 'govern peoples by your authority' (*regere imperio populos*): one possible intertext for that line is *De rerum natura* 5.1129–30, where Lucretius tells contemporary Romans that 'it is much better to live a quiet life as a subject than to want to govern by authority and hold sovereignty' (*satius multo iam sit parere quietum | quam regere imperio res uelle et regna tenere*). One may either stress here the presence of the Epicurean trace as a subversive element (as logically, perhaps, those should do who see the end in Epicurean terms) or see Epicureanism as here transcended. The choice is an interpretative one: the context itself fixes nothing.

In fact, the attempt to find a theory which will somehow exculpate Aeneas' final anger seems anyhow misconceived. More recent theories which attempt to read the *Aeneid* 'positively' or 'optimistically' feel able to incorporate in their interpretations an acceptance of the negative aspect of Aeneas' passion. The more, for instance, we feel in the closing lines that Turnus is a victim, not simply a criminal, the more we may be able to take his death as that of a Girardian scapegoat, and thus arrive at a sense of closural resolution.[26] My own view of anger in the *Aeneid*[27] is that attempts to draw a distinction between Aeneas' state at the end of the poem and Turnus' previous rages fail. Erler (1992*a*, 109–10) stresses that the *diathesis* of Aeneas is basically good, unlike that of Turnus; but this requires him to see the infuriation of Turnus in Book 7 as merely an example of 'working with' a previous disposition, which limits the sense we have in the Allecto scene of its tragic power.[28] The imagery of emotion in the *Aeneid* is overwhelmingly negative and Stoic; no one who wished to take a positive view of anger would use phrases such as 'inflamed by fury [or the Furies]' (*furiis accensus*).[29] But the *Aeneid* is certainly not Chrysippan, in that this imagery tends to presuppose division in the

---

[26] See Hardie (1993), and compare the reading of the end of the *Georgics* by Habinek (1990), taken with Thomas (1991*b*): a still more nuanced account is promised by Llewelyn Morgan in a forthcoming Cambridge Ph.D. thesis on the *Georgics*.

[27] My account here is, necessarily, brief and dogmatic: I hope to provide further detail elsewhere.

[28] See Feeney (1991), 169–71.

[29] On the attempt of Cairns (1989) to distinguish between *furor* and a more positive (!) *furiae*, see Thomas (1991*a*).

soul. Moreover the appetites and passions tend to be assimilated, rather than distinguished, and jointly opposed to reason, which attempts constantly to control them. This binary opposition within the soul between reason and emotional disturbance is consonant with the wider ideology of the *Aeneid*, with its stress on the imposition of order in the state and the world through forceful action, whether by Aeneas, Augustus, or Jupiter (see Hardie (1986)). It is possible to take the poem to be optimistic about the success of such control. But Virgil's work is full of scenes of lost control, where individuals or groups are carried away by emotion: Aeneas' last act is only one of many such scenes.[30] I read the *Aeneid* as simultaneously asserting the absolute necessity of emotional control and its complete impossibility. The way in which it does this is deeply embedded in a context of ancient philosophical speculation about the passions, but such a conclusion is obviously one no ancient and few modern philosophers would accept. Philosophy has to believe in solutions: literature often likes to stress that there are none.

I tried to make Epicurean anger relevant to the passions of literature, but failed. But I do suggest a different link with the themes of this volume. My failure mirrors the failure of the Epicurean doctrine itself: I cannot see coherence in the Epicurean treatment of the emotion. But there is no reason to think that a coherent account of anger which satisfies our intuitions can be given. Why should we think that the complexities of Western anger can be brought to order? To reverse my earlier argument, if there was an essence to anger, there might be a plausible aspiration to capture that essence in a theory: but anger is not like that. Our intuitions about anger are inherently incoherent and unstable: the problem of anger cannot be solved.[31] Or, to be precise, it cannot be solved philosophically without a simplifying revision of our intuitions that will fail to be persuasive to all but the most determined devotees of reason. From this point of view, literature is part of the problem. If it is a cliché to say that one cannot have literature without emotion, one cannot have the emotions without literature either. The ancient moralists

---

[30] See e.g. Aeneas in 2.314, 594–5, 776–7; 10.813 etc.; Coroebus in 2.407–8; Nisus in 9.424–6; Lausus in 10.811; the Trojans in 2.42–3, 244–5; Latinus and the Latins in 7.594–6, 599–600; the Trojans and the Rutulians in 12.313–15.

[31] See further Nussbaum (1994), e.g. 402–5, 507–10. This chapter was originally written before the appearance of Nussbaum's book (though several of her chapters had appeared already as articles), and I have not been able to revise it to take account of her dense and brilliant arguments.

were right: literature does not analyse the passions, it creates them, engendering in us a mass of conflicting intuitions. But already to talk of the problem of anger is to discount its value in our lives. Anger is fashioned by the stories we tell, but is also a vital element in those stories, in the way we make ourselves part of the world. And the complexities of our stories of attachment and involvement are preferable to any philosophical revision, even if that is the only hope for coherence. Even the Epicureans, perhaps the least post-modern thinkers the world has ever seen, could not get rid of anger: neither can we.

CHAPTER 2

Cicero and the expression of grief

Andrew Erskine

I

> What is not only more wretched, but also more repugnant or
> more grotesque than a man who is shattered, enfeebled and laid
> low by distress (*aegritudo*).[1]

So Cicero wrote in his *Tusculans*. The intensity of feeling in this
rhetorical question is no coincidence. Cicero knew from personal
experience the devastating effect of one particular form of distress –
that is grief, by which I mean the pain felt at someone's death. Not
long before he wrote the *Tusculans*, Cicero had had to cope with the
death of his only daughter, Tullia. So when he wrote about grief and
the passions in the *Tusculans*, it was not a subject of merely academic
interest to him. This is a point that should be remembered when we
read his account of the passions there.

Tullia had died in February 45 shortly after giving birth. For a
while Cicero had stayed at the house of his friend Atticus, but,
fortunately for us, on 6 March he left and so recommended his daily
correspondence with Atticus.[2] These letters give us a vivid picture of
his response to Tullia's death. He tells of the pain he feels as
memories gnaw at him, although it is interesting that he never
actually reports any memories of his daughter. In fact, after her
death, he never once mentions Tullia by name in any of his letters or
other writings.[3] Instead, he concentrates on his own suffering and his
attempts to 'cure' himself.

His grief is something which he has to fight against, a passion that
needs to be brought under control. 'When I am alone all my

---

[1] Cic. *Tusc.* 4.35. All references are to Cicero, unless otherwise stated.
[2] Shackleton Bailey (1966), 309.
[3] Memories: *Att.* 12.18. Numerous references to Tullia before her death up until *Att.* 12.5c
(probably June 46); *ad Fam.* 7.23.4 (Dec. 46), 6.18.5 (Jan. 45).

conversation is with books, but it is interrupted by fits of weeping which I struggle against as best I can. But so far it is an unequal fight.'[4] Or 'I do everything to bring composure not to my soul but at least to my face if I can. When I do this, sometimes I feel that I am doing wrong, but at other times I feel that I should be doing wrong if I did not' (*Att.* 12.14). So there is a certain ambivalence in Cicero's attitude: he should not yield to grief, yet at the same time it might be wrong not to express it. Later, in the *Tusculans* (3.61, 74), he was to argue that people mistakenly think that they have a duty to grieve. If Cicero cannot hide his face, then he hides himself. In his search for solitude he has been going into the woods from early in the day until evening (*Att.* 12.15). He is irritated when Marcius Philippus comes to stay the night, but relieved when Philippus limits his contact to a formal call and goes. The intensity of Cicero's grief was noted in antiquity and Plutarch reports that he divorced his new young bride because he felt that she was unduly satisfied at Tullia's death (Plut. *Cic.* 41). But he had other reasons for unhappiness and these all became focused on Tullia. He had divorced his first wife not long before; Rome was recovering from civil war; Caesar was now dictator.[5]

While he was trying to cope with his grief, Cicero sought comfort in solitude, choosing to live in the country rather than the city (*Att.* 12.15, 16, 18). The self-pity of his letters may suggest that he spent his time moping around in his country residence at Astura, but it is clear in fact that Cicero kept himself occupied. Nevertheless, the activities which he pursued were not a distraction from grief but rather ones which made grief their subject. He prepared to build a shrine (*fanum*) to his daughter, he read avidly, particularly philosophy and writings on grief, and he wrote a *consolatio* to himself and later other philosophical works.

Cicero's project of a shrine to his daughter appears in numerous letters. He is fairly sure what he wants the shrine to be like, so he does not discuss that.[6] What he is uncertain about is where it should go, so his letters to Atticus on the subject rapidly become very businesslike. Where the idea came from is unclear.[7] In order to

---

[4] *Att.* 12.15, trans. Shackleton Bailey, also 12.13.

[5] On Cicero's life and disappointments at this time, Shackleton Bailey (1971), 201–15; Rawson (1975), 203–29, esp. 222–9; Mitchell (1991), 263–88, esp. 283–8. Balsdon (1964), 173, is not entirely sympathetic when he suggests that Cicero may have been suffering from 'the emotional instability which sometimes besets the sexagenarian'.

[6] *Att.* 12.18.1, cf. 12.19.1 on pillars, 12.36 not like a tomb.

[7] Shackleton Bailey (1966), 404–13; Rawson (1975), 227–8.

convince a sceptical Atticus that such a shrine is a sensible idea, he says he can cite some writers he has been reading who support the plan (*Att.* 12.18.1). What is interesting here is the fact that Cicero is seeking practical help from his reading. The shrine was probably never built. It fades out of the letters while the discussion is still about the purchase of suitable land. Perhaps further reading of the philosophical literature dissuaded him. In the *Tusculans* Cicero reports Zeno's (Stoic) view that *aegritudo* (distress, pain) persists so long as the idea of the evil is fresh (*recens*). As an example he gives Artemisia, who, by building the Mausoleum, kept her grief for her dead husband alive and thus wasted away herself (*Tusc.* 3.75).

As early as his first stay with Atticus, immediately after Tullia's death, Cicero took to reading as a way of coping with his bereavement (*Att.* 12.15). He says that in Atticus' house he read everything that there was on the alleviation of grief (*Att.* 12.14.3). Here and elsewhere, he talks of his grief as if it were an unfortunate ailment that can be cured. The books of learned men are remedies. He is the brave invalid, taking his medicine (*Att.* 12.215, also 12.20.1). Again, it is important to notice that Cicero is reading these works, many of which would have been philosophical, for the practical help they can give him in overcoming his grief.

There was, of course, another reason for reading them, again a practical one – Cicero was writing his own *consolatio*, a treatise which is now lost. A work that is said to have had a particular influence on the composition of his *consolatio* is the *On Grief* (περὶ πένθους) of the Academic philosopher Crantor, written in the late fourth or early third century.[8] The precise nature of this influence is obscure because neither treatise survives. A common feature of the *consolatio* was to list examples of people in a similar situation in order to show that, if other people could endure it, so could you. Cicero's researches in this area were very thorough and he is constantly checking with Atticus the details of good Roman examples of children who predeceased their parents. 'I would like you to let me know in your next letter whether Cn. Caepio, father of Claudius' wife Servilia, died at sea while his father was still alive or after his death and also whether Rutilia died while her son, C. Cotta, was still alive or after his death. They are relevant to the book I am writing about the alleviation of mourning' (*Att.* 12.20.2,

---

[8] Plin. *Nat.* Pref. 22; on Cicero's *consolatio*, Philippson *RE* 8A, 1123–5.

also 12.24.2). Some such examples also find their way into the *Tusculans* (3.70).

This was not the first time that Cicero had written a *consolatio* (but it was the first time he had written one to himself). He had written one before Tullia's death to a certain Titius, consoling him for the loss of his children in an epidemic. It begins with a familiar theme – all men are mortal – then takes a not entirely tactful approach, arguing that it is better to be dead than living in these troubled times. Finally, he reminds Titius that there should be a limit to mourning.[9] This was not advice that Cicero himself took, and he had to be reminded of it discreetly by Atticus (*Att.* 12.20.1, 38a.1). But, as Cicero says in the *Tusculans*, those who comfort others are frequently laid low themselves when they are in the same situation, just as greedy men criticise greedy men. People spot the faults of others but forget their own (*Tusc.* 3.73).

II

So far, I have looked at Cicero's response to his daughter's death. I have tried to establish two things in particular: first, Cicero's personal experience of grief and, second, his conception of philosophy as therapy. It was therapy, not just because it was a distraction but, more importantly, because it could offer practical guidance. Both these points are relevant to understanding the *Tusculans*. This work, written in the flurry of philosophical activity after Tullia's death, devotes two books to the passions, with a significant proportion of this devoted to grief. Typically, this work has been studied simply as evidence for Greek philosophy, especially in the early part of this century. After a passing mention of Cicero's grief, scholars have got down to the serious business of working out what sources Cicero used.[10] But in fact, the account of the passions in the *Tusculans* is so coloured by Cicero's own experience that the two are virtually inseparable.[11] It was a product of Cicero's wide reading and recent

---

[9] *Ad Fam.* 5.16, cf., on a limit for mourning, *Att.* 12.10; for a contemporary *consolatio*, see Servius Sulpicius to Cicero, *ad Fam.* 4.5.

[10] Dougan and Henry (1934), vol. 2, xxx–xlvii, sum up some of the many arguments about possible sources, reflecting the emphasis on *Quellenforschung* current in late nineteenth- and early twentieth-century scholarship. More recent studies on the relationship between Cicero and Hellenistic philosophy are surveyed in Colish (1985), 65–79. Colish herself is interested in the way in which Cicero used Stoicism rather than which works he used. For the latter approach, see also Nussbaum (1990*b*).

[11] Cf. MacKendrick (1989), 163–4.

experience. As such it represents his own response to Greek philosophy on the subject, a response that is not always free from self-contradiction.

An examination of the *Tusculans* reveals the presence of Cicero's personal experience of grief. In some places, it is explicit, for instance, when he refers to his own attempts to cure himself of grief (3.76, 4.63). Elsewhere there are passages of striking intensity and vividness which seem to be the result of Cicero's own suffering and his reflection upon that suffering (3.25, 27; 4.35). At one point in his discussion of the Epicureans, he counters their position with an argument which appears to be drawn from his own experience of grief. The Epicureans suggest, he says, that, when faced with something that causes you grief, you should stop thinking about it and turn to pleasure instead. But, he argues, this is not possible: 'For when things which we consider to be evil are jabbing at us, concealment or forgetfulness is not within our power. These things tear us to pieces, they torment us, they stab us, they burn us, they do not allow us to breathe' (*Tusc.* 3.35). Surely he is thinking of himself here, remembering the hold that grief had over him in the months after Tullia's death (discussed in Section 1). Remarks such as these recall the pain expressed in his letters to Atticus. The memories gnawed at him and grief was something which attacked and had to be fought against, although in the *Tusculans* Cicero is, necessarily, more rhetorical.[12] Tullia's presence is also felt in the recurring example of the grieving parent (*Tusc.* 3.30, 58–9, 63, 70–1). The personal nature of the *Tusculans* is highlighted in the concluding sentence of the final book; the writing of the work had helped, he wrote, 'in my very painful sorrows and the various troubles which had surrounded me on all sides' (*Tusc.* 5.121).

But personal involvement also affects the amount of space which he gives to different aspects of the passions. He follows the Stoics in classifying the passions under four headings. Apart from *aegritudo* there are fear, appetite and pleasure.[13] *Aegritudo* is Cicero's translation of the Greek λύπη and it represents a shift in meaning, from 'pain' to 'illness'. Thus, ideas of curing are imported which were not

---

[12] Memories: *Att.* 12.18.1; grief fought against: 12.13, 14, 15; on rhetoric in *Tusc.*, see MacKendrick (1989), 163–8, but note also Douglas (1991), 67; Cicero on *Tusc.* as *declamatio*, *Tusc.* 1.7; 2.26.

[13] Fear = φόβος = *timor*; appetite = ἐπιθυμία = *libido*; pleasure = ἡδονή = *uoluptas* or *(gestiens) laetitia*; see *Tusc.* 3.23, 27; 4.13, 20, for the various translations of ἡδονή. On this fourfold classification, cf. D.L. 7.110, LS 65 A, B, E.

so apparent in λύπη. Then within these four categories numerous passions are placed, including grief, which is a subsection of *aegritudo*.[14] It is *aegritudo* which is singled out as Cicero's main concern – the other categories of the passions are relegated to Book 4 (see *Tusc.* 3.25). Cicero's priorities are made clear in the following passage:

> For while every passion is wretchedness, *aegritudo* is actually being put on the rack. Appetite involves eagerness, exuberant joy [i.e. pleasure] involves frivolity, fear involves humiliation, but *aegritudo* involves worse things – decay, torture, torment, repulsiveness. It tears and devours the soul and completely destroys it. Unless we strip it off and cast it aside we cannot be free from wretchedness. (*Tusc.* 3.27)

It is grief, and not *aegritudo* in general, that Cicero really has in mind here. He says that he is concentrating on grief in Book 3, because it is 'the greatest of all distresses' (*Tusc.* 3.81). So personal experience was important here – though it is worth pointing out a more mundane reason for the emphasis placed on grief. By this time, Cicero was exceptionally well read on grief.

But, when the Hellenistic philosophers who developed theories of the passions are examined, there is no sign that they gave grief the kind of prominence that Cicero did. In the *Tusculans* it is the Stoic account of the passions that most influences Cicero, but the Stoic concern is with the nature of the passions in general and the relationship of the passions with the soul and rationality. They are interested in grief only in so far as it is an instance of a wider problem. For them grief is just one passion out of many. Arius Didymus, in his summary of Stoic ethics, gives πένθος (grief) as one of ten types of λύπη – it is pain at untimely death. It is listed along with such feelings as malice, envy, jealousy and pity. The *On Passions* attributed to Andronicus is more thorough; the author has managed to list twenty-five types of pain, including grief (with the same definition). Diogenes Laertius, on the other hand, comes up with nine types of pain, but omits grief altogether.[15] This is not to say that nobody wrote about grief. Both Theophrastus and the Academic Crantor wrote works specifically on grief, their περὶ

---

[14] The four categories are named in *Tusc.* 3.23–4, but there is little notice of the individual passions until Book 4 where many of the subdivisions are given, 4.11–22. When Cicero gives these subdivisions, πένθος is translated as *luctus* (4.18), but in *Tusc.* 3 he is less precise and shifts between *dolor* (e.g. 3.55, 70), *luctus* (e.g. 3.58, 64, 71), *maeror* (e.g. 3.63, 71).

[15] Arius Didymus in Stob. *Ecl.* 2.92; Ps.-Andronicus, *On Passions* 2; D.L. 7.111.

πένθους.[16] But, in these cases, grief was treated separately and not in the context of an account of the passions. So when Cicero wrote about the passions, he was putting an unaccustomed emphasis on grief.

But Cicero's whole approach is different from that of the Greek philosophers he is discussing. Cicero is concerned with a particular problem and it is a practical problem. We suffer from passions such as fear, grief, anger and lust. How do we get rid of them? What Cicero is doing in Book 3 of the *Tusculans* is looking for a cure. He is interested in Greek writings on the nature of the passions, and *aegritudo* in particular, in so far as this helps to explain how to cure them. The Greek philosophers themselves studied the passions in the context of their psychological and ethical theory. They were interested in the cure of the passions, but this was part of a broader investigation, whereas for Cicero the cure was central. In what follows, I will avoid, as far as possible, the question of the extent to which he understood or misunderstood his sources and indeed what his sources actually were. My concern is with the way in which Cicero approached the subject and how his approach differs from that of the Hellenistic philosophers he had read. A problem that must be remembered here is that, although Cicero's text survives, the Hellenistic accounts are no longer extant.

The theme of Book 3 is that of putting an end to *aegritudo*, especially to grief. Cicero goes through a wide variety of different philosophical approaches to the nature of the passions and their control. He deals with Epicureans, Cyrenaics, Peripatetics (very dismissively), Academics and Stoics, assessing their various arguments. He sums up briefly at 3.76:

> These then are the duties of consolers, to uproot *aegritudo* completely, or to calm it, or to remove it as much as possible, or to restrain it and not allow it to spread further or to divert it elsewhere. Some, such as Cleanthes, think that the only duty of the consoler is to teach that it is not an evil at all; others, like the Peripatetics, that it is not a great evil. There are some who redirect attention from evils to goods, as Epicurus does. There are others, such as the Cyrenaics, who think that it is sufficient to show that nothing unexpected has happened. And Chrysippus thinks that the chief element in consoling is to relieve the mourner

---

[16] D.L. 5.44; Plin. *Nat.* Pref. 22; D.L. 4.27. None are known by Stoics. On grief in Greek philosophy, see Kassel (1958), 3–48.

of the opinion [that he should be mourning], in case he thinks that he is performing a just and obligatory duty.

Cicero concludes by saying that some people combine all these approaches as he himself did in his *consolatio*. He is interested in what the philosophical schools have to offer on the subject of the cure of grief and here he relates it explicitly to his own experience.

The Greek term which has been translated in this chapter as 'passion' is *pathos* (πάθος), but the various Greek philosophical schools in fact disagreed not only about how a *pathos* should be analysed but also about what it constituted. As Inwood (1985, 127) puts it, '*pathos* is a technical term whose meaning is determined by the theory in which it functions'. The Stoics were clear that all *pathē* were bad and that the wise man had no *pathē* at all; he had achieved a state of *apatheia*. But, when used by the Peripatetics, *pathē* described a much wider range of mental states and could more properly be translated as 'emotion'. The Peripatetics allowed that there were bad *pathē* which were not in line with reason, but there were also good *pathē* that were in line with reason.[17] Thus, in his search for a cure Cicero has to cope with the problem of assessing incompatible theories and relating them to each other. When he discusses the different options for curing the passions, his outlook is especially influenced by the Stoics, the school which had done most to develop a systematic theory of the passions. Cicero (*Tusc.* 3.22, 4.33) accepts as a basic premise the Stoic view that all passions are bad and so treats as ludicrous the Peripatetic position that some *pathē* are acceptable.

The early Stoics operated with the concept of a unitary soul and rejected the divided soul of Plato and Aristotle.[18] So, for the Stoics, the passions (that is, bad emotions) were not the product of a conflict between reason and the irrational which reason lost, but the product of a soul in which rationality was inadequately developed. Such a soul places value on the wrong things; instead of virtue it values wealth, health and other external things. In the psychological model presupposed, a passion involved a false belief that something was good or bad and this belief produced an alteration in the state of the

[17] See Arist. *NE* 1105b19–1106a13, 1108a31–b10.
[18] Later Stoics such as Posidonius and (probably) Panaetius seem to have adopted some form of the Platonic divided soul; see Gal. *PHP* Book 5, esp. 5.4.1–4, De Lacy (1978–84), vol. 1 312–13; also Rist (1969), 182–4, 211–15; Erskine (1990), 195–201. On current debate about the scope and nature of Posidonius' innovations, see Introd., Sect ii, text to nn. 23–4, and Gill, Ch. 11, Sect. iii, text to nn. 43–9. For the divided soul in Cic. *Tusc.* 4, see e.g. 4.10.

soul. Thus, in the case of λύπη / *aegritudo*, there is a false belief that
something, for instance the death of a relative, is bad and this leads,
under appropriate circumstances, to a contraction of the soul.
Chrysippus describes such a soul as diseased and says that, just as
there is an art for curing the body, so there is an art for curing the
soul.[19] This involves perfecting one's rationality and that means
learning to value the right things, as the good or wise person did.
Such a person would not be bothered by passions: for passions were
symptoms of a diseased soul.[20] But a Stoic would seek to cure his
soul not in order to get rid of passions but because a healthy soul was
the proper condition for a man's soul.

Curing the soul was clearly a solution to the problem of passions
as posed by Cicero, but it was very much an ideal solution. Few if
any were likely to achieve it. It is useful here to distinguish two
approaches to getting rid of the passions: one is the 'ideal' solution
outlined above, the other I will call the 'practical' approach. This
practical approach has a less long-term aim and seeks to cure
someone of a specific passion, such as particular feelings of grief or
anger. In Book 3 of the *Tusculans*, Cicero oscillates between the ideal
and the practical approach. He begins by arguing that it is philosophy which cures the soul. Through the study of philosophy
someone can become a good man and so have no passions at all
(3.1–7, 12–13; also 3.82–4). But Cicero is really faced with the
specific problem of curing *grief*. This problem is treated in a more
practical way. The first medicine is to demonstrate that the death is
not an evil or at least not a great one. To do this would require the
use of arguments such as those gathered together in Book 1 which is
devoted to refuting the proposition that death is an evil. In Book 3,
Cicero goes on to say that different methods of treatment are
appropriate to different cases. It might help, for instance, to know of
examples of people in a similar situation. But what appeals most to
Cicero is Chrysippus' idea that people feel that they have a duty to
grieve at something they think is bad. If the false judgement that they
have this duty is eliminated, then they can recover. But Cicero

---

[19] See Gal. *PHP* 5.2.20–5; *Tusc.* 3.1, and in later Stoicism, Sen. *Ep.* 8.2. For a similar idea
attributed to Democritus, see Clement Al., *Paed.* 1.6, DK B 31. See further Nussbaum (1994),
esp. chs. 9–10.

[20] On the Stoic theory of the passions, see LS 65; also Rist (1969), 22–36; Gill (1983a);
K. Campbell (1985); Inwood (1985), 127–81; Frede (1986); Nussbaum (1987b); see further
Introd., Sect. II, text to nn. 21–2, 28.

recognises that, although it sounds a good idea, it is not very practical, because it is difficult to persuade grief-stricken people to abandon this belief.[21]

Sometimes the ideal and the practical approaches converge, as when Cicero discusses Epicurus' idea that pleasure provides a distraction from grief: 'If you see any of your relatives tormented by grief, will you give them a sturgeon rather than a little Socratic treatise? Will you encourage them to listen to the sound of the water organ rather than of Plato?' (*Tusc.* 3.43). Not everyone may think that the answer to this question is quite as obvious as Cicero appears to imagine.

The shift from the ideal, curing the diseased soul, to the practical, eradicating individual passions, is made easier by Cicero's interpretation of the Stoic theory of the passions. The Stoics placed great emphasis on the analogy between the health and sickness of the soul and of the body. But Cicero goes further and mistakenly thinks that πάθος should be translated into Latin by *morbus*, disease, not a sense in which the Greek word was commonly used.[22] In the end, he does not use this translation himself, because he thinks it unsuitable in Latin. Instead he prefers *perturbatio*, 'disturbance' (*Tusc.* 3.7, also *Fin.* 3.35). For Cicero grief is something curable. This view is reinforced by his translation of λύπη by *aegritudo*, which substitutes 'illness' for 'pain'. The Stoics may have spent much time talking about the passions but they have little to say about their cure. Cicero goes so far as to say that the Stoic writings on the subject are 'minuscule', *perexigua* (*Tusc.* 4.9), and Galen makes the same point (*PHP* 4.7.23). And one would search the doxographical accounts in vain for material on curing individual passions. Why should there be this absence? Presumably, it is because it is not the passions themselves that are cured, at least not individually, but the soul. To cure a man of his grief would be only to tackle the symptoms; the problem lies in the soul. It is the soul that is diseased.[23] Chrysippus wrote four books on the passions; the last book was known as the θεραπευτικόν (therapeutic) or alternatively the ἠθικόν (ethical). But the surviving portions of this last book are not about curing individual passions

---

[21] *Tusc.* 3.77–9; I suspect that, in contrast to Cicero, Chrysippus' purpose was not to cure grief but to explain how grief comes to an end: when people no longer feel that they have a duty to grieve, then they stop grieving, *PHP* 4.12–17= LS 65 O.

[22] See LSJ, entry for πάθος; also Inwood (1985), 127–8.

[23] See Nussbaum (1987*b*), 138, 161–75, on interrelations between passions.

such as grief but about reason and restoring the harmony to the
soul.[24]

For philosophers such as the Stoics, whose aim was to understand
the passions, it was necessary to understand why and how passions
cease. Most people, after all, do not grieve forever. Such an enquiry
was undertaken not with the object of producing a cure, but in order
to achieve a satisfactory analysis of what a passion is and how it
worked. For those who believed that the human soul was divided, the
cessation of a passion (in the sense of a bad or unreasonable emotion)
did not present a problem – in time reason reasserts itself and brings
the irrational element, which is distressed (for instance), back under
its control. Once this has happened the passion has come to an end.
But this is not so easily explained by the Stoics with their unitary
soul. Over time, grief does cease, even though we still think that the
event that caused it is bad. Chrysippus seems to hold that some other
belief is involved; in the case of *aegritudo*, it is the belief that it is
appropriate to be distressed which fades.[25] What Chrysippus is doing
is seeking to explain how and why the passion ceases. Cicero, on the
other hand, is mainly interested in the practical side, the solution or
cure. Both would agree that if the belief is eliminated, then there is
no grief, but Chrysippus would see this as an explanation, whereas
Cicero would see it as a means of cure.[26] The Stoics may have
discussed this question of curing particular passions. But if they did,
it was peripheral to their main interest: the nature of the passions.
For them it was perfecting the rationality of the soul that was
important.

What I am suggesting here is that Cicero is presenting a collection
of arguments on the passions, the discussion of which is influenced by
Stoicism. But the problem he is posing is essentially his own – how
do you cure grief? To answer this, he has trawled through the
relevant philosophical literature for material on the passions and
λύπη in particular. He then applied this to his problem. For Cicero

[24] Gal. *PHP* 5.2.43–51; 4.1.14; 4.4.23; 4.5.13–14; 4.5.20–3; 4.6.12–14; 4.7.21; 5.2.22–4; 5.2.43;
5.3.13–14; 5.7.52.

[25] Chrysippus apparently acknowledged the difficulty raised for his theory by such
phenomena; see Gal. *PHP* 4.7.12–18; Inwood (1985), 146–55; also Gill, Ch. 11, Sect. 111, text
to nn. 43–5, which notes the question of the reliability of Galen's evidence on this subject.

[26] Cicero does not seem to pay sufficient attention to the difference between the type of belief
involved in passion and more everyday beliefs which can be abandoned as soon as someone
is taught that they are false. On Chrysippus' distinction between a *pathos* and other types of
error or mistake (*hamartēma*), which can more easily be changed, see Gal. *PHP* 4.2.24–7, De
Lacy (1978–84), vol. 1 242–5; also LS 65 A(7–8), J.

the cure is central, not peripheral, and the emphasis is firmly on grief. His approach in Book 3 is practical, as it tends to be in the other books in the *Tusculans*, for instance in Book 1, on not fearing death, and in Book 2, on the endurance of physical pain. This practicality may reflect Cicero's own attitude and particular circumstances, or it may be something distinctively Roman: the thought that philosophy should be useful. On the other hand, it may reflect a trend. Later Stoics, Musonius Rufus, Seneca, Epictetus, all adopt a more practical, moralising approach in which behaviour and attitude are as important as analysis.[27]

[27] My thanks to Theresa Urbainczyk and Christopher Gill for their invaluable comments.

CHAPTER 3

The subjugation of grief in Seneca's 'Epistles'

Marcus Wilson

I

The consolation is perhaps the paradigmatic instance of the therapeutic mode of philosophising.[1] Grief, like a disease, corrodes the soul which must be restored to its proper state of healthy equilibrium by applied remedies in the form of appropriate arguments and encouragements calculated to expel the disruptive passion. While the therapeutic metaphor serves to highlight an essential facet of Hellenistic and Roman philosophy, some of its implications are potentially misleading, in particular, the dichotomy it sets up between the sick, helpless patient and the healthy, proficient therapist. It presupposes a physician sufficiently calm and detached to make accurate diagnoses and offer apt and salutary counsel; a patient whose needs are primarily negative, to obtain release from pain and illness; a one-way process from which the sufferer, but not the healer, emerges healthier; a relationship of a basically professional type, a characterisation which may, in some cases, overshadow other aspects equally or even more philosophically significant (such as friendship).

Another dimension of the *consolatio* overlooked by the therapy analogy is that it is also a literary form. Since its intended audience is wider than the immediate addressee, its function is commonly not purely therapeutic; through allusion to other texts the context in which the advice is delivered may be stretched; the medical imagery may be diversified with other kinds of comparison; the language may not be precise and consistent but suggestive and ambiguous; tone may shift from composed to animated and vice versa; generic

---

[1] The therapeutic aspect of Greek and Roman philosophy is hardly a new discovery but has recently been brought into special prominence. Some relevant studies are Cushman (1958); P. Hadot (1987), 13–15; Nussbaum (1986*b*), (1990*b*), 1–6, and (1994). On the use of the medical metaphor in specifically consolatory literature, see the remarks of Morford (1973), 30–1.

conventions may not be followed so much as exploited or even remodelled; in suppressing one strong emotion, others may be vented or provoked.

Many of these qualities are evident in Seneca's consolatory writings, especially those of his *Epistles* (namely 63 and 99) that deal with the problem of grief. These cannot be read as isolated *consolationes* but must also be viewed as part of a collection concerned no less with the reformation of the author's self than with that of his correspondent.[2] 'I feel I am myself not being so much improved as transfigured', he writes (6.1). Against the picture of the philosopher as doctor should be juxtaposed Seneca's insistence that he, as Lucilius' adviser, is merely a fellow patient lying in the same hospital ward sharing information about his illness and its treatment (*tamquam in eodem ualetudinario iaceam, de communi tecum malo conloquor et remedia communico*, 27.1).[3] 'No doctor lives here', he later insists, 'only a sick man' (*non medicus, sed aeger hic habitat*, 68.9). This seems far more precise an analogy for Seneca's attempt to console Lucilius after the death of his friend, Flaccus (63), where he acknowledges that his own grief upon the death of Serenus was beyond his power to quell. He is himself one of those vanquished by sorrow (*inter exempla sim eorum quos dolor uicit*, 63.14). When subsequently in the final sentence he uses the first person plural jussive verb form ('let us imagine...', *cogitemus*) it is apparent that (as so often in the *Epistles*) he really does mean 'let us...'. The advice is directed at Seneca no less than Lucilius. If Seneca here must be likened to a physician, it is a physician himself severely affected by the same symptoms diagnosed in the patient.

II

The analogy of therapy can be seen to apply to *Epistle* 63, though not without an idiosyncratic twist; its pertinence to *Epistle* 99, a more complex and paradoxical consolatory text, is far more problematic. Marullus' son has died in childhood. Seneca does not write to the father immediately but only after it becomes known that his grieving is persistent. His opening words are aggressive and unsympathetic in

---

[2] The interrelation of epistles within the collection is a basic principle stressed by most modern commentators, e.g. Cancik (1967); Maurach (1970); Wilson (1987).

[3] Seneca frequently indicates that he does not regard himself as a Stoic sage (*sapiens*) but someone still on the road to wisdom, e.g. *Epp.* 6.1; 8.2; 57.3; 71.30, 35–7; 75.16–18; 79.11–13; 87.4–5; *Cons. Helv.* 5.2; *Ben.* 7.17.1; *Tranq.* 8.9; *Vit. Beat.* 17.3–18.2.

tone: 'Are you looking for consolation? Take some abuse instead' (*solacia expectas? convicia accipe*, 2). This opening is recalled (with the repetition of *expectare*) at the letter's close where any therapeutic intention is vigorously denied: 'I wrote this to you not thinking that you should look to me for a remedy at this late date ... but to reprove the brief delay during which you've lapsed from your true self ...' (*haec tibi scripsi, non tamquam expectaturus esses remedium a me tam serum ... sed ut castigarem exiguam illam moram qua a te recessisti*, 32). Though, as in *Epistle* 63, the principal theme here is 'grief', that is by no means the only strong emotion involved. As readers we are justified in wondering what feelings Marullus might have experienced on receiving such a communication, one calculated, it seems, to incite his emotions rather than produce any sense of serenity or resignation.

And what about Seneca? Does he not write passionately as if angered and exasperated by Marullus? By remarking in his introductory 'covering note' to Lucilius that in his letter to Marullus he has 'not followed the usual convention' (1), Seneca advertises how conscious he is that this is an unorthodox manner in which to accost the bereaved.[4] All Marullus gets is, instead of consolation, vituperation. His pain (*dolor*) is not assuaged but disparaged. What he needs is not healing but the cessation of healing. The relationship between *Epistles* 99 and 63 is characteristic of Seneca's strategy throughout the collection. *Epistle* 99 revisits the theme of grief broached in *Epistle* 63 but with this disconcerting departure: it turns back on itself to question the value of some forms of consolation as well.

In dealing with Marullus' grief, Seneca's argument unfolds in a manner which seems, at first sight, not especially logical. Numerous ideas are repeated at different stages rather than fully expounded all at once. For instance, the idea that in universal terms the length of a human life is minimal comes up in sections 10–11 to be recalled later in 31. The objection that Seneca, as a Stoic (of sorts), is too harsh and demanding (the charge of *duritia*) is raised and rebutted first in section 15 then later in 26. The importance of remembering shared happiness in the past instead of just lamenting present loss is found in

---

[4] Seneca similarly claims originality for his consolation to his mother (*Cons. Helv.* 1.2–3). There are references in ancient sources to an element of reproach and a severer tone in some other consolatory writings, e.g. Cic. *ad Brut.* 1.9.1; Sen. *Cons. Marc.* 4.1; Plin. *Ep.* 5.16.10. In none of these does this element seem to have completely overridden the essential aim of providing alleviation from suffering. There is no good reason to dispute Seneca's description of his procedure in *Ep.* 99 as novel.

4–5 and again in 23–4. The uncertainty associated with *Fortuna* enters on several occasions (3, 9, 22, 32). Insistence that for all born mortal, death is inevitable occurs in 6, 8, 9 and 22. The fact that the deceased was only a small child, a central issue, is handled discontinuously in sections 10–14, again in 22–3 and finally in 31.[5]

What is apparent, on the other hand, is a sophisticated rhetorical technique whereby the discussion oscillates between examining grief on an abstract and on a personal level. At the commencement of his letter Seneca quickly shifts the focus away from Marullus' specific loss to a hypothetical alternative: 'What would you do', he asks, 'if you'd lost a friend?' (*quid faceres si amicum perdidisses?*, 2). This, Seneca suggests, is the greatest loss possible (*quod damnorum omnium maximum est*, 3). Even then, protracted grieving would be inappropriate. He does not allow Marullus to concentrate on the deceased's age or blood-relationship to himself, on the image of his dead son. First Seneca seeks to establish the need to limit grief generally; only then, in this carefully defined context, will he address the specifics of Marullus' situation. This he approaches (though at a distance) in section 6, where he recalls that there are countless examples (*innumerabilia sunt exempla*) of fathers who buried sons but refused to let it disrupt the performance of their public duties.[6] These sons, though, are grown (*iuuenes*). Seneca comes no closer to Marullus' particular circumstances at this stage, quickly reverting to the discussion of mortality in universal terms (7–9). He continues to postpone confronting the question of the very young age of Marullus' son until section 10 where he imagines Marullus interjecting: 'But he was only a child when he died!'[7] Even here Seneca immediately redirects Marullus' attention away from present reality to the hypothetical: 'Let's pass over to someone who's grown old ... in how little does he surpass an infant!'

Seneca's plan of attack is to establish the general rule that lingering grief is always unwarranted, then to maintain that the young age of the deceased does not justify making an exception. Rather, he implies that the younger the age the less the grief is

---

[5] For a clear exposition of Seneca's arguments and their philosophical provenance, see Manning (1974).

[6] Seneca gives no details here, perhaps aware that he had previously done so in another consolation (*Cons. Marc.* 12.6–15). Other examples are given by Cicero, e.g. *Tusc.* 3.70. For a full catalogue see Erasmus' *De conscribendis epistolis*, Sowards (1985), 157–9. On fortitude at one's son's death as a stock theme of Greco-Roman moralising, see Gill (1994), 4613.

[7] Similarly, the addressee interjects at *Cons. Marc.* 21.1.

justified. Marullus' son, like any child, was of unknown potential and might have turned out unworthy of his parents (12–13). Seneca minimises the seriousness of Marullus' loss: 'It's not pain you feel; just a sting!' (*non est dolor iste sed morsus*, 14). Having weakened Marullus' defences by these comparatively subtle manoeuvres, Seneca moves in to deliver a lethal blow to his self-pity by means of a final broadside of crushing sarcasm: 'You yourself turn it into pain. Undoubtedly philosophy has aided you enormously if you can bear courageously the loss of a boy so far more familiar to his nurse than his father.'

Aware of the harshness of this last remark and anticipating its effect on Marullus, Seneca veers aside. He shifts ground at once in focus from the personal to the general, in tone from the abrasive to the conciliatory, in posture from offensive to defensive. He is probably right in thinking the reader may find his treatment of Marullus' grief unfeeling and redolent of the famed Stoic asperity. He takes pains to deny this. 'What? Am I now urging you to be hard of heart ...? Not at all' (*quid? nunc ego duritiam suadeo ...? minime*, 15). At this juncture, roughly the half-way mark, the epistle takes an introspective turn as the thought begins to range across more varied thematic terrain. Grief is no longer the sole issue. The author feels driven to justify and analyse his own stance, to explain his preference for the Stoic over the Epicurean approach to consolation. He proceeds to clarify his reasoning through a series of antithetical distinctions: between virtue and inhumanity (*uirtus* and *inhumanitas*, 15); between grief and the outward display of grief (*dolor* and *ostentatio doloris*, 16); between what is morally right (*quid oporteat*) and what is socially expected (*quid soleat*, 17); between nature and popular opinion (*a natura discedimus, populo nos damus*, 17); between two types of tears, those by which we are overcome and those which we indulge (*his indulgemus, illis uincimur*, 19).

With the reference to the boy (*puerum*) in section 22 the discussion becomes personal again, but the tone is now considerably more gentle than before. Marullus is advised to resign himself to the inevitable (*aequo animo excipe necessaria*) and to concentrate on the happy memories of the child talking and laughing (*sermones* and *iocos*, 23) rather than on his death. This particular 'movement' of the epistle (15–24)[8] is brought to a satisfying close with a redefinition of what counts as

---

[8] The implied analogy between the structure of Seneca's polythematic epistles and musical composition is deliberate.

inhumanity in the context of bereavement (the problem with which it began, 15) and a culminating antithesis (accentuated by chiasmus) between the two main motifs Seneca has introduced: weeping and remembering. 'To be extravagant in weeping but miserly in remembering is the sign of an inhuman soul ... We should persevere in remembering but make an end of mourning' (24).

The succeeding 'movement' sees the thought turned in yet another direction and the voice raised to a higher pitch as the imagined context of utterance is itself transformed. In section 25 Seneca turns aside from Marullus' particular plight to attack a consolatory argument he has read in the work of the Epicurean philosopher Metrodorus, which asserts the existence of a certain pleasure closely allied to sadness (*esse aliquam cognatam tristitiae uoluptatem*). To this tenet Seneca's hostility is undisguised. 'What is more disgraceful', he exclaims, 'than to hunt after pleasure in the midst of grief?' (*quid enim est turpius quam captare in ipso luctu uoluptatem?*, 26). This part of the epistle takes on something of the character of a heated debate between rival philosophical schools and brings out all Seneca's powers of dramatisation, evident in the abundance of rhetorical questions and direct speech. He addresses himself to Metrodorus rather than to Marullus: 'What? Do you say pleasure should be mixed with sorrow?' (*quid, tu dicis miscendam ipsi dolori uoluptatem?*, 27), where the *tu* is surely Metrodorus just as the second-person addresses in 28 refer to Metrodorus and his fellow Epicureans. Rejecting Metrodorus' therapeutic procedure as unfit, Seneca contrasts it with the sterner kinds of admonition he recommends as more likely to succeed in extinguishing grief.

> That kind of injury calls for more severe treatment. Give, rather, this advice: no awareness of evil reaches one who has perished; for if it reaches him, he hasn't perished. Nothing, I repeat, can hurt anyone who is not; if he's hurt, he lives.
>
> seuerius ista plaga curanda est. illud potius admone, nullum mali sensum ad eum qui perit peruenire; nam si peruenit, non perit. nulla, inquam, res eum laedit qui nullus est: uiuit si laeditur. (99.29–31)

This itself is an argument which would sound perfectly natural coming from an Epicurean.[9] Seneca is doing two things at once here:

---

[9] 'Nothing could be more clearly an application of the first Epicurean principle' (Manning (1974), 81). See also Lucr. 3.830–51, 885–7, 900–5; LS vol. 1, pp. 149–54.

on the one hand he is giving Metrodorus a lesson about what is most valuable in his own philosophy and, on the other, he is appropriating the most powerful Epicurean argument into his immediate campaign against Marullus' grief. (To say even this, of course, is too simple since it overlooks the roles of Lucilius and of posterity as addressees at the third and fourth remove.) It also stakes out an area of common ground between himself and Metrodorus. Seneca, now nearing the end of his epistle,[10] pulls together the discordant notes of his composition into an unexpected harmony.

> Let us also say this to the person who is lamenting and missing someone taken off at an early age: we all, young and old alike, in terms of the universe, are equal as regards the shortness of our lives. For out of all time less comes to us than what you would call the tiniest particle; for the tiniest is at least a particle. But this moment for which we are alive is the closest thing to nothing. And yet, such is our lunacy, it is expansively arranged.

> illud quoque dicamus ei qui deflet ac desiderat in aetate prima raptum: omnes, quantum ad breuitatem aeui, si uniuerso compares, et iuuenes et senes, in aequo sumus. minus enim ad nos ex aetate omni uenit quam quod minimum esse quis dixerat, quoniam quidem minimum aliqua pars est: hoc quod uiuimus proximum nihilo est; et tamen, o dementiam nostram, late disponitur. (99.31)

By switching (as at the end of *Epistle* 63) to the first person plural of the verb (*dicamus*), Seneca joins Metrodorus' voice with his own. Now they speak not at odds but in unison. In turning their attention away from their philosophical disagreements towards the specific source of Marullus' anguish, the death of a child, they at last reach the central issue about which the epistle has orbited. The two discourses, the philosophical and the consolatory, converge and, in defence of Marullus' peace of mind, Stoicism and Epicureanism enter into alliance. Simultaneously the perspective opens out to encompass all of eternity against which human life-spans are rendered microscopic. Human beings, young and old, share a common condition; distinctions between them are, from this vantage point, trivial.[11] This move, foreshadowed in section 10, works on the reader's mind more powerfully as a result of contrast with the narrow doctrinal debate

---

[10] The closure of the Senecan epistle, like the closure of the Senecan tragedy, always repays study. For some suggestions see Fowler (1989), 111–12.

[11] See *Epp.* 49.3; 71.15–16; 77.12; *Cons. Marc.* 21.1–2.

which precedes it in the text and because of the paradoxical qualities of the prospect it discloses: there is something less than the least; young and old are the same; nothing or next to nothing is extensively ordered; normal human behaviour is really madness (*dementiam*). Seneca tries to short-circuit our categories of understanding. Time itself we misapprehend. By making time here so conspicuous a concern, Seneca binds *Epistle* 99 more tightly into the rest of the correspondence where time (commencing in the first line of the first letter) is a continuing theme and motive for his reflections.

To complete the mood of conciliation, Seneca turns one last time to Marullus to explain why he has written to him in this way:

> I wrote this to you not thinking that you should look to me for a remedy at this late date (for it's clear to me that you've told yourself already whatever you're going to read) but to reprove the brief delay during which you've lapsed from your true self, and encourage you for the future so you uplift your morale against Fortune and foresee all her missiles not as things that might possibly strike but as things surely destined to strike. Farewell.

> haec tibi scripsi, non tamquam expectaturus esses remedium a me tam serum (liquet enim mihi te locutum tecum quidquid lecturus es) sed ut castigarem exiguam illam moram qua a te recessisti, et in reliquum adhortarer contra Fortunam tolleres animos et omnia eius tela non tamquam possent uenire sed tamquam utique essent uentura prospiceres. Vale. (99.32)

This carefully crafted sentence enacts the movement from negative to positive. Initially Seneca states what he has *not* been attempting (that is, to provide a remedy) but follows this up with a compliment to the effect that Marullus will, no doubt, have been thinking of the consolatory arguments for himself. (Note the implicit division here between a better and a weaker self.) Seneca then gives an account of what he *was* attempting to achieve. The first aim, as he expresses it, seems negative in tone ('to reprove', *ut castigarem*, recalling *castigentur*, 2) but this appearance is short-lived for the expected object of the verb, Marullus himself, is replaced by 'the delay' (*illam moram*) which is itself further qualified as 'brief' (*exiguam*). Marullus is mentioned only in the subordinate clause ('during which you've lapsed from your true self') where he is, for a second time, divided into better and weaker selves, the former being treated with implicit esteem. The next aim is entirely positive: to 'encourage' (*adhortarer* in contrast to *castigarem*). Now, as if taking fire from Seneca's encouragement,

Marullus ceases to be the passive recipient of advice and becomes instead the active subject of the verbs (*tolleres, prospiceres*). He is to raise his own spirits and anticipate Fortune's missiles for himself. Here, in the last half of the last sentence, Marullus' backward-looking sorrow gives way to forward-looking fortitude (*in reliquum, prospiceres*, emphatically positioned as the culminating word). Just as Seneca's attitude to Metrodorus changed from antagonism ('in no respect do I agree with what Metrodorus says', 25) to unanimity of purpose (31), so also has his attitude to Marullus finally swung from reprimand and abuse (*obiurgatione*, 1; *conuicia*, 2) to courtesy and involvement in a common cause. Previously Marullus was treated as the source of his own distress: 'you yourself turn it into pain' (*tu illum dolorem facis*, 14); 'bear it in an unmanly way' (*molliter ferre*, 1); 'absurdities of grieving' (*lacrimarum ineptias*, 2). Now the fault is displaced on to an external force, *Fortuna*, against which Seneca, Marullus, all mortals are at war. It is on the imagery of battle ('all her missiles'), not medicine, that the epistle leaves Marullus, Lucilius, us to ponder.

III

The ambiguity of the word *dolor* facilitates Seneca's blend within a single epistle of the literary form, the *consolatio* for Marullus' grief, with the attack on Metrodorus' philosophy. The term goes through several redefinitions. It is a physical pain more serious than a mere sting (*non est dolor iste sed morsus*, 14); it is the inner emotion, not the outward display of grief (*plus ostentatio doloris exigit quam dolor*, 16).[12] In section 28 Seneca plays on the technical Epicurean use of *dolor* as the polar opposite, in philosophical terms, of pleasure: 'There is a certain pleasure, you say, akin to sadness. We [Stoics] are allowed to say that but you [Metrodorus] are not. For you recognise only one good, pleasure (*uoluptatem*), and only one evil, pain (*dolorem*.) What affinity is possible between good and evil?'

Seneca's reliance on resonances from other texts underlines his fundamentally literary approach to his philosophical material. The consolatory arguments he employs are traditional and cannot help but remind the reader of earlier *consolationes*, including Seneca's

---

[12] The importance in Roman Stoicism of redescribing experience, of fitting different *lekta* ('ways of articulating') to the situation is emphasised by Long (1991), 119–20.

own.[13] Most importantly, we discover echoes of earlier Senecan epistles. The discussion of Metrodorus' views on consolation and grief was foreshadowed in the previous epistle (98.9) where a line was quoted from the letter he wrote to his sister after the death of her child. Seneca, it seems, has been perusing the correspondence of Metrodorus at around the time he composed *Epistles* 98 and 99; and earlier, judging by the quotations from his work at 79.16 and 81.11 of which at least the former is definitely attributed to a letter (*Metrodorus quoque in quadam epistula*). Part of Metrodorus' consolatory argument Seneca admires and this he works into *Epistle* 98; part, though, he finds repugnant and he expounds his objections in 99. Another allusion is even more pointed. The assertion in section 7 that 'the one you think has perished has been sent on in advance' (*quem putas perisse praemissus est*) unmistakably echoes the closing words and thought of *Epistle* 63: 'the one we think has perished has been sent on in advance' (*quem putamus perisse praemissus est*). The earlier expression is particularly memorable because of the alliteration, strong rhythm and conspicuous position at the very end of the text. We are, in this way, not so subtly invited to compare the two *consolationes*.

The two epistles do touch on a number of shared themes: the value of friendship (63.8–11; 99.2–4); the need to be grateful for the companionship of the past rather than complaining about present bereavement (63.47; 99.3–5); time (63.12–13; 99.10, 31); Fortune's violence (63.15; 99.32); the question whether any relation can subsist between grief and pleasure (63.5–7; 99.25–9). Despite this, it is the contrast between the two epistles that is more impressive. In 63 Seneca's tone is compassionate from the opening words in which he declares that he too is affected by news of the death of Flaccus, Lucilius' friend, to his admission of his own inconsolable suffering on the loss of Serenus (14–15) and his final exhortations to himself and Lucilius jointly (*cogitemus*, 15, 16). Seneca keeps his own past life out of *Epistle* 99, his relationship with Marullus being less close than that with Lucilius; his tone is mostly demanding and unsympathetic; though ideas from the earlier epistle are reintroduced, they are redeployed in response to very different circumstances. There is more conflict: between author and addressee; between Stoic and Epicurean systems of thought.

In 99, the marked resemblances between the Senecan epistle and

---

[13] For the topoi of the *consolatio*, see Kassel (1958); Manning (1981), 12–20.

Roman satire are more visible.[14] He attacks contemporary vice (his skill in which activity later won the praise of Quintilian, *Inst.* 10.1.129): 'Look at the youth of today', he writes, 'whom extravagance (*luxuria*) has flung out of the most noble houses into the amphitheatre; look at those who cater to their own or others' lusts in mutual shamelessness (*mutuo inpudici*), for none of whom a day goes by without drunkenness or the performance of some notable act of depravity' (13). The apparently orderless exposition, the contrived discontinuity of thought, is used to suggest an irritated, belligerent speaker, as in some of the early satires of Juvenal. For Seneca, satire is neither a literary exercise enjoyed for its own sake nor just a derisive tone of voice but a favourite and potent method of argument, a key weapon in his rhetorical armoury. He refutes his opponents by setting their behaviour or views in a context in which they can be made to seem utterly ridiculous, contemptible, barbarous or insane. He makes fun, in this way, both of Marullus' grief and Metrodorus' consolation. Marullus, for instance, is accused in section 2 of not having learnt that there are absurdities of grieving (*ineptias lacrimarum*). Metrodorus should be ashamed (*non te pudet ...?*, 29) to employ pleasure in conjunction with sadness. Seneca uses many expressions of the type: 'what could be more crazy/stupid/ignominious than ...' (5, 6, 7, 18, 20, 26). There is a certain propriety to be observed even in the act of grieving (*est aliquis et dolendi decor*, 21). Those who fail to see or meet this requirement locate themselves among the foolish (*inprudentium*, 21; *hoc prudentem uirum non decet*, 24) or less than human (*inhumani animi est*, 24).

Another satire-like effect results from Seneca's successive displacement of addressees. He begins by addressing in friendly terms his regular correspondent, Lucilius (1), but Lucilius soon gives way to Marullus (2) towards whom Seneca's tone is vehement and scolding. But the address to Marullus soon itself gives way to the address to Metrodorus (27) to whose yoking together of pleasure and sorrow Seneca makes no secret of his aversion. Now Seneca is sometimes angry with Lucilius for his philosophical backsliding (for instance, *Epistle* 60 which begins: 'I protest; I accuse you; I am furious!', *queror, litigo, irascor!*). However, the relationship he seems to have with Lucilius at this late stage of the correspondence does not allow the

---

[14] Roman satire sometimes adopts epistolary form. Horace's verse *Epistles*, similar to his *Satires* in style, seem to have influenced Seneca's epistolary practice. For other links between Seneca's philosophical works and satire, see Anderson (1982), 293–361; Braund, Ch. 4.

kind of sustained verbal assault with which Marullus is belaboured. Seneca wants to speak passionately against a grief which has degenerated to the stage of becoming, in his eyes, a vice. The substitution of addressee allows him to speak with more passion. This is not unlike what happens when a satirist changes his *persona* or otherwise achieves variations in intensity of feeling and tone by transformation of the relations between speaker and addressee. In fact, in the last sentence of *Epistle* 99, where Seneca explains why he has written this sort of letter (*haec tibi scripsi non ... sed ut ...*), it *is* as if he has stepped aside from a *persona* previously adopted to shock Marullus into self-examination. Seneca accepts fully the need for philosophical writing to engage the emotions, his own and his readers'. Defending the use of *sententiae* (94.28), he says, 'Those things require no advocate; they touch the emotions' (*adfectus ipsos tangunt*). Seneca's discourses of the passions are themselves passionate discourses.[15]

IV

When the voice of Stoicism is so agitated, there is little likelihood that the recipient of its guidance will speedily arrive at composure. Seneca's letter has done little to help Marullus find his way to inner calm; it seems to have been designed rather to stir him up (*tolleres animos*, 32). We should not take at face value the pretensions of the *consolatio* as a genre to be disinterestedly therapeutic in function. The way a Roman man copes with strong emotions, and, in particular, grief, is a crucial test of what sets him apart from the other sex and from alien cultural and ethical codes. In *Epistle* 63 Seneca made much of the observation that the Romans of old, the *maiores*, legislated a year as the limit for the mourning of women but set no limit for men because, he claims, they considered no time was honourable (13).[16] Thus, the male suppression of grief is depicted as being as much a part of the Roman moral tradition as of the Greco-Roman philosophical tradition. The first and greatest charge he

---

[15] For Seneca's employment of the rhetoric of *indignatio* see Anderson (1982), 423–8. Philosophy itself, for Seneca, resembles a passion. The originally Greek word, *philosophia*, he translates as a kind of *amor*, the 'love' of wisdom and the hankering after it' (*philosophia sapientiae amor est et adfectatio*, 89.4).

[16] Although Seneca addresses two *consolationes* to women, he is self-conscious about the social expectation that women are more prone to surrender to lamentation than are men: *Cons. Marc.* 1.1; 1.5; 16.1; *Cons. Helv.* 16.1–2. For discussion, see Manning (1973).

brings against Marullus in 99 is that the way he bears his grief is
unmanly (*molliter*, 1, 2).[17] Ostensibly preoccupied with grief, consolatory writings carry underneath a strong ideological imperative
concerned with self-definition and the fortification of identity. Marullus should behave like a man, not a woman; he should be treated
like an adult and not like a child who can be consoled with a biscuit
or like an infant which will stop crying if given milk (27). As human
beings do, he should remember the dead; not forget them as do birds
and wild beasts (24).[18]

Seneca devotes considerable attention to delimiting what sort of
behaviour, in the face of death and mourning, is or is not genuinely
human. To be extravagant in weeping but niggardly in remembering
indicates a less than human soul (*inhumani animi est*, 24); for Marullus
not to be moved by the loss of his son would be not virtuous but
inhuman (*inhumanitas est ista, non uirtus*, 15). 'Which is more bizarre or
inhuman' (*utrum tandem est aut incredibilius aut inhumanius*, 26), he asks
Metrodorus, 'not to feel sorrow or to go hunting for pleasure in the
midst of sorrow?' The consolation enjoins on the reader a recommit-
ment to the concept of *humanitas* ('civilised humanity').[19]

Excessive grief is also a special threat to such cardinal Roman
qualities as dignity, gravity and authority (*dignitas, grauitas* and
auctoritas). Each of these is invoked within the space of a few lines at
the end of the lengthy passage in which Seneca carefully distinguishes
between the two sorts of tears, those within and those beyond
physical control (*his indulgemus, illis uincimur*, 19). Only the latter type
is compatible with gravity (*licet, inquam, naturae obsequi grauitate seruata*,
21); such tears may flow without injury to authority (*salua* ...
auctoritate fluxerunt, 20) nor will they diminish humanity and dignity
(*illis nec humanitas nec dignitas deesset*, 20). These words carry with them
a whole Roman national identity. Seneca is relying on the emotional
pull they will exert on Marullus. It is also clear that he feels their
emotional pull himself.

Marullus' reaction, on reading Seneca's denunciation of his failure
to constrain his grief, can only be guessed at. Indignation? Anger?
Shame? Certainly not peace of mind. Given that the epistle has
evidently been devised with a view to inciting rather than soothing
his feelings, what, it might be asked, of the Stoic ideal of *apatheia*?
This Greek concept does not translate well into a Roman context.

---

[17] Cf. *Cons. Polyb.* 6.2; 17.2–6.   [18] Cf. *Cons. Marc.* 7.2.
[19] See *Cons. Marc.* 4.1; 7.1–4; *De ira* 3.26.3–4; 3.43.5; and see further Anderson (1982), 329–31.

The word, according to Seneca, cannot be translated at all.[20] He searches, in *Epistle* 9, for a Latin equivalent but, rejecting *inpatientia* because it may imply an inability to endure, ultimately decides that there is no single Latin word that will satisfactorily convey the meaning he wants:

> Ambiguity is unavoidable if we try to express succinctly in a single word the meaning of *apatheia* and render it as *inpatientia*. For it may be taken in the very opposite sense to the one we wish to denote. We wish to refer to someone who rejects every sensation of evil. It will be understood as referring to someone who is unable to sustain any such sensation.

> in ambiguitatem incidendum est, si exprimere ἀπάθειαν uno uerbo cito uoluerimus et inpatientiam dicere. poterit enim contrarium ei, quod significare uolumus intellegi. nos eum uolumus dicere, qui respuat omnis mali sensum; accipietur is, qui nullum ferre possit malum. (9.2)

What is revealing here is the way Seneca describes the meaning he *does* want to capture. Though the Greek word is an abstraction, he personalises it ('someone who', *eum . . . qui*). The most emphatic word he uses is *respuat* ('rejects'; literally, 'spits back'). It is the action of vigorous rejection that Seneca singles out as crucial.

The same point is made a few lines later where he is comparing the Stoics with rival philosophical schools: 'There is this difference between us and them: our wise man vanquishes every vexation, but feels it; theirs doesn't even feel it' (*noster sapiens uincit quidem incommodum omne, sed sentit; illorum ne sentit quidem*, 3). The metaphor here is martial ('vanquishes', *uincit*). Seneca's language suggests that, while he is striving to communicate the idea of a soul immune to disturbance (*inuulnerabilem animum . . . aut animum extra omnem patientiam positum*, 2), its attraction lies not so much in the freedom from perturbation as in the act of self-assertion involved in preserving it. Applied to the passions,[21] to the extent that the Stoics advocate extirpation of the destructive passions, Seneca is more interested in the act of extirpation than in the ideal state of serenity to which it

---

[20] Also of interest is Cicero's discussion of the Latin translation of *pathos* at *Tusc.* 3.7 and 23. The shift in emphasis and even meaning that occurs when Greek philosophical terms are transferred into Latin is commonly underrated. For an outline of some of the issues see Benjamin (1989), 39–59.

[21] On the Stoic attitude to the passions, see *Ep.* 116 and LS 65. For modern accounts, see refs. in Introd., Sect. II n. 22.

should lead. Seneca locates value in the heroism of the battle, not in enjoying the rewards of victory.

This is reflected in his treatment of grief. Some remedies, though efficacious, are rejected by Seneca on the grounds that they are either too passive or inconsistent with Roman dignity. Sorrow may be healed by the passage of time, but to depend on this, Seneca insists in *Epistle* 63, is dishonourable (*turpissimum*); the most disgraceful remedy for grief is weariness of grieving (*lassitudo maerendi*, 12). Lucilius should assert himself and abandon grief, not be abandoned by it (*malo relinquas dolorem quam ab illo relinquaris*, 12).[22] Similarly, with regard to Metrodorus' suggestion that there is a kind of pleasure associated with grief (99.25–9), Seneca shows no interest in whether or not it works as an antidote to the pain of bereavement but focuses exclusively on the fact that it is dishonourable (*turpius*, 26) in comparison with the more noble (*honestius*, 27) and dignified approach of the Stoics. As he says,

> Certain remedies, though beneficial for some parts of the body, cannot be applied to others through being, as it were, shameful and indecent; and what elsewhere might be of help without damage to one's sense of modesty becomes dishonourable by reason of the position of the wound.

> quaedam remedia aliis partibus corporis salutaria uelut foeda et indecora adhiberi aliis nequeunt, et quod aliubi prodesset sine damno uerecundiae, id fit inhonestum loco uulneris. (99.29)

Seneca employs the medical analogy in a way which reveals that it is, in the long run, inadequate. Healing is secondary to the preservation of modesty (*uerecundia*), to the shunning of anything shameful or indecent (*foeda et indecora*). To achieve a state of soul free of morbose passion is not the only nor the paramount goal. The means of quelling passion are more important than the end.

V

There is a tension (perhaps consciously foregrounded) between Seneca's adherence to Stoic theory and his Roman language and psychology.[23] This is reflected in two kinds of imagery. He does from

---

[22] Cf. *Cons. Marc.* 1.8; 8.3.

[23] I find it impossible to agree with Rist (1989), 2012, that: 'despite his high position in Roman society, we must also insist that with Seneca traditional Stoic thinking subordinates a purely "Roman" attitude'. Rist seems to me to have reached this conclusion by focusing on

time to time borrow from the philosophical texts with which he is familiar the commonplace comparison of philosophy with medicine.[24] But he had available to him a far more stirring and dramatic metaphor (not without philosophical antecedents) better attuned to gripping the attention of a Roman audience. 'To be alive, Lucilius', he writes, 'is to be in a war zone' (*uiuere, Lucili, militare est*, 96.5).

The imagery of battle in Seneca's prose has been called, without too much exaggeration, 'all-pervasive'.[25] According to this analogy the philosopher's role is more akin to that of a general exhorting his troops before entering into action than to that of a physician. It throws the emphasis not on knowledge, the superior expertise of the philosopher/therapist, but on the moral virtues of courage, perseverance and discipline of the embattled individual. It overcomes the glaring disadvantage of the therapy metaphor – that it leaves the 'patient' passive – by putting the onus on the addressee to become active, to become a willing participant in the fight. The philosophical life is not ultimately a matter of health but of struggle and conquest. It is a matter of dominion over the self. It is a matter of power.

In *Epistle* 63 Seneca writes that weeping is forgivable provided it is within limits and provided 'we ourselves suppress it' (*si ipsi illas repressimus*, 1). Recalling his own weeping for the loss of Serenus, he portrays it as a defeat inflicted by grief (*dolor uicit*, 14). In *Epistle* 98, discussing losses of things held dear, Seneca instructs Lucilius as follows: 'Of these things which seem so terrible, none is invincible (*inuictum*). Many men have conquered particular things: Mucius fire, Regulus the cross, Socrates poison, Rutilius exile, Cato death by the sword. Let us also conquer something' (*et nos uincamus aliquid*, 12). The language of subjugation similarly dominates the last sentences of *Epistle* 71:

> When will it come about that we can look down on Fortune, bad or good? When will it come about that, having crushed all the passions and brought them under our jurisdiction, we can say the words 'I have conquered'? Whom will I have conquered, you ask?

decontextualised doctrines without giving sufficient weight to the implications of the extremely resonant and often politically charged Latin in which they are embedded.

[24] See e.g. *Epp.* 7.1; 15.1–2; 53.6–7; 75.6–7; 78.3–5; 85.12.

[25] J. R. G. Wright (1974), 60. On military imagery in philosophical writing see Manning (1981), 62; on Seneca's use of it see Lavery (1980), 147–51; on Seneca's use of it in connection with control of the passions, see Inwood (1993), 171–2. At *Const. Sap.* 1 Seneca employs a contrast of martial and medical imagery to distinguish Stoicism as he sees it from other philosophical schools.

Not the Persians, not the most distant territory of the Medes, not
whatever warlike race lives beyond the Scythians, but avarice and
ambition and the fear of death which has conquered the world's
conquerors. Farewell.

quando continget contemnere utramque fortunam, quando continget omnibus oppressis adfectibus et sub arbitrium suum
adductis hanc uocem emittere 'uici'? quem uicerim quaeris? non
Persas nec extrema Medorum nec si quid ultra Dahas bellicosum
iacet, sed auaritiam, sed ambitionem, sed metum mortis, qui
uictores gentium uicit. Vale. (71.37)

A leading source of inspiration for Seneca's frequent use of
military imagery may be identified in the work of Quintus Sextius
who, despite writing in Greek, gave expression, Seneca tells us, to a
distinctively Roman morality (*Graecis uerbis, Romanis moribus philoso-
phantem*, 59.7).[26] Sextius' comparison of the wise man to a Roman
army marching in hollow-square formation (*quadrato agmine*, to
repulse surprise attacks) made a singular impression upon Seneca's
mind (*mouit me imago*, 59.7). In another epistle Seneca recounts the
way he feels after reading Sextius, probably hoping to produce a
similar reaction in his own readers in turn: 'I shall tell you the state
of mind I am in when I'm reading him. I want to challenge every
misfortune (*libet omnis casus prouocare*). I want to shout: "What are you
waiting for, Fortune? Fight me (*congredere*)! Can't you see I'm ready
for you?" I take on the spirit of a man who is looking for a way to
prove himself, to demonstrate his worth (*qui quaerit, ubi se experiatur,
ubi uirtutem suam ostendat*) ... I want something to conquer (*libet aliquid
habere quod uincam*), something to exercise my powers of endurance'
(64.4–5). Seneca's partiality for martial imagery is well adapted to
other aspects of his writing, in particular, his use of literary quotation, frequently from epic (especially Virgil); his use of historical
exempla, regularly involving Roman military leaders; and his philosophical emphasis on the person 'making progress' whose role
demands constant endeavour and a kind of unrelenting inner
heroism.

In highlighting the hierarchy of power-relations within the self, the
military analogy is sometimes augmented by a political one. At the
end of *Epistle* 114 the soul, in an extended allegory, is compared to a

[26] Manning (1981), 16–17, gives a concise and accurate account of the role played by the Sextii
in Roman intellectual life. See also Oltramare (1926), 153–89; M. Griffin (1976), 37–8;
Fillion-Lahille (1984), 256–7.

king whom the rest of the human organism obeys provided it rules with integrity and gives no orders to the body that are dishonourable or demeaning (*illi nihil imperat turpe, nihil sordidum*, 24). But if the soul becomes undisciplined, surrenders itself to desire or pleasure (*inpotens, cupidus, delicatus*), it turns into a tyrant and the passions run rampant like a rioting populace supplied with more largess than is good for it, sullying all that is beyond its power to consume (24). The world within contains opportunities for glorious campaigns and stands in need of strong government.

> Oh, in what a mighty error are those men caught who desire to extend their claims to dominion across the seas and think they have reached the pinnacle of success if, with their armies, they occupy many provinces, joining new ones to the old, but remain all the time ignorant of that other realm, enormous and on a level with the gods. The greatest empire is the empire of the self.

> O quam magnis homines tenentur erroribus, qui ius dominandi trans maria cupiunt permittere felicissimosque se iudicant, si multas milite prouincias obtinent et nouas ueteribus adiungunt, ignari quod sit illud ingens parque dis regnum: imperare sibi maximum imperium est. (113.30)

To be a physician of the soul may be a satisfactory occupation for a Greek, but such a humble conception of the role of philosopher does not satisfy Seneca. His is an imperial art, not a medical one.[27]

VI

Epistle 99 is unique among the *Epistles to Lucilius* in that it is not written to Lucilius. It is presented to the reader as having been originally composed for and sent to Marullus, then later incorporated into the material Seneca dispatches to Lucilius for his philosophical edification. Earlier in the correspondence Seneca had espoused the traditional conceptualisation of the letter as a conversation between absent friends: 'I want my letters to be … just like my conversation if we were sitting or walking together' (75.1).[28] The substitution as principal addressee of Marullus, a man with whom Seneca's relationship is not cordial and co-operative but strained and

---

[27] As further background to this comment, see the perceptive discussion of Braden (1985), 5–27. E. V. Arnold (1911), 239, pointed in the same direction.
[28] Cf. *Epp.* 38.1; 40.1; 65.2; 67.2. Malherbe (1988) collates ancient opinion on the epistolary genre.

antagonistic, upsets the previously established parameters of the correspondence and, in doing so, actuates a noticeable alteration in Seneca's epistolary style: his authorial voice becomes sterner; his philosophical posture becomes more bellicose. It is also through the presence of Marullus that Seneca is able to infuse into his writing here a striking, paradoxical discordance between content and form, between situation and tone. The letter is an impassioned attack on a passion; a non-consolatory consolation in which traditional consolatory motifs abound but the intention to console is denied (1, 2, 32).

The literary artifice apparent in the construction of this epistle makes it difficult to avoid the suspicion that Seneca has invented Marullus for the occasion; that he is a purely literary creation.[29] In no other of his *consolationes* does Seneca adopt anything like so hostile an approach; nor does any extant ancient *consolatio*, with the possible exception of Juvenal's mock-consolatory and very literary thirteenth satire, go so far in replacing solace with contumely (*solacia* with *conuicia*, 2).[30] That Seneca's epistle is written in response to an event almost identical with that which induced Metrodorus to compose his consolation (the mourning of a parent over the death of a very young son, 98.9) seems oddly coincidental. One senses here a more profound intertextuality between Seneca's work and that of Metrodorus, the details of which are now, along with the earlier text, lost to us.[31] While Seneca presents his disagreement with Metrodorus as a subordinate (though climactic) part of his epistle to Marullus, perhaps it is the main point, for which Marullus' bereavement is the fictional context and occasion. On this interpretation Seneca rewrites Metrodorus' consolatory case from a Stoic rather than an Epicurean, from a Roman rather than a Greek perspective.

[29] A Junius Marullus is recorded by Tacitus as consul-designate in AD 62 (*Ann.* 14.48.2). The name, however, is not uncommon and there is no other evidence to link this historical Marullus with the addressee of *Ep.* 99, despite the speculation of M. Griffin (1976), 92. Whether the *Epistles to Lucilius* are 'genuine' or 'fictional' is a long-debated question. Most scholars are now agreed that they were written with a view to publication. For a survey of opinion see Mazzoli (1989), 1846–50. See also Russell (1974), 72–9; M. Griffin (1976), 416–19; Wilson (1987), 119, n. 3.

[30] On Juv. 13 see Pryor (1962); Anderson (1982), 350–5; Morford (1973); and Braund, Ch. 4.

[31] Marullus is regarded as being philosophically knowledgeable in sections 14 ('Undoubtedly philosophy has aided you enormously if...') and 32 ('It's clear to me that you've told yourself already whatever you're going to read...'). The implication of the epistle is that he is an Epicurean or has, at least, Epicurean leanings; hence, Seneca's incorporation into his letter of detailed criticism of an Epicurean text is more telling than might appear at first glance. Perhaps, too, the contention (2–3) that the loss of a son is of little significance compared with the loss of a friend is deliberately provocative in alluding to the pre-eminent value placed by Epicureans on friendship.

In reading the philosophical discourse of the Roman period, as current emphasis on the analogy of therapy reminds us, it is necessary to relate the arguments to the particular parties and the situation in which they are involved. The consolation is typical in this respect. We should not forget, however, that the situation and even one or more of the parties may themselves have been fabricated in the author's imagination to create an arena for the interplay of philosophical ideas.[32]

[32] I am grateful to Charles Manning, Dougal Blyth and Peter Davis for their comments on an earlier version of this paper.

CHAPTER 4

A passion unconsoled? Grief and anger in Juvenal 'Satire' 13

Susanna Morton Braund

Anger is the passion which predominates in Juvenal's *Satires*. *Indignatio* is the driving force in the first two books, *Satires* 1–6.[1] The later *Satires* present a rejection of *indignatio* which is initiated obliquely in *Satire* 9, the last poem in Book III, and made explicit briefly for the first time at the close of *Satire* 10, the opening poem of Book IV.[2] *Satire* 13, the programme poem to Juvenal's fifth book, confronts the matter head-on, with an unsympathetic presentation of an angry man. This seems to invite reassessment of the angry speaker of the early books by offering a negative perspective on *indignatio*.[3] The treatment of the passion of anger in *Satire* 13, then, has tremendous significance for our understanding of the development of Juvenal's satire.[4] Here, however, the passion of anger concerns us in a broader sphere. The treatment of anger in *Satire* 13 demonstrates the vernacularisation of ideas about the nature and control of the passions which originate in the Hellenistic philosophical schools. That Juvenal not only incorporates such ideas into his satire but also exploits his audience's familiarity with them for satiric effect is an eloquent testimony to the interaction between different modes of ethical discourse.

The angry man in *Satire* 13 is Calvinus, the addressee in the poem, who has suffered a minor financial loss caused by fraud and perjury. Recent work has established that *Satire* 13 is an ironic *consolatio*, a mock-*consolatio* by the speaker to Calvinus in which the crime of fraud compounded by perjury is 'equivalent' to the death of a loved

---

[1] Established by Anderson (1982), 293–361; for an overview of *Satires* 1–6 see Braund (1988), 1–23.

[2] On *Satire* 9 see Braund (1988), 130–77; and for an overview of Books III and IV see Braund (1988), 178–89.

[3] As suggested by Anderson (1982), 351–5. On the significance and ambiguity of *dolor*, the word used by Juvenal to denote Calvinus' negative emotions, see n. 34 below.

[4] See Fredericks (1971), esp. 224–5.

one and the addressee's reaction of anger is 'equivalent' to the bereaved person's reaction of grief.[5] That is, in terms of the passions, anger replaces grief. It will be useful first to indicate how an appreciation of the *consolatio* tradition illuminates the choice of topics and structure of the poem before I proceed to a broader consideration of Juvenal's substitution of the passion of anger for the passion of grief. In showing how Juvenal adapts the structure and topoi of the consolation to his chosen theme, I shall not only draw together the work of other scholars[6] but also pay particular attention to the dynamics of the parody, as a preliminary to the broader discussion which follows.

I

The scene is set economically in the opening lines of the poem (1–18). Calvinus lent a small sum of money (at 71 we learn it was 10,000 sesterces) to a friend who failed to return it despite his sacred oath (*sacrum ... depositum*, 15–16); what is more, Calvinus has evidently attempted to seek legal redress, but without success, because the defrauder perjured himself and bribed the judge to secure an acquittal (3–4).[7] The speaker's words in the poem permit us to gauge Calvinus' reaction to these events. He reacts with profound anger. In response, the speaker offers him a 'consolation' which, if it were a conventional consolation, should aim to remove or calm his anger. As we shall see, the speaker's consolation proves

[5] For discussions of the ironic *consolatio* see (in chronological order of publication) Pryor (1962); Anderson (1982), 350–6 (first pub., 1964); Fredericks (1971); Edmunds (1972); Morford (1973). These differ on various points of interpretation. This chapter attempts a new and more thorough reading of the overall articulation of *Satire* 13 as a mock *consolatio* by superimposing the structure and detail of consolatory discourse on this satiric specimen and focusing particularly upon the points of deviation, where the parody is displayed.

[6] Cited in n. 5 above; of these, Pryor deals most helpfully with the adaptations, yet it is possible to provide a fuller analysis. For parallels in conventional consolations, see the compendious collections of material in Buresch (1886) and Esteve-Forriol (1962), and the philosophical overview of Kassel (1958).

[7] This interpretation treats lines 3–4 as significant rather than as inconsequential padding: it seems to me appropriate to regard all the material at the opening of a poem as potentially relevant to the scene-setting. Courtney's parenthesisation of *prima* (2) – *urna* (4) is unnecessary; see Pearce (1992) on the difficulties typically entailed in proposing parentheses in Juvenal. On this view, one might translate *crimine*, 6, as 'charge' and view *scelere* and *crimine* as an enumeration of the outrages which Calvinus has suffered, instead of appositional phrases as in Rudd's translation, 'this recent wrong – the crime of betraying a trust'. On the specific reference of line 4 to corruption of the legal process, see Courtney's note in his commentary (1980). Of the scholars who have discussed this poem, only Edmunds (1972), 62, even obliquely acknowledges this implication of Calvinus' resort to the law.

unorthodox and unsuccessful, while Calvinus' anger appears to increase during the poem until it develops into a desire for vengeance by the end.

In broad terms the poem has a structure modelled on a typical consolation. The bulk of the poem (1–173) closely resembles the typology of the consolation as prescribed by Menander Rhetor[8] and as determined in greater detail by Esteve-Forriol in his comparative study of prose and verse consolations in Latin literature: I use his categories of subdivision of material below.[9] The poem closes with a focus on revenge (174–249) which, not surprisingly, is outside the scope of prescriptions for consolation but which is highly appropriate to the topic of anger, as we shall see.[10]

A conventional consolatory speech has a bipartite structure, beginning with lamentation of the deceased then turning to consolation of those who mourn. In the first part, after introductory material, the speaker should focus upon the deceased, incorporating praise (*laudatio*), lamentation for the loss (*lamentatio / comploratio*), and sometimes a description of the death (*descriptio mortis*). Then the bereaved become(s) the focus of attention as the speaker turns to consolation (*consolatio*). 'Then, having amplified the lamentation as far as possible, the speaker should approach the second part of his speech, which is the consolatory part' (Menander Rhetor, *Treatise* 2, 413.21–3). Juvenal follows this broad pattern. The initial focus is upon the money (the object of loss), the events which brought about the loss and the act of perjury in court which followed the loss. Then the shift from lamentation to consolation is signalled explicitly at 120 with:[11] 'Here are some words of comfort . . .' (*accipe quae contra ualeat solacia ferre . . .*).

It is not only in broad structure that the poem resembles the conventional consolation. Many of the specific topoi recur, adapted for parodic, satiric purposes, and many of the precepts associated with various philosophical schools appear, again contributing to the parodic effect. A quotation from Cicero's discussion of the duties of

---

[8] The *logos paramuthētikos*, as prescribed at Menander Rhetor *Treatise* 2.9. The case for using these prescriptions as evidence for earlier educational and rhetorical practice has been made by Cairns (1972), esp. 31–3.

[9] Esteve-Forriol (1962); the evidence assembled does not feature Juvenal *Satire* 13.

[10] In this matter I disagree with Courtney (1980), 534, who sees 1–173 on the crime and 174–249 on vengeance as corresponding to the two themes of death and grief in a normal *consolatio*.

[11] The translation of Juvenal used throughout is that of Rudd (1991).

comforters (*officia ... consolantium*) will give an idea of the range of approaches to consolation available to the 'comforter' (*Tusc.* 3.76):[12]

> There are some who think it the sole duty of a comforter to insist that the evil has no existence at all, as is the view of Cleanthes; some, like the Peripatetics, favour the lesson that the evil is not serious. Some again favour the withdrawal of attention from evil to good, as Epicurus does; some, like the Cyrenaics, think it enough to show that nothing unexpected has taken place. Chrysippus on the other hand considers that the main thing in giving comfort is to remove from the mind of the mourner the belief already described, in case he should think he is discharging a regular duty which is obligatory. There are some too in favour of concentrating all these ways of administering comfort (for one man is influenced in one way, one in another) pretty nearly as in my *Consolation* I threw them all into one attempt at consolation; for my soul was in a feverish state and I attempted every means of curing its condition.

As we shall see, most, if not all, of these approaches are represented in *Satire* 13, but with a profoundly different effect from that of Cicero's *Consolation*. In Juvenal, the plethora of precepts is one of the various devices of parody.

The use of philosophical precepts at the start of a consolation was commended. Accordingly, philosophical material bulks large at the start of the poem. Lines 6–8 represent a practical application of the advice offered by the Peripatetics that the evil suffered is not great: 'However, you are not, as it happens, so badly off in financial terms that the weight of a moderate loss will sink you.' The speaker's message that Calvinus should not be surprised at such a loss resembles the view of the Cyrenaics that unanticipated misfortune strikes harder because of the failure to recognise the possibility that its cause could occur (8–10):

> What you've experienced
> is not an unusual sight; your lot is familiar to many;
> it is now quite commonplace, drawn from the middle of
> fortune's pile.

> nec rara uidemus
> quae pateris; casus multis hic cognitus ac iam
> tritus et e medio fortunae ductus aceruo.

[12] The consolation of Servius Sulpicius to Cicero on the death of his daughter Tullia (*ad Fam.* 4.5) is a classic example which incorporates a number of the points outlined here by Cicero. For modern assemblage and discussion of the philosophical material see Kassel (1958), and more briefly Manning (1981), 12–20, esp. 14, n. 14, which gives cross-references.

The speaker is amazed that Calvinus is amazed (*stupet haec...?*),
particularly at his advanced age of sixty (16–18): 'Does this come as a
shock to a man who was born when Fonteius was consul, and won't
see sixty again? Have you derived no profit from your long acquaintance with life?' Sandwiched within this material in 11–12 is an
appeal to proportion which resembles the view of the Academicians
who urged moderation of the emotions: 'Let's keep our grief within
reasonable bounds. A man's resentment shouldn't be *over*-heated, or
exceed the injury suffered.' After this concatenation of philosophical
precepts, the satiric frame is reasserted in 19–22 with an explicit
rejection of philosophy in favour of the school of common sense in
which life is the teacher (*uita ... magistra*, 22), a motif which will be
repeated at 120–5.[13] Whether or not we believe this rejection of
philosophy (and it seems that the speaker can have his cake and eat it
by invoking the philosophical precepts before preferring the school-
of-life approach), the speaker's claim to be offering the advice of the
plain man creates a tension with the rhetorical consolatory framework and signals the parody.

The material on the theme, 'you should have expected the like'
(23–37, resumed in 60–70), is reminiscent of the Pythagorean
doctrine *nil admirari* ('don't be dazzled by anything'), for example
(64–6): 'If I happen to find a totally honest man, I regard that freak
as I would a baby centaur, or a shoal of fish turned up by the plough
to its own surprise, or a mule in foal ...' This doctrine is crystallised
in the charge of *simplicitas* (naïveté) levelled against Calvinus at 35.[14]
This theme gives the speaker the opportunity to incorporate a set-
piece in which the corrupt and criminalised present is contrasted
with a (semi-)idealised primitive existence (38–59) when there was no
crime and therefore no punishment. (This point anticipates the
overall structure of the poem in which crime is followed by punishment.) As Pryor has observed, this passage describing the old days is
'a deliberately ludicrous caricature of the mythological common-
place-book'.[15] Its function here is to parody the recollection of the
pristine past, which was a commonplace of consolation literature.
Lines 60–70 resume the theme of 23–37 but now with obviously
unbelievable exaggeration which seems designed to point up the
parodic technique.

---

[13] On the dismissal of philosophy see Pryor (1962), 171.
[14] Pryor (1962), 172–3, sees *simplicitas* as one of the dominant motifs of *Satire* 13.
[15] Pryor (1962), 173.

Then in 71–4 the speaker attempts to set Calvinus' experience in perspective by comparing his minor loss of 10,000 sesterces with two greater losses, the first of 200,000 sesterces and the second of a whole chest full of money. This attempt at perspective is another standard tactic in consolation literature. It is an important element in Servius Sulpicius' consolation to Cicero on the death of his daughter (*Ad fam.* 4.5) and in the chorus on the alleviation of grief at Seneca *Troades* 1018–41. Moreover, it is presented in explicit and brutal (but hardly witty) form at the start of Seneca's pseudo-consolation in *Epistle* 99, an epistle which does not offer a standard consolation, as is declared explicitly at the outset (*Ep.* 99.2): ' "Is it a solace you are looking for? Let me give you a scolding instead! You are like a woman in the way you take your son's death; what would you do if you had lost an intimate friend?" '[16]

The next lines (76–85) replace the element of *descriptio mortis* (description of the death) standard in the conventional consolation with a description of the act of perjury, which we might label *descriptio criminis*. The vividness (*enargeia*) appropriate to such a description is present throughout, from the first word, *aspice* ('Look!', 76), and culminating in the citation of a perjurer's actual words (84–5). The use of direct speech seems to parody a feature of conventional consolations, the quotation of the last words of the dying person, for instance, Statius *Silvae* 5.1.170–96, where the *descriptio mortis* includes Priscilla's dying speech to her husband.

The following lines express perjurers' self-justifications (86–105) on the grounds either that there is no ruling force in the world which commands moral conduct or that it is worth risking the punishment of the gods. While this section seems to have no precise analogue in the conventional consolation, it does appear to parody the attempt to place the loss in the broader context of the role of fate or the gods in human affairs. The parody arises from the attribution of the various world-views to the perjurers, rather than to the fellow mourners, who, conventionally, might be the ones to offer a world-view to the prime mourner. If this displacement is accepted, it may also be possible to accept Pryor's view that the *laudatio* of money put into the mouth of a perjurer in 92–105 replaces the *laudatio* of the dead person.[17] Whether or not this is persuasive, it is certain that the speaker's dwelling upon the psychology and viewpoint of the

---

[16] For a full discussion of Seneca *Ep.* 99 see Wilson, Ch. 3.   [17] Pryor (1962), 175.

perjurer(s) is utterly inappropriate to a true consolation (it would be like offering the murderer's perspective while consoling the relative of the murder-victim). The breaking of the frame is a signal of the parodic process.

Line 106 resumes the topic of *descriptio criminis* ('description of the crime') from lines 76–85 by projecting future offences of perjury in which the perjurer will be even more brazen than before. Here the speaker returns to the consolatory framework by portraying the addressee's noisy reaction to the perjury: he is shown bellowing at the gods for their inaction over the perjury (112–19). His frenzy of noise resembles the initial grief of the bereaved, as shown in Statius *Silvae* 5.1.197–204. The hyperbolic description of his volume in lines 112–13, where he is compared with Stentor and Gradivus, adapts a feature of standard consolations whereby mourners might be encouraged to give up excessively noisy lamentation.[18] The explicit reference to Homer in line 113 suggests parody of another regular prescription, the use of quotations from poets: such quotations should be designed to alleviate pain, not to satirise the volume of the complaint.[19]

At 120 the speaker commences his *consolatio* (120–3):

> Here are some words of comfort that even a layman may offer –
> one who has never read the Cynics, or the rules of the Stoics
> (who apart from their shirt are Cynics too), or admired Epicurus,
> who took such pleasure in the plants he grew in his tiny garden.

> accipe quae contra ualeat solacia ferre
> et qui nec Cynicos nec Stoica dogmata legit
> a Cynicis tunica distantia, non Epicurum
> suspicit exigui laetum plantaribus horti.

This is advertised as a non-philosophical *consolatio*, which seems highly appropriate following the avowedly non-philosophical *lamentatio* established in 19–22, discussed earlier. The following two lines (124–5) reaffirm the speaker's stance of the plain man by indicating that only in complex cases is philosophy required; this, by contrast, is a straightforward case which even an apprentice can pronounce

---

[18] Cf. Lucian *De luctu* 15, also using the example of Stentor.

[19] See Homer *Iliad* 5.785–6, Stentor 'whose call had the power of fifty other men' and 859–61 where on being wounded 'brazen Ares screamed as loud as the shout of nine thousand men or ten thousand on a battle-field, when they join the clash of war'.

upon: 'Puzzling cases ought to be treated by medical experts; but *you* can safely trust your pulse to a pupil of Philip's.'[20]

This opening declaration to the *consolatio* section appears to reject a standard feature of the genre, that is, the explicit citation of philosophy as an aid to coping with pain. Yet the speaker confounds our expectations by deviating from his programmatic announcement. Even the formulation of his programmatic statement borrows from philosophical discourse the medical metaphor whereby illness of the spirit is described in terms taken from illness of the body.[21] And arguments familiar from the philosophical schools occur immediately in the first topic of this section, that a measure of perspective on the loss is necessary to indicate the triviality of the loss (126–34), specifically the arguments of the Peripatetics and Cyrenaics already noticed above in the discussion of the opening lines of the poem. The closure of this section is achieved by an adaptation of the topic of feigned and unfeigned tears (131–4): in the context of discussions of the expression of grief, the consoler urges that the mourner feel free to weep without restraint, provided the tears are genuine; feigned tears are condemned (for instance, Sen. *Ep.* 99.20). Here, the speaker declares he will not restrain Calvinus from his grief, because 'Tears are genuine when they fall at the loss of money' (*ploratur lacrimis amissa pecunia ueris*, 134). Transfer of the conventional topos to Calvinus' situation is enough to satirise him: the audience is invited to condemn the addressee for his inappropriate reaction to financial loss.

For the next section the speaker moves to a courtroom setting (135–61)[22] in order to facilitate a parade of examples of similar and worse cases which might sustain Calvinus to endure his pain, in accordance with conventional consolation technique and true to the Roman exemplary cast of mind. The comparison is announced explicitly at 144 with the word *confer*, 'compare', repeated at 154. But although he seems to promise a parade of individuals who had borne such sufferings bravely, designed as examples for emulation, in fact no individuals are named here (144–56).[23] Again, the speaker defeats our expectations.

---

[20] The contrast between 'medical experts' and 'a pupil of Philip's' seems slightly puzzling since Philip was a famous doctor in antiquity. It seems best to suppose that a strongly derogatory tone attaches to the pupil's status as an apprentice.

[21] Morford (1973), 29–31, discusses the use of the medical metaphor in consolation literature.

[22] The setting and, specifically, the example of perjury in 136–9 seem to confirm that Calvinus' experience included unsuccessful resort to law, as argued above, text to n. 7.

[23] Pryor (1962), 176.

The shift at 162 into a catalogue of 'freaks' of ethnographic phenomena which should not cause amazement when viewed in their usual, native context (162–73) has a dual function. Firstly, it reworks the Pythagorean doctrine about amazement from the opening of the poem (lines 23–37 and 60–70: discussed above, p. 72), thus consolidating the philosophical frame of reference for the *consolatio* section of *Satire* 13, as earlier in the *lamentatio* section. Secondly, it makes evident the speaker's parody of the conventions of the consolation and thereby his hostility towards the addressee. It achieves this effect chiefly through the fourth and final item in the catalogue of 'freaks', namely the pygmies (167–73). The fact that portrayals of battles between pygmies and cranes were favourites both in literature and in art seems to emphasise the extraordinary quality of this myth for the ancients.[24] But it is present here not simply for its classic extraordinariness but also for the particular symbolism which it conveys within the poem. As Pryor argues, Calvinus' loss is 'a pygmy loss' and must 'be reduced to its truly laughable size'.[25] And it appears that it is the speaker's use of this grotesque image to convey his by now not-so-ironic criticism of Calvinus which provokes Calvinus into an angry outburst.[26]

II

So far the speaker has continually exploited the conventions of consolation literature to raise and then disappoint expectations – until now. At this point, however, it becomes clear that his 'consolation' has proved to be no consolation at all. That is, it has utterly failed to alleviate Calvinus' sense of loss. The passion of anger is unconsoled. This is conveyed graphically at lines 174–5 where Calvinus bursts in with an angry exclamation in direct speech,[27]

<hr>

[24] See Courtney (1980), 554–5, for bibliography.

[25] Pryor (1962), 176. The tone of Juvenal *Satire* 13 is highlighted by comparison with Seneca *Ep.* 107, where a similarly trivial and unsurprising loss (the abscondment of slaves) is addressed in serious terms culminating in Seneca's Latin rendering of lines from Cleanthes' hymn to Zeus.

[26] See below on the connection here with Seneca *De ira*. Morford (1973), 32, also makes this connection.

[27] I interpret this as direct speech rather than the rhetorical figure of *anthupophora* (i.e. reply to an imagined objection), which is how Courtney reads it (p. 555 and p. 40). Brief interjections of direct speech feature in several of Juvenal's satires, for example at the close of *Satire* 1, and this feature suits a genre influenced by the Greek diatribe. Here, the attribution of 174–5 and 180 to Calvinus helps account for the content of the remainder of the poem.

asserting his desire to see the perjurer punished: 'What? Is this barefaced liar, this godless cheat, to get off scot free?' In these circumstances, it is no surprise to find that at this point the speaker abandons his attempt at consolation and the consolation structure which shapes the poem comes to an end. That is, the structure of the poem thus far has been illuminated by a study of the typology of the conventional consolation and by an exploration of the parody present here. But in the face of Calvinus' persisting anger, consolation is no longer appropriate. The speaker therefore adopts a different line, a line initially of direct attack on Calvinus for his unnecessary desire for vengeance followed ultimately by an apparent capitulation to Calvinus' views – the line of least resistance. It is as if he said, 'If my (parody of a) conventional consolation doesn't help you, then I'll give you a *real* "consolation" of the type you want to hear, a "consolation" which satisfies you in its promise of punishment and vengeance.' Furthermore, the structure of the poem suggests that the inappropriateness and ineffectuality of the speaker's consolation is what has provoked Calvinus' persisting anger. We may recall that right from the start the speaker was not sympathetic and immediately criticised Calvinus for his over-reaction. He indicated that anger is inappropriate because punishment will come to the wrongdoer through his guilty conscience. It is significant that this punishment is labelled 'vengeance' (*ultio*, 2), since this is the theme which re-emerges here in the finale of the poem. But here the speaker has changed his attitude: he seems to have abandoned the attempt at consolation for acquiescence in Calvinus' desire for vengeance. I shall argue that this shift in the speaker's stance will prove to be a further satiric tactic.

Despite the shift in the speaker's tactics away from the consolation framework in this final section of the poem (174–249), it will become evident that Juvenal continues to exploit the motifs of consolation discourse for satiric effect here. Thus, in reply to Calvinus' angry outburst, the speaker observes that even the ultimate punishment – execution – will not bring back his money (175–9). This is an adaptation of the consoler's argument that grieving – like taking revenge – will not bring back the loved one.[28] This provokes a further outburst of direct speech from Calvinus, who shouts that he simply enjoys vengeance (180): 'But revenge is an excellent thing,

[28] See Esteve-Forriol (1962), 150, e.g. Seneca *Ad Marciam* 6.2 with Manning (1981), 52.

sweeter than life itself.' This second violent intrusion by Calvinus
into the poem within seven lines compounds the effect of the first and
confirms that Calvinus is still in the grip of the passion of anger. The
persistence of his anger diminishes Calvinus still further, since,
whether or not the view that anger can be noble is subscribed to, this
anger cannot be described as noble. This, together with his advanced
years, perhaps renders Calvinus the irate and irascible old man of
New Comedy, an 'Old Cantankerous' for whom no sudden change
of heart will furnish a rehabilitation and reintegration into society.[29]

In reply (181–92) to Calvinus' second outburst, the speaker
identifies vengeance with anger (*irae*, 183) and then with pleasure
(*uoluptas*, 190), in an argument that the ignorant who demand
revenge lack wisdom (*sapientia*, 189) and morality (*rectum*, 189). He
fairly explicitly chides Calvinus for behaving like the ignorant (*indocti*,
181). In his assertion that neither Chrysippus, Thales nor Socrates
would behave like this, the speaker brings in the big guns of
philosophy on his side.[30] The use of the word 'old man', *senex*, in the
periphrastic reference to Socrates seems designed to deliver a
reproof to Calvinus, who was himself earlier described as a *senior* ('my
aged friend', 33) who ought to know better.[31] The speaker uses the
names of philosophers to chide Calvinus, finding it now expedient to
appeal to their authority. This runs counter to his earlier confidence
in the school of life and his avowed distance from philosophy asserted
at lines 120–5, and indicates a certain inconsistency. Then, to convey
his ironic tone towards Calvinus, he proceeds to assimilate Calvinus
to a woman on account of the pleasure (*uoluptas*, 190, and *gaudet*, 192)
which he takes in vengeance. This assimilation again recalls a
criticism of the recipient of the 'consolation' in Seneca's *Epistle* 99
where a man is chided for his 'womanish' behaviour (*Ep.* 99.2, 'you
are taking the death of your son over-emotionally', *molliter tu fers
mortem filii*, and 17, 'like a woman and with no backbone', *effeminatum
et eneruem*). The speaker has clearly abandoned his ironic approach
through the parody of the *consolatio* and has now embarked on much
more direct criticism of Calvinus.

---

[29] On the question of whether Knemon, the 'Old Cantankerous' in Menander's play, does
undergo a change of heart or remains isolated and alienated see Gomme and Sandbach
(1973), 267–9.

[30] Pryor's doubts about the presence of Thales the physicist in this triumvirate of philosophers
(1962), 177, are unnecessary since Thales was one of the Seven Wise Men (Plato *Protagoras*
343a2) and is cited as a stock type of philosopher from Plato onwards (*Theaetetus* 174a4).

[31] Cf. Fredericks (1971), 219.

The speaker proceeds to argue that the punishment delivered by a guilty conscience is worse than any punishments imaginable in the Underworld, an argument foreshadowed in lines 1–4. He illustrates his argument in two stages, first figuring the punishment of a man who *planned* a theft-plus-perjury (192–210) and second that of a man who has actually committed this crime (210–39). The terror and anxiety experienced by such men stands in stark contrast to a motif familiar in conventional consolations in which the blessed life enjoyed by the deceased is portrayed,[32] especially since the enjoyment is transferred to the addressee who is invited to enjoy the torments of the guilty. Moreover, the prediction that the perjurer will be haunted by visions of the addressee (217–22) represents a twisted and satirical version of the comfort which comes to the bereaved of seeing the deceased in their dreams.

Finally, as if worn down by Calvinus' continuing anger, the speaker appears to capitulate and adopt his addressee's standards (239–49). The final 'consolation' he offers is that the perjurer will carry on committing crimes and will be caught and punished in the end – which will bring Calvinus joy, in the end (*gaudebis … tandem*). In conventional philosophical terms, this is no 'consolation' at all, of course. In satirical terms, however, it is highly effective. By adopting his opponent's viewpoint, the speaker shows clearly how contemptible is the lust for vengeance. This technique of closure is not unique to *Satire* 13. Juvenal employed the same trope at the close of *Satire* 8 where, in the final seven lines, the speaker abandons the premise which he has accepted throughout the poem in order to argue against it (namely, that 'nobility', *nobilitas*, of the conventional (that is, inherited) kind exists) and delivers a *reductio ad absurdum* designed to deflate the pretensions of his worthless noble victims (i.e., with his assertion that all nobles are descended from shepherds or criminals if family trees are traced back far enough).[33]

Thus far we see that Juvenal has taken the conventions of the consolation in terms of both rhetorical structure and philosophical and rhetorical themes and applied them to a new context. The act of transference in itself would not have been startling, since it was widely recognised that consolations were useful for many circumstances other than mourning for the deceased. One of the clearest

---

[32] For the blessed life of the deceased see Esteve-Forriol (1962), 147–8, e.g. Sen. *Ad Marciam* 26, the emotional finale to the work.

[33] See Braund (1988), 121–2.

indications of the range of circumstances is found in Cicero at *Tusc.*
3.81: 'For there are definite words [of comfort] habitually used in
dealing with poverty, definite words in dealing with a life spent
without obtaining office and fame; there are distinctly definite forms
of discourse dealing with exile, ruin of country, slavery, infirmity,
blindness, every accident upon which the term disaster (*calamitas*) can
be fixed.' What all these circumstances have in common, of course, is
that they all cause distress. Cicero again is helpful in providing a
catalogue of the forms of distress (*Tusc.* 3.83): *at quae stirpes sunt
aegritudinis, quam multae, quam amarae!* 'But what are the roots of
distress, how numerous, how bitter! ... for envy is a form of distress,
and rivalry and jealousy and compassion and trouble, lament,
mourning, grief, vexation, torment and despondency.' The form of
distress in *Satire* 13 is anger. Seneca acknowledges the transferability
between grief and anger when he suggests that a person may be
deterred from lasting anger by use of the same words addressed to a
person experiencing lasting grief (*De ira* 3.27.4): 'The words so often
addressed to one in grief will prove most effective also for a man in
anger: "Will you ever desist – or never?"' (*quod in luctu dici solet
efficacissime, et in ira dicetur: utrum aliquando desines an numquam?*)

Furthermore, both grief and anger are passions which may be
designated by the single Latin word *dolor*.[34] Significantly, the word
dolor follows hard on the heels of *gemitus* ('grief') early in the poem as
we are introduced to Calvinus in 11–12: 'Let's keep our grief within
reasonable bounds. A man's resentment shouldn't be *over*-heated, or
exceed the injury suffered' (*ponamus nimios gemitus. flagrantior aequo |
non debet dolor esse uiri nec uulnere maior*). The word occurs again in the
speaker's ironic permission to Calvinus to let rip his grief over his loss
of money, provided that his loss is unparalleled, at 131–4:

> In such a bereavement,
> nobody feigns distress, or stops at ripping the neckline

---

[34] On the ambiguity of *dolor* and its relation to *indignatio* and *ira* see Anderson (1982), 316–17.
The same ambivalence as in the passages cited here is present at 9.90–1 where the speaker
says in apparent sympathy to his interlocutor Naevolus who has been raging angrily,
'Naevolus, the cause of your distress is justified' (*iusta doloris, Naeuole, causa tui*); at 10.315 *dolor*
designates the distress of the cuckolded husband, a distress which manifests itself in the
inflicting of physical pain and punishment in the quest for vengeance upon the adulterer.
The *Thesaurus Linguae Latinae* entry for *dolor* (III *passio animi*, i.e. passion of the mind) indicates
categories which relate to the cause of the passion, namely A loss, B injury and C love. In
practice, however, these categories may disappear as the different nuances of *dolor* shade
into one another. Here categories A and B are relevant, since it is not clear whether
Calvinus feels the loss or the injury more acutely.

of his clothes, or compels his eyes to squeeze a reluctant drop.
Tears are genuine when they fall at the loss of money.

> nemo dolorem
> fingit in hoc casu, uestem diducere summam
> contentus, uexare oculos umore coacto:
> ploratur lacrimis amissa pecunia ueris.

This apparent convergence is designed to lend a superficial plausibility to Calvinus' distress; the parody arises from the triviality of the
cause of his anger: it is shown by the speaker to be unjustified and
therefore inappropriate of consolation. The parody functions by
inviting the audience to make an implicit comparison throughout the
poem between the minor, everyday fraud and perjury of which
Calvinus complains and the forms of distress which constitute
suitable and justified causes for consolation such as those listed by
Cicero.

III

Satire 13, then, is a consolation for a trivial case of anger and hence a
parody of conventional consolations for distressing circumstances
which do merit consolation. The parody is marked in another way
too. An overview of *Satire* 13 indicates that the mock-*consolatio* is
unsuccessful. It fails to relieve Calvinus of his passion. Consider what
Cicero says about 'the duties of comforters' (*officia ... consolantium
Tusc.* 3.75): 'These are the duties of comforters: to do away with
distress root and branch, or allay it, or diminish it as far as possible,
or stop its progress and not allow it to extend further, or to divert it
elsewhere.' In contrast with Cicero's articulation of the theory of the
consolation of grief which prescribes such duties to the consolers,
Juvenal goes out of his way to indicate that his speaker in *Satire* 13 not
only fails to perform the duties of the comforter but actually inflames
Calvinus in his passion of anger. That is why Calvinus interrupts
with angry explosions in direct speech at 174–5 and 180, immediately
the formal 'consolation' is over: these explosions are clear signs that
his anger has not been consoled. Significantly, his anger recalls the
angry explosions which initiate Juvenal's first satire:

> Must I always be a listener only, never hit back,
> although so often assailed by the hoarse *Theseid* of Cordus?
> Never obtain revenge when X has read me his comedies,
> Y his elegies? No revenge when my day has been wasted . . .

The failure of the speaker/comforter is emphasised further by the fact that he ignores one of the basic precepts of offering consolation, that of choosing the right moment and in particular of not attempting consolation too early while the distress is still fresh. Cicero emphasises precisely this point with the example of anger taken from Aeschylus' *Prometheus Vinctus* (379–82) which he translates into Latin (*Tusc.* 3.76):

> But it is necessary in dealing with diseases of the soul, just as much as in dealing with bodily diseases, to choose the proper time, as was shown by the famous Prometheus, who after the words
>
>> And yet, Prometheus, this I think you know,
>> That speech can be a doctor to anger,
>
> replied:
>
>> Yes, if you apply the remedy at the right time,
>> And do not smash the worsening wound by force.

It seems interesting that Cicero introduces into his extended discussion of grief an example relating to anger: this suggests a certain interchangeability between the two passions. A similar point about appropriate timing is made by Seneca at the opening of *Epistle* 99 where he draws a distinction between the person in the first throes of grief and the person who is indulging in grief (*Ep.* 99.1):

> When a man is stricken and is finding it most difficult to endure a grievous wound, one must humour him for a while (*paulisper cedendum est*); let him satisfy his grief or at any rate work off the first shock; but those who have assumed an indulgence in grief should be rebuked forthwith, and should learn that there are certain follies even in tears.

The same precepts appear applied to anger at the very opening of *De ira* Book 3 where Seneca addresses the question of how to 'banish anger from the mind, or at least bridle and restrain its fury' (3.1.1). His discussion of the possible tactics is strongly reminiscent of Cicero's catalogue of the varied philosophical approaches to the consolation of grief quoted above[35] (*De ira* 3.1.1):

> This must be done sometimes plainly and openly, whenever a slighter attack of the malady makes this possible, sometimes secretly, when its flame burns hot and every obstacle only intensifies and increases its power; it depends upon how much

[35] Cicero *Tusc.* 3.76, quoted in text to n. 12.

strength and vigour it has whether we ought to beat back its attack and force a retreat, or should yield before it until the first storm of its fury has passed, in order to keep it from sweeping along with it the very means of relief.

Later he emphasises the folly of attempting to soothe an angry man in the first flush of a raging anger when he suggests that 'the best cure for anger is waiting (*maximum remedium irae dilatio est*), to allow the first ardour to abate and to let the darkness that clouds the reason either subside or become less dense' (3.12.4). Significantly, Calvinus' anger is fresh, since his loss is described as 'recent' (*recenti*, 5):[36] this is Juvenal's indication that any attempt to soothe his anger will be doomed to failure. This point is underlined when we recall that in his discussion of the consolation of grief Cicero includes a disquisition on the freshness of distress at *Tusc.* 3.75 which uses the same word, *recens*. In fact, the speaker's ironic words of solace and advice, far from soothing him, instead fuel Calvinus' anger by reminding him of the injury he has suffered and impel him to outbursts which reveal his enduring anger. What the speaker has done, in effect, is to indicate his lack of sympathy for Calvinus and this has incited him to further outbursts of rage. This is precisely contrary to Seneca's advice at *De ira* 3.40.1: 'To reprove a man when he is angry and in turn to become angry at him serve only to increase his anger' (*castigare uero irascentem et ultro obirasci incitare est*).[37]

And we are left in no doubt that Calvinus' anger *is* enduring. The speaker's final projection of Calvinus gloating over his enemy's ultimate bad end shows graphically how his anger persists (13.244–9):

> Our fraudulent friend will eventually step
> on a trap. He will face the gloomy dungeon and the hangman's hook,
> or else some crag far out in the Aegean – a rock that is thronged
> with important exiles. You will exult in the savage sentence
> imposed on the hated figure, and at last acknowledge with joy
> that neither a Drusus nor a Tiresias lives on Olympus.

Calvinus' utterly inappropriate and grim joy (*gaudebis*, *laetus*) in the perjurer's punishments combined with his late conversion to a belief

---

[36] In Stoic views on the passions, freshness was of central importance in the definition of what constituted a passion: see LS 65 B, C, D; Cic. *Tusc.* 3.74–5; Inwood (1985), 146–55; Nussbaum (1987*b*), 154–5, for discussion of the significance of the 'freshness' of a passion.

[37] One might draw a parallel with Seneca *Ep.* 99 where the reproof and anger offered to a man grieving to excess may only incite his grief still further rather than cure it.

in the existence of 'just' deities are simply new manifestations of his abiding anger.

The focus upon punishments and vengeance which forms the conclusion to the poem has another significance, too: it seems designed to invite the audience to *condemn* Calvinus' anger. The audience aligns with the speaker in seeing Calvinus' unholy enjoyment of the punishments the perjurer will inevitably, according to the speaker, suffer by persisting in his life of crime. Calvinus' abiding anger and perverted joy put him in precisely the same category as the ignorant (*indocti*, 181) and as women (189–92) who similarly delight in revenge (*gaudebis*, 247, deliberately echoing *gaudet*, 192).[38] The speaker, then, is playing the same ironic game as in *Satire* 9, where the addressee/interlocutor's flaws are displayed by the speaker without the interlocutor appearing to realise that anything is amiss.

IV

Thus far, it seems that Juvenal's parody functions by substituting one passion, anger, for another, grief, in a conventional rhetorical format. This theory holds as long as the combination of lamentation for the loss of money and consolation for anger follows the conventional pattern. But anger is not grief – and this, I think, explains the overall shape of the poem. What needs to be explained is the final section of the poem, the section which deals with vengeance, 174–249. This has no organic analogue in consolation literature, despite the presence noted above of certain consolatory motifs here. Yet this section does offer a perverted kind of consolation to the addressee, along the lines that the addressee will enjoy the perjurer's eventual come-uppance. What is noticeable is that from the point at which the theme shifts to vengeance (*ultio*, 174) onwards, Juvenal appears to echo or adapt material from Seneca *De ira* 3 about how to banish anger from someone else's mind, which is the nearest equivalent to the aim of consolation, namely, how to banish grief from (someone else's) mind. But whereas Seneca is offering serious prescriptions, Juvenal adapts this material about vengeance and punishment for satiric purposes, to display the inadequacies and flaws of Calvinus.[39] A brief examination of the most pertinent

---

[38] For a similar appraisal of the joy shown by Calvinus see Jensen (1981–2), 163.

[39] It is worth observing that Seneca admits that money is the focus and indeed the cause of a

material from Seneca will indicate the nature of Juvenal's adaptation.[40]

The final part of the poem is constructed as a reply to Calvinus' question whether the cheat will get away with his crime (174–5): the response is that he will suffer from his own guilty conscience. This much finds a close analogue in Seneca *De ira* 3.26.1–2 where Seneca puts these words into the mouth of the angry man: ' "I cannot be forbearing; it is difficult to submit to a wrong." ' (*'non possum', inquis, 'pati; graue est iniuriam sustinere'*) and ' "What then?" you say, "Shall the man go unpunished?" ' (*'quid ergo?' inquis, 'inpune illi erit?'*)[41] To this the reply is: 'The greatest punishment of wrong-doing is the having done it, and no man is more heavily punished than he who is consigned to the torture of remorse' (*maxima est enim factae iniuriae poena fecisse, nec quisquam grauius adficitur quam qui ad supplicium paenitentiae traditur*). That Juvenal was thinking of this passage of Seneca when he wrote this part of *Satire* 13 is strongly suggested by the fact that the examples used by Seneca appear to be the inspiration for those used by Juvenal. Seneca offers these illustrations of his argument that it is unjust to blame an individual for a fault that is universal: the unremarkability to his own people of the black Ethiopian and the red-headed German with his hair tied in a knot. These are close to Juvenal's examples of the remarkable which is unremarkable when set in its own context in 162–73, the lines which close the preceding section of the poem.

So far it would appear that Juvenal is following Seneca closely. The ironic element arrives in the finale to the poem, where Calvinus' enjoyment of his revenge is manifested in his gloating over the punishments to be suffered by the perjurer in the future. Here Juvenal is taking material from Seneca for adaptation. In order to demonstrate that anger is an evil, a passion, and not (potentially) beneficial, as Aristotle alleges (*De ira* 3.3.1), Seneca associates anger particularly with punishments (3.3.6):

> So that no one may wrongly suppose that at any time, in any place, anger is advantageous, its unbridled and frenzied madness

---

great deal of anger (*De ira* 3.33.1), but he belittles this, whereas Juvenal's speaker in *Satire* 13 ironically treats Calvinus' complaint with attention.

[40] It should be noted that Seneca sees anger as in conflict with sanity, whereas Juvenal sets up an opposition between the passion (anger) and the intellect in which the angry man is one of the *indocti* ('ignorant') who lack *sapientia* ('wisdom').

[41] The close resemblance to the explosive opening of *Satire* 1 (quoted above) with its cry for vengeance, marked by anaphora of *inpune* ('unpunished'), does not seem accidental.

must be exposed, and the trappings that are its very own must be restored to it – the torture-horse, the cord, the jail, the cross, the fires encircling living bodies planted in the ground, the drag-hook that seizes corpses too, all the different kinds of chains, the different kinds of punishment, the tearing of limbs, the branding of the forehead and the lairs of terrifying beasts – in the middle of these implements let anger be situated, while hissing dreadful, hideous sounds, even more disgusting than all the instruments through which it rages.

By portraying Calvinus' relish in the perjurer's punishments in the closing lines of *Satire* 13, Juvenal's speaker not only indicates his enduring anger but may provoke the audience's disgust (although not, perhaps, without an element of emotional satisfaction in the image of thieves ultimately getting the punishment they deserve). This is because his desire for revenge diminishes rather than magnifies Calvinus. Seneca's words at *De ira* 3.5.8 are pertinent: 'Revenge is the confession of a hurt; no mind is truly great that bends before injury. The man who has offended you is either stronger or weaker than you: if he is weaker, spare him; if he is stronger, spare yourself' (*ultio doloris confessio est; non est magnus animus quem incuruat iniuria. aut potentior te aut imbecillior laesit; si imbecillior, parce illi, si potentior, tibi*). Calvinus reveals that he is no 'great mind'.

Furthermore, in an ironic twist to Seneca's material, Juvenal hints that Calvinus' joy at the perjurer in prison resembles Seneca's picture at *De ira* 3.4.4 of the angry man as a captive of his own anger (*irae suae captiuus*) because of his desire for revenge and his view that the opportunity for revenge is one of the great blessings of power (*in magnis magnae fortunae bonis*). We are left with a picture of Calvinus captivated by the prospect of vengeance. Implicitly, Juvenal's speaker is inviting us to chide him with Seneca's salutary message to the angry man (*De ira* 3.42.2): 'Why do we, as if born to live for ever, take delight in proclaiming our wrath and in wasting the little span of life? Why do we delight to employ for somebody's distress (*dolorem*) and torture (*tormentum*) the days we might devote to virtuous pleasure?' and so on. Such a message is lost on Calvinus, doomed to a life of anger and hatred and irretrievably the prisoner of his passions.

The last eleven lines of the poem, then, offer 'therapy' of a non-doctrinaire kind in the form of ironic mockery of Calvinus.[42] Earlier

---

[42] On the therapy of the passions in Stoic thought see Nussbaum (1987*b*), esp. 129–44. On the

in the poem, the speaker has attempted the modes of consolation
prescribed for a passion: the arguments that his loss is not to be
regarded as an evil or a surprise and that he should not over-react
and so on. But when these appeals to reason fail, the speaker finally
appears to accept Calvinus' anger, to share in his angry outlook and
to whip up his feelings. This apparent acceptance is indicated by the
identification with Calvinus' viewpoint in the reference to the
defrauder as 'our perjurer' (*noster perfidus*, 244–5). In short, the
speaker has reversed the sequence appropriate to the soothing or
removing of anger: to be effective, he might have offered sympathy
with his passion initially then followed with the persuasion of reason.
This is an unorthodox consolation – as we might expect in the genre
of satire. And the effect of the satire is to condemn Calvinus' anger.[43]
This in turn implies a critique of the anger of the speaker of Books I
and II and indicates the distance which Juvenal has travelled in his
satiric development.

In conclusion, anger in Juvenal has been much studied in recent
years, but has not been widely considered as a passion in relation to
(Greco-)Roman philosophical discourse on the passions.[44] Analysis
of *Satire* 13 in this light proves illuminating. It illustrates both the
vernacularisation of philosophical theory on the passions whereby
such structures of ideas can provide a frame of reference within
poetry and the appropriation of rhetorical set-pieces concerned with
the passions by satirical discourse. It enhances our understanding of
the parody constituted by Juvenal's substitution of anger for grief in
the mock-consolation and permits a fuller appreciation than previously available of Calvinus' character, which is a character of
persisting and excessive anger. Finally, the study of anger as a
passion illuminates the dynamic development of Juvenal's entire
oeuvre, which appears to be an engagement with the passion of

concern with therapy of the passions see Fillion-Lahille (1984), 98–118, on the *Therapeutikon*
of Chrysippus, and its influence on Cicero and Seneca. Cf. Wilson, Ch. 3, text to n. 1.

[43] Marcus Wilson suggests that it may also be possible to read the end of the poem as a
catharsis of indignation which thus fulfils in an unexpected way the effect of consolation: it
offers a surrender to the pleasure of revenge, despite the intellectual condemnation of
revenge, which may purge the resentment. That is, the audience is, ultimately, drawn into
the passion of anger, which is always unfair (see e.g. Anderson (1982), 334–6). The same
combination of the ideas of consolation and pleasure in seeing the suffering of others is
found earlier in Seneca at *Troades* 1009–52, immediately following Hecuba's curse on the
Greeks (1005–8), epitomised perhaps by line 1013, 'Always, ah, always is grief malicious'
(*semper a semper dolor est malignus*).

[44] The exception here is Anderson, who opened up this entire area of enquiry in his ground-
breaking essay 'Anger in Juvenal and Seneca' (Anderson (1982), 293–361, first publ. 1964).

anger (never without the characteristic notes of ambivalence, even in *Satire* 1) followed by a critique of that engagement. It is hard to imagine any other passion providing such opportunities to a satiric poet.[45]

[45] I wish to express my thanks to everyone who offered comments on the (rather different) papers on Juvenal *Satire* 13 which I gave at Exeter during 1992 (July at the conference on the passions and December at the Research Seminar of the Department of Classics and Ancient History), to Christopher Gill for his comments on the first draft of this chapter and to Marcus Wilson for his subtle modifications and the references to Seneca's *Troades*.

CHAPTER 5

Passion, reason and knowledge in Seneca's tragedies

Alessandro Schiesaro

Mme Martin: Quelle est la morale?
Le Pompier: C'est à vous de la trouver.

(Eugene Ionesco, *La cantatrice chauve*)

'There is no such thing as a good influence, Mr Gray. All influence is immoral – immoral from the scientific point of view.' (Oscar Wilde, *Portrait of Dorian Gray*)

Tragedy and passions

I am painfully aware that the title of this chapter could well be the subtitle to a general essay on Senecan drama. This is a possible source of confusion I would like to dispel right away. It is true that the contrast between passion and reason is often named as the crucial tension animating these tragedies. But, as I am not attempting to offer here a general introduction, I do not focus primarily on the usual issues concerning the articulation of passions in the plays. My topic is more circumscribed: how passions can be described as the driving force not just behind the actions of characters but also behind the very existence of the tragedies, and especially how this genetic function is represented in the tragedies themselves.

Merely entertaining the hypothesis that passions might generate tragic poetry inevitably makes us face some familiar questions on the relationship between the tragedies and the rest of the Senecan corpus. One could claim that those questions are useless. Some critics could invoke the principle that we should read each tragedy as a separate and self-standing unit. Others could claim that the attempt to relate the tragedies, at any cost, to Senecan philosophy is a *petitio principii*: we ask how the tragedies can be compatible with the philosophy because we have already decided that they must be, since they were written by the same person. Yet, no reader of *Medea* or

Phaedra can avoid wondering how works of such extraordinary tropical luxuriance could have been penned by the very same author who fiercely (if anything *too* fiercely) advertises the virtues of stylistic restraint and expressive moderation. The fluid state of Senecan chronology in general, and not just that of the tragedies, makes it impossible to present a model of diachronic evolution, and compels us to read the corpus as an unnaturally static organism, with all its lines of tension prominently displayed and irresistibly attractive.

I divide my chapter into four parts. In the first (I), I attempt to read passages from two tragedies as reflections on the poetics of the tragedies. In particular, I focus on the way in which certain plays, especially *Oedipus*, seem to present an implicit view of the genesis of poetry, and of its relationship to passions and knowledge. In the next section (II), I connect the implicit poetics gleaned from the tragedies with the explicit remarks regarding the nature of poetry and poetic inspiration which Seneca offers at several points in his prose works. Next (III), I examine the effects that the tragic text might have on the audience. In particular, I investigate how tragedies could be deemed compatible with the Stoic requirement that poetry have an educational function. I conclude my paper (IV) by considering the way in which an understanding of the theory of passions and of the relationship of this theory to poetics can influence the interpretation of the plays and our assessment of their place and function in the Senecan corpus.

I

The poetics of passions 'en abyme'

Seneca's tragedies offer repeated and complex descriptions of the passions in action and of the effects of passions on both agents and victims. But I do not analyse here the passions which animate the characters themselves, for instance, Medea's and Phaedra's destructive love, Atreus' thirst for revenge, or Thyestes' quivering determination to resist passion. Rather, I look at the way in which these characters and their passions establish a connection between passions and poetic creation, and thus problematise the relationship between passions and aesthetic pleasure.

My assumption, which I will justify shortly, is that, at several critical junctures, the actions of certain characters embody reflections of the text on itself. While I cannot attempt here to provide a theoretical vindication of the notion of metadrama and of its importance in the analysis of the plays, I shall highlight some elements which are directly related to my investigation.

Senecan tragedy is a highly metadramatic form of theatre, one that often chooses to display its engagement in a self-conscious reflexion on its existence. In this respect, Seneca is no exception to the sustained metanarrative concerns that animate such works as Ovid's *Metamorphoses* or Lucan's *Pharsalia*.[1] After Virgil, poetry seems unable to resist the temptation to mirror in its own body the process of composition that lies behind it and the narrative mechanisms that make it possible. Succumbing to this temptation can produce the pleasing, if slightly dizzying, effect of the mirror reflecting its image on to another mirror, but it can also produce a sense of enclosure bordering on anguish. For such a mistake, after all, Narcissus dies.

Similar dangers await the critic; and it is better to admit from the outset that such a line of enquiry is far from risk-free. It does offer, however, considerable strategic advantages over approaching the tragedies by reference to the texts of Seneca's prose works, as if they could be considered a theoretical, systematic explanation of the more confused and dense universe of the tragedies.[2] At the least, if we are to connect the tragedies to the prose works, we should be ready to dispose of any hasty hierarchical assumption and to see the connection going both ways. There is no reason to believe that the explicit statements of the prose works should have a higher claim to validity than the tragedies, and should thus be used as a way to play down the potential disruptiveness of the tragedies. The order of my presentation reflects, rather, the suggestion that the opposite might well be the case.

In this chapter, I assume that the character who controls the dynamics of the actions on the stage with a degree of knowledge and power superior to his or her fellow-characters can be regarded – if contextual elements justify the hypothesis – as an embodiment of the playwright in the play, and can thus offer precious, if implicit, insights on its poetics. There are several candidates for this metadra-

---

[1] Among the bibliography on metanarrative and metadrama most useful at the theoretical level are: Hamon (1977), Prince (1977), Hutcheon (1980), Stam (1992). For Ovid, see Rosati (1983) and Hinds (1986); for Lucan, Masters (1992).

[2] The prose works, too, display significant oscillations, contrasting points of view, and, more importantly, severe efforts at normalisation, as Wilson shows in Ch. 3.

matic role, because several Senecan characters seem to wear the robe of the inspired poet in the process of creation. I comment briefly on *Medea* first, but my main focus is on *Oedipus*, a less typical and more complicated case.

In the prologue, Medea seeks to transform the storm of her emotions ('the mind stirs within', *mens intus agitat*, 47) into a plot of revenge. In doing this she is the prime mover of the play, and thus pre-emptively suspect of embodying a function inextricably associated with the author. Medea's decision to find a 'way' (*uia*) for her revenge, her selection of the most appropriate means, and her careful realisation of her plans all constitute the decision to have a tragedy and to represent it before our eyes. In this respect, Medea is similar to other central characters in Senecan plays: Juno in *Hercules Furens*, or Atreus in *Thyestes*. All appear on stage debating aloud their revengeful plots and voicing the tormenting doubts and emotions of creation.[3]

In search of inspiration for her actions, Medea invokes divine powers 'with an ominous voice' (*uoce non fausta precor*, 12). Now, while she prays that the Furies approach with their dirty hair and black torches, she imitates the poet's invocations for divine inspiration and concludes her proem, some thirty lines later, with an indication of the forces she intends to rely on to drive her actions, and the plot with them (45–52):

> Wild, unheard of, horrible evils at which
> heaven and earth alike shall tremble, my
> mind stirs within: wounds, slaughter, death,
> creeping from limb to limb. Too trivial are the acts
> I've rehearsed; these things I did as a girl. Let
> my grief rise to more deadly strength; greater
> crimes become me now that I am a mother.
> Gird yourself with wrath and prepare for deadly
> deeds with the full force of madness.[4]

> 　　　　　effera ignota horrida,
> tremenda caelo pariter ac terris mala
> mens intus agitat: uulnera et caedem et uagum
> funus per artus – leuia memoraui nimis:

---

[3] On the prologue of *Thyestes*, see Schiesaro (1992) and (forthcoming); for a more extensive treatment of the whole issue see my forthcoming monograph. The prologue to *Hercules Furens* describes various actions in the present and past tenses which the rest of the play will represent anew: Juno 'sees' in her words all the events that the play will then slowly unfold in front of its audience, see Shelton (1978).

[4] Translations of Seneca's tragedies throughout are modified from Miller (1961).

> haec uirgo feci; grauior exurgat dolor:
> maiora iam me scelera post partum decent.
> accingere ira teque in exitium para
> furore toto.

Medea seems to be aware of the essentially literary nature of her pursuit. Not only in the sense caught by Wilamowitz's dictum that she must have read Euripides' tragedy on herself,[5] but also because she explicitly hopes for a future of *literary* recognition for her deeds: 'let your repudiation be told as equal to your wedding' (*paria narrentur tua repudia | thalamis*, 52–3). The tragedy we are watching fulfils this wish.[6]

Passages such as these can tell us a great deal about how the author represents his own function. This does not mean, obviously, that they should be taken as public confessions of the historical author, or that, *qua* metadramatic, they should have a higher claim to authenticity than anything else said on the fictional stage of the tragedy. It only means that they represent important moments for the text to reflect on itself and on its poetics.

The *Oedipus* stages with great dramatic force the complex relationship between passions, poetry and knowledge. The play opens with Oedipus seized by an overwhelming fear of 'unspeakable things' (*infanda timeo*, 15), because of the oracle which predicted the monstrous deeds he has in fact already accomplished, and because of the sight of his city being slowly destroyed by the plague. While such a situation of objective distress should be confronted with reasoned poise, Oedipus is completely engulfed by passions, as he declares at 25–7:

> when you dread something huge, although
> you don't think it can happen, nevertheless you fear: I'm terrified
> of everything, and don't trust myself.

> cum magna horreas,
> quod posse fieri non potes metuas tamen:
> cuncta expauesco meque non credo mihi.

Jocasta's exhortation at lines 82–6 confirms that Oedipus' emotions are excessive, if not unjustified:

---

[5] Wilamowitz (1919), 3.162. This awareness of her being 'a Medea' (*Medea nunc sum*, 910), of being part of a literary universe, substantiates Medea's metadramatic character.

[6] Similarly, Atreus vows that his revenge must not be approved by anyone in future, but neither be passed over in silence (*age, anime, fac quod nulla posteritas probet, | sed nulla taceat*, 192–3).

> I think this very thing is regal: to face
> adversity, and the more dubious the situation and
> the more the greatness of empire totters to its fall,
> the more firm one stands, brave with certain foot.
> It's not manly to turn your back on Fortune.

> regium hoc ipsum reor:
> aduersa capere, quoque sit dubius magis
> status et cadentis imperi moles labet,
> hoc stare certo pressius fortem gradu:
> haud est uirile terga Fortunae dare.

This overwhelming fear is the real motor of the tragedy,[7] as Oedipus is spurred by it to engage in his painful search for truth through a tortuous path.[8] In the face of this new and powerful challenge, he will have to delegate his responsibilities more than once and will confess to the impotence of his vaunted rational abilities. The real breakthrough in learning the truth occurs only because of the elaborate magic rite organised by Tiresias and Manto and reported to Oedipus by Creon at 509–658. This powerful scene lies at the very centre of the play.

When Creon and Oedipus meet, the king asks his brother-in-law to reveal the results of his consultation with the inhabitants of the Underworld. The stichomythic dialogue (509–29) leading to Creon's long speech (530–658) can best be read alongside a similar exchange between the Fury and Tantalus in the prologue of *Thyestes*.[9] In *Thyestes*, Tantalus tries to resist the Fury's order to bring to Earth the 'crimes' (*scelera*) that actually constitute the play. His refusal to provoke 'crimes' (*scelera*) is a refusal to produce the words that recreate that 'crime' (*scelus*) in the play. In *Oedipus*, Creon begs for the right to be silent, and Oedipus, like the Fury, must persuade him

---

[7] Oedipus' emotional turmoil is represented fully in line with Stoic explanations of the functioning of passions (see Sect. III below). Although the text emphasises the quasi-irrational power of Oedipus' fear, his reaction contains a cognitive element in so far as it is caused by a judgement on a predicate, namely the prediction of the oracle; it is his judgement which is weak, in that it assents to an impulse which he should resist.

[8] Oedipus' first chance to discover the truth is vitiated by a residual trust in his reason. When Creon brings the convoluted prophecy (*uaticinium*) of the Pythia (211, 213–14), the king replies that he can easily handle the task, since this is precisely his prerogative: 'to understand ambiguities is a privilege granted to Oedipus alone' (*ambigua soli noscere Oedipodae datur*, 216). Oedipus' trust in his rational faculties outlasts even Creon's second and much more explicit description of a magical rite, as Oedipus boasts that he knows himself better than the gods do: 'but my mind is, rather, innocent and denies [the charge], known better by itself than by the gods' (*sed animus contra innocens | sibique melius quam deis notus negat*, 766–7).

[9] See Schiesaro (forthcoming).

with force. Just as the words of Tantalus come into existence only because violence overcomes his intransigence, Creon's revelation is similarly marked as a forced confession of truths which – he claims – should be left unsaid.

Creon's speech spans 128 lines, and I limit myself here to some specific observations. After the initial scene-setting, Creon reports the religious rite performed by a 'priest' (*sacerdos*, 548), soon referred to as a 'prophet' (*uates*, 552), who 'repeats a magic song and chants fiercely with rabid voice' (*carmenque magicum uoluit et rabido minax | decantat ore*, 561–2). Then, 'he sings again, and gazing at the ground, summons the shades with a tone deeper and wild' (*canitque rursus ac terram intuens | grauiore manes uoce et attonita citat*, 567–8), and evokes the ghosts of the dead. "'I am heard", says the priest, "I uttered prevailing words: blind chaos is burst open, and for the tribes of Dis a way is given to the upper world"' (*'audior' uates ait, | 'rata uerba fudi: rumpitur caecum chaos | iterque populis Ditis ad superos datur'*, 571–3).

The results of the prophet's invocation are tremendous: 'trembling' (*horror*, 576) occupies the grove, the Earth splits open (582–6), and there is a frightening triumphal procession of infernal creatures. 'Then grim Erinys sounded, and blind Fury and Horror, and all the forms which spawn and lurk amidst the eternal darkness' (*tum torua Erinys sonuit et caecus Furor | Horrorque et una quidquid aeternae creant celantque tenebrae* 590–1). There follow (592–4) 'Grief' (*Luctus*), 'Disease' (*Morbus*), 'Old Age' (*Senectus*), 'Fear' (*Metus*) and 'Pestilence' (*Pestis*). The prophet is not taken aback, unlike Manto.[10] Then other ghosts appear: Zetus, Amphion, Niobe, Agave with the Bacchants, Pentheus, a veritable catalogue of tragic figures. Last, apart from the crowd, Laius shows his face, and, speaking 'in a rabid voice' (*ore rabido*, 626), reveals the true state of affairs.

This scene powerfully re-enacts what poetry and poets do. The traditional connection between the magic and prophetic power of poets and of seers, crystallised in the use of *uates* itself, here finds a new contextual motivation. The *uates* who through his song can bring to life the frightening creatures buried in the Underworld is like the poet who, on the strength of his inspiration, gives life to the characters of tragedy. The regenerative powers of the *uates*[11] and the poet actually intersect in the parade of tragic characters described at

---

[10] 'My mind did not desert me. She who knew the rites and the arts of her aged father was amazed' (*non liquit animus. ipsa quae ritus senis | artesque norat stupuit*, 595–6).

611–18: both can reach a domain open only to a non-rational and frightening form of inspiration.

This view is strengthened by the structural links between Oedipus, the *uates* and, finally, Laius. Oedipus consults Creon, who turns to the priest, who is then able to interrogate Laius. As is fitting in a *mise en abyme*,[12] the inset scene is a microcosm of the larger framework, which makes reflection perceptible. Significantly Laius speaks with the same 'rabid voice' (*ore rabido*, 626) with which he had been summoned by the *uates* (*rabido* ...|... *ore*, 561–2). With different degrees of power and knowledge, these three characters all embody a desperate search for truth, the very search that motivates the tragedy from its inception. The plot of the play ultimately bends back on itself, as the search for truth is a search for poetry, but poetry is what the search is made of in the first place.[13]

In the light of the reading I am proposing, we can glean some points regarding the relationship between poetry, passions and truth. The uncontrolled fear that pushes Oedipus to search for explanations eventually leads him to discover in the frightening song of Laius the truth he was afraid to know. Passion leads to poetry, and poetry is revelation of truths which had been carefully hidden from the upper-world dominated by reason. As the *uates* literally finds a way for the creatures of Acheron to come back to Earth (572–3), so Laius gives a terrible and suppressed truth its chance to be voiced and heard. Poetry evokes the Erinyes, the new Muses of this poetry, but also the sources of a deeper knowledge, a knowledge which the proud rationality of Oedipus had not been able to reach.

Knowledge can be found in a poetry which is profoundly passionate in its origins and inevitably chthonic in its appearance. It is a knowledge which exists and acts instead of reason and against it. At the end of the play, Oedipus the cunning thinker and observer, the man boasting his ability to interpret 'traces' (*uestigia*, 768) in his

---

[11] Although the term *uates* does not appear to refer directly to dramatic poets, in Horace's *Letter to Augustus* (*Ep.* 2.1), 208–10, the tragic poet is equated to a magician (*magus*): 'poet who with inanities wrings my heart, inflames, soothes, fills it with false terrors like a magician, and sets me down now at Thebes, now at Athens' (*poeta meum qui pectus inaniter angit,* | *inritat, mulcet, falsis terroribus implet,* | *ut magus, et modo me Thebis, modo ponit Athenis*).

[12] The standard treatment of *mise en abyme* ('embedded' scenes or narratives) is Dällenbach (1977).

[13] This relationship is foregrounded by the fact that Oedipus had failed to draw useful conclusions from Manto's prophecy at 233–8, because at that stage he was still proudly relying on his rational abilities. He failed to understand the oracle himself, but he took reasonable and obvious steps towards solving the enigma.

search for truth, destroys the instrument and symbol of his reason. As he takes out his eyes, he transforms himself into another Tiresias, thereby implicitly recognising the superior cognitive power of the seer's blindness (971),[14] a power deeply rooted in the chthonic realm of blood and passions.[15]

Of the self-reflexive passages that I have, and could have, selected, the *mise en abyme* from *Oedipus* is the one that reaches deepest in the reconstruction of the process of poetic creation, and also the one that highlights most forcefully what begins to appear as the circular nature of that process. Fear will lead to poetry, and poetry will produce fear. But the metadramatic resonance of *Oedipus* is also different in important respects from that of other plays. Oedipus does not fully embody the functions of the playwright because his persistent trust in reason makes him unwilling to yield fully to the force of inspiration and poetry. In the end, poetry and truth will come from a real 'prophet' (*uates*).

Oedipus immediately rejects the truth which he is offered, relying on the deceptive evidence that Merope is married to Polybus. It will take a whole new act of the play for him to accept that he is indeed the culprit. This delay intensifies the sense of tragic irony that permeates the tragedy from its beginning. Now it is really only Oedipus, ever the cunning investigator, who still believes in reason and refuses to see the truth which the chthonic force of poetry offered. Oedipus is guilty because of his passions, since he yielded to the temptation of seizing power, and now is sadly wrong again because he denies that passions can give answers to his doubts. His tragedy dramatises the relationship between poetry, passion and truth: passion contains the seeds of truth and can lead to its full discovery.

We are now able to appreciate a fundamental difference in the way in which Oedipus fulfils his responsibilities as protagonist and prime mover of the tragedy in comparison to Medea or Atreus. He does not enjoy the privileged, omniscient point of view of the author in the way that Medea and Atreus do. Stirred by passion, he instigates a drama, but a drama he cannot control and which will eventually turn against himself. Medea and Atreus act within the plots they have constructed, while remaining unchallenged masters of their plans. Their authorial function, in other words, is always

[14] Cf. 'night' (*nox*, 977), 'darkness' (*tenebrae*, 999).
[15] Cf. the string of adjectives at 551–5: 'funereal' (*funesto*, 551), 'mournful' (*lugubris*, 553), 'squalid' (*squalente*, 554), 'deadly' (*mortifera*, 555).

foregrounded and never challenged. Oedipus, however, quickly reveals his true nature as an impotent spectator, repeatedly threatened by events outside his control. Thus, his plight dramatises one of the hermeneutic possibilities which we, as spectators, are offered. This tragedy represents the dangers of Oedipus' passions, and, at the same time, the futility of denying that passions have a valid claim to truth. Poetry is a passion, for the enthusiastic author who creates it, and for the audience which receives it.

II

The passions of the poet

In the process of representing the birth of their plots, Juno, Medea, Atreus and, to a certain extent, Oedipus reveal the passions of *furor*, *ira* and *metus* ('frenzy', 'anger' and 'fear') as the sources which will inspire their endeavours. These passages seem to amount to a strong case for the genetic connection between passions and poetry, in so far as they represent poetry as arising from a deeply passionate realm which has no room for reason. In his prose writings, Seneca confronts this very issue and tries to resolve the obvious tension with his teachings on passions produced by the connection between poetry and enthusiastic *furor*. I address especially these attempts at resolution, connect them with the metadramatic features I have already discussed, and try to reconstruct a Senecan theory of tragedy and tragic passions.

The connection between poetry and *furor* (in the sense of *enthousiasmos* or 'divine madness') dates back to Democritus and Plato. In the words from the *Phaedrus* (245a), which Seneca translates at *De tranquillitate animi* 17.10, 'in vain knocked at the doors of poetry a person of sane mind (*compos sui*)'. The enthused poet who transgresses his human limitations to reach out to the sublime nature of creation is mentioned several times by Seneca, and *De tranquillitate animi* offers a particularly interesting set of reflections. In the first chapter of the dialogue, Serenus voices his misgivings (1.14):

> Then again, when my mind has been uplifted by the greatness of its thoughts (*cogitationum magnitudine*), it becomes ambitious of words, and with higher aspirations it desires higher expression, and language issues forth to match the dignity of theme; forgetful then of my rule and of my more restrained judgement, I am swept

to loftier heights by an utterance that is no longer my own (*oblitus tum legis pressiorisque iudicii sublimius feror et ore iam non meo*).[16]

At the conclusion of the dialogue we find the *locus classicus* for the Senecan theory of the enthused poet (17.10–11):

> For whether we believe with the Greek poet that 'sometimes it is a pleasure also to be crazy', or with Plato that 'in vain at the door of poetry knocks the person of sane mind', or with Aristotle that 'no great genius has ever existed without some touch of madness': be that as it may, the lofty utterance that rises above the attempts of others (*grande aliquid et super ceteros*) is impossible unless the mind is excited (*mota*). When it has scorned the vulgar and the common-place, and has soared far aloft fired by divine inspiration, then alone it chants a strain too lofty for mortal lips (*aliquid cecinit grandius ore mortali*). So long as it is left to itself, it is impossible for it to reach any sublime (*sublime*) and difficult height; it must depart from the common track and be driven to frenzy and champ the bit and run away with its rider and rush to a height that it would have feared to climb by itself.

Although Seneca is not engaged here in an explicit declaration of poetics but is addressing most directly the issue of philosophical reflection, the presence of the Platonic quotation and the term *cecinit* ('chants', 17.11) suggests that the same state of enthusiastic lack of control lies behind artistic creation and philosophical excitement.

The idea that *megalopsuchia* ('greatness of soul') is inextricably connected with *megalophrosunē* ('elevation of thought')[17] and that the latter finds expression in the 'sublime' (*hupsos*) is rooted in Cleanthes' theory that poetry, thanks to metre, song and rhythm, is the only means which can adequately express 'divine greatness' (*theia megethē*).[18] Seneca, too, shares the idea that 'the beauty of things' generates enthusiasm, in *Epistle* 108.7:

> A certain number are stirred by high-sounding phrases, and adapt themselves to the emotions of the speaker with lively change of face and mind – just like the eunuch Phrygian priests (*Phrygii ... semiuiri*) who are accustomed to be aroused by the sound of the flute and go mad (*furentes*) out of order. The beauty of the subject matter ravishes and stirs those, not the jingle of empty words (*rapit illos instigatque rerum pulchritudo, non uerborum inanium sonitus.*)[19]

---

[16] Translations of Seneca's *Moral Essays* throughout are modified from Basore (1965).

[17] See 'Longinus' *On the Sublime* 7.3. The equivalent Latin terms are *magnitudo animi* ('greatness of soul') and *magnitudo ingenii* ('elevation of thought').

[18] *SVF* 1.486. Cf. Mazzoli (1970), 47.

The explicitly irrational overtones that mark the vocabulary of inspiration in this passage and make it so similar to its poetic counterparts are quite surprising in the light of the Stoic strictures against passions. While, in this particular context, the orgiastic frenzy of the converted is justified by their sources of inspiration, more complex problems arise if we try to apply this theory to poetry in general. Giancarlo Mazzoli (1970, 55–6) has argued that Seneca, following Posidonius' strictures against Chrysippus' theory of 'apathy' (*apatheia*), is here embracing Peripatetic elements, namely the notion that a controlled and moderate excitement can in fact lead to 'cheerfulness' (*euthumia*). According to Mazzoli, this explanation holds true for poetry as a whole. But even if this explanation can be considered satisfactory in the specific case of *philosophical* enthusiasm, it becomes much more difficult to apply it to poetry in general, since poetry is not bound to the exclusive representation of philosophical examples (*paradeigmata*). Cleanthes' *Hymn to Zeus* would plausibly fall into this category, but Seneca's tragedies, with their powerful representations of negative examples, are a different matter altogether.

This problem is highlighted by other Senecan passages which show a considerable degree of ambivalence towards poetry. At *De brevitate vitae* 16.5 (cf. *De vita beata* 26.6), Seneca attacks the frenzy (*furor*) of the poets which nurtures the errors of men by offering lascivious images of the behaviour of gods. Poets – as other passages make eloquently clear – are not bound by the respect for truth or morality.[20] Their inspiration is potentially dangerous precisely because it transcends, 'like an oracle' (*more oraculi*, *De brevitate vitae* 2.2), the limits of human rationality: this can lead to the possibility of speaking, 'with a voice greater than human' (*grandius ore mortali*, *Tranq.* 17.11), great philosophical truths, or, on the contrary, of depicting falsehoods in appealing terms. Like Hesiod's Muses, who can say many true things, but also many false things resembling truth (*Theogony* 27–8), the poets are ambiguous and ultimately unreliable sources who should constantly be checked for accuracy and moral worthiness.

I emphasise, again, the chthonic aspect of the ambiguous status of the poet, because it is the one that resonates most abundantly in the tragedies. When he describes the soul of the irate man, at *De ira*

---

[19] Translations of Seneca's *Epistles* throughout are modified from Gunmere (1962).

[20] Cf. *De beneficiis* 1.3.10, 1.4.5.

2.35.4, Seneca compares it with the terrible fictional Underworld created by poets:

> As is the aspect of an enemy or wild beasts wet with the blood of slaughter or intending slaughter; as are the hellish monsters of the poet's brain, fitted out with snakes and breathing fire; as are those most hideous shapes that issue forth from hell to stir up wars and scatter discord among the peoples and tear peace to shreds; as such let us picture anger.

He points out in *Ad Marciam* 19.4, that the whole apparatus of punishment in the Underworld is a sheer product of poetic craftsmanship:

> Reflect that there are no ills to be suffered after death, that the reports that make the underworld terrible to us are mere tales, that no darkness is in store for the dead, no prison, no blazing streams of fire, no river of Oblivion, no judgement-seats, no culprits, nor in that freedom so unfettered are there any second-time tyrants: all these things poets concoct playfully and distress us with groundless terrors (*luserunt ista poetae et uanis nos agitauere terroribus*).

Poets create fictional representations devoid of truth and use them to stir human souls with empty terrors; the close connection established here between 'play' and terrors is particularly striking.

Poetry springs from the same form of enthusiastic *furor* as that which generates the inspired sublimity of the philosopher, but it is not confined to great moral truths. Its morality and educational potential are linked to its contents: poetry can instruct, but can also deceive and misinform. It has a positive function when it celebrates the beauty of 'divine greatness' (*theia megethē*), as in Cleanthes' *Hymn to Zeus*. But what happens when it generates examples of vices, as do so many tragedies? How do these examples, presented through the powerful means of poetic expression, affect the audience? I will try to show that it is less easy than is often thought to reconcile these aspects, rooted as they are in the very nature of poetic passions.

III

Passions and hermeneutics: the audience

Much as they insist on the potential educational value of poetry,[21] the Stoics are also keenly aware of its possible dangers. For instance, Plutarch's *How the Young Man should Study Poetry* (*Quomodo adolescens poetas audire debeat*), which is very close, as far as we can ascertain, to traditional Stoic thinking,[22] expresses all these concerns very clearly. Poetry can be dangerous for the very same reasons that it can be useful: it is a form of expression which is more effective than prose. Cleanthes, as we glean from a reference in Seneca *Epistle* 108.10[23] and in Philodemus *De musica*,[24] formulated this thought with particular clarity:

> 'For', as Cleanthes used to say, 'as our breath produces a louder sound when it passes through the long and narrow opening of the trumpet and escapes by a hole which widens at the end, even so the confining rules of poetry clarify our meaning.'

There are two main ways in which poetry can be dangerous. First of all, listening to poetry produces pleasure in the listener, a passion which has to be accounted for, justified and contained. It is an irrational movement of the soul, and the Stoics must negotiate its existence by taking into account, on the one hand, the necessity to avoid passions altogether and, on the other, the potential benefit that the excitement of poetry can produce. Secondly, poetry can deceive the listener into endorsing morally objectionable ideas, and, by representing passions in the characters, it can induce passions in the audience.

These effects rest on the assumption that poetry itself can be analysed into two separate entities, matter and form, or – in Stoic terms – *logos* and *lexis* (a rhythmical pattern of sounds peculiar to poetic expression). Poetry, like music, to which Stoic authors often compare it, affects the hearer thanks to harmonious sounds and the

---

[21] De Lacy (1948), Tieleman (1992).

[22] De Lacy (1948), 250, n. 47. Nussbaum (1993), 122, too, uses Plutarch, with caution.

[23] Here, as elsewhere, Seneca offers examples of short *gnomai* effectively contained in a line or two, the equivalent, on a more modest scale, to the type of didactic poetry Cleanthes himself offers in his *Hymn to Zeus*. In such cases, the superior expressive and persuasive force of poetry is connected with a morally acceptable content.

[24] 28.1–14 Neubecker (1986) = *SVF* 1.486.

appropriately composed relationship among different parts,[25] and a well-crafted 'form' (*lexis*) alone can produce pleasure in the hearer irrespective of the content which it expresses. As an irrational movement of the soul, such pleasure should normally be avoided; but, if controlled and moderated, it can be justified because of its educational benefit, as long as the content of the poetry is morally acceptable. Only those still struggling in the way to wisdom, the *proficientes*, however, will need such inducements, which the wise person (*sapiens*) will normally eschew.[26] But it is the ability of poetry to produce pleasure *irrespective* of its moral contents which is a constant danger for educators to guard against.

At the level of *logos* (content), poetry appears again as a double-edged form of expression. For one thing, poetry can produce sympathetic passions, which makes it essential that the audience should restrain itself. The reader, says Plutarch (16e):

> will check himself when he is feeling wrath at Apollo on behalf of the foremost of the Achaeans ... he will cease to shed tears over the dead Achilles and over Agamemnon in the underworld ...; and if by chance he is beginning to be disturbed by their suffering and overcome by the enchantment, he will not hesitate to say to himself, 'Hurry eagerly to the light, and all you saw here learn by heart so that you may tell your wife hereafter' [*Od.* 11.223–4].[27]

Poetry can also represent immoral ideas and forms of behaviour (16d–e):

> Whenever, therefore, in the poems of a man of note and repute some strange and disconcerting [δυσχερές] statement either about gods or lesser deities or about virtue is made by the author, he who accepts the statement as true is carried off his feet, and has his opinion perverted [διέφθαρται]; whereas he who always remembers and keeps clearly in mind the sorcery of the poetic art in dealing with falsehood ... will not suffer any dire effects or even acquire any base beliefs.

A little later (17d) Plutarch quotes two short passages from the *Iliad* and Euripides' *Iphigenia at Aulis*, and comments:

> These are the voices of persons affected by emotion and possessed by opinions and delusions. For this reason such sentiments take a

---

[25] De Lacy (1948), 246 and n. 20; 248, n. 33.

[26] But the Stoics also hold that even the philosopher can derive 'joy' (*chara*), from poetry, a state of 'rational elevation' which derives from a correct judgement (of the contents of the poem): De Lacy (1948), 250 n. 48.

[27] Translations from Plutarch's *Moralia* throughout are modified from Babbitt (1960).

more powerful hold on us and disturb us the more, inasmuch as we become infected by their emotions (*pathē*) and by the weakness from whence they proceed. Against these influences, then, once more let us equip the young from the very outset to keep fresh in their minds the maxim that the art of poetry is not greatly concerned with the truth.

These two possibilities – that poetry will stir passions, and that the passions will give voice to wrong ideas – come closest to our present issue, for they are inevitable in tragedy. Plutarch gives an interestingly simple answer (18a–b). In the case of artists, such as painters, who depict unnatural acts (πράξεις ἀτόπους), for instance, Medea slaying her children, 'it is especially necessary that the young man should be trained by being taught that what we are to commend is not the action which is the subject of the imitation, but the art, in case the subject in hand has been properly imitated'.

While Plutarch insists on the fact that education and judgement must avoid the audience's endorsement of wrong ideas represented on stage, Strabo seems more confident that the text can safely orient the reactions of the audience. A pleasant *muthos* ('story' or 'plot'), he says (1.2.8), produces in the audience an impulse (*protropē*) towards that particular behaviour, while a frightening *muthos* exercises a deterrent effect called *apotropē*. This precise distinction, however, is undermined by the observation, in the same paragraph, that fear, too, can produce pleasure,[28] here called *ekplēxis* or *kataplēxis*. De Lacy notes that the term *ekplēxis* is found in the tract ascribed to 'Longinus', *On the Sublime* (1.4), precisely to describe the pleasurable excitement provoked in the audience by great literature, a state 'closely akin' to the *enthousiasmos* of the poet producing such literature.[29] Despite Strabo's apparent trust in the idea that the intrinsic shape of the text can produce the desired effect of *protropē* or *apotropē*, the representation of bad actions and bad passions in poetry never avoids the possibility of attracting and pleasing the audience, even if the author had intended to deter his audience from that wrongful behaviour.

[28] 'And what is new is pleasing ... and it is just this that makes men eager to learn. But if you add thereto the marvellous (*thaumaston*) and the portentous (*teratōdes*), you thereby increase the pleasure (*hēdonē*), and pleasure acts as a charm to incite to learning ... Now since the portentous (*teratōdes*) is not only pleasing (*hēdu*), but fear-inspiring (*phoberon*) as well, we can employ both kinds of myths [pleasing and fear-inspiring] for children, and for grown-up people too.'

[29] De Lacy (1948), cf. Russell (1964), 62. The connections between *On the Sublime* and the poetics of Senecan tragedy have been partially explored by Michel (1969).

So far, I have tried to show that Stoic theories on poetry fail to provide an adequate explanation of how the moral and educational value of poetry can be safeguarded in forms of poetry which represent negative *exempla*. The next step is to investigate the dynamics of aesthetic reception, of how the audience perceives poetry and is influenced by it.

The Stoic theory of passion posits a fundamental distinction between instinctive reactions and rational assent. When presented with a frightening appearance (*species*), any human being, wise or not, will receive an involuntary 'impulse' (*ictus*) which will make him or her react involuntarily. As Seneca points out (*De ira* 2.2.1), such reactions are not in the person's power and are therefore unavoidable (*quorum quia nihil in nostra potestate est, nulla quo minus fiant ratio persuadet*). Among the various examples of involuntary reactions, *De ira* includes episodes related to the effect of poetry and other forms of artistic expression (2.2.3–6):

> This [impulse of the mind, *ictus animi*] steals upon us even from the sight of plays upon the stage and from reading of old happenings. How often we seem to grow angry with Clodius for banishing Cicero, with Antony for killing him! Who is not aroused against the arms which Marius took up, against the proscriptions which Sulla used? ... Singing sometimes stirs us, and quickened rhythm, and the blare of the War-god's trumpets; our minds are perturbed by a shocking picture and by the melancholy sight of punishment even when it is entirely just ... It is said that Alexander, when Xenophantus played the flute, reached for his weapons.

This 'impulse' (*ictus*), however, is not a passion, because (2.3.1) 'none of those things which rouse the mind fortuitously should be called passions; the mind suffers them, so to speak, rather than causes them' (*nihil ex his, quae animum fortuito impellunt, adfectus uocari debet; ista, ut ita dicam, patitur magis animus quam facit*). Essential to the existence of a passion (*adfectus*) is the assent (*assensio*) which the receiver of such an *ictus* will or will not grant to the *ictus*. 'Passions', says Seneca (2.3.1), 'consist not in being moved as a result of impressions of things, but in surrendering oneself to them and following up this fortuitous movement' (*ergo adfectus est non ad oblatas rerum species moueri, sed permittere se illis et hunc fortuitum motum prosequi*). Of the involuntary reactions to poetry or painting, Seneca says (2.2.5):

Such sensations, however, are no more anger than that is sorrow which furrows the brow at the sight of a mimic shipwreck, no more anger than that is fear which thrills our minds when we read how Hannibal after Cannae beset the walls of Rome, but they are all emotions of a mind that would prefer not to be so affected (*motus animorum moueri nolentium*); they are not passions (*adfectus*), but the beginnings that are preliminary to passions (*principia proludentia adfectibus*).

If we apply this doctrine to the case of poetry, or, even more specifically, to dramatic poetry, we can say that the text produces an 'image' (*species*) which provokes an 'impulse' (*ictus*) of, for instance, fear, pleasure or hate; but that only when the mind has granted its assent to such an 'impulse' will poetry have produced a real 'passion' (*adfectus*). This structure seems in line with Plutarch's almost exclusive insistence on the fact that the audience should be educated to resist the 'impulse' of poetry, and entails interesting consequences for the critical interpretation of Senecan tragedy.

Before, however, turning to these consequences by way of conclusion, I would like to elaborate further on the dynamics of passions and on other Senecan passages which shed light on the relationship between poetry and *adfectus*.

In *Epistle* 115, Seneca criticises poetic endorsements of wealth (115.12): 'Verses of poets are added to the account, which apply the torch to our passions (*adfectibus nostris facem subdant*), in which wealth is praised as if it were the only credit and glory of life.' The torch is a remarkable metaphor for the *ictus*, since it implies not only the involuntary nature of the 'impulse', but also the intrinsic danger of the temptations.[30] As Seneca says in *Epistle* 7, 'there is nothing more dangerous to good customs than to indulge lazily (*desidere*) in some spectacles: then, in fact, vices creep in more easily through pleasure'. The 'impulse' can be resisted, but it is a dangerous temptation, because it is associated with the pleasure of poetry, the pleasure of hearing certain sounds and forms of expression, and (as Plutarch says) the pleasure essentially linked with the very act of mimetic representation.

In the following paragraphs, Seneca relates an anecdote from Euripides' career. Hearing some lines praising wealth,[31] the audience

---

[30] The torches are also traditionally associated with the Furies, whose connection with poetry are explored above.

[31] *Danae*, fr. 324 Nauck²; Seneca mistakenly attributes the lines to the *Bellerophon*.

rushed forward and tried to end the performance. Euripides came to the stage and asked them to wait and see what 'end' (*exitum*) that 'admirer of gold' would eventually get (115.15). This episode seems to point to the fact that, in order to preserve its educational value, tragedy must not only stage evil actions, but also show the retribution that they deserve. Again, we are confronted not so much with the fact that Senecan tragedy represents immoral conduct, as that it conspicuously fails to offer a convincing image of punishment.[32]

The relationship between passions and poetry established in the passages above implies a remarkable shift of responsibilities from the author to the audience. To be sure, the author is responsible for his intentions, and should be judged accordingly. But, whatever these intentions, the real burden of interpretation falls on the audience and ultimately lies outside the sphere of influence of the author himself. It is the *interpretative act* of the audience that in the end constitutes the educational outcome of a play, making even the best authorial intentions irrelevant. It is perfectly possible to assume that Seneca's intention in portraying Medea was to move his audience to a stern criticism of the passions which dominate her. But it is equally possible that a specific reader will end up feeling great sympathy for Medea, and thus forego any chance of being morally improved. In the hermeneutic process that links the author to his text and the text to its audience, there is a gap which makes the question of the educational value of poetry effectively aporetic.

Another section of *Epistle* 7, the famous letter on circus games, can provide an interesting confirmation that the theory of interpretation is heavily focused on the reactions of the audience. At 7.5 Seneca exclaims, 'Come now, don't you understand even this, that bad examples rebound on the agent? Thank the immortal gods that you are teaching cruelty to a person who cannot be taught to be cruel.' I am inclined to think that the person 'who cannot be taught to be cruel' is Seneca himself, caught, *malgré lui*, watching the slaughter of the arena. Unlike the crowd, Seneca is able to resist the *ictus* coming

---

[32] *Epistle* 108, too, acknowledges that *adfectus* may be stirred by poetry (108.11–12):
... but our minds are struck more effectively when a verse like this is repeated: 'he needs but little who desires little' or 'he has his wish, who wishes only for what is sufficient'. When we hear such words as these, we are led towards a confession of the truth. Even men in whose opinion nothing is enough wonder and applaud when they hear such words, and swear eternal hatred against money. When you see them so disposed, strike, keep at them, and charge them with this ... Preach against greed, preach against high living, and when you notice that you have made progress and impressed the minds of your hearers, lay on still harder.

from the performance because his moral principles lead him to deny his assent to such a monstrosity. But, again, the point is precisely that he is not influenced by the evil example in front of his eyes simply because his principles are *already* against it. If his principles had been different, the same 'text' could have caused very different results. This applies to the spectators of tragedy too. A negative spectacle will not likely affect the wise person (*sapiens*), but it might well invite a wrong assent from the morally weaker (*proficiens*) person, who is only 'making progress', let alone the 'foolish' (*insipiens*). And there are very few *sapientes* in this world.

Martha Nussbaum has recently argued that the Stoic project[33] of forming a 'critical spectatorship' escapes the seemingly insoluble contrast which Stoic sources delineate between the possible benefits and dangers of poetry. The 'critical spectator' will observe the tragedy with 'a concerned but critical detachment' and will analyse every aspect of the play with a reasoned coolness: 'the Stoics hope to form a spectator who is vigilant rather than impressionable, actively judging rather than immersed, critical rather than trustful' (1993, 137). I have a great deal of sympathy for Nussbaum's insistence on the spectator as the locus where these tensions are resolved. I am less optimistic than she appears to be about the idea that Seneca's tragedies can be seen as bearing out such a hypothesis. It is true that the insistence of many plays on passions highlights one of the elements crucial to the formation of a critical, detached spectator, who is reminded in the process of the existence of such mental processes. But I must dissent when Nussbaum claims that the repellent nature of many central characters discourages the audience's emotional identification, and even more when she invites consideration of the Chorus' moralising orthodoxy as 'a guide for the spectator's response' (148). Both claims are ripe for deconstruction, a process which would require analysis of each case in detail.

---

[33] Nussbaum (1993). Nussbaum distinguishes between two different Stoic views, the 'non-cognitive' and the 'cognitive', represented respectively by Posidonius (and, to a large extent, Diogenes of Babylon) on the one hand, and by Chrysippus, Zeno, Seneca, Epictetus on the other. The 'non-cognitive' position argues that emotions are non-rational movements which poetry can order by equally non-rational forces such as rhythm, harmony and melody. Proponents of the 'cognitive' line insist that emotions are evaluative judgements, and that poetry has an educational function in as far as it tries to modify those judgements. For the contrary case that Seneca's tragedies reject Chrysippus' theory of passions while embracing Posidonius' notion that irrational emotions have no cognitive value, see Pratt (1948). See further on Chrysippan and Posidonian psychology and the interpretation of Senecan tragedy, Gill, Ch. 11, Sect. III.

In general terms, however, I think it is reasonable to wonder whether the spectator's identification with such powerful characters as Medea or Atreus is really discouraged, especially when their apparent lack of reason is pitted against the commonplace superficiality or the moralising dullness of the characters who surround them, first of all, the Chorus. This is not to say that Nussbaum's solution might not have been the answer that Seneca himself would have given if asked how he would justify his poetic project. What he could not have said is that this solution actually works in the practice of his tragedies, that the philosophical infrastructure of his plays effectively avoids the possibility of a 'misinterpretation' which would transform his supposedly didactic project into a very dangerous source of passionate turmoil.

IV

The impossibility of tragedy

I hope that, so far, I have been able to make a case for the author's inability to control the moral lesson of the tragedies, a case based, as far as possible, on the dynamics of passions articulated by Stoic thought. I would like to reflect briefly, by way of conclusion, on the relevance of this approach to more general issues of interpretation relating to Seneca's plays and their position in his *corpus*.

The analysis of Stoic perception of literary phenomena offers a tempting way out of the polar opposition between reading the tragedies at all costs as the enactment of Stoic doctrines and reading them as a pointed and extensive refutation of those same doctrines. Whether Seneca must have meant us to disapprove or to approve of a certain character or set of actions, what the moral agenda of the play, if any, must have been, becomes, in a sense, irrelevant to the act of interpretation. I say this not just because intentionalism has become a suspect word in literary circles, but because the very explanation of how passions work and are perceived which Seneca offers makes the *effect* of a literary utterance necessarily *undetermined*. At the level of 'assent', which is the critical juncture in the development or forestalling of a passion, readers are left alone with their hermeneutic burden. They might have thoughtful teachers to guide them in the process, much as Plutarch recommends, but the author of the text, with his responsibilities and intentions, is inevitably out of the picture.

Actually, the situation is necessarily more muddled than this. The very form of tragedy imposes the representation of conflict, the battle between two sides. Their stances must be represented with equal accuracy and conviction if the play is to be effective.[34] Bad behaviour will be foregrounded, and represented with accuracy and artistic as well as psychological credibility. This fact alone introduces into the play a degree of openness and ambiguity that no firm authorial intention can ever dispel. As I said earlier, I find naïve the proposition that Seneca secretly meant his tragedy to be a refutation of the philosophical positions which he advocates in his prose. But for all the reasons listed above, Seneca's choice of the tragic form is inevitably a dangerous and ambivalent one. A full recognition of the double-edged powers of poetry, a recognition which could derive directly from the theoretical principles of Stoic poetics, would have perhaps recommended a different course of action. For instance, it would have supported an attempt at poetry along the lines of Cleanthes' *Hymn to Zeus*, where the pleasurable impact of poetry is put at the service of an unimpeachable moral lesson. But to mobilise the psychagogic qualities of poetry to represent negative passions meant an inevitable degree of ambiguity.

Seneca's tragedies do precisely what most (good) tragedies customarily do: they present a forceful 'display' (*phantasia*) of contrasting forces and passions and ask the audience, brought to 'ecstasy' (*ekstasis*), to examine their feelings and assumptions. This examination is all the more difficult (and rewarding) the more the poet has been able to make a compelling case for the very forces that constitute tragedy. This position is perfectly in line with what our Stoic sources have to offer by way of poetics, but, as I have tried to show, they do not offer anything more than a suspiciously circular argument, when they come to explain how, exactly, the fearful myths presented by tragedy can produce 'steering away' (*apotropē*) rather than 'incitement' (*protropē*). This is true in a particularly poignant way in the case of tragedies, including many of Seneca's, which blur the possibility of a clear-cut ethical reading by presenting figures such as Medea and Atreus deeply connected with the fascinating

---

[34] Nussbaum (1993), 108 and 143, discusses Aristotle's theory that tragic plots are predicated on the assumption that the reversals of fortune they represent constitute real evils. Tragic plots cannot therefore be 'ethically innocent' (108).

tension of poetic creation, for instance, or by depriving characters (such as the assistant and the Chorus in *Thyestes*) of much of the poetic credibility and ethical consistency that could make them powerful counter-examples. The audience, at least an audience of those 'making progress' (*proficientes*), will only be able to resist the wicked allurement of the various forms of tragic passion on the strength of previously held moral convictions, which can thus be tested and perhaps strengthened. Only in this very restricted sense does tragedy preserve an educational function, the only function which Stoicism is ready to grant it. But the risks implicit in writing tragedy are very considerable, all the more so in the case of Seneca.

What we end up with is the impossibility of Stoic tragedy: the wise (*sapientes*) will have no interest in it, and *proficientes* are as likely to be deceived by it as they are to draw useful precepts. As Seneca admits in one of his letters (29.1), 'truth should be told only to somebody who is going to listen' (*uerum ... nulli ... nisi audituro dicendum est*).

CHAPTER 6

Imagination and the arousal of the emotions in Greco-Roman rhetoric

Ruth Webb

I

The ability to arouse the emotions of an audience was vital to the ancient orator.[1] To achieve persuasion, he had to be able to move his audience as well as convince them by reasoned argument.[2] In this chapter, I take up one specific strand in Greco-Roman thinking on this subject: the use of 'vivid illustration' or 'imagination' (*enargeia* or *phantasia*) to make the audience 'see' situations in their minds and respond accordingly. This topic is handled in the treatises of writers such as Quintilian, Longinus and Menander Rhetor in a way that presupposes a background of philosophical psychology as well as of rhetorical method. Moreover, the authors of these treatises were themselves readers. Their precepts are based on their knowledge of the practice of earlier orators and, most significantly for the present discussion, they occasionally reveal their own emotional responses to the compositions of others. What emerges both from these autobiographical comments and from their statements about the device of *enargeia* is the presumption that the emotional responses of a reader or audience are highly predictable. This assumption is also clearly present in the typology of emotional responses, and of kinds of audience, in Aristotle's *Rhetoric* 2, a discussion that contains much that is relevant to the understanding of the social and cultural background to ancient rhetoric.[3] The Romantic idea that the power

[1] This article was begun with the support of the F. A. Yates Research Fellowship at the Warburg Institute and finished with the support of a British Academy Post-doctoral Fellowship. I am very grateful to the editors for their comments and to Jill Kraye, Nick Webb and Philip Weller for their advice.
[2] Fortenbaugh (1975) and (1979), 16–18, describes how, for Aristotle, emotional response is 'intelligent behaviour open to reasoned persuasion' and thus of comparable status to logical demonstration.
[3] See Gill (1984), 153. Fortenbaugh (1979) argues for the importance of the treatment of

of imagination on the part of the author and of the responding reader should be regarded as free, unlimited and unpredictable does not figure as part of this strand of ancient thought; and this fact, in itself, is relevant to the larger project of this volume, the understanding of the emotions in the ancient world.

II

The relationship between rhetorical theory and rhetorical practice is not, however, entirely straightforward and unproblematic and, as we see below, the theoretical treatments may ignore vital questions which arise when we try to envisage the actual presentation and reception of rhetorical works. The evaluation of the surviving speeches from this perspective presents its own problems. Although composed to be delivered on particular occasions, speeches of all kinds found wider audiences through circulation in written form. These published speeches would have been read outside the immediate context and unaccompanied by the orator's live delivery, a fact which might, in some cases, detract from their effect. The discrepancy between the effect of Galba's speeches when performed and the written versions, which lacked all the fire and spirit of the originals, was remarked upon by Cicero.[4] But Cicero attributes this discrepancy to Galba's lack of discipline and training, adding that the work of an orator who relies on his skill and judgement (*prudentia*) would not suffer in the same way. The implication is that the written version of a speech will retain the qualities of the original, even if it is not, in fact, identical.[5]

These problems are not usually discussed by the authors of rhetorical treatises whose precepts are directed towards performance to a live audience. Quintilian, for example, speaks to his readers both as a practising orator and as a reader of rhetoric and poetry; yet, when describing his responses to texts, he does so in terms of their direct impact on him, as if he were a member of a live audience, and not as a distanced reader reflecting on a text. The common

---

emotion in Aristotle's *Rhetoric* for the understanding of both ethics and philosophical psychology.

[4] Cic. *Brutus* 24.93. See also Quintilian's comments on the importance of delivery (*actio*) in *Institutio oratoria* (*Inst.*) 11.3.1–9.

[5] On the transmission of Cicero's speeches, see Humbert (1925), with further discussion in Nisbet (1992). On the performance and publication of epideictic speeches see Pernot (1993), 434–75.

practice of reading aloud would, in itself, have helped to preserve the oral nature of the text for the reader. Thus, the act of reading was assimilated to that of listening to a live performance in which the speaker communicated directly with the audience; and this remained the model of reception assumed by the rhetoricians in their discussion of written texts.[6] For Quintilian, the power of language to arouse *pathos* is vital to this immediate, even intimate, communication between speaker and listener.[7]

Only in rare cases, however, do we have both the text of a speech and an account of its effect on its original audience. Quintilian gives a fascinating analysis of his own reaction to a passage from Cicero's fifth *Verrine* – a speech which was never, in fact, delivered – which shows that a work could continue to have a powerful effect on audiences long after the original, or intended, one.[8] My first example, however, is from a very different type of composition – a letter sent by Aelius Aristides to the emperors Marcus Aurelius and Commodus requesting aid when the city of Smyrna was destroyed by an earthquake in AD 177 or 178.[9] Just over fifty years later, Philostratus, in his lively and anecdotal *Lives of the Sophists*, described the effect that this letter had had on its original audience. Aristides, he wrote, truly deserved the title of founder of Smyrna since it was due to his rhetorical skill that the city was rebuilt after this disaster.[10] He claims that Marcus Aurelius groaned out loud throughout his reading of the letter (whether he read it aloud or not is unclear) and that, at one point, he even shed tears which dripped onto the page. Such an open manifestation of emotion is all the more remarkable, given the account of Marcus Aurelius' composure elsewhere in the *Lives*.[11]

Whether or not Philostratus' account is historically accurate is of little importance. It does, however, illustrate the type of response to

[6] On the ancient practice of reading literary texts aloud, see Knox (1968).

[7] See Kirby (1990), 52. On the concept of language as power, rather than as an object of interpretation, in ancient literary criticism, see Tompkins (1980a), 201–32.

[8] Quint. *Inst.* 8.3.64–5; see Nisbet (1992), and text to nn. 29–38 below.

[9] On the dating of the events referred to in the letter see Behr (1981), 358, n. 1; for translation of the letter, *Oration* 19, see ibid., 10–13; for the text of the letter, see Keil (1898), 12–16: all further refs. to Ael. Arist. are to Keil (1898).

[10] Philostr. *VS* 582. This comment is typical of Philostratus' promotion of the civic importance of the Sophists. For a counterbalance, see Bowie (1982) and, on the limitations of Philostratus as a historical source, Jones (1974).

[11] Philostr. *VS* 561. See P. Brown (1992), 48–50. The Emperor's reaction to Aristides' letter has puzzled at least one modern scholar. In his notes to the passage, W. C. Wright suggested that 'either the Emperor was easily moved, or the rhythmical effect of this sentence is lost on us'. See W. C. Wright (1968), 216, n. 2.

Aristides' letter he considered appropriate. Menander Rhetor, writing in the fourth century AD, identified the arousal of pity (*eleos*) as the aim of such ambassadors' speeches (*presbeutikoi logoi*), addressed to emperors on behalf of earthquake-striken cities.[12] Philostratus' account shows precisely how Aristides' letter was supposed to have aroused the Emperor's pity to such a degree, since he cites the exact phrase which was supposed to have worked this dramatic effect: 'And the west winds blow through [Smyrna] as if through a wasteland' (ζέφυροι δὲ ἐρήμην καταπνέουσι) (W. C. Wright (1968), sect. 582, p. 214). Why did Philostratus identify these particular words as fit to move an emperor to tears? The image of the wind whistling through the ruined city is striking. Aristides plays on the topos of the opposition between urban civilisation and the vast uninhabited tracts beyond,[13] between the lost monuments of the city and the perennial forces of the elements. The simple, poignant phrase is equivalent in function to the vivid evocation (*diatupōsis*) of devastation which, according to Menander, should follow the speaker's elaborations on the subject of the city's cruel reversal of fortune. Menander recommends dwelling, in piteous tones (ἐλεεινολογησάμενος), on the loss of civic amenities, such as baths and aqueducts – the subject most likely to engage an emperor's interest (Russell and Wilson (1981), 180). Aristides, however, in the lines immediately preceding this phrase, simply mentions the results of the disaster in a few stark phrases. These phrases, however, clearly worked the same emotional effect as the more elaborate and explicitly emotive technique which Menander seems to recommend (Ael. Arist. 13, ll.3–9).

Some explanation of the power of Aristides' speech can be found by analysing his approach in the light of ancient philosophical and rhetorical theories of the imagination. Aristides opens his letter by attempting to express the magnitude of the disaster in general terms – the city which was once the glory of Asia and of the Empire now lies in ruins. But he quickly changes tone and addresses his audience directly, with an appeal to their personal experience: 'You have seen the city, you know the loss.'[14] He then exhorts them to recall their own experience of the city and their responses to what they saw there:

---

[12] Russell and Wilson (1981), 180. Menander does not mention this particular example but elsewhere cites Aristides as a model.

[13] This theme was to gain immensely in significance in the early Christian period with the paradoxical habitation of the desert, see P. Brown (1981), 8.

[14] Ael. Arist. 12, l.13: εἴδετε τὴν πόλιν, ἴστε τὴν ζημίαν.

Remember (ἀναμνήσθητε) what you said when you viewed it on
approaching, remember what you said when you entered, how
you were affected, what you did ... Which sight did you behold in
silence and not praise as befits you? These are things which even
after your departure you did not forget. All now lies in the dust.[15]

Rather than attempting to describe in detail the lost beauties of
Smyrna, Aristides refers his audience to their own memories of the
sight. By inviting them to summon up the mental images which their
visit had impressed upon their minds, he manages in a few words to
call forth an emotion whose intensity belies the apparent terseness of
the verbal expression. In terms of Aristotelian psychology, these
remembered images were the imprints (*tupoi*) left upon the mind by
sense perception,[16] an idea which is implicit in the term *diatupōsis*
used by Menander to refer to the verbal depiction of devastation in
the ambassador's speech. But, rather than using words to create an
impression of the city, Aristides relies on the images already stored in
the emperors' memories. Having summoned up these images, Aristides juxtaposes the stark phrase which Philostratus quotes, as if to
re-enact the moment of destruction in the emperors' minds. Alongside their memories of the city, he evokes the image of the wind-
blown wasteland. The power of the letter lies precisely in this
contrast between the past and present states of the city which
Aristides was able to evoke in the mind of Marcus Aurelius.

Philostratus credits Aristides not just with having aroused pity for
the victims of the destruction but with having implanted in his
audience a desire to restore the city to its former splendour. The use
of descriptive qualities in the letter is comparable to that in
Menander's recommendations for the *klētikos logos*, in which one
invites an official to visit a city. One should, he says, include an
ekphrasis of the city and the sights he will see on his journey (Russell
and Wilson (1981), 186–8). Such a device is only necessary, however,
if the addressee has never seen the city; for, if he has, he needs only
to be reminded of his existing knowledge to be filled with the desire
(*pothos*) to revisit it.[17] In both cases, the gulf between past experience
and present circumstance is momentarily bridged in the mind of the
recipient. An absent sight is recalled in order to inspire the audience

---

[15] Ael. Arist. 12, l.13 – 13, l.3; trans. Behr (1981), 10.

[16] See Arist. *De memoria* 450a25. For more practical discussions of memory as mental images,
see *Rhetorica ad Herennium* (*Rhet. Herenn.*) 3.16–24, and Quint. *Inst.* 11.2.

[17] For the suggestion that, for Aristotle, visualisation (*phantasia*) is a necessary precursor of
desire and movement, see Schofield (1979), 110.

to recreate the original experience from which the image derived, in this case by revisiting or recreating the city. The realisation of the gulf between past and present is intended to arouse emotion and so inspire action.

The power of visual images to make present what is absent is expressed with particular poignancy by Ovid in his poems from exile. Far from Rome, he can still 'see' before his eyes (*ante oculos*) his home, the city and the particular events (*singula facta*) of his past which are associated with the places in which they occurred (*suis locis*). The image (*imago*) of his wife is also visible, as if she were present (*coniugis sicut praesentis*).[18] The exiled Ovid, however, is unable to act to close this gulf and to realise his desire, so the effect of these intangible images is double-edged. For while they seem temporarily to enable him to transcend his condition as an exile, they cause him distress precisely because they remind him of the physical separation.

Like Aristides' *Letter to the Emperors*, Ovid's lament relies on the ability to summon up mental images deriving from past experience, and on the awareness of the gulf which separates these imaginings from present circumstance. Although both of these texts refer to personal memories, it is clear from Menander Rhetor's precepts for the speech of invitation and the ambassador's speech that it was thought possible to achieve through words alone a similar effect in the mind of an audience who had never seen the place in question.

III

'Longinus' discusses this phenomenon in both rhetoric and poetry under the heading of *phantasia*, or 'visualisation',[19] defined as occurring 'when, under the effect of inspiration and passion, you seem to see what you are speaking about and bring it before the eyes of your listeners' – a two-fold process whereby the orator himself visualises his subject-matter and thereby makes his audience see it through his words.[20] Unlike Quintilian, who uses quotations from both poetry and rhetoric to provide examples for the orator, Longinus makes a

---

[18] Ovid, *Tristia* 3.4.55–60; see also *Ex Ponto* 1.8.33–8. I am grateful to Don Fowler for pointing out this parallel. On this theme in Ovid, see also Viarre (1988), 102–4. For the association of memories of events with specific places, cf. the mnemonic techniques described by Quintilian and in *Rhet. Herenn.* (refs. in n. 16 above).

[19] *On the Sublime* 15. For this translation of *phantasia*, see Russell (1964), 120.

[20] Ibid., 15.1: ὅταν ἃ λέγεις ὑπ᾽ ἐνθουσιασμοῦ καὶ πάθους βλέπειν δοκῇς καὶ ὑπ᾽ ὄψιν τιθῇς τοῖς ἀκούουσιν.

distinction between the use of *phantasia* by the poet and the orator. In poetry, he says, the aim of this effect is *ekplēxis*, surprise or fear, whereas in rhetoric it produces *enargeia*, or vividness.[21] Both, however, aim to produce emotion (*pathos*) and excitement (*kinēsis*).

The process is explained at greater length by Quintilian who also associates *phantasia* and *enargeia* as cause and effect. Whereas *phantasia*, for Longinus, was a phenomenon experienced by speaker and audience, Quintilian uses the term in the plural form, glossed by the Latin term *uisiones*, to mean the mental images which the orator must be able to conjure up in his mind in order to create *enargeia*. In his treatment of emotion in Book 6, Quintilian describes the effect of *phantasia* from the point of view of the speaker:

> We name *uisiones* what the Greeks call *phantasiai* and it is through these that images of absent things are represented to the mind in such a way that we seem to see them with our eyes and to be in their presence. Whoever has mastery of them will have a powerful effect on the emotions. Some people say that this type of man who can imagine in himself things, words and deeds well and in accordance with truth is εὐφαντασίωτος [skilled in summoning up *phantasiai*].

> quas φαντασίας Graeci uocant (nos sane uisiones appellemus), per quas imagines rerum absentium ita repraesentantur animo, ut eas cernere oculis ac praesentes habere uideamur. has quisquis bene ceperit, is erit in adfectibus potentissimus. quidam dicunt εὐφαντασίωτον, qui sibi res, uoces, actus secundum uerum optime finget. (*Inst.* 6.2.29–30)

Quintilian is referring to a process analogous to that by which Ovid was able to recall the sights of his past. For Quintilian, however, this is part of the process by which an orator is able to move and persuade others; for, by summoning up an image of his subject in his own mind, he will ensure that his speech is vivid enough to produce a comparable image in the minds of his listeners. He demonstrates how to 'place something before the eyes' of an audience:

> When I am lamenting a murdered man will I not have before my eyes all the things which might believably have happened in the case under consideration? Will the assailant not suddenly spring out, will the victim not be terrified when he finds himself surrounded and cry out or plead or run away? Will I not see the

---

[21] On *enargeia*, see Zanker (1981); Meijering (1987), 29–53; and Lévy and Pernot (forthcoming). On 'Longinus', see further text to nn. 41–4 below.

blow and the victim falling to the ground? Will his blood, his pallor, his dying groans not be impressed on my mind? This gives rise to ἐνάργεια, which Cicero calls *illustratio* and *evidentia*, by which we seem to show what happened rather than to tell it; and this gives rise to the same emotions as if we were present at the event itself.

> hominem occisum queror: non omnia quae in re praesenti accidisse credibile est in oculis habebo? non percussor ille subitus erumpet? non expauescet circumuentus? exclamabit uel rogabit uel fugiet? non ferientem, non concidentem uidebo? non animo sanguis et pallor et gemitus, extremus denique expirantis hiatus insidet? insequetur ἐνάργεια, quae a Cicerone illustratio et euidentia nominatur, quae non tam dicere uidetur quam ostendere; et adfectus non aliter quam si rebus ipsis intersimus sequentur. (*Inst.* 6.2.31–2)

Quintilian begins this passage as if he were about to provide general instructions for the production of *enargeia* ('have before my eyes all the things', *omnia ... in oculis habebo*). But, in the very act of communicating in words his mental image of the murder, he demonstrates the effect to the reader so that the words 'this gives rise to ἐνάργεια' refer as much to the reader's experience of the preceding lines as to the effect of a hypothetical future speech on its audience. Above all, it is clear that the evocation of mental images in the audience was thought of as a means of working directly on the listeners' emotions, making them feel as if they were present at the scene (Schrijvers (1982)). Elsewhere, Quintilian describes such passages as penetrating the listener's emotions (*in adfectus penetrare*) and ensuring that the speech has mastery over (*dominatur*) its audience (*Inst.* 8.3.62, 67). This forceful expression of the emotional effect is echoed by Longinus in his discussion of *phantasia* in rhetoric: 'it does not just persuade the listener, but enslaves (δουλοῦται) him as well' (15.9).

Thus, Quintilian credits the orator with the power to implant images in the minds of his listeners, to communicate his vision of events to his audience through his words. Such vivid and evocative language is considered to be capable of creating images of absent things in the minds of others which are comparable to the memories which Aristides recalled to Marcus Aurelius and which Ovid summoned up for himself. The language used is similar in both cases. Both personal recollection, whether voluntary or prompted by another's words, and vivid language are spoken of as placing things 'before the eyes' (*ante oculos, sub oculos, ὑπ' ὄψιν*) and both have the power to move the person so affected. Several further rhetorical terms can be related to this concept. The word *diatupōsis* has been mentioned already; its equivalent, *hupotupōsis* is glossed by Quintilian as *sub oculos subiectio* or *evidentia* (*Inst.* 9.2.40); and one anonymous Greek source identifies *diatupōsis* as a means of arousing *pathos* ('emotion'), as was implicit in Menander Rhetor's instructions for the ambassador's speech.[22] An equivalent term to *diatupōsis* in Menander Rhetor is *ekphrasis*, defined in the *Progymnasmata* as a 'descriptive speech which brings the subject vividly (ἐναργῶς) before the eyes (ὑπ' ὄψιν)'.[23] What all these rhetorical techniques have in common is their effect on the audience. They may be extended descriptive passages or simple evocative phrases, such as Aristides' comparison of Smyrna to a wilderness or some of the examples of *phantasia* discussed by Longinus, but they all aim to affect the mind of the listener, evoking an image, thought of as an impression on the soul, and arousing emotion.

In the case of Aristides' letter, the emotional effect derived not just from the vivid evocation of a pitiful scene, but from Marcus Aurelius' realisation of the gulf between his memory and the present state of Smyrna. In the type of speech which Quintilian has in mind, such evocative passages were clearly thought to produce an effect on the audience which was comparable with that which the sight itself would have had. As Quintilian says, the audience is thought to be affected in the same way as if they had been present at the scene itself (*Inst.* 6.2.32, quoted above). This is, clearly, one means of ensuring that the listener feels personally involved in the case, as prescribed by Quintilian at the beginning of his discussion of emotion in Book 6 (6.2.6)

The emotions most frequently mentioned in the Latin rhetorical treatises in connection with *enargeia* and its related terms are pity (*miseratio* or *misericordia*) and indignation (*indignatio*), emotions which are entirely appropriate to the forensic orator's task of swaying an audience to one side of a case. These are the emotions identified in the *Rhetorica ad Herennium* as resulting from *descriptio*;[24] and Cicero in

---

[22] Anonymous, *Techne Rhetorike*, in Spengel and Hammer (1894), vol. 1, 393 ll.16–17: κινεῖ δὲ πάθος καὶ ἡ διατύπωσις.

[23] See e.g. Aphthonius, *Progymnasmata*, in Rabe (1926), 36.

[24] *Rhet. Herenn.* 4.39.51: 'By the use of this ornament [i.e. description] it is possible to arouse either indignation or pity (*misericordia*).'

De inventione identifies vivid accounts, which place scenes or events 'before the eyes' of an audience and make them feel as if they were present, among the means of arousing *indignatio* and *miseratio*.[25] Like Menander Rhetor, Cicero recommends that the orator should emphasise the contrast between the past and the present in order to arouse *misericordia*. A frequent example of a subject liable to arouse pity when described in detail is the sack of a city which is found in the *Rhetorica ad Herennium* as well as in Quintilian, who shows how one can increase the audience's feelings of pity by developing the details of the scene. Although, he says, the brief statement that a city has fallen contains implicit within it all the things which usually happen on such occasions, it penetrates the emotions less (*in adfectus minus penetrat*) than a developed and detailed account (8.3.67). Quintilian's remark might suggest that descriptions of the capture of cities were so commonplace that it was unnecessary to reiterate the familiar details on every occasion, an opinion which is clearly stated by Livy.[26] Indeed, as shown by Paul, this was one area of rhetorical training which influenced historiography so that the inclusion or exclusion of detail in such accounts would depend far more on the effect intended by the historian than on the amount of reliable information at his disposal.

IV

However, the precise type of emotion involved depends on the circumstances: the sack of a city or a murder might be used to arouse pity for the victims, or indignation against the perpetrator. It was with this latter end in mind that the fifth-century treatise on declamation by Sopater Rhetor recommended an *ekphrasis* of the sack of Thebes as a means of arousing indignation against Alexander, who was responsible for the sack.[27] But how could the orator ensure that his audience would be moved to the degree and in the way required? In Aristides' *Letter to the Emperors* (text to nn. 9–11 above) the emotional effect depended on the audience's own memories. Few authors of epideictic or judicial speeches would have had such

---

[25] Cicero, *De inventione* 1.54.104 (*indignatio*) and 1.55.106 (*miseratio*).

[26] See Paul (1982). Livy, 21.57.13–14, which Paul takes as his starting-point, makes it clear that he did not consider the repetition of details necessary in every case. See further on *aphēgēsis* (making a good 'story' in historiography), Wiseman (1993), 136–8.

[27] Sopater Rhetor, *Diairesis Zētēmatōn*, in Walz (1835), vol. 8, 210 ll.20–1.

precise knowledge of their audience's predispositions and previous experience. What effect might the description of a scene have on an audience who had never themselves witnessed it and who were perhaps – in the case of juries – subjected to competing visions of the same events? On the whole, the authors of treatises tend to speak as if the impact of vivid speech were entirely unproblematic, and as if the audience were bound to be affected as described. The examples mentioned by Quintilian of oratorical performances which failed to achieve their intended effect, often with humorous results, all involve non-verbal appeals to the emotions: the use of children or of props such as portraits and swords.[28]

Fortunately, we do have some relatively detailed accounts of the reactions of one Roman reader, Quintilian, to certain passages in Cicero which can point to some answers to this question.[29] Citing a passage from the *Verrines*, he asks:

> Who could be so incapable of conceiving [mental] images that, when reading that passage in the *Verrines* – 'there on the shore stood the praetor of the Roman people, shod with slippers, clad in a purple cloak and a tunic and leaning on this worthless woman' – he does not just seem to see the characters themselves, the place and their dress but even supplies for himself some of the things which are unspoken? I for my part certainly seem to see his face, his eyes, the couple's degrading caresses, the silent disgust and the frightened shame of those who were present.

> an quisquam tam procul a concipiendis imaginibus rerum abest ut non, cum illa in Verrem legit: 'stetit soleatus praetor populi Romani cum pallio purpureo tunicaque talari muliercula nixus in litore', non solum ipsos intueri uideatur et locum et habitum, sed quaedam etiam ex iis quae dicta non sunt sibi adstruat? ego certe mihi cernere uideor et uultum et oculos et deformes utriusque blanditias et eorum qui aderant tacitam auersationem ac timidam uerecundiam.[30]

Cicero's word-picture is economically drawn, each word contributing to the vignette of Verres. The passage does not make use of emotive figures; there is no apostrophe, no tricolon crescendo. But the physical details themselves were emotionally loaded for the

---

[28] *Inst.* 6.1.37–45. At 6.1.49 Quintilian demonstrates further his belief in the superiority of the spoken word over such theatrical effects by showing how they can be undermined by a single well-chosen remark from the opposing speaker.

[29] Quint. *Inst.* 8.3.64–5. This passage is discussed in Nisbet (1992).

[30] Quint. *Inst.* 8.3.64–5; Cicero, *Verrine Orations* 5.33.86.

Roman audience. As a Greek style of clothing, the cloak (*pallium*) could be a sign of moral laxity, the antithesis of the values represented by the traditional Roman toga,[31] a contrast which is underlined by the alliterative pattern (*praetor populi ... pallio purpureo*, 'praetor ... people ... purple cloak').

Cicero's deft sketch evokes for Quintilian far more than is stated explicitly. But he does not elaborate on the purely visual details of the scene evoked in his imagination, or on the aspects of the figures' appearance not mentioned in the text. Instead, he pays greatest attention to the ways in which the scene is brought to life for him and invested with movement and feeling. Interestingly, he supplies the scene with internal onlookers (*ii qui aderant*) to whom he attributes feelings with which, it is assumed, we are to identify.[32]

Quintilian presents his reaction as exemplary: not only should everyone see, but, he implies, they should react as he does. The individual reader – or member of the audience – might supplement the telling details of Cicero's sketch as he pleased, but the values depicted were clearly signalled in the details and the language used. It was vital for each reader or listener to respond and to feel personally involved in the scene for this technique of persuasion to be effective. But the possibility of a 'resisting reader', who refuses to react in the same way as the ideal or 'presumed' reader implied by the text and personified in Quintilian's imagined onlookers, is not entertained by Quintilian or Cicero.[33] This is not a matter of merely theoretical significance since, in order to be effective, the speech must have the intended effect on the audience.

Here, an understanding of the type of 'imagination' involved is important. The concept of the imagination referred to by Cicero, Quintilian, and even 'Longinus', is not the free, creative one of modern poetics which functions as a semi-divine, creative impulse in its own right, and whose products need only be internally consistent, without being caused by or aimed at the exterior

---

[31] See Cic. *Pro Rabirio Postumo* 25–7. I am grateful to Michael Koortbojian for discussion of this point.

[32] On a comparable use of onlookers in a different literary form, the Greek novel, see Morgan (1991). On the speaker's expression of his own emotions as an indication of what the audience should feel see James and Webb (1991). On the use of the 'internal audience', see also Levene, Ch. 7, Sect. II.

[33] Rabinowitz (1986), 117, uses the term 'presumed audience' to mean the ideal audience to whom the text is addressed, as opposed to the 'actual audience' of real individuals who may react in different ways or even reject the values implicit in the text.

world.[34] Rather, the ancient rhetoricians envisage a 'mimetic' imagination, based on a pre-existing reality and bounded by accepted truths and values which ensure that the orator could to some extent predict the reactions of his audience.[35] Quintilian more than once refers to the need to ensure that descriptions are in accordance with truth (*secundum uerum, ueri similia*), or credible (*credibile*). [36] To this extent, 'evocation' or 'imagination' in rhetoric is comparable to 'common place' (κοινὸς τόπος), the elaboration of commonly accepted ideas about a type of person.[37] As Quintilian says, one may introduce invented falsehoods into descriptions, as long as they are things which usually happen.[38]

V

In this sense, all appeals to the visual imagination in rhetoric relied, to some degree, on experience of shared cultural values. That appeals to such values were seen as an effective way of appealing to the emotions is clear from Cicero's discussion of *indignatio* in *De inventione*. This emotion can be aroused, he says, by referring to authority, by reminding the audience of the gravity with which the matter in question was regarded by their gods, their ancestors, rulers and lawgivers (1.53.101). In this way, by appealing to respect for tradition and religion, even a description of a landscape could be loaded with cultural meaning and used to arouse emotion. This is how Cicero uses the description of Henna in Sicily in the fourth *Verrine Oration*. He evokes the grandeur and fertility of the place with its precipitous cliffs, numerous springs and abundance of flowers, qualities which, he claims, guarantee the authenticity of the site as the place of Persephone's abduction.[39] Against this background,

---

[34] See Abrams (1958), 22, on the paramount importance of the creative imagination in modern expressive theories of poetics, and 281, on the need for internal consistency alone. See also Kearney (1988), 17, on the 'mimetic' paradigm of the pre-modern imagination as opposed to the 'productive' paradigm of the modern period; De Man (1984), 16, on the independence of the Romantic consciousness from the world of sense experience.

[35] See Pedrick and Rabinowitz (1986), 107.

[36] Quint. *Inst.* 6.2.30; 8.3.70; 6.2.31; see also n. 44 below.

[37] See e.g. Aphthonios, *Progymnasmata*, in Rabe (1926), 16–17; Webb (forthcoming), and Pernot (1986). See also Quintilian's discussion of behavioural indicators of character types, *Inst.* 5.9.12–15.

[38] Quint. *Inst.* 8.3.70: 'we may even invent fictitious events of the type which usually occur'.

[39] *Ver.* 4.48.107: 'Henna, where the events I am speaking of are reported to have taken place, is in a lofty and eminent place, at the top of which is a level plain with ever-flowing streams; it is surrounded by cliffs and cut off from all approach by its position. Around it are numerous

Verres' theft of cult statues is all the more worthy of indignation. The emotions aroused by this evocation of place thus shift from a sense of awe at the landscape and its associated narrative, to outrage at the contrast between the site and Verres' actions. At the climax of the passage, Cicero claims that his memory of the events not only moves him but makes him tremble physically (*De invent.* 50.110). Cicero later provides an explicit example of the use of *phantasia* in the orator's mind to produce vivid and emotive speech. In this case the image is said to derive from the speaker's own memory as Cicero recounts his recollection of how he was received by the priests of Ceres and the citizens. In so doing, he communicates to his audience his memory of their solemn appearance and their distress.[40]

There were, therefore, limits to the subject-matter of such evocations. If they were to be effective, they had to correspond to specific experiences, or to shared values and cultural norms which could be recognised by the audience and mobilised by the speaker. These latter had an emotive power, even if they were not upheld equally by all individual members of the historical audience. That orators did frequently overstep these boundaries, particularly in declamations on fictitious themes, is clear from the criticisms of Longinus and pseudo-Dionysius of Halicarnassus, among others.

Longinus makes a clear distinction between *phantasia* in rhetoric and in poetry. Poets were permitted to conjure up exaggerated scenes (μυθικωτέραν ... ὑπερέκπτωσιν) which went beyond the normal bounds of credibility (τὸ πιστὸν ὑπεραίρουσαν, *On the Sublime* 15.8). His first example of poetic *phantasia* is the image of the Furies described by Euripides' haunted Orestes and Longinus praises the way in which the tragedian was able to 'see' for himself, and thus make the audience 'see' the Furies (15.2). But such exaggeration is entirely inappropriate for the orator who should confine himself to what is 'practicable' (ἔμπρακτον) and 'in accordance with truth' (ἐνάληθες). Longinus accuses contemporary declaimers of stepping over these boundaries and of imitating Euripides' Orestes, without realising that, quite apart from the question of

lakes and groves with abundant flowers at all times of the year so that the place itself seems to confirm the story of the girl's abduction which we heard from our childhood.' I am grateful to E. J. Kenney for bringing this passage to my attention.

[40] *De Invent.* 50.110: 'I am thinking of the shrine, the place, that sense of awe. I can see it all before my eyes: that day when I came to Henna, the priests of Ceres were waiting there, wearing their fillets and carrying branches, the citizens also were assembled and, as I spoke, there were so many groans, so much weeping, that the city seemed to be filled with the most bitter grief.'

poetic licence, Euripides was depicting a character suffering from delusions (ὅτι μαίνεται).[41] In contrast, a proper rhetorical use of *phantasia* in combination with factual arguments (ταῖς πραγματικαῖς ἐπιχειρήσεσιν) will enable the orator to 'enslave' his audience.[42] This distinction between rhetor and poet corresponds to the standard rhetorical division between a narrative which is marvellous (*muthos*) and the 'true' or 'like truth'.[43] But Longinus combines the last two into one category emphasising that, for the orator, it is verisimilitude which counts above all.[44] The audience's presuppositions about what is plausible set the limits for what is acceptable in rhetorical visualisation.

The problem is raised in slightly different terms by pseudo-Dionysius of Halicarnassus. He advises against the use of *ekphraseis* of storms, plagues, famines, armies and deeds of valour which, he complains, have invaded declamation in imitation of history and poetry. His argument is not against such passages in themselves, nor does he claim that these *ekphraseis* are always inherently improbable. But, he points out, the authors of fictitious declamations have no agreed basis to limit their evocations of the sight: there is no particular or personal (*idios*) idea to which they can appeal. What is more, it is possible for the opponent to set out a counter-*ekphrasis* which is equally unfounded, so that there is no end to the waste of words.[45]

These passages all emphasise the necessity for the orator of producing an image which is not just internally consistent but which can be related to the audience's experience of, or beliefs about, the world. The 'realistic' (*veri similis*) in rhetoric is that which corresponds to such accepted truths and values rather than attempting to reproduce the reality described in its particularity.[46] The corre-

---

[41] 15.2. Orestes' visions were the stock example of illusion in Stoic epistemology (LS 39 A–B).

[42] 15.9; see pp. 117–19 above.

[43] On the terminology and the various systems of division, see Meijering (1987), 71–82. See also Wiseman (1993), 129–30; Morgan (1993), 189–90; Feeney (1993), 239–40.

[44] See text to nn. 35–8 above and, on the idea of rhetoric as directed at 'verisimilitude', i.e. a conventional understanding of what constitutes 'truth', see further Wiseman (1993), 142; Morgan (1993), 187–8; Webb (forthcoming).

[45] Pseudo-Dionysius, *Technē Rhetorikē*, in Usener and Radermacher (1929), 372: 'When orators compose declamations they do not have an idea (ἰδέαν) of the events which is agreed (ὁμολογουμένην) or particular (ἰδίαν) and they invent visions (ὄψεις) of plagues and famines and storms and wars which did not all occur in this way, as they themselves say. It is quite possible for the opposing speaker to relate these things in a different manner from his opponent … and this draws out the speech needlessly.' See also Russell (1983), 2.

[46] See refs. in n. 44 above.

sponding conception of truth, as what is likely to have happened in the past, or to happen again in the future, is the same as that underlying ancient historiography.[47] The audience of a forensic speech, or even in some cases an epideictic speech, needed to be able to recognise and evaluate the significance of the situations evoked by the orator. Although any evocation of an image in the mind of a listener could be termed a *pathos*, since it was thought of as having a physical impact, the precise emotional effect of such images depended on such acts of cognition on the part of the audience – the recognition of the incongruity between Verres' rank and his actions or of the gap between the past and present states of the city of Smyrna. As with Aristotle's categorisation of the emotions and the means of arousing them, this means that much of the effect of such passages was determined by the cultural knowledge shared by speaker and audience.

[47] See Woodman (1988), 27, on Thucydides, and 201–3, on ancient conceptions of truth. See also A. Cameron (1989), 10, on history, poetry and rhetoric, and Wheeldon (1989). For some qualifications of the linkage between historiography and rhetoric in this respect, see Moles (1993), 103–7, 116–18.

CHAPTER 7

Pity, fear and the historical audience: Tacitus on the fall of Vitellius

D. S. Levene

I

For the Roman historians, no passion is more prominent than fear. Fear for them is perhaps the single most important influence on the behaviour of individuals and states. It is often a negative force, deterring people from courses of action that they might otherwise entertain. But it can sometimes cause activity too. A country may be led to attack its neighbour through fear; fear can decide the outcome of a battle or a siege. Fear of assassination may lead a ruler into tyranny; yet it may be fear that drives the hand of the assassin.[1] When a historian wishes to analyse a situation, or explain a policy, he will very often do so at least partly in terms of fear.

Pity is less central. It probably appears less often than, say, anger or hatred as an explanation for action. Yet it too has an important role to play when, for example, people consider whether defeated opponents should be spared, with the concomitant idea that, if so, they may live to fight again, or, alternatively, may transfer their allegiance to the victor out of gratitude. Here, pity or the absence of pity may be presented as the key that will change the course of history.

Does the portrayal of these emotions in the Roman historians owe anything to philosophy? Many of the chapters in this volume are concerned with philosophical influences on Roman literature, and one might hope to find such connections here. Stoicism, in particular, has a distinctive attitude towards the passions, is certainly important for understanding many Roman writers, and has indeed at times been claimed to have influenced various of the major

---

[1] See Martin and Woodman (1989), 253, on the way in which rulers' and subjects' fears are bound together; more generally Heinz (1975), 30–73.

historians.[2] Is there anything of Stoicism in their accounts of pity and fear?

It is hard to find it. Both pity and fear were roundly condemned by the Stoics.[3] For Roman historians, however, pity is almost always a positive trait.[4] With fear, of course, they are closer to Stoic views. It is hardly surprising that historians writing in a culture that set a high premium on military virtues should often present fear as something to be condemned. Yet such condemnation is far from universal. Fear is frequently attributed to characters in what seem quite neutral contexts, without any obvious indication that it is a defect. Still more significantly, historians will sometimes present fear as explicitly positive. Most famous, for example, is Sallust's account of 'fear of the enemy' (*metus hostilis*) as something that kept the early Romans virtuous.[5] Livy takes this theme up at 1.19.4, with the additional twist that he there presents 'fear of the gods' (*metus deorum*) as a desirable alternative;[6] while Tacitus (*Ann.* 6.51.3) applies a similar idea to Tiberius, and claims that it was fear that until the end of his life kept him from indulging his vicious character.[7]

Thus there seems to be little influence of Stoicism; but what of other philosophical schools? Epicurean theories of the passions are less prominent in surviving accounts of their doctrines, but one can piece together evidence for their views. They seem to have applauded pity, and to this extent are similar to the historians (D.L. 10.118). However, they, like the Stoics, generally condemned fear, as not being conducive to *ataraxia*;[8] hence the reasons that led us to discount Stoicism as an influence should lead us similarly to reject Epicureanism.

Much closer is Aristotle. Though there is no clear account of pity in his ethical writings, there is a famous discussion of courage and

---

[2] E.g. Pantzerhielm-Thomas (1936); Walsh (1958) and (1961), 46–81; cf. André (1991).

[3] On fear, see e.g. Cic. *Tusc.* 2.11; 4.64; Epict. 4.7; D.L. 7.112–13: on pity e.g. Cic. *Mur.* 62–3; *Tusc.* 4.56; Sen. *Cl.* 2.4–6; D.L. 7.111; 7.123. See Sandbach (1975), 59–62.

[4] A general condemnation of pity is put into the mouth of Caesar by Sallust (*Cat.* 51.1–4); but this is a deliberately paradoxical passage, which can hardly be accepted at face value; it is moreover subsequently undermined by the author (*Cat.* 54.2–3).

[5] *Jug.* 41.2; *Hist.* 1.11–12; the idea itself is, of course, an ancient commonplace (Earl (1961), 47–9).

[6] Ogilvie (1965), 94–5; cf. Levene (1993), 136.

[7] 'Finally, with shame and fear gone, he simply followed his own character, and abandoned himself to both crime and disgrace.' See also Heinz (1975), 42–53.

[8] Epicur. *Sent.* 10; Lucr. 2.16–19; Cic. *Fin.* 1.49. See Bailey (1947), 796–7; Mitsis (1988), 71–4, 90–1.

fear at *NE* 3.6–9. The details are not always coherent,[9] but Aristotle certainly believes that true courage does not involve the total absence of fear; rather the brave man fears only those things that it is appropriate to fear, and reacts to those things in an appropriate manner (*NE* 1115b15–19). This doctrine of the mean can be applied to other emotions, including some (such as pity) that Aristotle does not treat in detail.[10] All of this seems closer to the Roman historians' pragmatic approach to pity and fear than does any other doctrine so far considered.

However, we should not deduce from this that the historians were influenced by Aristotelian ethics directly. True, from the first century BC onwards Romans were acquainted with Peripatetics (M. Griffin (1989), 7). Whether the actual writings of Aristotle were much studied by Romans is more dubious: Cicero *Top.* 3 says not, and there is little in the Latin writers of the next hundred years to suggest that things changed later. Even Seneca does not show any deep acquaintance with Aristotelian philosophy (Gottschalk (1987), 1140–1). For our purposes, it is especially noteworthy that Cicero, even when purporting to give an account of Peripatetic ethics in *Fin.* 5, does not refer to the doctrine of the mean. Admittedly, Cicero's account is based not on mainstream Peripatetic thought but on the syncretic account of Antiochus of Ascalon (*Fin.* 5.8; 5.75); but this may itself suggest that Aristotle's own thinking on the subject was relatively unfamiliar (Barnes (1989), 86–9). We may add that, while Aristotle's broad approach is fairly similar to those of the historians, the detailed examples that he provides of appropriate and inappropriate types of fear are not correlated especially closely to the attitudes of their narratives.[11]

It is more likely, therefore, that such views are part of a general cultural complex that is emerging separately in Aristotle and the Roman historians. It may be that this part of Aristotle's ethical doctrine is attempting to provide a philosophical grounding for non-philosophical views (Fortenbaugh (1975), 12–16). But it is also the case that aspects of Peripatetic ideas filtered into wider culture via

[9] The problem arises not least because Aristotle seems to wish to treat courage as a 'mean' of two separate passions, fear and confidence. See Pears (1978); Urmson (1988), 63–5.

[10] *NE* 1106b18–23. However, at 1115a5 he inconsistently implies that all the virtues will receive a detailed treatment, something that is not true of pity.

[11] For example, the popular notions of 'fear of the enemy/the gods' (text to nn. 5–6 above) have no place in Aristotle. On the other hand, Aristotle's distinction between incomplete types of courage at *NE* 3.8 is hard to trace in the historians.

their influential work on rhetorical theory (Solmsen (1941)). This, however, introduces a further consideration. Up to now we have been treating pity and fear solely as qualities by which we can analyse characters' motives and judge them morally. But in rhetorical theory an additional element is highlighted: the emotions of the audience itself. Aristotle gives an extremely precise dissection of fear and pity (among other emotions) in the *Rhetoric* (2.5; 2.8); and the avowed aim is to explain how they may be aroused in the listeners (*Rh.* 1383a8–12). The arousal of emotions in the audience becomes a major theme of later rhetorical writings; Cicero and Quintilian are especially clear examples.[12] All of this is well known, and has been much discussed; as too has the even more famous application of similar criteria to poetic criticism by Aristotle in the *Poetics*, where, of course, it is precisely pity and fear that are identified as the emotions that it is characteristically tragedy's object to arouse.[13]

How do the ancient theorists believe that these emotions are to be induced in the audience? Once again, the answer is famous: the hearers are to be encouraged to identify with the emotions experienced by the participants in the events about which they are hearing. In the case of oratory, Aristotle suggests that the audience should imagine itself as directly affected by what is described.[14] This will often mean taking over the emotions of the orator.[15] Oratory is by its very nature generally concerned with real people, and it is relatively easy to see how an audience might find the situation personally affecting. But in less topical genres, such as tragedy, and even in narrative genres, a similar effect can be achieved. *Enargeia* often performs a central role here: the vivid description breaks down the barriers between the audience and the characters and encourages the former to share the viewpoint of, and hence to empathise with, the latter.[16]

This account, however, needs a certain qualification: pity and fear do not seem to be emotions that are aroused in an identical manner in an audience. The most plausible account of what it is for members

---

[12] See e.g. Cic. *de Or.* 2.185–216; Quint. 6.1–2.

[13] *Po.* 13–14. Pity and fear were regularly linked together, especially in discussions of literature: see Halliwell (1986), 170; also Nehamas (1992).

[14] See e.g *Rh.* 1382a24–32 (on fear); 1385b15–19 (on pity). Also Cic. *de Or.* 2.211; Quint. 6.2.34.

[15] This does not often emerge in Aristotle, who seems rather to envisage the speaker himself remaining calm while inducing emotion in the audience (see Gill (1984), 151–5), but it is important in later theory: e.g. Cic. *de Or.* 2.189–90; Quint. 6.2.3; 6.2.26–36.

[16] Gorg. *Hel.* 9; Arist. *Po.* 1462a14–18 (cf. *Rh.* 1386a32–5); *Rhet. ad Her.* 4.68–9; Horace *Ars* 99–104; Quint. 6.1.31–2; 6.2.29–36.

of an audience to fear is, as discussed above, for them to place themselves imaginatively in the position of a character, who either actually does fear for himself or at least is in a position where such fear would be appropriate. But for an audience to pity, no such emotion need be experienced by any character in the work at all: one can respond directly to the portrayal of the fearful (or otherwise wretched) character's plight.[17] The two emotions are still, of course, closely related, and the one will often lead to the other (a point well brought out by Halliwell). But the methods by which they are aroused in the audience would appear to be fundamentally different: with fear, one takes over a character's emotion directly; with pity, one responds to his plight sympathetically – but from the standpoint of an observer.

However, there is a further consideration, which is sometimes overlooked. Writers on rhetoric, as pointed out earlier, often argue that the best way to induce emotions in an audience is for the orator himself to display those emotions: and this is true of pity as well as of fear.[18] This may suggest that, even in narrative genres, pity may be aroused in an audience by a similar method to that of fear: namely, by persuading them to take over the emotions of a character who is pitying another character. As I show later, this method may become especially desirable when the character to be pitied is one to whose plight the audience might not automatically respond with sympathy. By showing him through the eyes of someone who is actually pitying him, one can instil in the audience a similar emotion.

This type of pity and fear may be described as 'audience-based'. We may distinguish it from the type discussed at the start of the chapter, which is essentially concerned with explaining and evaluating the behaviour of those who are subject to these emotions, and which may be called 'analytic'. The importance of the latter in the historians was described earlier; but the presentation of history in a 'tragic' fashion, which meant above all the describing of events in a sensationalist manner likely to arouse the 'tragic' emotions of pity and fear in the audience, was, plainly, also a widely accepted technique;[19] it is indeed used by some as a criterion of good historical writing.[20]

---

[17] On this analysis of 'audience-based' fear, and its consequent asymmetry with pity, see Lucas (1968), 273–5; Russell and Winterbottom (1972), 87; and esp. Halliwell (1986), 175–9.

[18] E.g. Cic. de Or. 2.189–90; cf. Rhet. ad Her. 2.50.

[19] So much is uncontroversial; for the more difficult problem of whether there was actually a school of 'tragic history' see e.g. Walbank (1972), 34–40; Fornara (1983), 120–34.

[20] E.g. Cic. Fam. 5.12.4–5; D.H. Th. 15; Plu. de Glor. Ath. 347A–C.

But what precisely is the relationship between these two forms of emotional presentation? Some might think that the two are most likely to be operating at different times, and that primarily 'analytic' passages are not those which are aimed at generating emotions in the audience. Thus Christopher Gill, in a series of articles, distinguishes what he calls 'character-viewpoints' from 'personality-viewpoints', and argues that they have broadly different and indeed contradictory effects.[21] The former entail looking at a character from outside, and detailing his traits in a clinical and often moralistic fashion; the latter approach is more psychological, and involves the adoption of a character's viewpoint, without judging him according to external standards. A treatment of pity and fear that encourages an audience to take over those emotions can be seen as a particular example of Gill's 'personality-viewpoint'. On the face of it, such a treatment seems unlikely to encourage that same audience to engage at the same time in an analysis of historical causation (Gill (1990), 2–8).

However, the ancient sources do not support such a clear-cut distinction. When Aristotle in the *Poetics* speaks of the arousal of emotion in the audience, his fundamental assumption is that it is primarily generated by the audience's perceptions of the moral qualities of the story.[22] This view is implied in the *Rhetoric* also, and derives, more generally, from Aristotle's broadly 'cognitivist' account of emotion. Emotions are based on one's analysis of the situation: if that analysis is accurate, one's emotions are appropriate and justified; an inaccurate assessment of the situation would lead to inappropriate and unjustified emotions.[23] But in either case emotion may be seen as firmly rooted in reasoned perception of the sort that I have associated with an 'analytic' approach. Such a 'cognitivist' account was adopted by other philosophers, notably the Stoics, who (with the distinguished exception of Posidonius) saw the passions as arising from reason – albeit mistaken reason (Introd. Sect. II); and this view of emotion often appears to underlie non-philosophical discussions of literature also (Lada (1993), 113–19).

Looking specifically at historiography, a comparable point emerges from Polybius' criticisms of Phylarchus:

---

[21] Gill (1986), (1990); cf. also (1983*b*), (1984).

[22] Arist. *Po.* 1452b28–1453a22; see also Fortenbaugh (1975), 35, 50–3; Halliwell (1986), 158–9, 162–7.

[23] Arist. *NE* 1106b21–3; see Halliwell (1986), 195–6. The analysis need not be conscious; on the contrary, the mark of a virtuous man for Aristotle is his ability automatically to perceive the situation and to feel the appropriate emotion. See Fortenbaugh (1975), 70–5.

He is keen to excite his readers' pity and make them sympathise
with what he describes; so he introduces women embracing altars,
with hair dishevelled and breasts bare, and moreover the tears
and laments of men and women being led away in the company
of their children and aged parents. He does this through his whole
history, trying always at every point to make us visualise dreadful
scenes ... A historian ought not to be shocking his readers by
telling tall tales through his histories. (2.56.7–10)

At first sight, it might seem as if Polybius is making a point similar to
that of those theorists who claimed that the arousal of emotion is
liable to interfere with the audience's rational judgement.[24] But in
fact this is not the chief thrust of his attack. It is not that emotion *per
se* is inimical to rational analysis, but rather that the attempt to excite
emotion is liable to lead a writer into falsehood; in a subsequent
comment he does seem to allow that 'tragic emotions' can sometimes
play a useful role for the historian: 'In any case, with most of his
tragic reversals, Phylarchus just tells us the story, without suggesting
why things are done and to what end; and without this it is
impossible to feel either legitimate pity or proper anger about any
events' (2.56.13). This has various implications. First, it confirms that
Polybius, like Aristotle, is adopting a broadly 'cognitivist' approach
to emotion. His distinction between 'legitimate' and 'illegitimate'
emotions, as he later makes clear, is that the former are based on a
complete understanding of the circumstances of the case, the latter
on a partial view only. But, more interestingly, he also appears to
suggest that these 'audience-based' emotions have in themselves a
valid role to play in historiography. Provided that the author arouses
appropriate emotions in the audience, by ensuring that the characters
with whom they are encouraged to sympathise actually deserve their
sympathy, 'audience-based' emotions are not only derived from, but
may reinforce and underpin, the moral and historical analysis.

But Gill's arguments still have something to offer. Implicit in them
is the claim that it is not *only* analysis of morals and causes in the
Aristotelian or Polybian sense that can generate an emotional
response in the audience: such 'audience-based' emotions can also be
aroused independently of the 'analytic', for example, by a narrative
method that leads one to identify with a particular character.[25]

---

[24] See e.g. Gorg. *Pal.* 33; Quint. 6.2.5–6.

[25] One might argue that, even in such cases, emotions are still based in cognitive perception,
as they are connected with the adoption of a particular viewpoint; however, it is a rather

Indeed, this can itself be supported from the ancient critics: note, for example, the important role allotted to *enargeia* ('vivid illustration'), or the possibility of audience identification with a character who is pitying another leading to sympathy with the character pitied (both discussed in text to nn. 16–17 above). We may also observe the significant distinction at Aristotle *Poetics* 1453b1–3 between pity and fear that arise 'from the spectacle', and pity and fear that derive from the 'arrangement of events' – the former category suggesting that Aristotle (though disapproving of it) sees the possibility that the method of presentation may alone suffice to produce emotions in the audience (Halliwell (1986), 64–5). 'Audience-based' pity and fear, then, sometimes derive from 'analytic' emotions, but sometimes also emerge independently; likewise, naturally, not *all* 'analytic' presentations of these emotions are such as to invite audiences to take on the emotions themselves. Therefore such an external, 'analytic' viewpoint can indeed, as Gill argues, conflict with independently derived 'audience-based' emotions.

But one further point should be considered. Polybius' account has shown 'audience-based' emotions that are not only derived from cognition, but actually influence it, by supporting the 'proper' picture of historical events. What then of independently derived 'audience-based' emotions? It can be plausibly argued that these, too, have 'analytic' implications, inducing a particular picture of the moral circumstances.[26] For example, the fact that a character attracts audience sympathy may itself be taken to imply that his moral position is such as to deserve sympathy; this may imply a particular 'external' assessment of the situation.[27] If a historian sets this approach, with its own analytic force, against a straightforwardly 'analytic' approach, he can exploit the tension between these two modes of presentation, either to show one or other as ultimately

different sort of cognitive perception from the essentially explanatory and moral analysis discussed so far, which usually seems to be assumed by Aristotle and Polybius.

[26] This is, in fact, implicit in some of Gill's discussion: e.g. his idea that a 'personality-viewpoint' is associated especially with the expression of 'morally non-standard and problematic' views (Gill (1990), 6–7, 30–1). But, as Polybius suggests, and as I hope to demonstrate, 'personality-viewpoints' need not only be questioning: they can encode positive and indeed quite conservative values, and the questions, if any, arise only if those values clash with others in the work.

[27] For a more extended discussion of the derivation of cognition from emotion, see Lada (1993), 116–19, citing ancient sources and modern psychological theory. Nussbaum's controversial interpretation of Aristotelian *katharsis* as a cognitive clarification produced by pity and fear (Nussbaum (1986a), 388–91; also (1992), 143–50) would point to a similar conclusion; but see *contra* e.g. Lear (1988).

inadequate, or even to leave the 'correct' analysis open. In the second part of this chapter I shall seek to demonstrate that Roman historians did indeed exploit these two modes of presentation for the purposes of complex analysis, taking as a case-study Tacitus *Histories* 3.36–86.

II

Both fear and pity play a prominent role in the second part of Tacitus *Histories* 3. This is partly because fear is one of the chief characteristics of Vitellius, as Tacitus presents him; Suetonius, by contrast, has little or nothing of this, and indeed is even ready to show Vitellius as unreasonably confident (for instance, *Vit.* 8). But Tacitus does not limit himself to giving an account of Vitellius' fear. As we shall see, he goes further still, and sets the whole action surrounding the fall of Vitellius against an intricate network of both fear and pity involving all the participants.

The sequence begins with the immediate aftermath of the Flavians' sack of Cremona. The focus now moves to Vitellius (36–9), but at a time before he hears about this major blow to his cause. The result is that the reader sees his behaviour here in an ironic light: the danger facing him is far greater than he realises.[28] Fear and pity only enter the picture in 38–9, where his brother Lucius persuades him to take action against Junius Blaesus. Here the two emotions combine to explain Vitellius' murder of Blaesus. The fear is explicit,[29] the pity implicit in his brother's appeal on behalf of his son. But both emotions are shown as utterly misplaced. Blaesus, as Tacitus explicitly tells us, is not a threat to Vitellius (39.2). Despite what Lucius says here, Vespasian is; and Vitellius' ignoring of this threat, as was said above, looks particularly ironic in the light of the defeat at Cremona, and in conjunction with his failure to take the recent defections from his forces seriously (Fuhrmann (1960), 271–2). That this shows Vitellius in a poor light is undeniable, especially when we

---

[28] Dio, by contrast (if Xiphilinus' summary is to be believed), moved directly from the battle to Vitellius' reaction to it (64.15–16).

[29] 'He [Lucius] was not afraid or nervous for himself, but was begging and weeping on behalf of his brother and his brother's children. There was nothing to fear in Vespasian ... the enemy to beware was in the city and their very bosoms ... The Emperor nervously hesitated between crime and terror ... so he decided to employ poison.' (*non se proprio metu nec sui anxium, sed pro fratre, pro liberis fratris preces lacrimasque attulisse. frustra Vespasianum timeri ... in urbe ac sinu cauendum hostem ... trepidanti inter scelus metumque ... placuit ueneno grassari*, 38.3–39.1)

add that the murder of Blaesus to which these misplaced emotions lead is so clearly presented as an atrocious abuse of power.

Additional interest is provided by one striking sentence (39.1):

> The Emperor nervously hesitated between crime and terror. On the one hand, putting off Blaesus' death might bring on him swift ruin; but on the other to order it openly might cause dreadful resentment. So he decided to employ poison.

> trepidanti inter scelus metumque, ne dilata Blaesi mors maturam perniciem, palam iussa atrocem inuidiam ferret, placuit ueneno grassari.

Tacitus' phrasing here is complicated and initially misleading. The implication of 'between crime and terror' (*inter scelus metumque*) seems at first sight to be that fear might keep Vitellius from crime. This reminds us of the more positive forms of the emotion in the Roman historians, where people are deterred by fear from immoral actions (text to nn. 5–7 above). But, as is indicated by the word 'hesitated' (*trepidanti*) and the first part of the 'might' (*ne*) clause, Vitellius is fearful either way: he has been affected by Lucius' speech, and is afraid not to commit the crime, as well as to commit it. Ultimately fear simply leads him to commit the crime covertly, rather than openly. The reader is again invited to analyse and judge Vitellius; and his fear is seen as all the worse through being a perverted version of the familiar moral deterrent.

Overall, therefore, this is an example of an 'analytic' treatment of pity and fear, combining explanation and evaluation. There is no idea that the audience might sympathise with emotions that are presented as so plainly out of place and immoral. It is true that there is a strong rhetorical context: as with the textbook rhetorical audience, pity and fear are awakened in Vitellius by Lucius' speech, which even employs the orator's standard trick of introducing a child.[30] But the readers are distanced from any direct access to the emotional effect of such a speech, partly by the fact that it is in *oratio obliqua*, but more importantly by the fact that, before it begins, Tacitus has told us that Lucius had ulterior motives in making it, and that Vitellius was already predisposed to accept its conclusions. Both orator and hearer are compromised in our eyes from the start.

At 54 we return to Vitellius, who has now learned of the Cremona disaster. Tacitus treats his response with great and ironic detail:

---

[30] 38.2: 'Clasping his [the Emperor's] son to his bosom'.

Vitellius suppresses the report of the defeat, even killing the spies who tell him the truth, and fatally damages his own cause in the process (54). At last he accepts the situation, and acts – but his actions are again shown as quite inappropriate (55–6). In the course of this Tacitus describes his fear:

> Moreover, panic showed in his face and walk ... He was terrified at every new setback, but was indifferent to the supreme crisis. It was open to him to cross the Apennines with his army's strength undivided, and to attack the enemy while they were exhausted by the winter and their lack of supplies. Instead he wasted his forces, and surrendered his soldiers, who were fiercely ready to resist to the last, to slaughter or capture. (56.2–3)

Just as before, this fear is misplaced, and ignores the real danger, an understanding of which could have led Vitellius to act more rationally. This time it does not have as strong an explanatory role; it is clear that, even before he is shown as afraid, Vitellius is behaving irrationally and failing to see what is in his best interests. But it is still, fundamentally, an 'analytic' treatment: if we do not see the fear as the cause of his irrational behaviour, it is still a close concomitant of that behaviour, the unreasonableness of which is the chief focus of the passage. With Tacitus' ironic dissection of Vitellius' faults to the fore, there is yet again no idea that he might be an object of sympathy.

Yet not only Vitellius himself, but also his followers are of interest here. At 55.3, his senatorial supporters are described as being afraid of him ('many were attracted through ambition, more through fear'); but at 58.2–3 the situation changes:

> Their pretence of duty, which originated in their fear, had turned into real support. Most of them pitied not Vitellius, but the calamitous position of the Emperor. But he was there himself to work on their sympathies with his looks, words and tears. He was lavish with his promises and knew no restraint, as is typical of a man in a panic. He even wanted to be called 'Caesar', although he had previously scorned the title. But now he was attracted by the superstition of the name, and when one is afraid one is unable to distinguish sensible advice from vulgar gossip.

> ea simulatio officii a metu profecta uerterat in fauorem; ac plerique haud proinde Vitellium quam casum locumque principatus miserabantur. nec deerat ipse uultu uoce lacrimis misericordiam elicere, largus promissis, et quae natura trepidantium est, immodicus. quin et Caesarem se dici uoluit, aspernatus antea,

sed tunc superstitione nominis, et quia in metu consilia pruden-
tium et uulgi rumor iuxta audiuntur.

The first point to make is that Tacitus is using pity and fear to
demonstrate Vitellius' progressive loss of control. His followers move
from fearing him to pitying him, and, correspondingly, he is shown
as increasingly subject to fear. It is less and less the case that Vitellius
is capable of exciting terror in others, and more and more that he is
in a position where he needs to be afraid, and where he is thus an
appropriate recipient of compassion. A similar idea appears at 59.1:
'The capture of Mevania terrified Italy, because the war seemed to
be beginning anew; but the panicky departure of Vitellius solidified
support for the Flavian party.' The Italians' fear of Vitellius' forces is
counteracted by Vitellius' own terror, which makes his weakness
apparent, which in turn explains the general move to support
Vespasian.

But there is another aspect to this passage. While Vitellius' fear, as
presented above, is treated by Tacitus in an 'analytic' manner, his
followers introduce a further consideration. For the first time, we see
Vitellius through the eyes of other people who are sympathising with
him, and this is a viewpoint that it is possible to share, at least
partially. It is true that Tacitus is still treating Vitellius' fears in an
ironic manner. As in 38, there is a rhetorical context that is undermined by its presentation. Vitellius' speech is described rather than
being shown directly; as a result his attempt to gain sympathy looks
excessively calculating. Moreover, his promises, and his acceptance
of the name 'Caesar', are clearly presented as the irrational products
of his fear.

Likewise, his followers are not presented in a wholly attractive
manner. The senators in particular are initially reluctant followers
(55.3), and have their contributions imposed on them (58.2); and
they, along with the knights, are the ones who soon lose their
enthusiasm for him and drift away after his speech – their pity is
suggested by Tacitus to be an 'ill-considered impulse' (58.4). The
knights come across slightly better, in that their contributions are
voluntary. However, although Tacitus expresses contempt for the
mob,[31] when it comes to Vitellius' freedmen he shows them in a far
better light. He indirectly praises their support ('the more distin-

---

[31] Also 58.1: 'He was deceived by appearances into calling a craven mob (who were not going
to dare anything more than words) "an army" and "legions"'.

guished the friend, the less loyal', *amicorum quanto quis clarior, minus fidus*),[32] and describes their spontaneous offers of money and help (58.2). The latter passage comes immediately before his description of the growing sympathy for Vitellius in the passage above. There is, likewise, no suggestion here that these supporters, unlike the upper-class ones, are subject only to a temporary passion in their pity for Vitellius.

The result is that the 'internal audience', composed of observers within the work, the people through whose eyes we view Vitellius here, are at least partly ones whose point of view we have no reason to reject: we can see Vitellius as genuinely deserving of pity, since they pity him. In effect, *this* audience is adopting an 'audience-based' viewpoint, and since our picture of Vitellius is partially mediated via them, we may begin to do the same.

How does this relate to the 'analytic' view of Vitellius that Tacitus has been establishing until now, and which, as I argued above, he continues to establish even in this passage? In one way it reinforces it, by emphasising the weakness that leads his followers to drift away. But in another respect it jars slightly: by showing Vitellius as relatively sympathetic, it works against the 'analytic' viewpoint, which has been treating him entirely critically. However, Tacitus smooths over the potential clash, by making it clear that the sympathy that Vitellius' supporters feel for him is limited to the office, not the man; this draws on the common feeling in the ancient world that a great fall from power is in itself deserving of pity (Dover (1974), 197). In this way it is possible, it seems, to despise Vitellius for his fear, while sympathising with him as a falling emperor. But this is always vulnerable to the objection that Vitellius the man and Vitellius the emperor are not separable; and Tacitus introduces an element that brings that problem to our attention, as he shows Vitellius now through his cowardice taking on the imperial title that he had previously rejected. How far audience sympathy for Vitellius can potentially extend is still left open.

Shortly after this, we are returned far more insistently to the idea of Vitellius as an object of pity. The theme is brought in at 65.2: 'Their expressions were witnessed by those watching at a distance,

---

[32] Wellesley (1972), 155–6, claims that we should understand 'he was thought to be' (*habebatur*) here, and that this represents not Tacitus' view of the imperial freedmen, but rather Vitellius' mistaken view. Such a reading is, however, difficult to sustain when 'he was' (*erat*) would make equally good sense (Kühner and Stegmann (1955), 551).

Vitellius' downcast and degenerate, but Sabinus seemed not scornful, but closer to compassion' (*uultus procul uisentibus notabantur, Vitellii proiectus et degener, Sabinus non insultans et miserantis proprior*). It might seem that Sabinus' viewpoint is one that we are disposed to accept, even though the actual description of Vitellius as 'degenerate' (*degener*) carries moralistic overtones that would seem to make him an inappropriate object of pity. However, we do not see Vitellius through Sabinus' eyes as he pities him; rather we see both of them from the point of view of observers, who regard Sabinus as 'closer to compassion', but whose view of Vitellius is the moralistic one mentioned above. Hence there is no invitation to the readers that they themselves should pity Vitellius.

Yet the idea that he is pitied is now there; it is continued by 66.1–2, where he is advised that Vespasian would not spare him even were he to surrender, and Tacitus sums up with the key phrase 'so danger comes from pity' (*ita periculum ex misericordia*). As Wellesley says, 'the phrase is excessively obscure'; the most likely sense is 'danger from throwing himself on Vespasian's mercy'.[33] Tacitus is insisting more and more on the idea of Vitellius as an object of pity, even at the cost of straining the Latin. As in 65, there is no suggestion that this pity is to be taken over by the reader, as the thought is only coming up in *oratio obliqua* as part of a potential strategy to be rejected. But Tacitus has just before shown us Vitellius' weakness and lack of direction,[34] and the treatment of pity reinforces this. As before, we see more and more the diminution of Vitellius' status, as he becomes a person to whom pity might be applied.

But in the following sections (67–8) the idea of pity is taken up by Tacitus with much greater length and complexity, when Vitellius attempts to abdicate his power. Here again, he is pitied, and we see in this his weakness and powerlessness (a theme ironically reinforced by 68.3, where his followers will not allow him to abdicate, and instead force him to return to the palace). But Tacitus' handling of the theme of pity moves the passage far more strongly in the direction of an 'audience-based' approach. Again, we have a rhetorical context, with Vitellius addressing the crowd; again, we see him through the eyes of the bystanders. But, much more than any passage that we have considered so far, the reader is encouraged to

---

[33] Wellesley (1972), 163; cf. *OLD* s.v. *misericordia*, sense 2.
[34] Esp. 63.2: 'He was so overcome by sloth that, if others had not remembered that he was Emperor, he himself would have forgotten it.'

identify fully with those bystanders and to share their pity for
Vitellius. Although the Romans often reacted to changes of fortune
such as Vitellius' with, for example, ridicule or amazement (cf. 84.5
and text to n. 52 below), Tacitus does not allow for such a reaction
here. 'No one could have been so indifferent to human tragedy as to
be unmoved by that scene' (*nec quisquam adeo rerum humanarum immemor
quem non commoueret illa facies*, 69.1); the reader is implicitly included.
Moreover, the description stresses the *appearance* of the scene – note
'that scene' (*illa facies*) – and this 'vivid illustration' (*enargeia*, text to n.
16 above) encourages audience involvement with the characters. The
word 'scene' (*facies*) and the phrase 'they had never seen or heard of
such a thing' (*nihil tale uiderant, nihil audierant*), help to emphasise that
the bystanders are an audience, rather than actors (they are, rather
oddly, implicitly distanced from the soldiers and people, who behave
rather differently).[35] The readers consequently will merge this position with their own, since they can see both themselves and the
internal audience as pure observers.[36] It is true that the people are
said to react inappropriately to Vitellius' departure – but their
inappropriate reaction is not pity, which is confirmed in this way as
an appropriate reaction.

The position of Vitellius here reinforces this. He is explicitly said
(unlike at 58) to be saying things appropriate to the situation.[37] More
importantly, in both his departure from the palace and his speech, he
is linked as an object of pity with his family, and in particular with
his mother and children, the only members of it who get any detailed
description, and who are clearly deserving of total sympathy. We
may compare 2.64, and indeed 3.66 just before this passage, where it
is made clear to Vitellius that his son has nothing to hope for in the
event of Vespasian's victory. The doom that hangs over them is plain
from the reference to his mother's timely death,[38] and from the
funeral imagery describing their departure; the pathos of the diminu-
tives referring to his son is also striking (the boy was in fact killed by
Mucianus shortly after the Flavian victory (4.80.1; Wellesley (1972),

---

[35] The response of the soldiers and people has been shown at 67.2 just before: 'The people
shouted words of inappropriate flattery; the soldiers maintained a threatening silence.' Cf.
also 68.2: 'with even women watching'. On the 'audience' theme in general, see Borszák
(1973), esp. 65–6.

[36] See Davidson (1991), esp. 14–16, on the way in which Polybius' readers' view of events
merges into that of the internal audience.

[37] 'He said a few words suited to the sad occasion' (68.2).

[38] 'She had the good fortune to die a few days before the destruction of her family' (67.1).

164)).[39] Vitellius' family, and hence Vitellius himself, are to be seen here as rightly pitied by the internal audience, and hence by the readers.

But Tacitus pulls us still closer towards an 'audience-based' treatment of Vitellius here, because the Emperor is not only appealing for pity, but is himself one of those who are pitying his family.[40] That pity is shown as his private reaction, not simply as part of his speech, and hence is treated as genuine.[41] Vitellius' love for his family has consistently been his one attractive trait; Tacitus has made relatively little of it before now, but here it dominates the picture of him.[42] As we adopt the viewpoint of the internal audience, as described earlier, we also adopt the near-identical viewpoint of Vitellius himself. The pity for him that has been built up as a result of seeing him through the eyes of pitying observers is now turned into a more direct and unmediated sympathy.

As before (p. 140 above), sympathy with Vitellius is tied to the idea of him as a falling emperor. What is said to excite the bystanders' pity is the idea of the former master of the world reduced to such ignominy;[43] and they contrast his public abdication with the violent and private ends of Julius Caesar, Gaius, Nero, Galba and his heir Piso (68.1). However, this time it is in practice impossible to distinguish the man from the office, since the whole presentation of Vitellius here is such as to invite sympathy for him. To sympathise with Vitellius as emperor is now to sympathise with him as a man (Briessmann (1955), 80).

[39] 'He descended from the palace wearing a black cloak, with his sorrowing household around. His little son was borne in his litter as if in a funeral procession' (*pullo amictu Palatio degreditur, maesta circum familia; ferebatur lecticula paruulus filius uelut in funebrem pompam*, 67.2).

[40] 'His mind was crushed by pity and concern that by persisting in warfare he would leave the victor less well-disposed towards his wife and children. He also had a mother who was old and weak' (*obruebatur animus miseratione curaque, ne pertinacibus armis minus placabilem uictorem relinqueret coniugi ac liberis. erat illi et fessa aetate parens*, 67.2). (Vitellius speaking): 'Let them only remember him, and pity his brother, his wife, and his children of tender years. As he spoke he held out his son, commending him to them individually and collectively'. (*retinerent tantum memoriam sui fratremque et coniugem et innoxiam liberorum aetatem miserarentur - simul filium protendens, modo singulis modo uniuersis commendans*, 68.2).

[41] Contrast Dio/Xiphilinus 64.16.5, for whom this scene is described only to demonstrate Vitellius' inconsistency, and who of his pity for his son says only 'he held him out to them as if to invite pity'.

[42] Vitellius has earlier acted to protect or honour his family at 1.75.2; 2.59.3; 2.89.2; 3.38; Suetonius by contrast removes any indication of this attractive side to Vitellius, and actually shows him as cruel towards his family (*Vit.* 6, 7, 14).

[43] 'The Roman emperor, until recently the master of the whole human race, was leaving the house of his power and departing from the principate through the people and the city' (68.1).

It is against this background that we reach the famous scene of
Vitellius' death (84–5). The most striking aspect of Tacitus' account
here is the extent to which he uses *enargeia* to present Vitellius' fears
in the most vivid light – especially at 84.4:

> He returned to the huge, deserted palace. Even the lowliest slaves
> had slipped away, or else were avoiding meeting him. The
> loneliness and the silent rooms terrified him; he tried locks, he
> shuddered at the emptiness.

> in Palatium regreditur uastum desertumque, dilapsis etiam infimis
> seruitiorum aut occursum eius declinantibus. terret solitudo et
> tacentes loci; temptat clausa, inhorrescit uacuis.

The reader is invited in effect to look at things through Vitellius'
eyes, and hence to adopt his fearful viewpoint. The scene is dramatic
and affecting, and clearly follows up the 'audience-based' approach
to Vitellius: the audience empathises with his fears, and pities him.

Added to this are various indications that Tacitus is, even in the
humiliation of Vitellius' death, seeking to remove the worst indignity.
In comparison with the accounts of Suetonius *Vit.* 16–17, Dio/
Xiphilinus 64.20–1, and Josephus *BJ* 4.651–2, Tacitus softens the
sense of moral degradation with which they surround his person.
Although Tacitus has earlier made a good deal of his gluttony,[44] he
now, unlike the other writers, does not refer to it.[45] Suetonius and
Dio/Xiphilinus both describe his sordid hiding-place in some detail
(the former has him hiding in the porter's lodge (*Vit.* 16), the latter in
with the dogs (64.20.1–2)); Tacitus calls it only a 'shameful hiding-
place' (*pudenda latebra*, 84.4). Tacitus does not show anything of his
calculating and degrading attempts to avoid capture by disguising
himself. He says nothing of his fortifying himself with a moneybelt,
pretending to be someone else, and then claiming to have information 'vital to Vespasian's safety' (Suetonius). He says nothing of his
deliberately dressing in rags (Dio); Tacitus refers to his 'clothes in
tatters' (*laniata ueste*, 84.5) while he is dragged to execution, but the
implication is that they were torn in the course of his flight or arrest.
Such descriptions would involve an overtly moralistic approach to

---

[44] E.g. 1.62.2; 2.31.1; 2.62.1; 2.71.1.

[45] Josephus *BJ* 4.651 actually describes him going to his death after emerging drunk from a
lavish banquet; Suetonius does not have him initially wandering around alone, but
accompanied by his pastry-cook and chef (*Vit.* 16); both Suetonius *Vit.* 17 and Dio/
Xiphilinus 64.20.3 have him mocked for his fat stomach.

Vitellius that would hinder the audience from sharing his fears and pitying him.

In fact, Tacitus even includes the occasional element that might justify a favourable moral reaction. Vitellius' final words are one example, which not only remind us of his earlier imperial status, but are also presented as having a certain nobility of their own.[46] Another is the account of the route he took to his death, in which he is implicitly linked to the deaths of Galba and Sabinus.[47] Although Vitellius had opposed both men, Tacitus did not show him as directly implicated in the deaths of either: the dominant impression is thus the link between their unjust deaths and Vitellius' own impending doom.[48] We can contrast Dio/Xiphilinus 64.20.2–3, who uses a similar effect partly to set Vitellius' degradation against his earlier glory, but also to remind us of his vices ('They led out of the palace the man who had revelled there').[49]

But also found in the passage are occasional hints at moral criticism of Vitellius from a more 'analytic' standpoint. These, consequently, jar against the 'audience-based' approach which the bulk of the passage is establishing; they are more like Tacitus' adverse comparison of Vitellius' death with Otho's in Book 2.[50] We can see this at 84.2 in the phrases 'endemic restlessness' (*mobilitate ingenii*), 'he feared everything, but distrusted most his immediate surroundings' (*cum omnia metuenti praesentia maxime displicerent*), and especially 'typically of one in a panic' (*quae natura pauoris est*), which suggests a rather clinical, external view of Vitellius' fear. 'Shameful hiding-place' is similarly moralistic; so too the phrase 'one comment

---

[46] 'One comment he made showed a mind not entirely degraded: as a tribune mocked him he replied that even so, he had been his Emperor' (*una vox non degeneris animi excepta, cum tribuno insultanti se tamen imperatorem eius fuisse respondit*, 85). This is also found in Dio/Xiphilinus 64.21.2, but not Suetonius, despite his usual interest in 'last words' (apart from *Vit.*, only *Tib.*, *Claud.*, and *Dom.* lack this information). Doubtless Suetonius did not wish to include anything that would conflict with his picture of Vitellius as totally vicious.

[47] 'Vitellius was compelled by his enemies' swords to lift his head and face the insults; then to watch his statues as they fell, and above all the rostra or the place of Galba's murder. Finally they forced him to the Gemonian Steps, where the body of Flavius Sabinus had lain' (85).

[48] See 1.41, 49; 3.74–5. Rademacher (1975), 248–9, argues that the description of the death of Vitellius in general recalls that of Galba. Cf. also 3.86: 'People cannot claim credit for their treachery who betrayed Vitellius to Vespasian after earlier deserting Galba.'

[49] Baxter (1971), 105–7, argues that the whole of the last section of the book is set up so as to recall the fall of Troy in *Aeneid* 2. By linking Vitellius to Priam, Aeneas, and the Trojans in general, Tacitus reinforces his presentation of him as a sympathetic figure of tragic stature.

[50] 'Their deaths, for which Otho won a splendid reputation, but Vitellius a most infamous one' (2.31.1).

he made showed a mind not entirely degraded' implies a general criticism of Vitellius – the clear suggestion is that degeneracy was more typical of his character. We may add that, directly before this passage, Tacitus has shown the heroic last stand of Vitellius' soldiers, and the implicit contrast is not to Vitellius' credit.[51] These factors are not prominent enough to wipe out the audience's sympathy; but they do raise the idea that there is something problematic about an 'audience-based' approach to such a fundamentally unattractive figure.

There is, moreover, a further complicating element. Here, as before, Vitellius is seen through the eyes of an internal audience. But whereas previously the internal audience pitied him, and hence encouraged readers to adopt the same viewpoint and do the same, now Tacitus tells us that Vitellius' degradation was so great that there was no place for pity; instead the onlookers taunted him.[52] The fact that Vitellius is described as a 'spectacle' (84.5) might seem to suggest that we are once again (cf. text to n. 36 above) to see this internal audience as pure observers like ourselves, and consequently merge our viewpoint into theirs, which is fundamentally an 'analytic' one.[53] Against this might be the ironic comment on the mob with which Tacitus concludes the scene (85): 'and the mob reviled him when killed with the same perversity that had led them to support him when alive' (*et uulgus eadem prauitate insectabatur interfectum qua fouerat uiuentem*). This might lead us to see the internal audience's own viewpoint as flawed. True, we have already seen (text to n. 35 above) that Tacitus' internal audiences are not necessarily identical with any particular group of onlookers, even if that group is referred to in the same passage; but one could argue that here the fact that both the internal audience and the mob are described in comparable fashions as hostile to Vitellius means that it is difficult to separate them from each other.

But more significant still is that just a few lines earlier Tacitus has presented the viewpoint of a similar internal audience as highly questionable (83):

> The people stood by as spectators to the fighting; just like in a
> show in the arena, they supported first one side, then the other

---

[51] The final sentence, directly before this passage, particularly points the contrast: 'even as they fell they were concerned to die honourably' (84.3). See Wellesley (1972), 186.

[52] 'Many taunted him, no one wept: the disfigurement of his death had wiped out pity' (*multis increpantibus, nullo inlacrimante: deformitas exitus misericordiam abstulerat*, 84.5).

[53] See Keitel (1992) for the general significance of the theme of 'spectacle' in Vitellius' story.

with cheers and applause. Whenever one side went under, the onlookers demanded that those who had hidden in shops or had taken refuge in houses be dragged out and slaughtered; and they themselves kept most of the booty ... The whole city's appearance was cruel and distorted ... You would believe that the city was simultaneously in the grip of rage and lust: there was every vice of luxurious living, every crime of the most brutal sack ... It was as if this were an extra Saturnalian festivity: they rioted and revelled, caring nothing for either side, but rejoicing in their country's ruin.

aderat pugnantibus spectator populus, utque in ludicro certamine, hos, rursus illos clamore et plausu fouebat. quotiens pars altera inclinasset, abditos in tabernis aut si quam in domum perfugerant, erui iugularique expostulantes parte maiore praedae potiebantur ... saeua ac deformis urbe tota facies ... quantum in luxurioso otio libidinum, quidquid in acerbissima captiuitate scelerum, prorsus ut eandem ciuitatem et furere crederes et lasciuire ... uelut festis diebus id quoque gaudium accederet, exultabant, fruebantur, nulla partium cura, malis publicis laeti.

Here the people of Rome are seen in an extended image as an audience; but to be an audience when atrocities are actually being performed in front of one's eyes is clearly presented as an abominable thing. Moreover, such audiences do not limit themselves simply to spectating, but also egg on the participants,[54] and even seek to profit by the destruction. Tacitus implicitly confirms that the reader should not seek to identify with such internal viewpoints by using the second person 'you would believe' (*crederes*): the reader's view of such events ought to be very different.[55] Specifically, the *enargeia* and the stress on the appearance of the scene, once again, invite the reader to feel the sympathy that the internal audience do not. When Tacitus then treats Vitellius' humiliation, likewise, as a spectacle observed by an audience, this continues the same theme; given that an internal audience composed of the citizens of Rome has so recently been shown as corrupt, the idea of accepting as valid another such audience's view of Vitellius (especially in the context of a largely sympathetic presentation) can only jar.

---

[54] A touch manifestly derived from the behaviour of real Roman audiences, especially at gladiatorial contests; see Sen. *Ep.* 7.2–5, taken with Ville (1981), 442–5.

[55] See 'Longinus' *On the Sublime* 26.1; also Gilmartin (1975), 116.

III

So, through Tacitus' handling of pity and fear, two very different pictures of Vitellius dominate at different times, but are finally brought into direct conflict. One is the 'analytic' picture, treating his fears as part of the explanation for his cruel and ineffectual behaviour, and implicitly or explicitly criticising them in a moralistic fashion. The other is the 'audience-based' picture, which leads us to sympathise with those fears and pity him. We adopt the latter not least through accepting the viewpoint of the internal audience; at the end that internal audience would seem to turn us back towards the 'analytic' picture, but only at a time when its own status has been rendered problematic.

Moreover, as was argued earlier, the 'audience-based' treatment has an analytic force of its own: by suggesting that Vitellius is a character to whom pity may legitimately be given, Tacitus indicates that his fears do not set him as far beyond the pale as the 'analytic' treatment implied. In addition, the 'audience-based' mode is linked to the idea that Vitellius deserves sympathy as a falling emperor. This attitude is a traditional one in historians faced with a leader's demise (p. 140 above).[56] At the same time, it can hardly be divorced from its contemporary political resonances, encoding as it does the status of the emperor and his significance for the Roman world. But Tacitus blurs the distinction between sympathy for Vitellius as Emperor and sympathy for him personally; he then sets the 'analytic' against the 'audience-based' mode at the end, placing such an attitude in opposition to the highly undeserving character of Vitellius himself. The problem of the 'bad emperor' is thus starkly raised.

What, then, does this case-study tell us about ancient historians' use of pity and fear? To begin with, it seems broadly 'Aristotelian', in that the arousal of emotions in the audience is not opposed to a moralistic, 'analytic' treatment, but may form part of it. As before, however, we should not assume that this is due to direct philosophical influence on historians (text to n. 11 above). Nor should one even deduce from this some Hellenistic school of 'Peripatetic historiography':[57] many historians, including Thucydides well before the

---

[56] Ancient writers tended to present the fall of even morally dubious leaders in 'tragic' guise. See, for example, Polybius on the fall of Philip V (23.10–11, followed by Livy 40.3–24); cf. Walbank (1938).

[57] See the debate on 'tragic history' (n. 19 above), and esp. Walbank (1972), 34–7.

Peripatetics, can be argued to exhibit similar traits, and, once again, it may well be that the Peripatetics were seeking to give a philosophical form to non-philosophical beliefs.

But perhaps the most significant conclusion, if Tacitus here is taken as representative, is that historians linked emotion to reason more closely than by simply deriving the former from the latter. While it is true that, as he moves towards an 'audience-based' portrayal of Vitellius, Tacitus excludes some of the negative features found in other versions of the story, he does relatively little to provide a positive reason, in the 'analytic' sense, for audience sympathy. This sympathy may encode political attitudes, as was argued above, but it is not fundamentally determined by external moral criteria. Rather, Tacitus approaches the issue in the opposite way: instead of establishing Vitellius as a character of greater stature than might originally have been implied, and allowing our sympathies to follow this revised perception of him, he arouses our sympathies in ways that are not primarily related to a reasoned morality at all, by the use of the internal audience and *enargeia*. Thus, Vitellius' standing is improved in our eyes precisely because of the sympathy that has been generated for him.

Such a technique is found in other literary genres also (and indeed may even be implicit in Aristotle, as Lada (1993), 116–19, suggests); but to discover it in historians is especially noteworthy. A principal aim of historiography is the explanation, interpretation and understanding of the world of the past. The arousal of the 'tragic emotions' in historical works has often been treated as something essentially divorced from this: a purely literary matter which, while making those works more attractive to read, interferes with, or is at best irrelevant to, the rational part of a historian's work. We can now see that the 'audience-based' approach to the passions is far from being inimical to historical analysis: it can lie at its very heart.[58]

---

[58] I should like to thank for their help Helen DeWitt, Andrew Laird, John Moles, Leighton Reynolds, Tony Woodman, the late Michael Woods, the participants in the Newcastle Narrative Seminar, and above all Chris Pelling and the Editors.

CHAPTER 8

All in the mind: sickness in Catullus 76

Joan Booth

If in recalling former kindnesses there's pleasure
    When a man reflects that he has been true,
Nor broken solemn promise nor in any pact abused
    The gods' divinity to fool his fellow men,
Then many joys remain in store for you, Catullus,   5
    Throughout a long lifetime from this thankless love.
For whatever kind things men can say or do
    To anyone, these you have said and done,
But invested in a thankless mind they have all been wasted.
    So now why torture yourself any more?   10
Why not harden your heart and tear yourself away from her
    And stop being wretched against the gods' will?
It's difficult to cast off long love suddenly.
    It's difficult, but this you must somehow do.
This is your only chance. To this you must win through.   15
    Possible or not, this you must achieve.
O gods, if you can pity or have ever brought
    Help at last to any on the point of death,
Look on my wretchedness and if I have led a decent life
    Take away from me this deadly disease,   20
Which, like a paralysis creeping into my inmost being,
    Has driven from my heart every happiness.
I do not now ask this, that she love me in return,
    Or, what's impossible, that she be chaste.
I pray to be well myself and cast off this foul sickness.   25
    O gods, grant me this for my true dealing.

Siqua recordanti benefacta priora uoluptas
    est homini cum se cogitat esse pium
nec sanctam uiolasse fidem nec foedere in ullo
    diuum ad fallendos numine abusum homines,
multa parata manent in longa aetate, Catulle,   5
    ex hoc ingrato gaudia amore tibi.
nam quaecumque homines bene cuiquam aut dicere possunt

aut facere, haec a te dictaque factaque sunt.
omnia quae ingratae perierunt credita menti.
    quare iam te cur amplius excrucies?   10
quin tu animum offirmas atque istinc teque reducis
    et dis inuitis desinis esse miser?
difficile est longum subito deponere amorem,
    difficile est, uerum hoc qualubet efficias:
una salus haec est. hoc est tibi peruincendum.   15
    hoc facias, siue id non pote siue pote.
o di, si uestrum est misereri aut si quibus umquam
    extremam iam ipsa in morte tulistis opem,
me miserum aspicite et, si uitam puriter egi,
    eripite hanc pestem perniciemque mihi,   20
quae mihi subrepens imos ut torpor in artus
    expulit ex omni pectore laetitias.
non iam illud quaero, contra me ut diligat illa,
    aut, quod non potis est, esse pudica uelit.
ipse ualere opto et taetrum hunc deponere morbum.   25
    o di, reddite mi hoc pro pietate mea.

                    (Catullus 76 (trans. Lee (1991), with minor variations))[1]

I

First, I give a fairly bold paraphrase of this poem, with supplements and comments to clarify what I think is the sequence of thought (this, together with the tone, especially of lines 1–16, is a matter of some controversy; see Powell (1990), 199–200).

'If there is any pleasure to be had' (the tone seems sceptical, implying 'and I doubt it')[2] 'from reflecting that one has in the past honoured all the obligations of a personal relationship' (we are meant to think of formal Roman friendship), 'you, Catullus, can already count on enough pleasure to last you a lifetime from your unrewarded love (1–6). For the fact is that [in that love] you have acted entirely dutifully [by friendship's standards] (7–8). But this has not been appreciated [by your beloved] (9), so why continue to torment yourself [by persisting with this special, friendship-like love which in the present – whatever its dubious future benefits – gives you nothing but pain] (10)? Why don't you make a clean break from her?' (that is, Lesbia; she is pointedly not named, but it would be

---

[1] Most of these were kindly communicated to me privately by Mr Lee after discussion.
[2] Cf. the frequent use of *si qua fides* to hint at the dubiousness of what is being suggested; see further Booth (1991), on Ov. *Am.* 2.6.51.

perverse to think of the woman in this poem as anyone else.) 'It's the only right thing to do (11–12). But it's hard to put a sudden end to long-standing love [because it is not, after all, *just* a form of friendship]' (13). (*Miser* in line 12, translated 'wretched', not only suggests general misery but is also often a near-technical term for 'afflicted with erotic passion'; and it thus seems to indicate that Catullus' thoughts are turning more towards sexual desire at this point. But his love is not necessarily, by implication, 'redefined' in line 13 as 'sexual passion only'.[3] The tacit acknowledgement is rather that it is a complex thing, with a sexual *as well as* a spiritual aspect; cf. lines 23–4.) 'Yes, but you must do it, whether you "can" or not; your very survival depends on it' (14–16). (In line 15 Catullus has introduced the idea of survival with the Latin *salus* – Lee translates 'chance' – which means both 'salvation' and 'health', and the notions of sickness and recovery pervade what follows.) 'Gods above, deliver me, desperate and deserving as I am (17–19), from this deadly disease' (*pestem perniciemque*, literally, 'plague and bane') (20), 'which, like a paralysis creeping through my body, has made my life a misery' (20–2). (This is probably not so much a genuine appeal to the divine, in simple faith, as a despairing plea for a miracle from any superhuman power which is capable of one.)[4] 'I have written off the idea of Lesbia ever satisfying my desires in either spiritual love' (*diligere*, the verb Catullus uses for 'love' in 23, is the one used to denote specifically non-physical affection at 72.3–4) 'or sexual love' ('chaste' in the context of 24 means having a single sexual partner, that is, Catullus himself); 'please gods, just let me recover; I think I deserve it in return for doing all that was right myself' (25–6).

Although this celebrated poem has been subjected to numerous scholarly analyses, the language of disease pervading the last third has generally been treated rather dismissively by critics: Catullus 'can diagnose his malady, even wish to be cured of it', says one, without deigning to tell us what it is;[5] 'Catullus means, of course, his infatuation', says another, as if we should know;[6] and yet another refrains from comment altogether.[7] The implication of all this is clear: it is his *love* which Catullus is depicting as a disease, and there

[3] Wiseman (1985), 168.
[4] See Williams (1968), 411–12; Syndikus (1987), 29–30.
[5] D. A. Kidd (1963), 300.
[6] Quinn (1970), on line 20.
[7] Lyne (1980), 29–33.

is nothing particularly unusual or mysterious about it – in fact, the thing is too obvious for words.[8] However, despite the long literary pedigree of the idea of love as a disease before Catullus (see Sect. II below), I question whether this is true. Rather, I suggest that Catullus' use of the language of disease here gives us, by the end of the poem, an unprecedentedly deep insight into the nature of the condition which he is desperate to be free of and which unglossed 'love', even if it is understood to be love of an intense and complex kind, may not adequately describe. This is not to say, of course, that the portrayal of love as a sickness in previous amatory writing, or indeed elsewhere, is irrelevant to Catullus 76. On the contrary, the frames of reference offered by poetry, Hellenistic philosophy (whose relation to Roman literature is a central concern of this volume) and even medicine can perhaps help us to grasp more fully what Catullus is trying to convey.

II

The literary portrayal of love as a sickness is traditionally traced back to seventh-century BC Greek lyric. After that, it appears in Greek tragedy, in Hellenistic poetry of both personal and non-personal kinds and in early Latin elegiac epigram. All these manifestations of the love-sickness motif (occurring in the types of poetry whose conventions Catullus in 76 might, on the face of it, be most expected to have followed) have one, very notable, common feature: the sickness they depict is physical. It takes two basic forms: (i) some sort of transient fainting fit, and (ii) a more lasting kind of psychosomatic illness which does not respond to medical or magical treatment. The individual symptoms of (i), brought on by the sight and sound of the beloved, are first described by Sappho (fr. 31. 1–16; translation and text as in D. A. Campbell (1982)):

> He seems fortunate as the gods to me, the man who sits opposite you and listens to your sweet voice and lovely laughter. Truly that sets my heart trembling in my breast. For when I look at you for a moment, then it is no longer possible for me to speak; my tongue has snapped, at once a subtle fire has stolen beneath my flesh, I see nothing with my eyes, my ears hum, sweat pours from me, a

---

[8] See Kroll (1929), on line 15; Commager (1965), 97–8; Moritz (1968), 57 (a reference to the 'medical conceits' of the prayer). Copley (1949), Wiseman (1985), Skinner (1987), and Newman (1990) are among the few dissenters; see text to nn. 29–31 below.

trembling seizes me all over, I am greener than grass, and it seems
to me that I am little short of dying.

φαίνεταί μοι κῆνος ἴσος θέοισιν
ἔμμεν' ὤνηρ, ὄττις ἐνάντιός τοι
ἰσδάνει καὶ πλάσιον ἆδυ φωνεί-
σας ὑπακούει

καὶ γελαίσας ἰμέροεν, τό μ' ἦ μὰν   5
καρδίαν ἐν στήθεσιν ἐπτόαισεν·
ὡς γὰρ ἔς σ' ἴδω βρόχε', ὥς με φώναι-
σ' οὐδ' ἒν ἔτ' εἴκει,

ἀλλὰ κὰμ μὲν γλῶσσά <μ'> ἔαγε, λέπτον
δ' αὔτικα χρῷ πῦρ ὑπαδεδρόμηκεν,   10
ὀππάτεσσι δ' οὐδ' ἒν ὄρημμ', ἐπιρρόμ-
βεισι δ' ἄκουαι,

κὰδ δέ μ' ἴδρως κακχέεται, τρόμος δὲ
παῖσαν ἄγρει, χλωροτέρα δὲ ποίας
ἔμμι, τεθνάκην δ' ὀλίγω 'πιδεύης   15
φαίνομ' ἔμ' αὔτ[ᾳ.

This catalogue of pathology is imitated very selectively in Latin
before Catullus by the epigrammatist Valerius Aedituus (fr. 1
Büchner),[9] and more comprehensively by Catullus himself to describe the effects on him of the sight and sound of Lesbia (Poem 51;
translation by Lee (1991)):

That man is seen by me as a god's equal
Or (if it may be said) the gods' superior,
Who sitting opposite again and again
Watches and hears *you*

Sweetly laughing – which dispossesses poor me   5
Of all my senses, for no sooner, Lesbia,
Do I look at you than there's no power left me
<Of speech in my mouth,>

But my tongue's paralysed, invisible flame
Courses down through my limbs, with din of their own   10
My ears are ringing and twin darkness covers
The light of my eyes.

Leisure, Catullus, does not agree with you
At leisure you're restless, too excitable.
Leisure in the past has ruined rulers and   15
Prosperous cities.

---

[9] See text and trans. in Quinn (1969), 13. Aedituus is conventionally dated c. 100 BC, but Ross
(1969), 141–3, would place him fifty years earlier.

Ille mi par esse deo uidetur,
ille, si fas est, superare diuos,
qui sedens aduersus identidem te
    spectat et audit

dulce ridentem, misero quod omnis   5
eripit sensus mihi. nam simul te,
Lesbia, aspexi, nihil est super mi
    <uocis in ore>

lingua sed torpet, tenuis sub artus
flamma demanat, sonitu suopte   10
tintinant aures, gemina teguntur
    lumina nocte.

otium, Catulle, tibi molestum est.
otio exsultas nimiumque gestis.
otium et reges prius et beatas   15
perdidit urbes.

Catullus' final stanza (often thought exceedingly puzzling and even wrongly placed) is correctly explained as his own recognition that personal damage of a far more fundamental kind than that he has just outlined can come of dallying in love, which he equates with being 'at leisure', 'having nothing (else) to do'.[10]

Form (ii) of the sickness motif, the psychosomatic illness which does not respond to medical or magical treatment, is found even earlier than the archaic Greek period in love-songs from ancient Egypt (1300–1100 BC), for instance:[11]

> Seven days since I saw my sister,[12]
> And sickness invaded me;
> I am heavy in all my limbs,
> My body has forsaken me
> When the physicians come to me,
> My heart rejects their remedies;
> The magicians are quite helpless,
> My sickness is not discerned.
> To tell me 'She is here' would revive me!
> Her name would make me rise;
> Her messenger's coming and going,

---

[10] See D. A. Kidd (1963). Cf. Plu. fr. 136 Sandbach (from *De amore*): '[Love] robs people of their means of life, their homes, their marriages and their positions of authority.'

[11] Trans. Lichtheim (1976), 185, quoted in Griffiths (1990), 350.

[12] Ancient Egyptian culture did not exclude love-affairs between siblings.

That would revive my heart!
My sister is better than all prescriptions,
She does more for me than all medicines;
Her coming to me is my amulet,
The sight of her makes me well!
When she opens her eyes my body is young,
Her speaking makes me strong;
Embracing her expels my malady
Seven days since she went from me!

In Greek, this form of the theme first appears in a fragment of
Archilochus (fr. 193 West): 'Miserable I lie with longing, lifeless,
pierced through my bones with pains sent by the gods.' In Hellenistic
literature (where the possibility of Egyptian influence cannot be
entirely ruled out)[13] more detail is given. Theocritus' Simaetha,
deserted by her lover Delphis, is afflicted by a 'burning disease'
(καπυρὰ νόσος) which turns her pale, makes her hair fall out and
reduces her to skin and bones (*Id.* 2.85–90); she also experiences a
fleeting Sapphic type of swoon when the said Delphis turns up at her
sick-bed (104–10). Callimachus diagnoses love as the cause of similar
symptoms in a man (*Epigr.* 30 Pfeiffer). In addition, Greek poetry
offers two interesting variations of the motif. Apollonius' Medea in
Argonautica 3 seems to be suffering from a combination of both types
of sickness (676, 681–7, 755–66, 962–6; the bug later visited on
Virgil's Dido at *Aen.* 4.1–5, 66–7, 76 was clearly of much the same
strain), and earlier, in Euripides' *Hippolytus*, Phaedra, driven to
something like anorexia by her erotic passion for her stepson
(131–40), becomes weak, pallid and wasted (173–5)[14] – psychological
cause, but physical effects. The cure for this type of love-sickness is
often left unspecified; but it is implied in the Theocritean poem and
made explicit in the Egyptian one that only the beloved can effect it
by responding to the lover's needs.[15]

What is striking about Catullus' use of the sickness motif in 76 is
not so much its affinities with these earlier poetic treatments as its
divergence from them. Most importantly, Catullus claims no physical
symptoms of any kind; and he positively rules out the possibility of

---

[13] See Griffiths (1990), 363–4; also West (1969).
[14] On Phaedra's love as sickness, see also *Hipp.* 40, 269, 279, 283, 477, 729–30, 769; Toohey
(1992), 280–1, diagnoses Phaedra's affliction as a manic type of psychosis. Cf. also Soph. *Tr.*
445.
[15] For further examples of love as a sickness in Hellenistic poetry and for alternative remedies,
see Griffiths (1990), 355–7; also La Penna (1957), 208; Funke (1990), 13–19.

being cured by his beloved's response (23–4). The non-physicality of his sickness is made clear by his *likening* it to the very physical disability of paralysis, which is presented as an actual symptom of his love in Poem 51 (cited above). He now refers to Poem 51, through close and concentrated verbal echoes, to show how different is the condition which afflicts him here. At 51.9–10 his tongue alone 'is paralysed' (*torpet*), while fiery sensation remains 'in his limbs' (*sub artus*); but at 76.21 his sickness as a whole is like a 'paralysis' (*torpor*) creeping through 'the depths of his limbs' (*imos ... in artus*). What is physical, localised and transitory in 51 is non-physical, deeply generalised and progressive in 76 (line 22 makes it clear that the very core of Catullus' emotions has been affected).[16] Other, less intrinsically significant, verbal echoes of 51 in the immediate vicinity also play their part in keeping that poem in mind: note the echo of *misero* at 51.5 in *miser* at 76.12, and *miserum* at 76.19; and of *eripit* at 51.6 in *eripite* at 76.20. Perhaps Catullus is referring also to the Sapphic model for 51, when he implies that he is 'on the point of death' (18). The oblique suggestion seems to be that he is as utterly sapped of emotional strength as Sappho was of physical vigour. It already looks clear that the 'deadly disease', the 'foul sickness', that Catullus is suffering from in 76 is of a very different nature from that found in the earlier lyric-elegiac and epic-tragic tradition. But he makes reference to the traditional treatment of the idea, especially in his own poetry, to highlight the unusualness of what he is saying here.

It would be wrong to suppose, however, that non-physical (or at least neutral) versions of the notion of love as a sickness are not found before Catullus. In New Comedy simple metaphorical forms of the motif, with no mention of physical symptoms, are common. For example, Plautus speaks of a 'cure' for the 'sickness' which is love (*Cist.* 74, 'If a doctor should come who can effect a cure for this disease ...', *si medicus ueniat qui huic morbo facere medicinam potest ...*). Terence asks 'What sort of sickness is this? Are people so changed by love that you would not recognise them?' (*Eu.* 225–6, *quid hoc morbi est? adeone homines immutarier | ex amore ut non cognoscas eundem esse?*).[17] The Roman dramatists' thinking and expression in these instances could

---

[16] I.e. his heart, *pectus*; this connotes in Latin, as in English, both the seat of feeling and the power-house of the body (for ancient thinking on the physical importance of the heart see Frede (1987*a*), 230, and the ambiguity helps to strengthen the analogy between Catullus' present condition and physical paralysis.

[17] Cf. Caecil. *com.* fr. 262 Ribbeck; see also Fantham (1972), 18.

be subject to some philosophical influence via Greek New Comedy (on this, see text to n. 42 below) which they imitated closely. But, for the moment, the points to be made are: (i) that comedy offers nothing akin to Catullus' careful likening of his own non-physical sickness to a specific physical one; and (ii) that the tone of the non-physical versions of the love-sickness motif in comedy is, unsurprisingly, comic.[18] Later, in Augustan lyric and, especially, elegy (where the influence of comedy in turn may be a factor[19]) the non-physical, purely metaphorical conception of love as a sickness is as common as the physical one,[20] the *pièce de résistance* being Ovid's *Remedia Amoris*. Here too, the tone is essentially light-hearted: the elegiac lover, for all his postures of suffering, is perceptibly a figure of fun.

Instinctively, the modern reader does not laugh at Catullus' sickness in 76. Why not? Instinct – especially modern instinct – should perhaps be checked. Fortunately, this is easily done through closer scrutiny of some items of Catullus' vocabulary. *Morbus* (25) itself need not detain us, for it is a stylistically and emotionally neutral word in wide general use, both literal and metaphorical.[21] *Pestis* and *pernicies* (20), translated 'deadly disease', and *taeter* (25), the epithet of *morbus*, translated 'foul', are more revealing. These three terms are very rare altogether in lyric and elegy and are never used of love either there or in comedy, the genres which characteristically treat love – and love-sickness – humorously. In comedy and the lampoons of Catullus himself, they are used with comic tone, mostly as terms of abuse directed at, or descriptive of, individuals.[22] The same is broadly true of satire, though the humour there is generally more sardonic.[23] *Pestis* in epic and tragedy is occasionally used

---

[18] Eubulus, fr. 67 Kock, 'Hidden love, ghastly disease' (λαθρίαν Κύπριν, αἰσχίστην νόσον), may seem to suggest otherwise; but parody of epic language is generally common in the fragments of Eubulus, and this could be an example of it.

[19] It is increasingly being realised that the Augustan elegists may have drawn directly on *Roman* comedy; see J. Griffin (1985), 198–210; Yardley (1987); Booth (1991), 31–2 and 154 (on Ov. *Am.* 2.12.9–10).

[20] For non-physical love-sickness see e.g. Tib. 2.5.109–10; Prop. 2.1.57–8; 3.24.17–18; for physical love-sickness see e.g. Hor. *Carm.* 1.13.5–6 (taken with Nisbet–Hubbard's note (1970)); Prop. 1.5.21–2; Ov. *Ars* 1.729, 733. For further examples of the theme in elegy see La Penna (1957), 206–7, and in later Greek erotic literature, ibid., 208; also Maehler (1990); Griffiths (1990), 359.

[21] The imagery of disease was by no means confined to amatory contexts in either Greek or Latin: see Harvey (1971); Fantham (1972), 14–18.

[22] E.g. Pl. *Ps.* 204 (*pestis*), 364 (*pernicies*); *Mos.* 593 (*taeter*); Ter. *Ad.* 189 (*pestis*), 188 (*pernicies*); Catul. 69.9. (*pestis*), 27.6. (*pernicies*).

[23] E.g. Hor. *Ep.* 1.15.31 (*pernicies*); Juv. 4.84 (*pestis*), 6.418 (*taeter*). Horace uses *taeter* twice at least semi-seriously in condemnation of sexual lust (*S.* 1.2.33, 3.107).

figuratively of love, but never light-heartedly; the afflictions which it denotes are those of Dido, Phaedra and Medea.[24] All three words are also used both literally and figuratively in non-amatory contexts in epic, didactic and tragedy, but again with an invariably serious tone.[25] Both *pestis* and *pernicies* are used figuratively in the high poetic genres for 'doom', 'danger' or 'disaster' in general;[26] and the two are used together by Cicero, in the same alliterative phrase as we find in Catullus, of Catiline and other threats to public order and security.[27] *Taeter* in the most elevated types of poetry connotes putrefaction and is applied particularly to foul odours, corpses and blood.[28]

Instinct is right then: these are serious words. The deep gravity of tone combined with emphatic non-physical conception is what makes Catullus' language of sickness in 76 unique in the poetic tradition, and it continues to look as if he was using such language to depict a love-related condition outside the imagination or interest of other poets. Some scholars have indeed thought that the words are simply too strong to denote mere love – even bitterly disappointed love –. and have explained their significance differently. It has been claimed, for example, that Catullus' sickness is the moral guilt he feels about continuing to love Lesbia, when, by rights, he should not;[29] that his likening of his love to a sickness is his way of trying to excuse his moral guilt to the gods;[30] and that the language of sickness is used to condemn his love as a moral wrong, but with a self-satirising irony.[31] The actual words may be capable of any of these connotations, as suggested by Horace's condemnatory use of *taeter* ('foul') specifically

---

[24] Dido: Virg. *A.* 4.90; Phaedra: Sen. *Phaed.* 210; Medea: V. Fl. 8.165.

[25] *Pestis* signifies, literally, 'plague'/'pestilence', usually of a widespread kind (Ov. *Met.* 7.553; Luc. 6.89, 97; V. Fl. 4.482, 491; Sil. 14.582, 613; Sen. *Oed.* 55, 589); figuratively, it signifies any kind of harmful substance or creature, especially poison and snakes (e.g. Virg. *G.* 3.419; Luc. 6.681; 9.805; Stat. *Theb.* 2.282; Sil. 3.201; Sen. *Oed.* 152). Notice the interesting hybrid at Ennius, *Alcmaeo* 24–5 'Bring me help, rid me of this *pestis*, this flaming violence which is torturing me' *(fer mi auxilium, pestem abige a me | flammiferam hanc uim, quae me excruciat)*, where 'it is not clear whether Alcmaeo is referring to the flames of the Furies' torches or the fever from which he is suffering' (Jocelyn (1967), on *Alcmaeo* 24–5). In view of the mention of 'torture' *(excruciat;* cf. Catullus 76.10) as well as 'plague' *(pestem)*, it seems possible that Catullus had the phraseology of this passage in mind.

[26] E.g. Enn. *trag. fr.* 230 Jocelyn *(pernicies)*; Lucr. 3.326 *(pernicies)*, 347 *(pestis)*; Virg. *A.* 1.712 *(pestis)*; Ov. *Met.* 9.200 *(pestis)*; Luc. 1.649 *(pestis)*; V. Fl. 7.334 *(pestis)*; Sil. 5.498 *(pestis)*; 12.337 *(pernicies)*; Sen. *Med.* 670 *(pernicies)*; *Her. F.* 1084 *(pestis)*.

[27] *Catil.* 1.33; *Rab. Perd.* 2; *de Off.* 2.51.

[28] E.g. Lucr. 2.415, 510; Virg. *A.* 10.727; Luc. 1.618; V. Fl. 4.183; Stat. *Theb.* 2.674; Sil. 5.67.

[29] Copley (1949), 39.

[30] Wiseman (1985), 168.

[31] Newman (1990), 322–3. Newman sees Catullus as a satirist in his love-poems no less than his lampoons, if I interpret his view of the sickness language in 76 correctly.

in relation to sexual mores (n. 23 above); but there are logical objections to each of them in the context of the poem. It is enough to mention here their common weakness, which is that they all fail to explain why Catullus should have bothered to liken his morally wrong love or his sense of guilt to a particular physical condition – creeping paralysis.

III

Rejection of these interpretations, however, does not preclude the possibility that Catullus presents his condition as sickness because he regards it as some sort of personal moral failing. '"Catullus the philosopher"', we are told, 'would be a challenging thesis, but perhaps it is time it was written.'[32] I do not propose to write it here, but, given Catullus' own emphasis on the psychological rather than physical nature of what ails him, it is entirely appropriate to consider whether his concept of mental sickness in this love-poem has anything in common with that of the Hellenistic philosophers, especially the Stoics, for whom the idea of mental or psychic sickness was fundamentally important. For the Stoics, the 'passions' (*pathē*) are the product of sickness of the psyche (LS 65 R–s). In orthodox Stoic theory, passions are 'rational', in the sense that they involve explicit or implicit beliefs (in Stoic terms, 'assent' to rational 'impressions') about the value of the objects of passions such as desire or fear. But passions are 'irrational' (contrary to right Reason), in that the beliefs involved are misguided.[33] In Stoic thought only virtue is genuinely good and desirable, and all other objects of desire are 'matters of indifference' (*adiaphora*). To bring one's will into line with virtue can also be conceived as obedience to Nature or the divine will. Since, for the Stoics, all psychological experiences are physical events, the 'sickness' of the psyche which produces passions is itself physical (it can be described as a kind of 'flaccidity', *atonia*); and it may manifest itself in distinctive physical symptoms. But the only cure for this soul-sickness is philosophical: a rational effort of will is required from the 'sick' person to initiate progress towards the recognition that virtue is the only good, through which alone this 'sickness' can be cured.[34]

---

[32] Newman (1990), 339.
[33] See Introd., Sect. II, text to nn. 21–2.
[34] See LS 65, esp. D, L, R–T; Cic. *Tusc.* 4.23–32; Gal. *PHP* 4.6.1–11, De Lacy (1978–84) vol. 1 270–3; 5.2.1–51, De Lacy ibid. 294–305. See further Inwood (1985), ch. 5; Frede (1986);

Despite the fact that orthodox Stoicism maintained that human psychology is strongly unified, Stoics did not wholly deny the phenomenon of inner conflict, and of what Aristotle (*NE* 7) called *akrasia* ('weakness of will'). As Christopher Gill brings out later in this volume, there was debate within the Stoic school about how such conflict was to be understood and how much division of the soul was required to explain it. Chrysippus, the main theorist of the school, argued that it was to be explained, essentially, by unrecognised changes in beliefs (and in the passions dependent on beliefs). He also acknowledged that passionate responses, though deriving originally from the person's beliefs, could fall outside his or her control at any given moment (like running legs rather than walking ones). For instance, in judging that sexual satisfaction is a good, I desire it, and, once I have desired it, I may not be able to stop (even if I in some sense want to), for the desire can acquire its own psychophysical momentum. Posidonius, a later head of the school, argued that these conflicts can only be explained by assuming conflict between distinct parts of the soul, or, at least, between the person's beliefs and his or her 'affective motions' (*pathētikai kinēseis*). However, for both Stoic thinkers, passions and the conflicts that they generate derive, in essence, from misguided beliefs, and require change in belief (above all, belief about what is good and worth pursuing), if such passions are to be 'extirpated'.[35]

As regards the passion of love, the Stoics, perhaps surprisingly, apparently approved of one form of sexual love: the 'beauty'-inspired erotic liaison, usually, but perhaps not exclusively, homosexual, whose objectives were to help the beloved towards virtue, for which he (or she) was naturally endowed, and, perhaps more importantly, to establish 'friendship' (*philia*) between the parties through the beloved's reciprocation.[36] This type of love the Stoics regarded as completely in accord with Nature, but 'ordinary' heterosexual love they classified as a morbid passion.[37] Chrysippus himself regards the lover as a perfect example of a person deaf to Reason and convinced

---

Nussbaum (1994), chs. 9–10. On Roman reception of the Stoic idea of 'therapy' of passions, see Erskine, Ch. 2; Wilson, Ch. 3.

[35] See Gill, Ch. 11, Sect. III, text to nn. 43–5. See also LS 65 G, I–Q, Gal. *PHP* 4.5.19–7.44, De Lacy (1978–84) vol. I 262–91. See further Gill (1983a); Gosling (1987) and (1990), ch. 5; Price (1995), ch. 4.

[36] See Schofield (1991), 22–56, 112–18. The basic pattern is clearly Platonic: see Price (1989), chs. 2–3.

[37] LS 65 E; cf. Muson. *Discourse* 12 (*On sexual indulgence*) in Lutz (1947), 85–9 (with translation).

of his own inability to cast off his passion (he quotes from Euripides in support of his point: 'Even when censured Cypris does not let go; | if you use force she loves to strive the more').[38] Cicero, after expressing some scepticism about the very existence of Stoic ideal love,[39] and confessing to finding more sense in Epicurean distaste for all erotic passion, does not hesitate to condemn 'ordinary' love in broadly Stoic terms:

> But above all [the lover] must be warned how great is the madness (*furor*) of love ... the disorder of the soul (*perturbatio*) in love is in itself foul (*foeda*) ... and this too, which is said of every disorder, must be pointed out: none is ever anything but a matter of belief (*nisi opinabilem*), an exercise of judgement (*nisi iudicio susceptam*), a free choice (*nisi uoluntariam*). (*Tusc.* 4.75–7, with omissions)

We can now return to Catullus 76 and consider whether the poet's presentation of his condition as a sickness there is understandable within a Stoic context – whether Catullus himself offers anything like a Stoic analysis of his situation as a whole. Superficially, it seems that he does: he recognises the deleterious effect of sexual love; his conflict with divine will (what Nature orders) in pursuing it; the difficulty of breaking off something which has got a hold; and the imperative need to make himself do this however impossible it may seem, if he is to recover. But Chrysippus would have dismissed him as a hopeless case. Catullus does not accept the Stoic view that the love which aims at ethical friendship is Natural and, therefore, to be engaged in, while the love which aims at simple sexual fulfilment is not Natural and therefore to be extirpated. Rather he sees the one type of love as indivisible from the other and both, therefore, to be given up when they cause him personal distress, which he perceives as a bad thing. This is a double rejection of the Stoic idea of Reason. He does not see sickness of soul as the cause of the love which pains him, but equates the passion of love itself with sickness – though not much can be made of this, since Cicero falls into the same 'error'.[40] More importantly, he implies, through the Latin terms he uses for 'deadly disease' (see text to nn. 4–6, 21–30 above) and his *likening* of that disease to a progressive physical paralysis, that he regards his love-rooted distress as something inflicted on him from outside and not

---

[38] Gal. *PHP* 4.6.30, trans. De Lacy (1978–84) vol. 1 267 (= Eur. fr. 340 Nauck).
[39] *Tusc.* 4.68. Cf. the debate at Plu. *Amat.* 750c–752c.
[40] *Tusc.* 3.7; 4.23; see also Nussbaum (1987*b*), 130, n. 2.

generated by his own psyche. The Stoics would have told him that, on the contrary, it was 'all in his mind' and that the feeling of paralysis was *truly* physical, in the sense of being part of his psychological (that is, psychosomatic) experience.

His inability to desist from love, despite his recognition of the need to do so, looks far more like a claim to be subject to (non-Stoic) *akrasia* than an admission of an original error of judgement about the desirability of requited love which has resulted in difficulty in controlling the concomitant passion ever after. Quite unlike the Stoic, who knows that there really is no such word as 'can't', Catullus finally gives up the effort to effect a cure by himself, looking instead, without much confidence, for a god-sent miracle in return for his good behaviour. There is no awareness here that virtue is its own reward and that nobody *owes* him anything. When Catullus finally wishes 'to be well', he gives no indication of looking for anything more than to be cured of his pernicious love for Lesbia and its consequences. He seems nowhere near accepting that satisfied love is not itself a good, nor is the 'happiness' which eludes him.[41] To be truly 'well' in Stoic terms is to be unaffected by such 'irrational' desires.

Although Catullus, therefore, is obviously trying to depict through the language of disease a serious psychological affliction, he clearly does not think of it as a sickness which is 'all in the mind' in the Stoic sense of being a chronic condition which involves aberrations of judgement. The Stoic remedies of self-help and moral-intellectual effort are no good for it: the Stoic perspective helps us, at least, to see what Catullus' sickness is *not*. Whether he was consciously applying Stoic language and ideas for this purpose is questionable. The Greek writers of New Comedy knew the Hellenistic Stoics at first hand and could easily have absorbed some of their attitudes and expression.[42] Could Menander's, 'It is difficult, Phanias, to break off long intimacy in a short time' (fr. 544 Körte, ἔργον ἐστι, Φανία, | μακρὰν συνήθειαν βραχεῖ λῦσ' ἐν χρόνῳ) perhaps be an example of this? And could Catullus' almost verbatim version of the same sentiment at 76.13 perhaps indicate that he in turn learned a kind of Everyman's Stoicism from New Comedy? It could; but equally there is

---

[41] *Laetitia*, the word he uses for 'happiness', is the one Cicero uses at *Tusc.* 4.68 of the enjoyment which goes beyond what is Natural, and interestingly he uses it in direct connection with sexual 'lust' (*libido*).

[42] See further Preston (1916), 3–14.

nothing exclusively and characteristically Stoic about the sentiment or the language, and the notion could be merely proverbial.[43]

On the face of it, Catullus would seem more likely to have engaged with the rival Hellenistic philosophy of Epicureanism. Not only was he a poetic contemporary of Lucretius, the most artistically accomplished of all Epicurean believers, but he was also, almost certainly, an intimate of Philodemus of Gadara, writer of witty elegiac love-epigrams as well as Epicurean treatises.[44] The Epicureans believed that pain itself was mostly 'all in the mind' and presented their philosophy as a cure for it;[45] but, on the whole, the language of disease is not so pervasive in their thought as it is in that of the Stoics. Still, it might be useful to offer their perspective on Catullus' love-related anguish.

The Epicureans teach that human desire should be limited to that which is 'natural and necessary' in pursuit of the only good, which is pleasure.[46] Pleasure is absence of pain. False perceptions of pleasure result in pain. The ultimate pleasure is the static one of *ataraxia*, 'tranquillity of mind', which results from absolute physical and mental contentment. But, for this to be achieved, certain natural and necessary desires which result in kinetic pleasure must be satisfied, for instance, the desire for food to relieve hunger. The desire for food of a special kind or in lavish quantities, though natural (because it is for food), is not necessary (because it goes beyond what will merely relieve hunger). The belief that satisfaction of such unnecessary desires constitutes pleasure is false (LS 21 B, C, I). Once someone has a true understanding of what pleasure is, he can avoid much pain, and he should also be able to use recollection of past pleasures and anticipation of future ones to counteract any pain (LS 21 T).

Epicurean hostility to love is notorious (D.L. 10.118). Epicurus himself is on record as saying that simple satisfaction of sexual desire

---

[43] What is more, the Stoics were clearly taken with some sayings in comedy; see e.g. Chrysippus' famous quotation of Menander fr. 702 Körte (*ap*. Gal. *PHP* 4.6.34): 'I got hold of my mind and stuffed it in a pot', trans. De Lacy (1978–84) vol. 1 277. Cf. Men. fr. 569 Körte, *ap*. Plu. fr. 134 Sandbach (from *De amore*). Stoic 'sermons' in Roman satire also draw material from comedy; e.g. Hor. *S*. 2.3; Pers. 5.

[44] Some scholars have contended that Catullus shows a general inclination towards Epicurean thinking throughout his oeuvre; e.g. Neudling (1949), Giuffrida (1950) (the latter work is known to me only by report).

[45] The idea was in fact almost a general philosophical cliché; cf. Cic. *Tusc.* 4.58–62, Muson. fr. 36 in Lutz (1947), 135 (with translation). See further Gill (1985), 320; Annas (1989), 146.

[46] For the sake of brevity, I follow Annas (1989), 151–3, and I interpret rather than summarise some of the most important source material here.

might at best do 'no harm' – it may fall into the category of the natural and necessary relief of pain – but is never in itself 'advantageous' (LS 21 G). Fulfilment of the sexual desire which is accompanied by intense erotic emotion (conventionally called 'love') is one of the things falsely believed to be a pleasure, for it is not 'necessary', and results in pain and loss of tranquillity. Lucretius' lurid depiction (4.1073–191) of the besotted, demented, insatiable, physically, morally and financially ruined, stressed and deluded lover is primarily designed to demonstrate this Epicurean truth, though it draws on some of the age-old stock motifs and imagery of amatory literature. Interestingly, Lucretius resorts to a metaphor of progressive disease in his description of obsessive sexual love: it is 'an ulcer' which 'becomes active and established, if nourished' (*ulcus enim uiuescit et inueterascit alendo*, 1068). The frenzy (*furor*) and suffering (*aerumna*), he says, get worse unless treated with some sort of counter-irritation or distraction (1069–72).[47]

How receptive to this kind of analysis, then, does Catullus look in 76? There is certainly Lucretian vividness in his imagery of progressive disease, and his implicit admission of love's disastrous domination of his life concisely testifies to the truth of Lucretius' larger-scale picture. In particular, his final plea merely 'to be well', rather than to have his love satisfied, sounds very like aiming at the Epicurean ideal of 'tranquillity'. But Catullus has some very un-Epicurean conceptions of how this is to be achieved. Bitter irony seems to underlie his initial airing of the idea that consolation may be had from recalling past pleasures (past 'good deeds' are what he actually mentions at 76.1, but these appear to have counted as 'pleasures' for the Epicureans;[48] the Epicureans did not, however, have a monopoly of the notion of assuaging present distress by recollection of past probity,[49] and Catullus' oblique criticism on this point may not be directed *exclusively* at them).

Catullus seems to equate pleasure mainly with positive happiness (76.1, 22) rather than with the absence of pain which leads to *ataraxia*. Even at the end (25), where he seems closest to Epicurean enlightenment, we can still doubt whether he accepts that obsessive love of any woman, rather than of this particular woman, is a worthless

[47] For this strategy, cf. Cic. *Tusc.* 4.74; see further Nussbaum (1989), (1994), ch. 5.
[48] LS 22 G: 'They themselves [the Epicureans] in fact say that it is more pleasurable to confer a benefit (*eu poiein*) than to receive one (*eu paschein*).'
[49] See Powell (1990), 200.

thing in itself, and that fulfilment of this brings no 'pleasure' in the Epicurean sense. But by far his most obvious disengagement from the Epicurean point of view is to be seen in his appeal to the gods. It shows neither the general acceptance of personal responsibility for the 'health' of one's soul (demanded by the Epicureans as much as the Stoics); nor, despite its unoptimistic tone (see text to n. 4 above), willingness to give up quite completely, as an Epicurean would have done, the idea of any superhuman agency intervening to benefit man.[50] The Epicurean perspective, then, at least confirms that Catullus does not regard his mental sickness as the sort of moral-intellectual failing which philosophy might remedy (the much-vaunted Epicurean distraction-therapy, in particular, he never considers).[51] But whether he was actually trying to encourage his readers to adopt an Epicurean perspective (rather than, or as well as, a Stoic one) is hard to tell.

If, however, his sickness is one beyond philosophy, would it come within the ambit of medicine? The physicians of classical antiquity, no less than the philosophers, to whose art they considered their own to be very closely related,[52] were aware of the interaction of mind and body, and they certainly recognised mental illnesses and symptoms besides plain psychotic madness (which can obviously be discounted in Catullus' case). One is the chronic mental dejection, accompanied by digestive difficulties and physical prostration, which is called 'melancholy' (*melancholē*) and thought to result, as its name indicates, from an excess of black bile; and another is irrational fear accompanied by physical symptoms (Hp. *Epid.* 7.86). On the other hand, general states of neurosis, including what would now sometimes be called 'endogenous depression' (that is, depression with no obvious external cause) and other personal difficulties in coping with life, were thought to be more the province of philosophers, who, as we have seen, regarded them as moral-intellectual, not medical, problems.[53] To view Catullus' emphatically non-physical sickness temporarily through a Greek or Roman doctor's eyes is a way of seeing yet again what it is *not*. He is not suffering from 'melancholy': his 'paralysis', as his simile indicates, is *wholly* mental. Nor is his

---

[50] On Epicurean (complex) beliefs about the divine, see the useful discussion, with examination of the primary sources, in LS, vol. 1, 144–9.

[51] See e.g. Cic. *Tusc.* 3.33.

[52] See Gill (1985), 320–1; Frede (1987a).

[53] See Gill (1985), esp. 317 (on melancholy), 322–3 (on neurosis).

irrationality of a phobic kind. And if he had presented the doctors of his time with his symptoms, they would probably have referred him to a philosopher for the sort of treatment that we know he does not find helpful.[54]

IV

From all the negatives, however, which literary, philosophical and medical perspectives on Catullus' sickness have produced, it is possible to assemble a number of positives. The sickness is to be identified with an externally generated emotion: love of a complex kind, both spiritual and sexual, unsatisfied and unsatisfying, yet irresistible. But it also embraces the wider effects of this love, which are mental, not physical. It is a condition of the psyche which is serious and has gradually been getting worse: it is, in short, a progressive mental *crippling*. It has taken over Catullus completely, and makes him feel that life is not worth living. He considers it to be utterly beyond his ability to control or remedy. Moreover, to be cured is not to be granted the positive happiness which would come if his beloved suddenly reformed, but is to return to a normal and tranquil state of mind, and nothing short of a hardly-to-be-expected miracle can bring that about. By the end of the poem we can see, then, I suggest, that the 'foul sickness' of which Catullus is desperate to be healed is *both* the emotion of love *and* the mental crippling which has in his case resulted from it – in other words, cause and effect to the sufferer are, realistically, indistinguishable. The poem is a grim rewriting of lines 13–16 in Poem 51 (see text to n. 16 above), which has been kept in mind from line 17 onwards here: having nothing to do (that is, being susceptible to love) results in being able to do nothing. Had Catullus presented his condition to a modern doctor, it might well have been diagnosed as a classic case of reactive depression, that is, depression with a clearly identifiable external cause (by contrast with endogenous depression). This is not an illness (though its victims frequently feel bad enough to believe themselves ill) but a completely normal and appropriate human response to a

---

[54] Had Catullus been able to consult Oribasius (fourth century AD) or Paulus of Aegina (seventh century AD), he would, apparently, have been regarded as mentally disturbed in the modern psychiatric sense of the term; see Griffiths (1990), 362–3. Contrast Plu. fr. 136 Sandbach (from *De amore*), where the claim is made that a man in love should be treated *as if he were* mentally ill – the implication being that in fact he is not.

deeply distressing situation, such as bereavement, or, indeed, emotional rejection or betrayal.[55] If I am right in thinking that Catullus was using the language of sickness in 76 to try to convey the essence of this kind of human experience – something far more serious for those who suffer it than 'the purely nervous malaise of disappointed love'[56] – we classicists have to face up to the awful possibility that for once a Roman poet, all by himself, was trying to say something strikingly original and even, in a sense, true.[57]

[55] I am grateful to Dr John Hilliard and Dr Rosemary Mason for discussing with me the modern clinical terminology of depression.

[56] Such is the intuitive diagnosis of Powell (1990), 220, n. 2: more on the right lines than most, but still over-dismissive. Syndikus (1987), 28, also seems to have an inkling of what Catullus is really trying to say, though he does not go beyond generalities ('The special feature of Catullus' assertion is the expansion of metaphor to represent a condition that threatens to destroy one's whole existence', my trans.).

[57] I should like to thank the participants in the Exeter conference for their valuable reactions to the original draft of this chapter. Here, I have included new material and attempted to clarify some points, but my conclusion remains the same.

CHAPTER 9

'Ferox uirtus': anger in Virgil's 'Aeneid'

M. R. Wright

I

Achilles' slaying of Hector and Odysseus' massacre of the suitors link the themes of anger at the close of the Homeric poems with Aeneas' response to Turnus in the last lines of the *Aeneid*. Karl Galinsky has studied this in detail, but he also introduced briefly the Greek philosophical tradition, as well as Roman legal practice, to justify Aeneas' enraged killing of Turnus as wholly appropriate in these contexts. Michael Putnam has taken issue with this stand, claiming that, on the contrary, Aeneas' final action is reprehensible, to be condemned in Stoic terms as incompatible with wisdom, revealing lack of moderation, moral blindness and ultimate failure as either heroic or Roman *exemplum*.[1]

My purpose is not to attempt to solve the problems inherent in the last lines of the *Aeneid*, but to mediate on the controversy of principle that underlines the particular disagreement between these two points of view. This involves reopening and broadening the discussion by suggesting the use of a variety of passages from the poem as a whole to show that Virgil is interested in the psychology and physiology of anger primarily in their contribution to the development of epic character and action. In this the Homeric precedents are of crucial importance, but they have been filtered through the general under-standing of human passion and motivation developed by Plato and especially by Aristotle; these philosophically based conclusions are still of relevance and interest to contemporary psychological theory.[2] The Stoics, however, in their condemnation of all passion as

---

[1] See Galinsky (1988), Putnam (1990); also Galinsky (1994), Putnam (1995), ch. 8. See also Fowler, Ch. 1, Sect. IV; Gill, Ch. 11, Sect. IV.

[2] See Averill (1982), Hillman (1992), Madow (1972), Nesse (1991), Stearns (1975) and Tavris (1982). Hillman actually sums up his thesis within an explicitly Aristotelian framework as being the most appropriate for a contemporary theory of emotion.

intellectual error, mental illness and moral collapse, deliberately restricted the evidence of empirical observation in the interests of ethical consistency, and did so in a manner that set their theory at variance with poetic insight and representation.

The method adopted in this chapter, therefore, is to place the phenomenon of anger in an Aristotelian rather than a Stoic or legalistic framework. Aristotle's analysis of anger is, I would maintain, the most viable and perceptive ancient account in its own right; it links the preceding Greek epic and philosophical traditions to the subsequent Hellenistic theories and it provides a basis for understanding the literary treatment in the ancient world of what is empirically familiar and generally presupposed, though I am not claiming that Virgil based his treatment of anger in the *Aeneid* directly on any Aristotelian or Peripatetic texts. The application of the Aristotelian mean of 'righteous anger' to both sides of the conflict in the second half of the *Aeneid* – to Aeneas' allies the Etruscans as 'righteous anger' (*iusta ira*) and to the Italians' leader Turnus as 'fierce virtue' (*ferox uirtus*) – serves as an effective way to reassess Aeneas' role in the tragic conflict involved in the Trojan settlement in Italy.[3]

II

Anger is a practical passion, and the only one that has a meritorious aspect in the inheritance of both epic heroism and the psychology of Plato and Aristotle. It also involves a rational element to a much greater extent than other passions, not merely in the accompanying beliefs about present and future good and evil, but also in the nexus of judgements required in any particular situation in which anger arises, and in the part played by imagination. Heraclitus, significantly for his attested influence on Stoicism, was unusual among pre-Hellenistic philosophers in condemning anger (in the form of *thumos*), because, in his view, it consumed mental energy to no purpose, and so contributed to psychological failure at the expense of enlight-

---

[3] *Ferox uirtus* is from the compliment of Latinus, king of Latium, to Turnus as a young man of outstanding spirit and 'fierce virtue' (12.19–20). The phrase implies an aggressive courage and anger that are to be commended. 'Righteous anger' (*iusta ira*) is similar in meaning, but with less aggression implied. It is used in the context of the Etruscan retaliation on their enemy Mezentius (10.714), whose cruelty Evander had earlier recounted in detail (8.481–8). (Numerical references without a title refer to book and line of Virgil's *Aeneid*; translations given are my own.)

enment.[4] The subtle Aristotelian treatment of the passion on the other hand, deriving in part from Plato, allowed for righteous anger as a mean between under- and over-reaction, which was justified in exacting appropriate retribution, and it is in this context that the Virgilian *iusta ira* and *ferox uirtus* are best interpreted. In addition, Aristotle assimilated the biological aspect to the related cognition in the application of his theory to a broad range of common experience. The Aristotelian involvement of mood and disposition also provided the basis for the two kinds of related therapy: the replacement of erroneous judgements by those that are morally correct, and the assuaging of physical excess as a precondition for individual autonomy and serenity.

In a famous passage in *Republic* 4, Plato distinguished anger (understood as *thumos*) from hunger, thirst, fear and greed; when reason and such appetites conflict, anger sides with reason and is its natural ally. Furthermore, when someone thinks himself wronged it is said: 'his *thumos* seethes, grows fierce and becomes the ally of what is judged to be just, and in noble souls it endures and wins victory, and will not desist until it achieves its purpose, or dies, or is recalled and calmed by reason'. In the *Philebus*, anger was again differentiated from hunger and thirst, and put in the category of mixed pleasures and pains. These belong to the soul and form its own emotional response, deriving judgement from reason and in turn spurring reason to initiate action. The *Politicus* (like the *Republic*) concluded by finding harmony in state and individual in the 'interweaving' of the courageous and the sophronic (moderate) elements: 'The soul full of vigour and courage will be made gentle by its grasp of truth and will then become a willing member of a community based on justice.'[5] While recognising well enough that *thumos*, like its analogue the army, may usurp the role of reason, ally with lower elements and become lawless, Plato claimed it as a positive and necessary force for good when it supports reason, guards against external attack and internal insurrection, and motivates both state and individual to persevere and conquer. This ambiguity in anger, inherent in its position between reason and appetite, which made it a force for both good and ill, was developed by Aristotle. The two aspects of anger, however, were later separated off in Hellenistic philosophy, so that

---

[4] See fr. 85: 'It is hard to fight against *thumos*; whatever it wants, it purchases at the expense of *psuchē*.'

[5] See Plato *R.* 440c–e, *Ti.* 70d, *Phlb.* 47e, *Plt.* 309d–e.

anger became an intellectual fault for the Stoics, explicable solely in terms of erroneous judgement, but mainly physicalist in Epicureanism, where emotional characteristics were derived from the preponderance and interaction of particular atomic groupings within the psychosomatic construct.

Aristotle's interest in anger ranged from the early treatment in the *Topics* (where anger was said to involve pain along with the belief that one has been slighted) to the late *Rhetoric*. Here it received detailed treatment with a number of other passions, for clearly, if the orator is to be skilful in arousing and manipulating the passions of his audience, he needs to understand the circumstances, moods and dispositions relating to them, as well as the various physiological, social and moral states involved. On this basis, anger was described as 'an impulse accompanied by pain towards a conspicuous revenge for a conspicuous slight' concerning self or friends. *De anima*, on the other hand, defined passions in general as 'formulae in matter', looked for accounts of them in terms of efficient, material and final explanations, and then took anger, in particular, as the combination of two necessary ingredients: the 'final cause' in the philosopher's definition as 'desire for retaliation' and the 'material cause' of the biologist's 'boiling of blood around the heart'. The main treatment, however, came in *Nicomachean Ethics* 4.5, supplemented by extensive comments in books 2, 5 and 7.[6]

From this comprehensive Aristotelian evidence, which takes into account the literary and philosophical inheritance as well as physicalist and general empirical observation, it is possible to set up some criteria to provide a standard by which the treatment of the passion of anger in Virgil's literary text may be assessed. Primarily, there has to be an initial offence, serious and threatening. This might take the form of an open unjustified insult, or unfairness, ingratitude, lack of co-operation, obstruction or negligence of some sort, which is directed against oneself, or by transference against family or friends or country. The core of the offence is that it is blameworthy, and entails humiliating social consequences for the individual offended; it may often be exacerbated when it is unexpected, should it arise, for

---

[6] See Aristotle, *Top.* 127b30–1 and 126a10; *de An.* 403a25–8; *NE* 1103b18–22, 1105b26–8, 1108a4–11, 1125b26–1126b10, 1130a31, 1138a9, 1149b20–3; *Rh.* 1378a30–1380b10. The word translated by 'anger' in Aristotle is *orgē*; *mēnis* is used for the wrath of Achilles and of gods in the *Iliad*; *cholē* is more a medical term; and *thumos*, giving the physical location in the heart area, connects with the aggressive impulse sometimes translated as 'spirit'.

example, from a quarter where respect rather than insult would be the norm. If anger is to be strictly applicable, the one who perpetrates the offence and so becomes the target for retaliation should be an identifiable, present, responsible rational agent, and of comparable social status. In other cases, when emotion is directed at objects or animals or young children, the response is more like irritation, for these annoy, but cannot really offend; and, when the target is not individualised or accessible, indignation rather than anger arises.

From a psychological point of view, the mood which provokes the anger may be temporary, or aggravated by particular circumstances:

> So when people are sick, poor, in love, thirsty, or in general in a state of unrequited desire, they are hot-tempered and easily provoked, especially towards those who belittle their current predicament... for they are guided in each case towards their own particular anger by their present suffering. (*Rh.* 1379a15–22)

But the temporary mood arises from a *disposition* that is prone to anger, and this will be more permanent. Aristotle suggested that impulsive youth and crotchety old age are that way inclined, but the tendency may also be inherent in the individual's physical structure (a point the Epicureans were to take up) – some people move naturally to angry outbursts, as others are more cowardly or too apathetic.[7] Aristotle also proposed (in *Nicomachean Ethics* 2.1) that such a disposition (*hexis*) may be fixed by behaviour patterns. Passions often act like crafts and virtues in this respect: as one becomes skilful in pottery by making pots, and just by doing just acts, so a disposition to anger may be developed or aggravated by continually indulging loss of temper without restraint. In these circumstances the disposition accounts for the passion, and this in turn can be the stimulus to wrong action; in the example of anger, the disposition is the underlying cause, and a particular offence the immediate cause, of the physical assault that commonly accompanies it.

---

[7] Cf. *NE* 1108a4–11 and 4.5 *passim* with Lucretius 3.296–309, where the corresponding animal paradigms of lion, deer and cow are cited. Lucretius' description of the character which is too apathetic and bovine is close to Aristotle's 'lack of anger' (*aorgēsia*); here, cf. the 'placid heart', *sedato corde*, of Latinus, 12.18.

III

When the *Aeneid* is read in the light of this Aristotelian theory, a salient point that emerges right at the beginning of the poem is that a permanent disposition towards anger is a divine characteristic: 'Do gods in heaven have so much anger in their hearts?' (*tantaene animis caelestibus irae?*, 1.11).[8] But this is not a righteous or moderated anger. Gods and goddesses over-react at any injury (*iniuria*) from mortals that threatens their status, and respond immediately with cruel retaliation. Such is the death which Minerva inflicts on Ajax (1.41), Triton on Misenus (6.173), and Jupiter on Salmoneus (6.586); Cybele, on the other hand, prefers to wait for the exact moment (*promissa dies*, 9.107) that will hurt Turnus the most.

In particular, the vicious anger of Juno (*saeuae Iunonis ira*, 1.4) is central to the action of the poem. It is aroused in circumstances of threats to her honour rather than of objective moral offence, and at the outset the offences perpetrated by the Trojans against her status are listed:

> The reasons for her anger and the cruel bitterness had still not passed from her mind; deep in memory were implanted the judgement of Paris, the insult in the rejection of her beauty, her hatred of the race, and the seduction and honouring of Ganymede.

> necdum etiam causae irarum saeuique doloris
> exciderant animo; manet alte mente repostum
> iudicium Paridis spretaeque iniuria formae
> et genus inuisum et rapti Ganymedis honores.   (1.25–8)

She has the inherited family *disposition* to this particular passion, as her brother later comments: 'You are truly sister of Jupiter and second child of Saturn – so great are the waves of anger that you set turning in your heart' (*es germana Iouis Saturnique altera proles – | irarum tantos uoluis sub pectore fluctus*, 12.830–1). The immediate offence which hardens her disposition, already greatly affronted and deeply resentful, and which gives the impulse to a violent outburst, is the idyllic scene of the Trojans sailing on a tranquil sea from Sicily to Italy. This voyage is to initiate a train of events that will eventually lead to the destruction of Juno's favourite city, Carthage. The

---

[8] Servius understands mind (*animus*) as *thumos* here; 'in heaven' (*caelestes*) emphasises the surprise that they should be subject to the same passion as the 'lower spirits' (*inferi*), notably the Furies.

eruption of her anger at this sight takes the form of a vicious speech
(the first means of retaliation, as Aristotle had noted), and then a
cruel plan of action, expressed physiologically in a context of
destructive bodily heat.[9]

The *cognitive* aspect of anger also emerges here. The example of the
irate goddess illustrates the ways in which Aristotle perceived the
intellectual element of this passion. There is the firm belief, based on
evidence real or imagined, that an offence has been committed, a
judgement made that the offence or insult was deliberate, and the
specific target, the offender, recognised as responsible. The intellectual aspect is also revealed in the detailed strategy, cunning and
bargaining with which Juno carries out her retaliation on Aeneas and
the Trojans through the poem, and in her finally succumbing to
persuasion: 'Juno agreed to these conditions and happily changed
her attitude' (*adnuit his Iuno et mentem laetata retorsit*, 12.841). Juno thus
presents a classic case of Aristotelian anger taken to vicious excess.
First, she has a disposition prone to temper; then, when she meets
with a series of offences that are viewed as threatening to her status
and person, her inward resentment is exacerbated. A final incident
drives her to erupt, almost literally to 'burn up', but there is sufficient
control of her rational faculties for her to plot revenge with cunning.
Eventually, having achieved most of her objective and pleased with
the outcome, she ostensibly yields to reason and withdraws from the
scene.[10]

Aristotle, in his discussion of the cognitive aspect of anger, also
highlighted the influence of counter-persuasion or counter-evidence
to affect judgements and assessments so that the anger might be
assuaged. This was a key feature of the *Iliad* as various attempts were
made to bring Achilles back into the fighting. Phoenix, for example,
used the precedent of Meleager as a means of persuasion in *Iliad* 9,
and, although Achilles was not won over from his anger at this stage,

[9] See 'on fire because of these' (*his accensa*, 1.29), 'with heart inflamed' (*flammato corde*, 1.50),
'grim Juno blazes' (*urit atrox Iuno*, 1.662). On speech as the first retaliation, see *Rh.*
1380b18–19 (Achilles' well-known substitute for assault in *Il.* 1); on physical retaliation, *NE*
1130a31, and on the biological heat, *de An.* 403a25–32. There is a similar description of
Juno's instrument, the Fury Allecto, in charge of 'anger and treachery' (*irae insidiaeque*), who
'burnt up in anger' (*exarsit in iras*, 7.445).

[10] On the pleasure principle, see Aristotle *NE* 1126a21–2: 'revenge provides release from anger
by substituting pleasure for pain', and *Rh.* 1378b6–10: 'pleasure accompanies anger because
people dwell on their revenge in their thoughts'. Thus Aeneas in the 'Helen' episode: 'it will
give pleasure to have satisfied my mind with avenging fire' (*animumque explesse iuuabit* | *ultoris*
flammae, 2.586–7), and 'glorying in pleasure' (*laetitia exsultans*, 12.700).

the embassy would have had no point if there were not some expectation that anger is amenable to reason.[11] Conversely, as Aristotle was aware, skilful oratory can stimulate anger, not so much by mindless rabble-rousing as by the presentation of argument and evidence to support a case for retaliation. This can be seen in two examples of the epic topos of breaking a truce: the disguised Juturna in *Aeneid* 12 makes a sophisticated speech appealing to intellect and emotion to arouse the anger of the Rutulians, whereas Athena had personally tempted Pandarus in *Iliad* 4 with a suggestion of future fame and lavish gifts.[12]

In his discussions on anger, Aristotle at one point analysed a situation in which there might be no possibility of redress, or in which the retaliator could not match the offence because of physical weakness, inferior status, or force of circumstance. The offended then has to ignore or make light of the offence, or transfer the retaliation, 'taking it out' on a more innocent but more vulnerable target, or else turn it inwards to fester as resentment or hatred. When people suppress anger, they are not susceptible to reason because the complaint is not obvious, and, Aristotle suggested, 'to digest one's anger within oneself takes time; those like this are most troublesome to themselves and to those dearest to them'. He recognised that self-directed anger may lead eventually to self-mutilation and even suicide, a further wrong in itself and a crime against the community in the loss of a valued individual. Perhaps Aristotle had in mind Electra (where years of resentment and the thwarted desire for revenge subverted her youth and beauty) or Ajax (whose self-disgust at his failure to redress the insult to his honour led to suicide), but the idea is applicable also to Dido.[13] Her verbal assault on Aeneas consumes all her physical strength, and yet fails. Her inner conflict is then well described: 'Her anxieties double, again love rises up and rages, swirling in a great flux of anger' (*ingeminant curae, rursus resurgens*

---

[11] Different (unsuccessful) methods of persuasion were used in turn by Odysseus, Phoenix and Ajax. In the *Aeneid*, Charon's anger is overcome by persuasion, supported by the evidence of the golden bough: 'then his swelling heart settled after his anger' (*tumida ex ira tum corda resident*, 6.407).

[12] Cf. *Il.* 4.93–103 with *A.* 12.229–37, and Aristotle on the use of rhetoric to arouse anger, *Rh.* 1380a2–3.

[13] See *NE* 4.5, and 1138a9 in 5.11. Dido blames herself ('die as you deserve', 4.547), although the poet exonerates her ('since she died not by fate nor by a death deserved', 4.696). Amata, Latinus' wife and mother of Lavinia, is in some respects a similar case: she blames herself for the war between Trojans and Italians (12.600), and anger against herself drives her to suicide.

| *saeuit amor magnoque irarum fluctuat aestu*, 4.530–1). This is followed by an impassioned but rational assessment of her predicament, the listing and elimination of possible courses of action, and the final acceptance of suicide as the only available course of action. Famously, for her as for Ajax, the inner resentment, finding no release, continues even after death.[14]

The philosopher's explanation of anger as 'desire for retaliation', which was shown to involve cognitive elements of belief, judgement and assessment, needs to be complemented, as Aristotle recognised, by the biologist's answer. The physical aspect is revealed in the open and immediate response to a threat which is perceived as coming from a particular individual, and, in the metabolism of the person offended, the response translates into a strong impulse to action. As such, it is healthy and normal, a survival mechanism brought into play when one's status or security is threatened. The virtue of courage needs anger as a stimulant, but one who fails to respond, 'turning the other cheek', is to be despised as simple-minded, servile, and vulnerable to exploitation.[15]

The physical effects of the stimulus to anger usually involve increased bodily heat. The blood around the heart seethes, the face takes on a heightened colour and the eyes flash, while the arm has added strength consequent on the release of energy. A similar description is found in contemporary psychiatry:

> If we get angry our body prepares for action. More sugar pours into our system so we have more energy. More blood, containing needed nourishment, is circulated by increasing the blood pressure and making the heart beat faster. More adrenalin is secreted, to dilate the pupils of the eyes and make us see better, and to mobilise other such needed activities.[16]

Usually this build-up is discharged in an immediate reaction, and the body soon returns to normal. It is the contrasting 'cold' response which is a sickness, where the outward effects are a frown, clenched fists and stiffened muscles. Further, if one continues to be inwardly obsessed with the offence there is no relaxation, and retaliation, when it comes, is long drawn out and often cruel.[17]

[14] See *Od.* 11.563–4, *A.* 6.469–72.

[15] See *NE* 1108a4, 1126a3–8; cf. the language of Plato *R.* 375b–e, 440c–d and *Plt.* 307e.

[16] From Madow (1972), 73; Madow is Professor of Psychiatry and Neurology at the Medical College of Pennsylvania.

[17] The physical effects of the 'hot' and 'cold' responses are listed in detail in the pseudo-Aristotelian *Physiognomica*, a treatise which was very popular in the Middle Ages and which

When retaliation is swift, effective and justified there are psychological and social advantages. The pain arising from the disgrace which ensues on the offence turns to pleasure when the retaliation is successful. 'Revenge is sweet' ('sweeter than honey' in the Homeric phrase),[18] and, once the present pleasure has counterbalanced the previous pain, there is a restoration of the body's equilibrium. Similarly, on the social level, when the offence has been avenged, whether verbally in a public apology, by compensation, or in some appropriate physical retaliation or punishment, justice is seen to be done and social harmony re-established. But if there is further counter-aggression then a vendetta results, and, where the emotion is extended from an individual to a crowd, collective anger at a perceived offence becomes a riot, and, on a national scale, leads to war.

In the *Aeneid*, in some contexts the impulse to action is provided by the aggravation of anger from an outside source (as rumour rouses Iarbas to his diatribe against Jupiter) (*[fama] aggerat iras*, 4.194), or internally, as when the boxer Entellus works himself up to return to the fight after a fall: '... he roused strength from anger' (*uim suscitat ira*, 5.454). This considered entry into a state of rage and its subsequent enhancement is the way in which the warrior acquires the impetus to engage in the horror of battle. It is, as such, a survival mechanism, and is not necessarily reprehensible in itself, given the need for defence against attack. The deliberate arousal of anger as a stimulus to action is, after all, a standard aspect of military training (and sports coaching). The two major combatants in the *Aeneid* act in this way: 'No less [than Turnus] did Aeneas meantime, ruthless in his mother's armour, sharpen the spirit of war and rouse himself with anger' (*nec minus interea maternis saeuus in armis | Aeneas acuit Martem et se suscitat ira*, 12.107–8).[19]

The same principle is at work on a broader scale in the various descriptions of riots in the poem. The first instance is in a simile of a Roman assembly when the crowd grows violent and rage (*furor* as an

---

influenced Descartes' *Les passions de l'âme*. On malingering retaliation, see *NE* 1126a13–21, Calchas on the postponed revenge of kings, *Il.* 1.80–3, and the 'promised day' of Cybele's action against Turnus, *A.* 9.107.

[18] *Il.* 18.110, quoted by Plato *Phlb.* 47e and Aristotle *Rh.* 1378b7; on the 'pleasure principle', see n. 10 above.

[19] Servius takes 'ruthless' (*saeuus*) as 'brave' (*fortis*) here, and contrasts Aeneas' need to make a deliberate effort to be angry with the more spontaneous outburst of 'anger' (*furor*) in Turnus.

intensified form of *ira*) provides weapons (*furor arma ministrat*, 1.150). In Book 5, the Trojan women in their frustration at always being on the move (which Juno uses for her own ends) make torches from the hearth fires and rush off to burn the ships, driven on by rage (*actae furore*, 5.659). In Italy, the Latin women, led by Amata, are angry at the wrong done to Turnus by Aeneas' betrothal to Lavinia, and the resulting *ardor* and *furor* drive them to take to the hills and act like Maenads. Then the local country people are enraged at Ascanius' shooting of a pet deer, and 'anger made a weapon of what anyone could find' (7.508). A last example here is the Rutulians' preparation for war on hearing of Aeneas' arrival: 'Anger is roused by the sudden shock. Weapons in hand they call for in haste, for weapons the young men clamour' (*arrectae stimulis haud mollibus irae, | arma manu trepidi poscunt, fremit arma iuuentus*, 11.452–3).

In the individual then, in the group and in the nation, *ira* and *furor* can be seen to act as survival mechanisms, providing the stimulus to aggressive and defensive action when a perceived wrong threatens status or security.[20]

IV

It has been shown from Plato and Aristotle that the praiseworthy anger which characterises heroic temper, and which is necessary for this survival of individual and state, can be taken to excess. Then it subverts rather than supports reason, so that the mind is no longer in control and no opportunity is available for rational decision-making; purposeless aggression ('the madness of war', *insania belli*) results. This is how Aeneas and Turnus appear in their first participation in the action of the poem; the language is similar, and the impetus to irrational action is presented in both cases as the result of an extraordinary intervention during a deep sleep. Turnus is visited by the Fury Allecto, who, on Juno's orders, is intent on initiating hostilities between the Trojans and Italians. When snubbed by Turnus, she blazes into anger (*exarsit in iras*) and hurls a firebrand at him. He awakes ready now to fight: 'Weapons in madness he roars for, weapons he looks for by the bed and through the house; love of steel rages and the cursed madness of war, anger above all' (*arma amens fremit, arma toro tectisque requirit; | saeuit amor ferri et scelerata insania*

---

[20] In this sense of aggressive urge, *ira* may be applied to animals, e.g. wolves (2.355 and 9.62), a snake (2.381), a boar (10.708); and a bull (12.103).

belli, | *ira super,* 7.460–2). The scene recalls the apparition of Hector with his admonition to Aeneas on the night the Greeks invaded Troy, and Aeneas' morning awakening:

> Weapons in madness I seize, yet with no rational plan for weapons, but the spirit burns to round up a gang of friends to fight and rush with them to the citadel; rage and anger drive the mind headlong, and glorious death in battle is the only thought.

> arma amens capio, nec sat rationis in armis,
> sed glomerare manum bello et concurrere in arcem
> cum sociis ardent animi; furor iraque mentem
> praecipitat, pulchrumque mori succurrit in armis.   (2.314–17)

The physiological aspect of such anger increases in proportion to its vehemence, with a marked rise in bodily heat, especially in the blood or the heart area. Modern medical practice recognises this as heightened blood pressure and *angina pectoris*, but a second area affected is the head, with the symptoms of red eyes, flushed cheeks and sharp pains gripping the temples or going through the head.[21] The Homeric description of an angry Agamemnon (from *Iliad* 1.104) is given added significance in the Aristotelian (and medical) context of the raised temperature, in Virgil's lines on Turnus: 'He is driven by this rage, sparks fly from all his face as he burns, and his flashing eyes dart fire' (*his agitur furiis, totoque ardentis ab ore* | *scintillae absistunt, oculis micat acribus ignis,* 12.101–2). Aeneas also appears literally 'on fire', the effect enhanced by his splendid armour, but here a simile adds a sinister note:

> The top of his head is burning, the plume of his helmet is on fire, and the golden boss on his shield spouts leaping flames; it is like the blood-red glow of comets portending disaster on a clear night, or the star of Sirius that brings thirst and plague to suffering humanity, flooding the sky with a grim and menacing glow.

> ardet apex capiti cristisque a uertice flamma
> funditur et uastos umbo uomit aureus ignis:
> non secus ac liquida si quando nocte cometae
> sanguine lugubre rubent, aut Sirius ardor
> ille sitim morbosque ferens mortalibus aegris
> nascitur et laeuo contristat lumine caelum.   (10.270–5)

---

[21] See Aristotle *de An.* 403a22–32; Madow (1972), 73–4 (referring also to the colloquial phrases 'pain in the neck', 'blowing one's top'); and Hillmann (1992), ch. 10, 'Emotion and Physiological Location', quoting Darwin (126): 'until the bodily frame is affected one cannot be said to be enraged'.

So far Aeneas and Turnus have been portrayed in accordance with the Aristotelian pattern, comparable in that their anger stimulates aggression and they are affected by accompanying biological changes, which will give them the strength needed for great deeds of retaliation. In the two characters, the anger may initially overwhelm reason under what is presented by the poet as extraordinary influence, but only temporarily. Turnus' complex psychological state, for example, is described in terms similar to those used for Dido:[22] 'In one heart – sense of honour, grief and madness mingled, love harassed by rage, and awareness of true worth' (*uno in corde pudor mixtoque insania luctu | et furiis agitatus amor et conscia uirtus*, 12.667–8). Yet, in his case, the maelstrom of emotions clears, reason regains control (*discussae umbrae et lux reddita menti*), and a conscious, courageous decision is made. Similarly, Aeneas shows, at first, frustration and anger when Lausus dares to stand in the way of the pursuit of the wounded Mezentius:

> Aeneas is enraged ... higher and higher swells the anger of the Trojan leader, and the Fates draw to the end the threads of Lausus' life; for Aeneas drives his powerful sword straight through the young man, and buries it up to the hilt.

> furit Aeneas ...
> ...saeuae iamque altius irae
> Dardanio surgunt ductori, extremaque Lauso
> Parcae fila legunt; ualidum namque exigit ensem
> per medium Aeneas iuuenem totumque recondit. (10.802, 813–16)

But, immediately afterwards, the mood changes – Aeneas expresses pity for the dying boy, praises his courage and loyalty to his father, and allows him honourable burial.

This matching of the psychology of anger for Aeneas and Turnus continues through from their first appearances to the final engagement of their two armies:

> Both keyed up, Aeneas and Turnus tear through the battle-lines; now, now anger seethes within, hearts that do not know how to bear defeat are breaking, now with all their strength there is a rush to wound.

> non segnius ambo
> Aeneas Turnusque ruunt per proelia; nunc, nunc

---

[22] Cf. Dido's conflict of emotions (4.530–1) and the comparable psychic state of Mezentius (10.870–1).

fluctuat ira intus, rumpuntur nescia uinci
pectora, nunc totis in uulnera uiribus itur.   (12.525–8)

Here the concept of 'unconquerable hearts' introduces the final
question of Virgil's understanding of 'righteous anger' (*iusta ira* and
ferox uirtus), and the relevance of this to the Aristotelian virtue of the
midway disposition (the *mesē hexis*) between excess and deficiency.
Aristotle had defined the virtuous ('mean') state as that in which one
is angry 'as one should be' (*hōs dei*), that is, with an appropriate
target, in the proper circumstances, for an appropriate duration and
in a fitting manner. In situations where such conditions are fulfilled
the anger is praiseworthy and the consequent retribution duly
exacted, but where there is excess or deficiency of any one criterion,
then there is moral failure and censure is deserved.[23]

It is particularly on this issue that the Stoics parted company not
only with Peripatetic theory but also with the evaluation of epic and
tragic heroism and with ordinary human behaviour. If passions are
to be described in terms of corrupt judgement and mental sickness,
then a Stoic is clearly right to demand their eradication. But this
closes off the central part played by anger in heroic character and
action, and in that conflict of principle which confirms their enduring
interest.

There are two occasions when it seems that Aeneas is following a
pattern of aggressive action beyond the restraints of reason, and,
therefore, reprehensible in Stoic terms. In the last book, after the
Italians have broken the treaty and Aeneas has been wounded, he
returns to the fight in a mood like that of Achilles:

> Then it is that anger swells ... now indeed he charges into the
> middle ranks, and, with the War-god on his side, starts a cruel
> and indiscriminate massacre, a terrifying figure giving his anger
> free rein.

tum uero adsurgunt irae ...
iam tandem inuadit medios, et Marte secundo
terribilis saeuam nullo discrimine caedem
suscitat, irarumque omnis effundit habenas.   (12.494, 497–9)

The language of his final killing of Turnus is similar: 'Burning with
rage and terrifying in his anger ... he buries his sword deep under
the heart of his opponent in ferment' (*furiis accensus et ira | terribilis ...
ferrum aduerso sub pectore condit | feruidus*, 12.946, 951–2).

---

[23] *NE* 4.5. See also text to n. 6 above.

This looks like the unacceptable face of anger, beyond the Aristotelian mean and into its violent 'excess', the only form of anger recognised by the Stoics. Yet the choice of the adjective 'in ferment' (*feruidus*) here for Aeneas, and its strong position at the beginning of the line, is immediately reminiscent of the great exemplar, Hercules, similarly described as raging (*furens*) and showing raging anger (*feruidus ira*), as well as grinding his teeth, in his pursuit of the monster Cacus. This account in Evander's earlier narrative of the physical manifestations of Hercules' anger showed how the passion had to work through the body to provide the stimulus for the muscular effort required to shift the massive flint-rock above the cave of Cacus, and then to overcome the monster with bare hands.[24] As a result of this victory, Hercules received from a grateful people the divine honours of altar, sacrifice and banquet near the future site of Rome. Aeneas had been invited, quite literally, to follow the example of Hercules, and, like him, and as a forerunner of Romulus and of Augustus himself, he was due to be taken into the company of the gods as fitting recompense for his part in the Roman foundation. If Putnam is right to tie Virgil to the blanket disapproval of anger required by the Stoics, then the poet would be presenting Hercules and Aeneas as well as Turnus as outright Stoic failures in the expression of their heroism; and this is surely questionable.

When Cicero compared the Peripatetic view of anger unfavourably with that of the Stoics in his discussion of passions in *Tusculans* 4, he called anger the most degrading of vices, and the clearest manifestation of madness (*insania*). He quoted with approval Chrysippus' official Stoic definition of courage (*fortitudo*) as a 'disposition of soul in suffering and enduring', involving an aspect of reason which did not require the support of anger, and which rejected its physiological changes (heightened colour, flashing eyes, heavy breathing) as incompatible with a sound mind. In general, Cicero tends to emphasise the mental disorder that the Stoics find in the passions by translating the Greek *pathos* (which is neutral in its root meaning of 'being affected' in some way) by the Latin words 'sickness' (*morbus*) and 'disturbance of mind' (*perturbatio mentis*). Here, somewhat unfairly, he uses the phrase 'war-like anger' (*bellatrix*

---

[24] See 8.225–71, esp. 228–30; there is a comparable description of Dido's outward appearance (flushed cheeks and red eyes) indicative of her increased physical strength as 'furious' (*furibunda*) she runs through the palace, climbs the high funeral pyre and unsheathes the sword, 4.641–6.

iracundia) for the Aristotelian mean, which, in Virgil, appears more accurately as 'righteous anger' or 'fierce courage'. Cicero concedes that, if anger could be justified, and if some irascibility does indeed characterise the heroic temper, then the Stoics would be involved in a contradiction, forced by their strict dichotomy to admit that vice is virtue.[25]

To support the Stoic position that anger is not an essential ingredient of courage Cicero cites a series of examples of victors from the Roman past who showed no emotion in their struggles. In addition, he gives as an illustration from epic the duel of Ajax and Hector in *Iliad* 7, in which the two combatants address each other with calm courtesy before engaging, and even during the fighting show no anger or frenzy.[26] The problem here, of course, is that this incident is more in the nature of an interlude, ending in an honourable draw and exchange of gifts. If the fighting throughout the poem and the final duels were conducted in a similar fashion, the audience would soon lose interest. Indeed, without the wrath of Achilles there would be no *Iliad*, and the *Odyssey* would fail in structure and purpose if an angry Odysseus did not exact final retribution on his wife's suitors.

When it comes to an assessment of Virgil's position, it is clear that he is explicitly aware of the Homeric precedents in presenting anger as an aspect of heroic character and as a major stimulus to heroic action, with the accompanying mental attitude and physical features that the passion entails. In the *philosophical* groundings of the anger attributed to mortal and immortal agents and portrayed in a wide range of circumstances, the various Aristotelian criteria may profitably be applied without the need to claim any explicit derivations. If the *Aeneid* is freed from close linkage with Stoic theory on this issue, there is an opportunity to show that Virgil is sensitive to the special status that the passion has in the philosophical as well as epic tradition; that he makes use of the opportunities which Aristotle established for analysing both the physiological and cognitive aspects of anger, and that his poetry provides a context for a recognised psychological mechanism for individual survival and social justice.

---

[25] *Tusc.* 4.48–54, 79–80; on the disposition to anger and the problems with the translation of *pathos*, see Cicero *Fin.* 3.32 and 35, and the commentary of M. R. Wright (1991).

[26] *Tusc.* 4.49, *Il.* 7.211; the only Virgilian example comparable to Cicero's cold historical figures is that of Brutus condemning his sons to death (6.817–23), which the poet implicitly criticises.

CHAPTER 10

'Envy and fear the begetter of hate': Statius' 'Thebaid' and the genesis of hatred

Elaine Fantham

HATRED. A mental state of revulsion from something that offends us – a dislike or feeling of ill will, intensified by the desire to harm or injure or make a speedy end of the object hated ... this applied in chief to hatred of persons by persons, at the root of which lies *the desire to destroy*. (W. L. Davidson, *Hastings Encyclopaedia of Religion and Ethics*)

In discussing the treatment of psychology (or ethics) in Roman creative literature it is not always easy to reconcile the approach of philosophers, whose primary interest is in the reception of Hellenistic ethics and psychology, with that of literary interpreters who start, as I do, from the desire to understand the motivation of a poetic text. Previous work on Senecan tragedy and Lucan[1] has made me sceptical of claims for a primarily ethical and specifically Stoic motivation of their tragedy and epic: instead, their characterisation appears to me rooted in the psychology of the poetic tradition and the ethics of a Roman cultural code that was only partly affected by Stoicism. However, even without positing a Stoic purpose, the student of Lucan and Seneca must recognise that Stoic conceptions of the human mind and human behaviour contributed to the way in which both poets retell both myth and history.

I

This chapter focuses on Statius' *Thebaid*, a work written a generation after Seneca and Lucan and clearly reflecting their influence. Statius himself came from a different milieu from that of the Annaei, more Hellenic, and at the same time more concerned with professional

---

[1] See Fantham (1982) and (1992a).

technique and the literariness of poetry. Yet the single extended study of his epic in English, Vessey's *Statius and the 'Thebaid'*, identifies the poem as a Stoic epic. Vessey bases this claim on very little argument beyond the eschatology of a fated sequence of events (*fatorum series*) that entailed each successive disaster.[2] But a far more distinctive aspect of Stoic doctrine is its psychology. Passions dominate Statius' poem and fuel each new phase of its action, but is their representation Stoic? The Stoics believed that the soul had a single nature. In its most extreme form, Stoic theory argued that passion in the soul afflicted and destroyed its reason, in turn infecting the reason of others and blighting its environment. Hence, a truly Stoic epic would surely have to represent all passions as destructive both of the psyche and of the society in which they are harboured.

In contrast, Greek popular morality, as reflected in tragedy and in the ethical writings of Aristotle, accepted the loyalties and enmities of communities, clans and other groups, and singled out only the extreme and isolated passion of an Ajax or a Medea for condemnation. To understand how hatred functioned in Greek tragedy, one must consider the language used to describe the passion and the gestures and behaviour associated with it, invoking the incidental judgements of chorus and onlookers and matching them against the views of the origin and social function of hatred found in oratory and popular ethical texts. For Aristotle, emotions such as anger and hatred could be 'reasonable', warranted by certain types of provocation and useful in ensuring the defence of innocence and punishment of evil. Socrates (or Plato who recreated him) may have been the only major thinker who did not tolerate the negative passions of anger, envy, vengeance and hatred as useful forces in certain circumstances of the life of man and society.

Let us ask first where hatred belongs in the chart of the emotions. Aristotle recognises it as a passion distinct from anger and envy, but treats anger as the dominant passion.[3] Cicero's advocate Antonius in

---

[2] Vessey's over-schematisation is criticised by both Ahl (1986), 2810, and Feeney (1991), 338 n. 38. Billerbeck too (1986) finds few traces of Stoicism in Statius, and even her Stoic interpretation of Menoeceus must be disputed (see n. 54 below).

[3] See Arist. *NE* 2.5, 1105b21–3: 'By *pathē* I mean appetite, anger, fear, confidence, envy, joy, affection, *hatred*, longing, emulation, pity ...' In 1107a 9–11, he mentions 'emotions whose very name connotes baseness, e.g. spite, shamelessness, envy'. Does this extend to hatred? Cf. also *Rh.* 2.4. 1381b30ff.:

the nature of enmity (*echthra*) and hating (*misos*) is evident from the opposites [of what has been said about friendship (*philia*)]. Anger, spite and slander are productive of enmity. Now anger comes from what affects a person directly, but enmity also from what is not directed

De oratore groups together hatred, anger and envy – though *inuidia* is something more than envy – and ventures that *inuidia* ('ill will') is perhaps the strongest of all emotions.[4] Given the concern with anger in both the philosophical and the rhetorical tradition founded by Aristotle, I hoped that analyses of anger in the *Rhetoric* or *Nicomachean Ethics* might cast incidental light on hatred and help me to understand how the philosophical tradition distinguished between the two levels or modes of passion. What these *pathē* have in common is ill will directed at an individual; where they differ seems to be in motivation, duration and degree. Can one feel anger without hatred? Surely. Can one feel hatred without anger? Perhaps not: we will see that hatred is often defined as anger grown chronic. What other causes of hatred are there besides anger? Ancient texts often explained hatred as arising from other passions, such as envy and fear, so that it came to be included by the Stoics among secondary passions, 'that have [the dominant passions] as their reference'.[5] What circumstances or relationships foster hatred? Different passages in the expository texts touch on these questions without offering explicit or consistent answers.[6]

Alongside these psychological questions were more important ethical issues, many of them raised in the dispute between radical Stoic thought and Aristotle's successors in the Peripatetic school who believed there could be such a thing as reasonable and even useful emotions. For the Stoics all emotions were 'unreasonable', that is, *pathē* in the strong sense of sicknesses or disturbances of the reason. It will greatly affect the representation of hatred in Roman literature that Stoicism, the predominant school of philosophy at Rome, saw any degree of anger as a mental sickness, to be inhibited even on the

---

against himself: for if we suppose someone to be a certain kind of person, we hate him. And anger is always directed at individuals, while hate is directed also at types ... anger is accompanied by pain, but hate is not accompanied by pain: for the angry person is himself pained, the one who hates is not. One who is angry might feel pity when much has befallen, but one who hates under no circumstance; for the former wants the one he is angry with to suffer in his turn, the latter wants [the detested class of persons] not to exist. (trans. Kennedy)

[4] See *De oratore* 2.206, starting with the antithesis of love and hatred, but associating anger and envy with hatred: ('love') *amor* ('hatred') *odium* ('anger') *iracundia* ('envy') *inuidia*. *Inuidia* itself is paired with 'pity' (*misericordia*), because these two emotions are the basis of the final denunciation or appeal in Roman judicial oratory. See also 2.208: 'If you were to exaggerate whatever is ruinous or harmful to the audience (jury), it creates hatred; but if you build up something harmful to good citizens or to those whom one should least harm, then even if no such bitter hatred is stirred up, it arouses a hostility not unlike ill will (*inuidia*) or hatred.'

[5] See Stobaeus 2.88, 8ff., = LS 65 A.

[6] See nn. 3–4 above and nn. 9, 10, and text to n. 45 below.

battlefield or when one faced the raping of one's wife or murder of one's child.

But if the Romans knew and repeated the Stoic doctrine, they found it difficult to apply consistently. Thus, Cicero closely associates his rather perfunctory account of hatred in the Stoicising *Tusculan Disputations*[7] with the issue whether anger is a prerequisite for successful combat – in battle or the arena. He denies that anger had a role to play in the just retributive killings by Roman heroes known to his audience through Ennian epic or the *fabula Praetexta*: but, in at least one case, the text he cites and his own characterisation weaken Cicero's ethical claims.[8]

Seneca, focusing in *De ira* on Stoic values in a civilian context, also comments more than once on the undesirable nature of hatred, but is even more concerned with the non-moral problems of being hated.[9] Seneca's personal situation and temperament fully explain why he was less concerned in his moral essays with the evil of hating than with being hated.[10] The additional factor in his own life was the correlation between hatred and power. Living at the mercy of a capricious emperor, Seneca himself enjoyed sufficient power and wealth to provoke others' fear and envy. Thus, he was vulnerable to the emperor's hatred for his wealth or his political opposition to imperial decisions, but scarcely less vulnerable to the envy of the powerless for the same wealth and his deceptive appearance of power.

---

[7] See *Tusc.* 4.21, where it is a desire (*libido*) and defined as anger grown chronic (*ira inueterata*).

[8] That of Lucius Brutus, *Tusc.* 4.50. In *Tusc.* 4.21 hatred is grouped with anger, explosiveness, enmity, strife (*ira, excandescentia, inimicitia, discordia*), as a form of passionate desire; but the same passage contrasts raw instantaneous anger with hatred, as anger inured by time (*ira inueterata*); and makes a further distinction between hatred and *discordia*, which is applied to an even more bitter and deep-felt form of ill will. But Cicero's correct Stoic position in theory should be contrasted with his contemporaneous political advocacy of just hatred and rejection of ethical wisdom (*sapientia*) when liberty is at stake in e.g. *Phil.* 13.6 and 16: 'We feel hate and fight in anger, arms cannot be wrenched from our hands ... we would rather suffer the worst hardships than be slaves.'

[9] In *De ira*, Books 1–2, Seneca argues at length against the usefulness of anger in battle (1.12–13). On hatred, he adds these points: the good man does not hate (1.14) and must punish without feeling hatred (1.15); the loathsome features of enmity are incurable once it has hardened from anger into hatred (3.41); hatred is implacable (3.42) and ends in evil delight in the enemy's suffering (3.43). *Epp.* 14 (10–11) and 105 expand Seneca's arguments on the relationship between hatred and the fear and envy felt towards (and sometimes by) those in power.

[10] On the reciprocity of hatred and other negative emotions, see e.g. Sen. *Ep.* 14.10: 'According to the old proverb, we must avoid three things: hatred, envy and contempt; but we have to beware that the fear of envy [being envied] carries us away into contempt [being despised].' *Ep.* 105.3 elaborates the hazards of being feared by slave or citizen, and the inevitable fear that comes from knowing that one is feared.

Lucretius' Epicurean account of the development of society had incorporated the cycle of power, envy, fear and, by implication, hatred, into his account of the rise and fall of absolute rulers.[11] But when Seneca came to write his tragedies, such as *Thyestes* or the incomplete *Phoenissae*, which influenced Statius' *Thebaid*, he was less concerned with the hatred felt by oppressed subjects than with a more extreme form of hatred, based on the contest of equals or near-equals for absolute power. As a poet, he subordinates the legitimate loathing felt towards a tyrant to the unnatural horror of enmity between close kin. Certainly, when Seneca's Eteocles speaks of hatred as the corollary of royal power (*Phoen.* 654–5, cited in text to n. 29 below), he is thinking of the fear-driven hatred of his subjects. But Seneca shows us that power, the desire for power, drives Eteocles' own brand of hatred: although Eteocles (like Atreus) enjoys sole power at the expense of his exiled brother, his passionate enmity will not be satisfied by any extreme of revenge, and is scarcely ended by the death of its object. This is a hatred so deep it can only be resolved by the death *of the hater*.

Seneca is important as the first surviving moralist to experience at close hand the relationship between power and hatred under the principate: he had lived under two tyrants (Caligula, Nero) and been exiled and recalled by the gullible Claudius, who was manipulated by unscrupulous wives and freedmen. After him, other, less political, figures such as Plutarch and Epictetus would also study the patterns of power, jealousy and fear. Hence their work, and that of other imperial authors of this age, renews and develops discussion of the origins of hatred from the other passions that are felt by both the weak and the strong.

But no explicit and extended treatment of hatred and its causes has survived from the periods of Classical Greek and Roman poetry. How then can the modern reader reconstruct this or any other aspect of ancient psychology? Before applying English terms such as 'hatred' or 'enmity' to gloss the speech or action of ancient epic or drama, he or she must take into account the different semantic ranges of the Latin and Greek terms that together cover the spectrum of passion, and examine the range of patterns of behaviour associated by the texts with these terms. It is then possible to move

---

[11] Cf. Lucr. 5.1120–51, especially the role of envy (1125–32) and fear (1140) in the murderous deposition of kings by the common people, because 'whatever is too greatly feared, is trampled with glee', (*cupide conculcatur nimis ante metutum*, 1140).

cautiously forward from the influential Greek versions of the relevant myths to the representation of these passions in the analogous sections of Roman drama and epic.

Thus, my approach to Statius' Theban epic is based on a multiple approach to those Greek tragedies in which hatred seems to be a driving force. The Sophoclean tragedies and Euripides' *Medea* provide both precedents and points of comparison for the power-mad peer hatred of the Theban brothers in Euripides' *Phoenissae*, the late tragedy which seems to have been a model for both Seneca's and Statius' account of the sons of Oedipus.

After outlining what can be learnt from the related Greek and Roman tragedies in the first part of this chapter, we are ready to consider Statius' own genre. I preface the case-study of hatred in the *Thebaid* with some comments on the role of this passion in the *Aeneid*, which deeply influenced the architecture of Statius' war epic and his representation of both human and superhuman embodiments of hatred.

II

The tragic tradition

Since one of the difficulties in recognising hatred or enmity arises from what psychologists call denial – the shame felt by scrupulous men at admitting to themselves and others that they feel enmity or are acting from hatred, rather than from moral indignation or a desire to redress injustice – there may be an additional advantage in returning to Greek tragedy. Although the rhetorical texts of both Greece and Rome display uninhibited hatred, scholars of Greek epic and tragedy have stressed the overt acknowledgement of hatred as a distinctive feature of Greek heroic culture. Stanford tells us, commenting on Sophocles' *Ajax*, that 'in heroic Greece it was considered a virtue to hate enemies';[12] and Dover (1974, 181–2) asserts that 'Athenians took enmity much more for granted ... it was not the Athenian custom to disguise hatred'. Whether we regard the overt hatred expressed by Sophocles' Electra or Ajax or Philoctetes as 'heroic' or 'Athenian', there is no doubt that, as Blundell (1989) has shown, preoccupation with enemies, with enmity and the reciprocity

---

[12] Stanford (1963), 224, commenting on 1336. See also his Appendix F on anger and related terms.

of hatred, is a powerful force in Sophoclean tragedy, perhaps even more dominant than in the surviving Euripidean corpus. As is implied by Blundell's title, *Helping Friends and Harming Enemies*, such hatreds are usually the corollary of loyalties, whether to friends or community. The language of hatred in *Ajax* or *Medea* is closely intertwined with the dramatisation of the ethics of friendship (*philia*): thus, the passion is presented in terms that allow the hater to represent his hatred as 'reasonable'. Gill has argued cogently that, where the hatred involved is so unnatural that it seems unreasonable even to the hater, a special kind of explanation must be supplied in the form of a curse, or guilt-induced madness, that may be personified by a Fury or Furies. A Medea about to kill her children or an Eteocles resolved to kill his own brother will go as far as she or he can to render this (essentially self-destructive) enmity intelligible in terms of social rights and wrongs. But, ultimately, the division of the hater's own personality, and the externalisation of his passion, become a necessary strategy for warranting the action that passion demands.[13]

Lexically, three main roots in Greek cover the range of emotions from routine distaste through aversion to loathing and from routine political opposition or rivalry to murderous hatred. Although they overlap, each root has its own range of usage. In both prose and verse, *echthros*, *echthairein* and *apechthanesthai* ('enemy', 'hate', 'be hated') denote the second category of enmity, the emotion felt towards tyrants, competitors and obstacles to a dominant life-goal. Blundell (1989, 37, 39) notes that 'enmity may range from passionate hatred to blunt acknowledgement of conflicting interests'. Thus, the axiom of Bias of Priene cited by Aristotle *Rh.* 1389b23–5, 'always love as if you were going to hate and hate as if going to love', recognises that this kind of enmity will be terminated by self-interest such as the uniting of former rivals against a common enemy. In domestic and foreign politics alike, such enmity is regular and reversible and something less than we understand by hatred.

Similarly, the verbs *misein* and poetic *stugein*, with their cognates, cover a range of distaste from the trivial to the obsessive. *Misein* ('hate') serves for Aristotle as the opposite to *philein* ('like', 'love'), positive and negative emotion defined in part by the categories of

[13] See Gill (1990), 25–8, on Eteocles in Aeschylus' *Seven Against Thebes* and Medea; and Gill (1983*a*), (1987) for a more detailed analysis of the Medea-monologue discussed on p. 195 below.

persons who are the objects of the affect. As *philein/philia* are felt
towards our own – family, friends, fellow citizens – so *misein/misos* are
used for aversion and fear felt towards the other – women,
foreigners, helots. Such aversion can be trivial: the corpus of
Euripidean fragments is saturated with non-significant uses of *misein*
to register lack of sympathy or disapproval for groups, or their
behaviour.[14] Such hackneyed phrases would seem to mean little
more than a child's petulant 'I hate broccoli', and contribute nothing
to understanding hatred as a passion. Yet the same vocabulary is
used to voice Hippolytus' pathological horror of women. What
distinguishes the singular passion of his misogyny in the extant play is
not a different lexicon but the combination of this with other features
that we shall find significant in tragic and epic haters. Thus,
confronted by the nurse, he begins with a conventional expression of
aversion; but, as her purpose is made clear, this turns to loathing,
and he curses her and her sex with a hatred that he himself conceives
as insatiable.[15] This aversion to an alien class of persons is an entirely
different form of hatred from the enmity of the brothers in *Phoenissae*,
and the difference is clearly shown by the lexicon of the two plays.
Phoenissae is marked by the recurrence of *echthros* (also the noun
echthra, 'enmity', 374) with no instance of *misein* cognates, and one
isolated incidence of *stugein* ('hate') – to which we shall return – in
1,700 lines.

The size of the Euripidean corpus, and the comprehensiveness
of modern computer search, allow the reader to observe general
lexical patterns of this type; for the actual behaviour of those who
hate, we should look to both Sophocles and Euripides. The most
persistent carriers of hatred, Ajax, Electra, Philoctetes, are proud
figures humiliated and powerless, and it is powerlessness to obtain
revenge that has nourished their hatred. But this is not the whole
story. In Sophocles' *Ajax*, the dominant Agamemnon hates Ajax
more brutally, even after his death, than Ajax's rival and peer,
Odysseus. The fullest demonstration of the psychology and ethics of
hatred is given by the debate between Odysseus and Agamemnon
over the body of Ajax. Here the 'proper circumstances for hatred

---

[14] See e.g. Eur. fr. 528.1, *Erechtheus* fr. 50.30 'I hate women who choose their children's lives
before honour', fr. 886.1; 905.1, 'I hate a sophist who is not wise in his own case.'

[15] Contrast *Hipp.* 639, 'I hate a clever woman', with 664–6, 'Be damned: I will never be sated
with hating women, even if someone claims I say it always and incessantly: for they too are
always evil.'

and enmity' are defined, and a criterion emerges for measuring extreme hatred that will be used more than once by Seneca and by Statius in the *Thebaid*: extreme hatred pursues the hated one even in death and violates the ordinances of the gods to satisfy its passion. When Agamemnon is led by hatred of Ajax to refuse burial to his old enemy and gloat over his power to harm the corpse, it is Odysseus who argues that to deny the dead hero burial harms not Ajax but justice and the laws of the gods (*Ajax* 1332–45). Besides debating the ethical issues here, Sophocles is also portraying the different moral natures of Ajax's two enemies. The rival Odysseus abandons enmity for pity at Ajax's madness and observes the moral law of respect for the dead; but the brutal Agamemnon is moved only by Ajax's previous impotent enmity to the Atreidae, and seizes on his power as commander-in-chief to exploit his hatred without restraint.

In the Theban myth, as told by Sophocles and Statius, the offence of Creon is materially the same as that intended by Agamemnon; but in *Antigone* Creon acts from the bitterness and insecurity of a new tyrant without authority rather than from personal enmity. A mixture of fear and pride drives him to extend his punishment of the dead traitor to anyone who gives him burial. He had seen Antigone as a welcome bride for his son until her defiance turned his fear to hatred, intensified by jealousy of his son's love when Haemon tries to support her action; it is then that he calls her *misos* ('hated one') to Haemon's face (*Ant.* 760). In the *Thebaid*, as we shall see, Creon's denial of burial will be both a product and a source of hatred: the act that renews the conflict after the death of the brother-enemies. But, throughout the epic, burial and treatment of the dead constitute a locus for the exercise of love or hatred, and a testing of the ethical limits of enmity. It is for this reason that I have put particular emphasis on the issue of hatred in the last scene of the *Ajax*.

I return now to Euripides, using the fully drawn figure of Medea to illustrate how Euripides represents hatred and the hater, before moving to the Theban brothers of the *Phoenissae*. We think of *Medea* as a revenge play, and in both Euripides and Seneca one may choose to stress anger and resentment (*orgē/cholos* : *ira/dolor/furor*) rather than hatred itself, but the figure of Medea, like Electra, shows how a woman's powerlessness has turned anger into hatred. For want of resolution in violence, the thwarted passions of these women develop an almost toxic condition, made more incurable by the external compulsion to conceal them. Thus, Medea's anger cannot be brought to an end: it is *duskatapaustos* (109).[16]

Medea's language also exemplifies how the hater's emotions spill over from their direct object (Jason) to self-hatred and hatred of those who should be dear: she calls both herself (113) and her children (36, 117) 'hateful' (*stugeros*). Her passion is expressed in curses, the most violent verbal manifestation of hatred, comparable to a murderous attack. Indeed, in tragedy and epic the curse is not just an effect of passion: it is a cause and vehicle of destruction. When Medea cries out, 'let the whole family perish' (πᾶς δόμος ἔρροι, *Med.* 114) – a curse also used by Eteocles to express his hatred at *Phoen.* 624 – the curse itself goes into action: in this mythic world it is, paradoxically, both an admission of impotence and a potent, unstoppable force.[17]

In the presence of the man she hates, Medea will neither address him nor refer to him by name: indeed, she treats him as not there, referring to him in the third person (for instance, 'speaking to a bad man/husband', *kakou pros andros*, 498). Typically, the hated enemy is referred to only as 'this person' (*hode/hēde*); or by the relationship that he has betrayed: 'but I hate my husband' (ἀλλ᾽ ἐμὸν πόσιν | μισῶ, 310–11). When Medea does name Jason, it is to Aegeus, the outsider, as she simulates the reasoned indignation of a person wronged ('Jason wrongs me, having suffered no harm from me', 692) and, more blatantly, when she has established a rhetoric of enmity (cf. 734; 'my enemies', ἐχθροὺς τοὺς ἐμούς, 767; 'harsh to enemies and kind to friends', βαρεῖαν ἐχθροῖς καὶ φίλοισιν εὐμενῆ, 809) to lend justification to her intent: 'after throwing the whole family of Jason into confusion I shall leave this land' (795).

Jason likewise refuses to name her; in a movement to be repeated in many other plays, he can only convey his bitter passion by echoing her own denunciation and crediting his own emotions to all men and gods: 'O loathed creature, O most hated woman, to gods and me and to the whole race of men' (1323–4). Only in their final exchange is hatred made explicit face to face: 'The gods know your despicable nature.' 'Hate on! I loathe your

---

[16] Cf. 93–5, 117–20, 195–200 and the Chorus' allusion to incurable (*dusiatos*) anger and insatiable (*akoresta*) grudging (635).

[17] In the same way, it was believed that the hateful words of *iambi* such as those of Archilochus had the power to destroy, and legend ascribed to his poems the deaths of Lycambes and his daughters. See Lefkowitz (1981), 27; the theme is explored in Elliott (1960).

bitter utterance.'[18] This direct sensory revulsion, like other allusions to physical aspects of the hated person, is a psychologically acute insight: the hater loathes the sight and sound of those she hates. During the action Medea's passionate hatred has developed from sullen silence to voicing her desire for revenge (767), and then to increasingly obsessive concern with her enemies. The audience is shown how the thought of their gloating mockery drives her on to each destructive act and to the climactic internal conflict of her great monologue (1021–80).

In fact, Medea's speech of decision to kill her children is not strictly a monologue, and Gill (1987, 25–8), in a comparison between the parallel scenes of Euripides' and Seneca's *Medea*-plays, stresses the 'other-related character of the concerns' that fuel her inner conflict in Euripides. Despite the uncertainties caused by varying scholarly excision of parts of this text, it remains the complex speech of a complex person, unable to reconcile her role as mother and avenger, or to dissociate herself completely from the avenging anger (*thumos*). Even the moments of self-address can be seen as part of her sequence of responses to the other people of her world, her husband and her children (ibid. 30–1).

In contrast, the Medea of Seneca's play seems to stand outside herself; Gill notes the features of apostrophe to her passions (909, 916 etc.), and of a self-consciousness that casts self-description in narrative form, employing the third person (910, 927, 948 etc.). He shows how Seneca has subordinated the conflict between maternal and avenging impulses to a sharper clash, between moral and immoral responses, and has marked Medea's determined immorality (*scelus*, 923, 932 etc.) and her 'akratic' acknowledgement of a force that she does not wholly accept. After the onset of madness (958), Medea acts out the infanticide that she has conceived in sanity, finding a resolution between her sense of guilt and her willed immorality by reinterpreting the infanticide as both her crime and her self-punishment, to fuse her moral and immoral responses to the situation (Gill (1987), 31–6).

For the present argument, it is important to amplify Gill's helpful analysis of the Senecan scene, starting from Medea's first words addressed to her *animus* (*thumos*) as itself maddened: 'Why do you delay, my spirit ... you are still in love, mad spirit' (*quid anime cessas?*

---

[18] *Med.* 1373–4. I follow most modern editors in adopting Weil's emendation στύγει (imperative) for στυγεῖ ('you are hated').

... | *amas adhuc furiose*).[19] She is already conscious of her madness (*furor*) at 909, and of the divorce from her own *animus* in 917–19: 'my fierce spirit has, deep within itself, decided on something or other, but does not yet dare to confess it to itself' (*nescioquid ferox | decreuit animus intus et nondum sibi | audet fateri*). The strain of her mental disintegration, conveyed by her image of the storm-tossed sea (939–44), leads to a last resurgence of human tenderness, before *dolor* and *odium* (grief and hatred) take control (952) in the form of her old Erinys, the consequence of her fratricide. 'Grief grows up again and hatred boils; the old Fury looks again for my unwilling hand [or action]. Anger, I follow where you lead' (*rursus increscit dolor | et feruet odium, repetit inuitam manum | antiqua Erinys – ira, quo ducis sequor*, 952–4). Now her madness takes the form of hallucination (958–69), only remitted briefly when she strikes her first child (969–71), but reviving with the second killing (976–7, 982–7). Thus, Seneca sees the passion of hatred as the last step before madness, and depends upon this madness to explain the fact of unnatural crime.

This pointed sequence of hatred, madness and murder is strangely paralleled, twice over, in Seneca's *Hercules Furens*. Instead of Lussa, the personification that interrupts Euripides' drama to bring on Hercules' dementia,[20] Seneca presents the hero's madness and its cause in two phases. First, Juno in the prologue stresses the intensity of her hatred: 'My hatred will not pass away so easily: my violent spirit will urge on undying anger' (27–8), and, 'Anger, go on, go on and crush him as he dares great deeds: confront him, tear him to shreds with your own hands: why do you delegate such great hatred?' (75–7).[21] As part of her rising passion she invokes 'Crime, Impiety, Delusion and Madness ever armed against itself' (98) to destroy him, and calls on the Erinyes ('handmaids of Pluto', *famulae Ditis*, 100). Both she and they must first become crazed in order to madden Hercules, and she reproaches herself for failing to reach this madness ('What, not yet mad?', 109). Later, despite an apparent

---

[19] Sen. *Med.* 895–7, accepting Bentley's masculine *furiose* ('mad', 'frenzied') in 897 (with Leo, Zwierlein and most recent editors) over *furiosa*, the common reading of the MSS.

[20] Euripides inserts at *Her.* 823–73 a dialogue between Iris and Lussa, in which Lussa describes how she will cause Hercules' homicidal madness, employing the first person singular, 'I will first kill his children' (865), to affirm her responsibility.

[21] *non sic abibunt odia: uiuaces aget | uiolentus iras animus* (27–8) ... *perge ira, perge et magna meditantem opprime, | congredere, manibus ipsa dilacera tuis: quid tanta mandas odia?* (75–7)

change of plan,[22] she declares outright that she will direct the maddened Hercules' weapons to complete his crime (118–20).

The link between hatred and madness, madness and crime is renewed when her threats are enacted by Hercules' dreadful insanity. Delusions set in at 939, but he does not speak of the Erinyes until 982–6. As in Medea's case, this leads immediately into the language of hatred, as he turns on (his own) children: 'See how the offspring of the hated tyrant cowers, the abominable brood! This hand will soon restore you to your [dead] father.'[23]

In both Senecan dramas, the expression of hatred precipitates or signals the madness that commits the tragic crime. We can see the passion as the internal force that Seneca's figures apostrophise, or again as an external force, which in Hercules' case is represented both by the half-allegorical Juno of the prologue and by the Erinyes who appear to both hero and goddess. This changed representation of passion, in its equation of hatred with madness, as in its equation of crime with madness, is certainly compatible with Stoic thought.

Euripides' portrayal of the mutual hatred of the Theban brothers in the *Phoenissae* follows the pattern of his *Medea*, and again supplies fruitful comparisons for their treatment in both Seneca and Statius. Although Euripides puts the brothers' only stage encounter early (446–637), they are represented in narrative, through the speeches of the two messengers, before (1217–77) and after (1336–1446) the fatal combat. A preliminary scene between Polynices and Jocasta comments on the nature and origin of the brothers' passion. While Polynices includes himself with his brother, seeing the worst aspect of their hatred in their kinship itself,[24] Jocasta first passes judgement on his hatred alone, ascribing it to the ousted brother's envy (539–40), then includes Eteocles in her reproaches: the folly of two men contending for a single prize is the most hateful of evils (580).

Once Eteocles has entered, the brothers communicate only through Jocasta. Neither names the other. To Eteocles, Polynices is 'this man'. He addresses him only when ordering him to leave, which he does four times.[25] As Polynices calls on the gods for justice, Eteocles breaks in 'they loathe you' (606, the only instance of *stugein*

---

[22] On the ambiguities of these lines and the disputed text in 108–9 (*nobis/uobis, furis/furit*) and 112 (*uota mutentur mea/odia mutentur mea*), see Fitch (1987), 153–5.

[23] *ecce proles regis inimici latet | nefandum semen; inuiso patri | haec dextra iam uos reddet* (*HF* 987–9).

[24] 'How dreadful is enmity, mother, between kindred and dear ones' (374).

[25] 'This man' (*hode*), 451, 511, 514, 523. Polynices uses the same form at 473, 479, 481 and 487. Eteocles uses the second person for the first time at 593, then at 604, 613 and 636.

in the play), and the dialogue reaches the final stage. At the high point
– a stalemate like the last encounter of the *Medea* – Eteocles answers
Polynices' threat to kill him by acknowledging the passion ('desire',
erōs, 622) of his own murderous intent,[26] and cursing the whole family
(624). Before their next (off-stage) encounter, Eteocles will extend his
hatred beyond death, prohibiting the burial of his (still living) brother
and imposing this decree upon Creon; even so, his passion spills over
into mistrust and abuse of both Creon and Teiresias.

The patterns that we saw in *Medea* are confirmed in the messenger
speeches. When Eteocles proclaims the single combat to the armies, he
wears his public face and speaks of his brother by name and as
kinsman; there is neither abuse nor accusation. Polynices is equally
correct and – for once – praises his brother's speech (1237). But when
the messenger calls Jocasta to intervene, she never doubts that they
will fight to the death, and that she and Antigone must perish over
their bodies.

In the narrative of the combat (1357–1426), each brother symme-
trically appeals to his warrior goddess (Hera, Athene) to help him kill
his brother, acknowledging the relationship he will violate (1363–6,
1373–6). They fight without quarter, like wild boars;[27] as Eteocles
strips the armour from his wounded brother, Polynices exploits his
feigned helplessness to strike a deadly blow. Only after his brother's
death does Polynices forget his hatred and speak with pity, recalling
the tragic coincidence of *philia* and *echthra* which he lamented at 374:
'Mother, he became my enemy but he was once dear' (*philos*, 1446).

Besides the expression of hatred in word and action, Euripides
calls on several symbols of hatred that Statius will use repeatedly to
articulate the violent passions of the *Thebaid*. We might note the
allusion to the gorgon as symbol of the hated enemy's face,[28] the
Homeric similes of animal hatred (1298, 1380, 1573–4), and the
association of the final combat with Ares and Hades (1576).

Seneca's setting of the confrontation scene is more oblique,
avoiding direct exchanges between the brothers even to the end.
Both brothers are present from the beginning but Jocasta speaks to

---

[26] Compare hatred as 'desire' (*libido*) in Cic. *Tusc.* 4.21, n. 7 above.

[27] *Phoen.* 1371–2, echoed by *Theb.* 11.524–35. Euripides also compares the brothers to twin
beasts (1298) and lions fighting in their lair (1573).

[28] 'Stop your dreadful glare and gasps of anger. | You are not looking at the throat-severed head
| of a gorgon, but looking at your brother who has come. | And you as well; turn your face to
your brother | Polynices', Jocasta to the brothers, *Phoen.* 454–8, trans. Craik. For the gorgon
face as symbol of the enemy, including enemy kinsmen, see Fantham (1992*b*), 101–2.

each in turn; as in Euripides, neither brother names the other and Eteocles addresses Polynices only to order him into exile (652, repeated at 662).

What is conspicuous is how Seneca again holds back the language of direct hatred until the last phase, substituting vocabulary of moral condemnation such as 'crime, evil, guilty' (*scelus, nefas, nocens*). The noun *odium*, the only Latin equivalent of 'hatred', is reserved for Eteocles' final self-assertion: for him (even more than in Euripides) power is all. 'He who fears to be hated does not want to be king: the god who created the universe produced those two evils, kingship and hatred, together: I think it the mark of a mighty king to suppress even men's hatred.'[29] We do not know how this unfinished play would have continued or reached its climax, but the climax of the present text is the yoking of hatred with the prize of kingship.[30]

III

The epic tradition

If Statius absorbed from Euripides and Seneca the characterisation of his hateful brothers, the Theban tragedies are not the sole source of the role played by hatred in his epic. It is from his revered Virgil that he developed the whole infernal and supernatural apparatus of the war – hatred and conflict.[31] In this connection, Virgil's Book 7 is the most influential, as peaceful peoples are driven to war by the cumulative evil generated by Allecto at Juno's command. Juno herself is the main vehicle of hatred in the *Aeneid*, marked by three of the thirteen instances of *odium/odia*;[32] and it is she who invokes Allecto, the loathed deity whom even her own kinsmen abhor, because Allecto can send loyal brothers to arms against each other

---

[29] *regnare non uult, esse qui inuisus timet.* | *simul ista mundi conditor posuit deus* | *odium atque regnum: regis hoc magni reor* | *odia ipsa premere* (654–7).

[30] This restriction of its use is also true of Seneca's other hateful brother, Atreus. The word *odium/odia* is held back until the climax of his premeditation of the crime (*Thy.* 323, 329) when he declares it his mission to carry on active hatred. *odium* serves as leitmotif on two more occasions: in the deception scene at 493–4 and 511, and when Thyestes learns of his children's murder: 'Is this how you lay down your hatred? (*sic ponis odia?*) Yet I beg my brother for their burial which can be granted without cancelling your crime or hatred (*odium*)' (1025–8).

[31] For the multiplicity of influences on Statius, compare Feeney (1991), 344 n. 107: 'Statius has two mighty progenitors, Vergil and Ovid, together with two godfathers, Seneca and Lucan, and a grandfather, Homer.'

[32] 1.668; 5.786; 7.298. To her the Trojans are 'the loathed race' (*gens* | *stirps inuisa*, 1.28; 7.293).

and pervert families with hatred.[33] Besides Juno and Allecto, only
evil men hate or are hated: the tyrants Pygmalion (1.361) and
Mezentius (10.692, 853, 905), the demagogue Drances (11.122) and
the lying Sinon, who first claims to have become hated for defending
the dead Palamedes, then falsely swears 'let it be right to hate the
Greeks!' (sit fas odisse uiros, 2.158). Dido's curse, like that of Oedipus
in Thebaid, imposes hatred between others, in this case, the enmity in
war of her descendants against those of Aeneas (4.623). Turnus,
Aeneas' other great adversary, vents his passion in fighting and
begins his last day of life implacable with burning passion,[34] but ends
it begging Aeneas to 'carry hatred no further'.[35]

Of course, Virgil represents many forms of passion close to hatred,
such as blood-lust and rage, through terms for anger and madness
(ira, rabies and furor), by epithets, and more indirectly by speech and
behaviour such as we have seen in tragedy. But he sets the pattern
that will be observed by Senecan tragedy and Statian epic, reserving
the single name of hatred for significant and climactic moments. We
should note too how rare is a speaker's overt declaration of hatred,
as opposed to the poet's own interpretation of his warriors and
contenders. Virgil imposed a decorum on his heroes that might yield
instant fury or indignation, but was sparing in suggesting personal
animosity. And he put those who hated their brothers among the
damned in Tartarus.[36]

---

[33] See A. 7.571, 'loathed deity' (inuisum numen); 327, 'even her father Pluto and her sisters hate
her' (odit et ipse pater Pluton, odere sorores); 336–7, 'You can make brothers who are united by
love go armed into battle and destroy homes with hatred' (tu potes unanimos armare in proelia
fratres | atque odiis uersare domos). As both Whitman (1987) and Rieks (1989), 33–7, have
shown, Virgil's Furies, e.g. Discordia (6.280), are only extensions of the bad pathē (ira, furor,
dolor) whose destructive effects Virgil records more literally throughout A. Virgil's Juno is
clearly a major influence on the representation of Juno in Seneca's HF, discussed in text to
nn. 21–3 above: it is Allecto that underlies Juno's invocation of the famulae Ditis in HF 100.

[34] 'Spontaneously, he burns implacably, and rouses his spirit' (ultro implacabilis ardet | attollitque
animos, 12.3). Cf. 12.9 'Turnus' violence swells up' (gliscit uiolentia Turno); while implacabilis,
like its synonym implacidus ('rough', 'ungentle'), stresses the incurable and unrelenting aspect
of hatred, the verb gliscere (swells) conveys the tumid growth of hatred or blood-lust seen as
libido ('desire'). Both words are used by Statius in imitation of Virgil: see implacabilis ardor
('implacable passion'), Theb. 1.440, and n. 60 below on gliscere.

[35] ulterius ne tende odiis (12.938). Does Aeneas feel hatred, or is this only the bias of Turnus,
interpreting his enemy in his own terms? Aeneas' state of mind in this final act of killing is
the key to the most important modern disputes over Virgil's ethical and political viewpoint:
see Galinsky (1988) and Putnam (1990), esp. 18–19. Putnam usefully correlates the
psychology of anger in Virgil and Senecan tragedy; see also Fowler, Ch. 1, Sect. IV; Wright,
Ch. 9; Gill, Ch. 11, Sect. IV.

[36] A. 6.608: 'here were those who hated their brothers while they were alive' (hic quibus inuisi
fratres dum uita manebat).

But Statius' Thebans were neither Roman ancestors, nor 'heroes' in our modern sense, whose behaviour had to meet a certain level of nobility.[37] The only inhibition upon his display of hostility between warriors or armies was the need to reserve a climactic level of animosity for the inborn and curse-begotten hatred of the sons of Oedipus. The epic announces its theme as 'alternate kingship fought over with impious hatred' (*alternaque regna profanis | decertata odiis*, 1.2), and devotes its opening movement to demonstrating the genesis of Statius' 'more than civil war' in the three realms of gods and men and underworld deities. Even before the first Book is out, we may feel that Statius' war against Thebes is the most over-determined conflict in antiquity – except perhaps the start-up mechanisms of Eumolpus' *Bellum civile*.[38]

I would like to focus on two dimensions of hatred and related passions in the *Thebaid*. The first concerns the diverse strands of passion which Statius feeds into his war narrative, as he strategically distributes surges of anger, blood-lust and hatred through the action up to and beyond the deadly combat of the brothers. The second is the relationship between hatred and supernaturally induced madness, *furor*, that we have already seen in Seneca's criminal protagonists and Virgil's counter-heroes, and the degree of responsibility attributed by Statius to those driven by *furor*.

There can be no doubt about the importance of human hatred as a driving force in the *Thebaid*; in Vessey's analysis of the humours of the leading mortals, he assigns bitterness and hatred to Oedipus, tyranny (but also hatred) to Eteocles, vengeance and envy to Polynices, and anger to Tydeus.[39]

But hatred and kindred passions animate the gods above even before the appearance of Oedipus and his hateful sons. The grievous anger of Bacchus (11) and the work of savage Juno (12) precede the first human reference, namely that to the unrestrained anger of

---

[37] A reader has reminded me that the figures of Lucan's civil war were also Romans and ancestors of the poet's generation; but, in their vulnerability to hatred and other passion, they are clearly to be contrasted with the republican ancestors. Only Cato is shown as free from selfish passion, but Lucan's own rhetoric makes even Cato's patriotic *uirtus* ('courage') alarmingly passionate.

[38] Note that the crowd of personifications in Petronius' travesty of civil war epic (*Satyricon* 119–24) presupposes that divine personifications of evil and hatred were already a feature of epic a generation before Statius.

[39] Vessey (1974), 66. This is borne out by the blazons of their shields and helmets in *Thebaid* 4. To Polynices' Sphinx and Tydeus' Mars (111), add Hippomedon's representation of the Furies at the wedding night of the Danaids (133).

Tydeus (1.41). At 50, Oedipus in rage at his sons' treatment invokes
the Dirae, and Tisiphone in particular, and in 88 the action passes to
the infernal realm, and to Tisiphone, the personification of vengeful-
ness.[40] With Tisiphone, Statius comes very near to allegory, portraying her in the first full characterising description (*notatio*) of the
epic: her conventional head-snakes, arms and blazing torch en-
hanced by the iron glare (*ferrea lux*) of her eyes and her flesh bloated
with pus and venom.[41] From the poison of her instigation spring the
passions of the brothers: fury, envy at the other's success, and fear,
the parent of hatred:

> Immediately passions are stirred beneath the brothers' breasts,
> and their inherited madness takes over their hearts, and envy
> distressed by good fortune and fear, the begetter of hate. *From this
> source* comes the savage love of ruling, and the violation of their
> turns, and ambition intolerant of the second claim, and the
> sweeter charm of one man standing at the peak of power, and
> strife, the companion of divided rule. (*Thebaid* 1.123–30)

What is this *furor*? Schetter's extended discussion is refined by
Venini.[42] They agree in the range of *furor*, which covers noble
madness, such as prophetic inspiration and heroic self-dedication
(*deuotio*), as well as routine blood-lust in battle and frenzied rage or
hatred.[43] They agree that, in Statius, it is possession by a supernatural being that renders the crazed person out of control (*inops
animi*); but Venini, at least, argues that Statius always makes clear the

[40] Statius calls her *debita uindex*, 'the due avenger' (1.80), just as Virgil calls her the Avenger in
A. 6.570.

[41] 1.103–13. Here the reader should recall Seneca's *notatio* of Anger at *De ira* 2.35.5. He
compares the face of an angry man to 'infernal monsters girded with serpents and with fiery
breath, just as the most loathsome goddesses of the underworld emerge to stir up wars and
spread discord among nations and tear apart peace' and leads on to what seems to be an
inaccurate quotation of *A.* 8.702–3, describing Bellona and Discordia. The face of anger is
that of a Fury. Hence Vessey (1982), 574, calls Tisiphone 'a *figura* of hatred and madness'.
Whitman (1987), 45–6, 55–7, cites both the Senecan *notatio* and the early books of *Theb.* as
examples of 'allegorical tendencies' rather than outright allegory, while Rieks (1989), 25–37,
speaks without qualification of the allegorisation of these evil *pathē* in both Seneca and the
poetic tradition before and after Virgil.

[42] Schetter (1960); Venini (1964), 201–13. On madness in general in Statius, see Hershkowitz
(1994), (1995*b*). Feeney (1991), 348, notes that Statius leads from the personified passions into
a 'naturalistic account of the brothers' discord' but misses the importance of the political,
power-focused, language that follows.

[43] For the link between *furor* and hatred, cf. with 1.126–7, 5.74–5, 'everywhere fierce hatred
and *Furor* and discord reclined even in the very bed'. *Furor* is closely associated with hatred
of the brothers at 7.515, 525; 11.329, 382, 440, 538–9, and (*post mortem!*) 12.444; with the
hatred of Creon at 12.593 and 660. Elsewhere, it most commonly denotes the lust to kill,
whether general or specific.

natural propensity of the human agent for the passion and the actions performed in a state of *furor*. Thus, the brothers' behaviour following the lines which we have discussed is the immediate outcome of Tisiphone's infection, but is also generated by their natures. As Oedipus declares, 'The young men's spirit will not be slow to follow: you will recognise the pledge of my paternity' (1.86–7).

In 1.127 Statius connects the list of passions to specific behaviour with *inde* ('from this source'), an ambiguity designed to blur the distinction between Tisiphone and the bad *pathē* as cause of the hostile actions. Here, the raw emotions are realised in terms of the power-struggle, the obsession with undivided rule, that the poets Seneca and Lucan recognised in Euripides' *Phoenissae*.[44] But note that Statius provides psychological motivation for hatred in the emotions of fear and envy (which Seneca and Plutarch also present as the source of human hatred).[45] For, despite Statius' wording, both *inuidia*, the painful jealousy of Polynices, and *metus*, the fear felt by the tyrannical Eteocles, are to be seen as causes of hatred. Alongside these three negative passions, he adds the evil passion of desire for power (*regendi saeuus amor*) and, matching Eteocles' fear, Polynices' fretful hope (*spes anxia*, 1.322).[46]

But when the poet intervenes in person, rebuking the brothers for their anger (1.155–6), he adds a further motivation besides Oedipus' curse and its infernal agent: the very palace and crown of Thebes are polluted and create hatred, because they have been 'bought at the cost of dreadful frenzy' (*furiisque immanibus emptum*, 1.162–4). The discord and physical separation of the brothers enable Statius to multiply the scene of the action: while his council of the gods gives prominence to Juno's hatred of Thebes (256), on earth Polynices has travelled through a hurricane to reach the porch of Adrastus' palace at Argos. Here, his first act will be to fight with the unknown Tydeus who tries to share his shelter, in mutual and eager hatred (*alacres odio*, 425, cf. 441).

At this point, one could protest that the fight for a shelter in a

---

[44] Cf. 1.150–1, 'naked power drove the brothers to arms' (*nuda potestas | armauit fratres*).
[45] Sen. *Ep.* 14.14–16; 105.10–14; Plutarch, 'How to Profit from your Enemies', *Moralia* 86b–92a.
[46] The last is developed more fully in a new analysis of Polynices' passions in 2.318–20: 'resentment and crazed anger consumed his heart, and the most grievous passion inflicted on mortal cares, hope long delayed' (*exedere animum dolor iraque demens | et qua non grauior mortalibus addita curis | spes, ubi longa uenit*).

palace porch may be a fine symbol of Polynices' greed for sole tenancy of the throne, but the anger of Polynices and Tydeus, though *furor* (1.438), is not hatred. It is quickly dispelled and yields to an equally passionate friendship that will be the most positive aspect of Polynices' character. What the episode does contribute is Tydeus himself, a man driven by anger and so a new source of hating, who will constantly provoke others to warfare and ultimately break the bounds of human decency in victory over an enemy warrior who has not offended against him or the code of battle. The implacable passion[47] of the two newcomers, whose hatred violates the calm of Adrastus' sleep (1.440-1), is there to mark their future careers, and to foreshadow the course of the epic, not to describe the relationship between them. But, by this point half-way through his first book, Statius has set the scene with the forces of hatred in Argos as well as in Thebes, and on Olympus as well as in the infernal realm. It is as though hatred has run mad in the epic, passing beyond the predictable confines of personal grievance to become a self-prolifer-ating infection beyond control.[48]

Thus, the second book introduces new forces for hatred. We meet, in sequence, Laius, driven from Hades to haunt his grandson;[49] Eteocles, roused by Laius from sleep to war-lust; Polynices, torn by resentment, anger and hope (318-20); and Tydeus, who arrives as a provocative envoy to Eteocles, and receives a tyrant's answer. The failure of Eteocles' ambush on the returning envoy serves to renew anger in both Thebes and Argos. Book 3 opens with the accusations and suicide of Maeon, Eteocles' first tyrannical denial of burial (85-98) and the mourning of the bereaved Thebans. In this scene, as in Aletes' brief secondary narrative of the slaying of Niobe's children (3.195-7), mourning is given its rhetorical function of generating *inuidia* ('envy' or 'resentment'), the hatred of those who have suffered against men seen as the cause of suffering.[50]

[47] *implacabilis ardor* (440), a phrase that echoes Turnus' mood in *A.* 12.3; see n. 34 above.

[48] If passion is inherently beyond control within the person, Statius is true to Stoic doctrine in representing it as infecting the body politic and even (by association, *sumpatheia*) nature itself.

[49] This is modelled on the prologue to Sen. *Thy.*, in which Tantalus is driven by a speaking Fury to approach his grandson's palace and infect it against his will.

[50] Cf. 3.214-15, 'these things the old man said and greatly exaggerated the wickedness of Eteocles, calling him cruel and unspeakable, and declaring he would be punished for it', with Cicero's model account in *De oratore* 2.201 of how Antonius roused the *inuidia* ('resentment') of the bereaved families against the commander responsible for their kinsmen's deaths.

Twice, in Book 3 before the expedition sets out, and in Book 7 after the funeral games for Archemorus, Statius constructs a similar sequence that moves from Jupiter's initiative to Mars and his retinue and to the impact of Mars on both warring forces.[51] Mars' role as an embodiment of war-lust, the bloodthirsty charioteer associated with northern Thracian tribes and a personified retinue of terror and panic, originated in the *Iliad* and persists in the *Aeneid*.[52] Thus, Virgil's divine craftsman Vulcan actually separates Mars from the national gods of Rome at Actium in the description of the shield of Aeneas, and sets him between the two naval forces with the Dirae, Discordia and Bellona (8.700–3). Later, Turnus enraged is compared to Mars with his escort of Dread, Anger and Treachery (*Formido, Irae, Insidiaeque*, 12.332–6). Lucan echoed Virgil's more cautious use, evoking Mars only in the climactic simile that compares Caesar's violence in battle at Pharsalus to the god himself (7.567–73).[53]

Statius' Mars is both allegorised and dramatised from the beginning; but there is an escalation both in personnel and in hostility from Jupiter's first initiative in Book 3 to the renewal of desire for war in Book 7. In Book 3, Mars is sent to disturb the inclinations of men for peace so that they will loathe safety (231), and this is shown in parallel action on earth. At one level, Tydeus passes through the Peloponnese, inflaming the communities with hatred of Thebes (3.338), and Statius dilates on the resentment and anger and passion for war that he provokes. At the other level, it is Mars who excites men's hearts, filling them with love of himself. He drives his chariot attended by Fury, Anger, Panic and Rumour, and, while his charioteer lashes Rumour to spread true and false tales, the god himself, filled with hate (*infestus*), belabours her with his spear (3.420–31). In the seventh book, Mars appears in two instalments: first in an almost allegorical tableau at the shrine which he inhabits, surrounded by his retinue of hate-related abstractions, Assault and Wickedness and blood-red Anger, Fear, Treachery, Discord, Threats, most grim Valour (*uirtus*) and gleeful Frenzy and armed Death;[54] then in action, sending Panic ahead from the Isthmus to

[51] On Mars' two levels of being, as allegory and as anthropomorphic Olympian, see Feeney (1991), 367–74.

[52] *Il.* 4.439–40; 5.890ff.; 13.299ff.; *A.* 12.332–6.

[53] Such a mythological simile is rare in Lucan, but is anticipated by the somewhat apologetic comparison of the preparations of the two Roman armies before Pharsalus to the gods arming before the gigantomachy (7.144–50).

[54] Most sinister and significant is the juxtaposition of *uirtus* and *Furor*. Although Billerbeck

outdo Rumour and provoke men and animals alike to violence
(7.105–9).

Parallel but completely independent is Tisiphone's appearance at
7.466–9; her mission is restricted to the sons of Oedipus. Given the
brothers' mutual hatred, it is sufficient that she fills each with
thoughts of his brother enemy, and both of them with the thought of
Oedipus, while Oedipus himself, roused from his confinement,
renews his appeal to the Furies.[55]

Thus, two sources of supernatural provocation are operating in
counterpoint, and, throughout the epic, Mars' provocation of blood-
lust (*furor* and *ira*) will act as a warm-up for the climactic intervention
of Tisiphone. Their effects consistently coincide with the difference
between the honest battle of ordinary mortals and malevolent,
dehumanising hatred. Indeed, for all her vivid personification and
purposive actions, Tisiphone should be identified with the *furor* she
implants in guilty men, that is, with hatred.[56]

Statius' seventh book, then, shares the function of Virgil's seventh,
but motivates his outbreak of hostilities with both Olympian war-lust
and infernal hatred. When Tisiphone's infusion of hatred suffers a
set-back from Jocasta, whose reproaches to Polynices shame him and
his army,[57] Tydeus serves his structural purpose as a force for
conflict. Full of just anger, he reminds the army of their ambushed
comrades, and Polynices of the risk of entering Thebes under safe
conduct from a treaty-breaker. As a climax, he renews hostility in
Polynices with the suggestion that he will put himself in the power of
his brother's hatred (*possessum odiis*, 551). The thought of hatred
begets hatred.

When the army decides again for war, the Fury seizes her

(1986), 3143–4, argues for the Stoic conception of *uirtus* as inspiring the self-dedication of
Menoeceus in Book 10, Ahl (1986), 2848, 2900, more persuasively, argues for Statius'
negative interpretation of both *uirtus* and the Menoeceus episode: 'one's *uirtus* is measured
by one's ability to destroy'. As Feeney (1991), 383–5, shows, *uirtus*, 'death-besotted valour',
will prove kin to *Furor* in the suicide of Amphiaraus and the death-scene of Tydeus (cf. 9.6,
discussed below), as well as the *deuotio* of Menoeceus. It is not Stoic *uirtus* but a very different
quality that animates these heroes: Stoic redefinition of *uirtus* as moral constancy or
endurance left it open to moralists to condemn the brute military valour that traditional
epic still called by the same name.

[55] 'Tisiphone, shaking her twin snakes, runs wild in both camps; she hurls brother against
brother, and father against both: he [Oedipus] aroused, wanders far from his inner retreat
at home, appeals to the Furies and asks to have his eyes back' (*it geminum excutiens anguem et
bacchatur utrisque | Tisiphone castris; fratrem huic, fratrem ingerit illi, | aut utrique patrem: procul ille
penatibus imis | excitus implorat furias oculosque reposcit*).

[56] See Feeney (1991), 346–56, and Venini (1970), on 11.84, and 414.

[57] Statius almost schematically marks the barometer at 7.531, 'instantly anger dwindles'.

opportunity to play Allecto, and in Virgilian mode causes the first bloodshed by provoking the sacred tame tigers of Bacchus to attack the Argive warriors. Once Aconteus has wounded them, and is in turn killed by a priest of Bacchus, all hope of parley is dismissed, and a chaotic battle breaks out. Each of these stages has been marked by the language of anger and the revived force of Mars (7.562–704).

Feeney's important discussion has brought out how Statius colours even the relations of other beings outside Thebes with hostile motives, with hatred, jealousy and rage. This is fully displayed at the opening of Book 8, when Dis, angry that Amphiaraus has been engulfed by the earth and intruded upon the Underworld, protests at the violation of his grim neutrality, his 'restless calm' and his liberty to 'loathe the daylight' (8.44–5).[58] Hating his brother Jove, and grieving at his unequal share of Persephone's year (63–4), he is himself an analogue for the sons of Oedipus.[59] Now – for the second time – Tisiphone is sent back to earth to produce a new kind of evil that will amaze him and provoke her sisters' envy.

Thus, in this proem to the next phase of the epic (Books 8–12) the prospectus is set by Dis, and by the forces of malevolence. The brothers' combat is to be the 'first omens of his hatred' (*nostrique haec omina sunto prima odii*, 69–70), preceded by the cannibal savagery of Tydeus, and the hubris of Capaneus.

Before the brothers' final duel, only one episode will express the full force of hatred. This is the death of Tydeus. Once Enyo renews the fighting, Book 8 is devoted to Tydeus' *aristeia*. When Tydeus confronts and aims at Eteocles, Tisiphone prevents the great moment that could have ended the war. She deflects Tydeus' spear-cast to reserve Eteocles for combat with his abominable brother (687). And it is Tisiphone who sends Tydeus' own war-lust over the brink into inhuman hatred. When he is wounded by Melanippus and tries to retaliate, he precipitates his own death from loss of blood by the sheer violence of his spear-cast, and is dragged from the combat. First, the excess of hate in his character spills over into self-hate; repudiating burial and loathing the body that has merely retarded his fighting spirit, he asks only for the head of his enemy. As he gloats

---

[58] *quid me otia maesta | saeuus et implacidam prohibet perferre quietem | amissumque odisse diem?* But Statius does everything to assimilate Hades' position to that of Polynices, as he asks, 'Which brother has inflicted these battles on me? ... the third lot has cast me down defeated from the mighty vault of heaven' (36, 38–9).

[59] Feeney (1991), 350–2; he also notes the same brother-rivalry in *Virtus'* appeal to Menoeceus (385).

over the severed head, maddened with anger and joy, he swells with lust.[60] Yet Statius gives his word that Tydeus' hatred would have been content to gaze at his decapitated enemy. It is again Tisiphone who demands worse.[61] Statius postpones the horror – so that Pallas herself recoils from her protégé as she sees him suck his enemy's blood and gnaw his brain.

This grisly climax leads to one of Statius' most telling phrases. Tydeus has violated the laws of hatred, *fas odii* (9.4). Even the utterly ruthless Mars, intent on the work of slaughter, turns away, offended by Tydeus' valour (*uirtus*), and steers away his frightened team, while Eteocles compares him to a wild beast, whose naked hatred (*nuda odia*) does not need weapons. Is Statius simply recognising a limit on hatred, as recent critics suggest,[62] or is he establishing a new standard, a new absolute for hatred? Normal battle-lust observes the code in treatment of the dead, but when hatred is truly intense, every code is violated. Hatred itself is *nefas*.

There had been no personal enmity between Tydeus and Melanippus, not even an angry exchange of Homeric taunts. Melanippus' offence began five minutes before his death, but Tydeus hates him because his spear-cast was both furtive and fatal to the champion who could never have been defeated face to face. Surely Statius, like Virgil, has pointedly limited his attribution of hatred to evil creatures and flawed or wicked men?

In the last two books, Statius must achieve a climax of fraternal hatred and show how – against all hope – hatred renews itself and proliferates like a hydra head. It will not cease until Creon dies forty lines before the epic's close.

How can the poet convey the horror of the brothers' mutual loathing after so much anger and bloodshed? He redoubles the supernatural intervention: Tisiphone's great speech (11.76–112) is a key to Statius' interpretation of evil and the Furies' role as embodiment of human evil. The brothers' natures were always prone to

---

[60] The verb is *gliscere* ('swell'), limited in Statius to description of passion, whether battle-lust or hatred (see n. 34 above): it is used in its physical sense only to describe the swollen skin of Tisiphone (1.107). With 8.755, cf. 9.871, the boldness of Parthenopaeus and 12.635, the battle-lust of the Athenians. (At 3.73, where the MSS are divided between *gliscis* | *gestis* ('you swell'/'you desire'), the former may be the correct term for Eteocles' lust for power.)

[61] 'The unhappy man was satisfied; but avenging Tisiphone demands more' (*infelix contentus erat: plus exigit ultrix* | *Tisiphone*, 8.757–8).

[62] Dewar (1991), 59, defines this as 'the limits placed on *odium* by *fas*', and quotes Lactantius, 'hatred should end with death'. Feeney (1991), 360, speaks of 'the poem's clearest example of the Ovidian bounds of definition'.

hatred (*Theb.* 1.86–7); now the Furies are to assimilate themselves to the brothers' passion and to fulfil it in mutual murder.[63] Tisiphone and Megaera each dog their own fighter like insidious seconds: Statius lists the forces struggling to prevent the abominable duel – the common people, Jocasta, Antigone, even Oedipus, and, for Polynices, Adrastus. Jupiter himself averts his eyes and orders the gods to hold aloof.

As the brothers face each other, their words reflect their loathing: confrontation in battle is the only kind of law and compact possible to them (11.390). At this 'vast war of a single womb', all the gods of proper war, Mars, Virtus, Bellona and Pallas with her gorgon – the face of war-rage in so much ancient epic[64] – flee, leaving the field to the Stygian sisters, and the Theban ghosts (410–15).

The combat itself follows the Euripidean contours. At its heat, men can see only the anger and incandescent hatred blazing through the brothers' helmets: they fight like wild boars, and, charged with hatred by the Furies, no longer need the Furies to drive them. The dying Polynices powers his last failing thrust with *odium* (566); Eteocles' last words threaten to sue for his kingdom before the court of Hades and his last act is to fall so as to crush his brother's body (573).

One positive counter-force Statius did reserve for this crisis. Although piety could not overcome hatred in the sons, their father is softened: Oedipus acknowledges the victory of Nature in his own tears for his sons (607).

This passage is perhaps the best key to the problem of human responsibility: here Oedipus claims that it was frenzy (*furor*) and an Erinys who provoked his curse:

> Which of the gods was it who stood by me as I prayed and dictated to the Fates the words snatched from me? It was Frenzy and the Erinys, and my father and mother and the kingdom and my gouged-out eyes: I did nothing.

> > quisnam fuit ille deorum
> qui stetit orantem iuxta praereptaque uerba
> dictauit fatis? Furor illa et mouit Erinys
> et pater et genetrix et regna oculique cadentes.
> nil ego.   (11.617–21)

---

[63] 'Let us fit ourselves to their hatred and to their clashing arms' (11.100–1). For the trans., see Venini (1970), on 11.100; for the evolution of the Furies to represent 'every evil of which human beings are capable', Feeney (1991), 376–7.

[64] Cf. Euripides' symbolic use of the gorgon for the face of the hated brother in *Phoen.* 456–7, n. 28 above.

But if we scrutinise Statius' opening account in detail, the assignment of responsibility is more complex. After describing the avenging Furies (*dirae scelerum*) in Oedipus' breast (1.52) Statius gives him speech. He calls on Tisiphone, 'often accustomed to my invocation' (*multum mihi consueta uocari*),[65] to give her support to his perverted prayer, 'if it is worthy and what you yourself would suggest to me in my frenzy' (*si digna precor, quaeque ipsa furenti | subiceres*, 1.73–4). This becomes even stronger in his final appeal: 'grant me the evil I would long to see' (*da ... quod cupiam uidisse nefas*, 85–6), words that seem finally to weigh the balance of responsibility towards Oedipus. Whatever the weight of past crimes, known and involuntary, that have formed his nature, the present Oedipus wills the evil of hatred between his sons, and Statius makes his responsibility overt.[66] Thus, his denial after the event in 11.621ff. would seem no more convincing than Agamemnon's denial in *Iliad* 19.86–8 on which it is modelled: 'it is not I that am to blame, but Zeus and Destiny and the sky-borne Erinys: they all put a savage frenzy (*atē*) into my mind at the assembly'.

The reader's first reaction is to see Oedipus as deceiving himself in this speech of remorse. But a return to the lines introducing Oedipus' first appearance (1.52ff.) shows that Oedipus' mind was already possessed by the Furies when he called upon them to fulfil the curse on his sons. Ultimately, it is a false distinction to assign responsibility by separating the human agent from the personified passion that informs his acts.[67]

Despite the apparent return of human tenderness, Oedipus cannot shed his guilt, which revives his anger and turns into the very Statian form of self-hate and attempted suicide. As he again invokes the Furies (631), it is left to Antigone to restrain him, while Jocasta stabs herself.

---

[65] 1.58. Statius recalls this in 11.105, where Tisiphone confirms that Oedipus has constantly invoked the Furies.

[66] Cf. Ahl (1986), 'By the end of the prayer he most certainly has taken upon himself the guilt of wishing for their destruction ... reverting to primitive hatred and vengeance.'

[67] I owe this reinterpretation to Anna Wilson's clear-headed arguments during the discussion following the paper at the Exeter conference on the passions. In mythic terms, Oedipus must have been in the Furies' power from the moment that he killed his (unidentified) father at the crossroads.

IV

All passion spent?

The brothers are dead, but hatred lives on, and is now transmitted to Creon with his assumption of the throne. This supernatural motivation enhances his natural motive of bitterness at the futile death of his son Menoeceus, and he turns first on Oedipus, then on the body of Polynices. Antigone speaks for Statius in associating Creon's actions with the contamination of the Theban throne: 'are you turning against him *from hatred and the power of kingship?*' (11.724).

The theme of hatred has become more frequent, just when we might expect it to fade out. Fittingly applied to the refusal of the wood of Eteocles' funeral pyre to burn his brother ('here are the brothers once more ... their obstinate hatred lives on, it lives!'),[68] it is more contrived in the ironic portrayal of the competition between Argia and Antigone to claim credit for burying Polynices ('so great their cries of conflict you would think it anger or hatred between them', 12.461–3). The Argive women themselves appeal to Theseus on the grounds that war and former hatred have ended between their cities: 'yes, we have been at war, but the hatred has lapsed and grim death has buried our anger' (12.573–4). But hatred still lives in Creon's Thebes, and Theseus' response to their appeal from the altar of Clemency must be another war, however just, and more speeches of denunciation.

In the last battle against Creon, Theseus claims that Nature and all the gods are on his side, whereas Creon is led on by Poenae and the Furies (12.645–6). Isolated by the loathing of both armies (*hinc atque hinc odia*, 758–9), Creon challenges Theseus and dies by Theseus' spear. Only now that all the male royalty of Thebes have perished can hatred end and give way to the mourning that ends the epic.

This is the course of Vessey's Stoic epic, with its fated sequence of events (*fatorum series*), incurring each successive disaster. We have seen that its psychology and moral causality can be called Stoic, or perhaps post-Stoic, to the extent that the evil of the epic derives from human passion run amok. But it is difficult to recognise either the Stoic or any other philosophical system in an action so dominated by

---

[68] *ecce iterum fratres ... uiuunt improba odia, uiuunt* (12.423, 441).

destructive forces. It is surely in conflict with any Stoic conception of deity that Statius shows passion poetically unleashed among the superhuman beings, both Olympian and infernal, and goes so far in extending the allegorical intervention of god or daemon against men.[69]

To the extent that Statius' portrayal of men is compatible with Stoic psychology, and that both the poet and the Stoics stop short of continuous allegory in their treatment of gods and daemonic beings, this is surely because post-Virgilian epic and later Stoicism are separate but equal representatives of pagan thought in their time, before the fourth century and the Christian psychological allegory of Prudentius.

Let us return to seeing Statius in his own terms. His epic presents a world in which human hatred is the central proliferating power of evil that only piety and clemency can bring to an end. The characterisation of the *Thebaid* may be grotesquely negative, more black than white; but its point of view is both moral and retributive, leaving the world to those who punish the guilty without animosity and deal with their neighbours unmoved by envy, anger, fear or the hatred which they generate.

---

[69] Recent critics have been more cautious than Whitman (1987) and Rieks (1989) in assessing the Stoic use of allegory and its influence on subsequent epic and tragedy. Neither the Epidrome of the etymologising Annaeus Cornutus (see Most (1989)) nor the allegorising of the non-stoic Pseudo-Heraclitus should be read as evidence for systematic Stoic allegorisation of gods and supernatural beings, still less for their allegorical interpretation of Homer (Long (1992)).

CHAPTER II

Passion as madness in Roman poetry

Christopher Gill

... Aeneas stopped his right hand; and now, now Turnus' speech had begun to affect him and make him pause, when he was struck by the unhappy baldric of Pallas ... when he drank in the spoils that reminded him of his savage grief (*saeui monimenta doloris*), then, inflamed by fury and terrible in his anger (*furiis accensus et ira | terribilis*) ... boiling (*feruidus*), he buried the sword full in Turnus' breast. (Virgil, *Aeneid* 12.945–51)

I

Introduction

The passage cited above, Aeneas' killing of Turnus at the end of Virgil's *Aeneid*, has served in recent years as a focus for debate on the project which is central to this volume.[1] The project is that of trying to place the representation of the passions in Roman literature in its contemporary intellectual context, in a way that can help to inform our interpretative responses to this representation. In this chapter, my contribution to this debate is to highlight a pattern in Roman poetry to which the killing of Turnus seems (at least partly) to belong, and to explore the shaping influences on this pattern. The pattern that I have in view is one in which the figure's surrender to emotional forces, following inner conflict (in some cases, 'akratic' self-surrender),[2] generates a certain kind of madness. This kind of madness is not the 'raving' insanity, involving fundamental changes in physical state and perception, that is a recurrent feature of, for

---

[1] On this debate, see Fowler, Ch. 1, Sect. IV; Wright, Ch. 9, text to nn. 1, 24–6; and text to nn. 96–104 below.

[2] 'Akratic' (from the Aristotelian term, *akrasia*, roughly 'weakness of will', *NE* 7) signifies that which is done against the agent's better judgement. See further e.g. Gosling (1990), part 2; Price (1995), 1–7.

instance, Greek tragedy,[3] but a more fully psychologised, and moralised, madness. The state of mind involved is marked, in general, by violent, often fluctuating emotion, and sometimes by defective or strained reasoning and miscommunication with other people. Also, and perhaps most significantly, it is sometimes recognised as 'madness' by the person herself, who thus partly distances herself from what she too sees as an (in some sense) 'irrational' state of mind.[4] As this summary suggests, I have in view a set of (partly overlapping) 'family' resemblances, rather than a wholly uniform type. But I think that this set of resemblances has a special interest for the project of correlating literary and conceptual patterns of thinking about the passions in this period.

As regards the latter project, my approach contains what might seem to be a rather surprising combination of emphases. On the one hand, my interest in the literary pattern outlined derives partly from the fact that (as argued later) the pattern seems to be shaped by one of the two main strands of contemporary philosophical thinking about the passions, namely the Stoic, as distinct from the Aristotelian. On the other hand, I suggest that, in the *Aeneid* and Seneca's tragedies (the texts I am mainly concerned with), philosophical influences converge with literary and ideological ones to produce the relevant pattern. The methodological points I want to make are linked with these two emphases in my account. On the one hand, when looking for intellectual influences on literary patterns, we need to identify features which are sufficiently determinate in themselves and well marked as features of the relevant text to enable us to discriminate between possible intellectual influences. On the other hand, we should be ready to accept that the literary work may combine these features with other strands (in a new but coherent synthesis) in a way that reshapes their meaning in comparison with the intellectual source. A further caveat follows from the latter point. Determining the intellectual source which (perhaps in combination with other sources) informs a literary pattern cannot, by itself, *settle* questions of interpretation (if anything can), especially in a work as complex as the *Aeneid*. There is no substitute, as regards interpreta-

---

[3] On this point, see text to nn. 14–17 below.

[4] This pattern constitutes a subdivision of the presentation of passion as madness (i.e. of the moralised and psychologised kind outlined here) which, as Fantham brings out (Ch. 10, text to nn. 19–23, 41–8, 55–6), forms a pervasive strand in Roman poetry; see also Hershkowitz (1994), (1995).

tion, for a sustained, responsive reading of the work as a whole. But discussions such as those offered in this volume can play a crucial role in helping interpreters to reflect on the literary and conceptual patterns that should inform such readings.[5] This is the kind of contribution that I seek to make here in exploring the pattern outlined in Senecan tragedy and Virgil's *Aeneid*.

II

Seneca's 'Phaedra' and 'Medea'

I begin by exploring two Senecan versions of the pattern in view. Seneca is taken first, out of chronological order, because his work provides examples and explanations of this pattern which are, in some ways, more straightforward than those in the *Aeneid*. This pattern is presented in an extended form in *Phaedra*, and appears in an abbreviated form within the final monologue of *Medea*. In the prologue of *Phaedra*, we are shown Phaedra thinking her way into her passionate love for her stepson, Hippolytus, (which she herself sees as criminal) through quasi-justification, by reference to the continued absence of her husband Theseus and her family's tendency to love in a criminal or misguided way.[6] When the nurse urges self-control, emphasising the unnaturalness of Phaedra's lust (165–77), Phaedra replies with these famous words: 'I know that what you say is true, nurse; but frenzy (*furor*) compels me to follow the worse course of action … What could reason (*ratio*) do? Frenzy (*furor*) has won and rules, and a powerful god [*Amor*] dominates my whole personality (*tota mente dominatur*)' (177–9, 184–5). Although the nurse counters that such talk of the divine power of love is simply the rationalisation of lust (*libido*), and warns Phaedra of the dangerous consequences of acting on her feelings, Phaedra continues to present herself as wholly under the domination of love, *amor*, the power of which could only be counteracted by suicide (195–7, 216–19, 253–4).

Subsequently, Phaedra is presented as acting uncontrollably in the grip of her passionate love, which she continues to regard as

---

[5] For a similar (but more sceptical) view of the scope and limits of what we can achieve in literary interpretation by highlighting ancient philosophical parallels, see also Fowler, Ch. 1, Sect. IV.

[6] She is thinking of her mother Pasiphaë and her sister Ariadne; see esp. 91–2, 96–8, 113–14, 127–8.

illegitimate and unnatural; this passion is described, by Phaedra herself and others, as 'madness'. The nurse characterises in this way Phaedra's intense, feverish behaviour and the gesture with which she throws off her female dress and longs to put on hunting clothes (both features based, though with significant modifications, on Euripides' surviving *Hippolytus*).[7] Phaedra describes her own love in these terms, when about to declare it to Hippolytus: 'the heat of love burns my maddened breast (*pectus insanum*)' (640–1). When Hippolytus rejects her love with violent intensity, Phaedra reiterates the thought that (like other members of her family) 'we pursue what we should avoid, but I am not in control of myself', and insists that she will pursue him 'madly' (*amens*) in spite of his rejection (698–703). In this scene and subsequently, the use of the language of madness in self-description is sometimes coupled with the expression of shame at her passion. Thus, when Hippolytus threatens to kill her after her declaration of love, she says, in so doing, 'you cure my frenzy (*furorem*). This is more than I could have prayed for: that I should die at your hands with my shame preserved (*saluo … pudore*)' (710–12). The latter comment implies a mixture of passionate lust and shame or guilt; and this combination of reactions is strongly marked in the final scene when she kills herself on stage following Hippolytus' death at her instigation. The chorus describe her as entering 'in a demented state' (*uecors*, 1155); and, in her final address to the remains of Hippolytus, she tells him both that, 'I shall punish myself on your behalf with this hand' and, 'I shall follow you madly (*amens*) through rivers of fire' (1176–80). Similarly, she tells herself: 'die, if you are chaste, for your husband [as punishment for her unlawful love], if you are unchaste, for your love' (1184–5). Finally, she discloses to Theseus that she falsely accused Hippolytus of the crime 'that I myself had madly absorbed in my crazy mind' (*demens pectore insano hauseram*, 1193).

Although there are certain relevant general similarities between the plots of *Phaedra* and *Medea*,[8] the closest parallel to the pattern

---

[7] 360–403, esp. 361: 'there is no end to mad flames (*flammis … insanis*)'; 363: 'the frenzy (*furor*) is betrayed by her face'; 386: 'with an insane state of mind (*mente non sana*), she rejects her normal clothes'. Cf. E. *Hipp.* 176–238, which, however, does not contain the language of madness or the stress on 'cross-dressing' (the latter is underlined in the chorus' description of Hercules in the grip of love, 317–24).

[8] Like Phaedra in 85–128, but more strongly, Medea activates her own passion, by self-exhortation to crime and frenzy (41–55, esp. 51–2; 120–36, esp. 122–4). She is urged to control herself by the nurse, esp. 150–4, 157–8, who describes her as 'mad' (*demens*, 174), but she rejects this urging. She is subsequently described by the nurse as showing the violent

outlined in *Phaedra* comes in the great monologue near the end of *Medea* (893–977). On the face of it, it is surprising that a figure as resolutely evil as Seneca's Medea should be presented as surrendering to 'mad' passion against her better judgement rather than out of deliberate policy. But in the final monologue, we find both akratic self-surrender and, as in the last scene of *Phaedra*, a complex fusion of self-acknowledged 'madness' and guilt. Medea, having arranged the death of Jason's new bride and father-in-law, urges herself to an unparalleled (*haut usitatum*) form of vengeance against Jason (893–901). As elsewhere, she draws on her own self-image as an evil and violent person as a source of motivation for the kind of frenzy (*furor*) and crime (*nefas*) that she is trying to generate.[9] The outcome is a plan which she embraces, eagerly, as the 'ultimate crime' (*ultimum ... scelus*): that their children be killed, as a substitute for the children of the marriage between Jason and his new bride, whose procreation has been pre-empted by Medea's murder of the bride (919–25).

It is the formulation of this plan that activates in Medea a sustained phase of inner conflict, between herself as 'mother' and her 'motherly duty' (*pietas*), on the one hand, and, on the other, the 'mad frenzy' (*demens furor*), 'bitter grief' (*dolor*) and 'anger' (*ira*) of the outraged 'wife' (*coniunx*, 926–44). This conflict is expressed partly in third-personal self-description (926–8, 937–44, also 951–3),[10] and partly by Medea taking on the 'voice' of one or other of the two aspects of herself, sometimes appealing directly to the other aspect.[11] It is in the continuation of the latter dialogue that she finds a kind of resolution of this conflict, by reconceiving the surrender to passion as a way of appeasing her guilt at her former crimes, especially her killing and dismemberment of her brother. Calling her children to her, in an appeal against her bitter grief (945–7), she is answered by the voice of her anger, recalling that, as an exile, she (though not Jason) will be deprived of the children anyway, and insisting that they should 'die' for the father as well as the mother (948–51). She

agitation that constitutes 'the face of frenzy' (*uultum furoris*, 382–96, esp. 396), cf. *Phaedra* 360–86, esp. 362–3; Medea herself envisages no limit to her 'frenzy for revenge' (406); see also, on her 'madness', 673–4, 849–56.

9   902–15, esp. 909, 915; see also refs in n. 8 above. Seneca's Medea thus displays the self-consciousness sometimes noted as characteristic of her (e.g. Gill (1987), 32–4), which is taken as an index of the 'metadramatic' status of Senecan figures by Schiesaro, Ch. 5, Sect. II, esp. text to nn. 3–6.

10 On this mode and its literary background, see Gill (1987), 33–4.

11 See 929–32, esp. 'ah, mad frenzy!' (930), answered by 933–6, 944 ('yield to motherly duty, bitter grief', *cede pietati, dolor*), also 945–7, 948–51.

then (third-personally) describes the resurgence of her anger as the act of 'the ancient Fury' (*antiqua Erinys*) seeking again her 'unwilling hand'. This seems to resolve the conflict: she now declares, 'anger, I follow where you lead', and, speaking with the voice of anger, expresses pleasure at having generated two children 'for punishment' (*in poenas*, 952–7).

The nature of the 'punishment' involved is clarified in the final phase of the monologue, in which she presents herself as 'mad' in a (partly) new sense. She seems to see a crowd of Furies with flaming torches, and also her dismembered brother who 'looks for punishment' (from her, 958–64). She gives it willingly: 'my breast lies open to the Furies' (966); she urges her brother to leave her after using 'this [her] hand, which has drawn the sword – with that victim [her child], I appease your shade' (967–71). In effect, she resolves the conflict between anger and mother-love by reconceiving the infanticide (and the punishment of Jason of which this is the vehicle) as a form of *self*-punishment for the crimes in which she has previously gloried.[12] The combination of passion (in this case, bitter anger) and guilt embodied in this final stage resembles that in the final scene of *Phaedra*.[13] More generally, the monologue as a whole exhibits another version of the pattern displayed in *Phaedra*, in which akratic surrender to passion generates what the person concerned sees as a kind of madness.

III

The Senecan pattern: shaping influences

In exploring the nature of, and possible influences on, this pattern, I begin by underlining significant differences between the pattern examined in these Senecan plays and those found in certain relevant types of Greek and Roman poetry. I focus on the presentation of madness, and akratic self-surrender, in Greek tragedy, and of akratic self-surrender in some earlier Roman poetry. My initial aim is to highlight the significance of the fact that the pattern outlined above is *not* present in these works.

[12] For her previous glorying in crime, see 904–15; also 124–36. For fuller analysis of this final move and the monologue as a whole, see Gill (1987), 31–6, esp. 36; also Rambaux (1972), esp. 1021–3.

[13] Cf. esp. *Phaedra* 1176–7, 1181: 'with this hand I shall punish myself on your behalf ... let me appease your shade (*placemus umbras*)', with *Medea* 969–71: 'use this hand, brother [to take punishment] ... with that victim I appease your shade (*manes tuos | placamus*)'.

In a full-scale study of Greek tragic madness, Ruth Padel takes as central to the genre the type of raving, god-induced madness, marked by physiological changes (such as rolling eyes and foaming mouth), distortions in perception and identification, and violent behaviour, that we find in Aeschylus' Io, Sophocles' Ajax, and Euripides' Heracles and Agave. One of her key claims is that Greek tragic madness is conceived as an occurrent state, not deriving from deep-rooted features of the personality. It arises, typically, from outside, either from divine intervention or from a special set of pressures, such as those operating on Orestes when he sees the Furies after murdering his mother.[14] Although this claim, arguably, needs to be refined, Padel's account highlights the dominance in Greek tragedy of a kind of madness that is significantly different from that examined in Seneca.[15] If there is a Greek tragic antecedent for the latter type, it falls within what Padel (1994, 194–6) calls 'hyperbolic' not 'real' madness, in which the language of madness is used to characterise behaviour that is not of the raving, god-induced, type just described. This category includes certain striking instances in which it seems natural to say that the figures who are so described are *in some sense* 'mad', even though their actions fall outside the normal limits of Greek tragic madness. These instances include the chorus' characterisation of the embittered (but sane) Ajax in Sophocles' *Ajax*, and of Eteocles in Aeschylus' *Seven Against Thebes* as he insists on going to kill, and be killed by, his brother.[16] It is conceivable that these and other tragic cases may have served to shape the special type of (psychologised and moralised) madness that we find in Seneca, though I see no special reason to think so. But Padel's study, none the less, brings out the fact that the kind of madness which figures so prominently in these two Senecan plays is, at most, marginal to the Greek tragic genre.[17]

---

[14] Padel (1994), esp. chs. 2, 4, 7, 8, 18, 20, 21 (the last challenging psychoanalytic readings which present Greek tragic madness as deriving from the personality of the figure involved); also (1992), ch. 8.

[15] This madness does, of course, also figure in Seneca, in *Hercules Furens*, though Fantham suggests that it is at least partly psychologised there (on the divine as well as the human level), Ch. 10, text to nn. 20–3.

[16] See S. *Aj.* 609–16, 639–40, taken with Winnington-Ingram's analysis of Ajax's 'megalomaniac pride' (1980), 47, n. 109, also 32–8, 42, 47–56; and A. *Th.* 653–719, esp. 653, 686–8, 692–4, taken with Long (1986b). A further suggestive instance is the half-madness of Pentheus in E. *Ba.* 810–46.

[17] See further, on Padel (1994) and the conception of the cultural function of Greek tragic madness implied in her account, Gill (1996b), esp. sect. IV; also, on the distinctive character of Greek tragic psychological agency-*cum*-passivity, Gill (1990), esp. 17–31.

Padel's claims about Greek tragic madness also help to explain why, in Greek tragedy, akratic self-surrender is not presented as generating 'madness', in any sense. The two Greek tragedies most clearly relevant to this point are, as it happens, the ones most relevant as background to the two Senecan plays: Euripides' surviving *Hippolytus*, especially Phaedra's great speech, recounting her attempts to cope with her passionate love for her stepson (373–430, esp. 391–402), and his *Medea*, especially the great monologue (1021–80). Both these plays show the central figure, in these speeches, distancing herself from one or other aspect of herself, or from a possible response. Medea's monologue displays one of the two ways of doing so noted earlier in Seneca's *Medea*, the adoption of the 'voice' of one of her possible selves, sometimes addressing the other possible self directly.[18] But in neither Greek play does the figure concerned use the language of madness to distance herself from her passionate love, her anger or her restraining mother-love.[19] Nor is either figure characterised by others in those terms, even in the type of language that Padel associates with 'hyperbolic' madness.[20] It is worth noting (and, obviously, bears on the comparison) that in neither Greek play can we say, without qualification, that we find akratic self-surrender. Phaedra's great speech identifies what she sees as the only effective way of not acting on her love, namely suicide.[21] Medea, famously, at the close of her monologue presents her 'plans' (in the translation that I would prefer) as 'mastered' by her anger (*thumos*), and distances herself in other ways from this anger. But, at an earlier, and (I think) decisive, moment of her speech, she has reaffirmed this anger, and its grounds, dissociating herself from 'the cowardly self' (τῆς ἐμῆς κάκης) who admits 'soft arguments' against this anger (1049–55). The subsequent comment about her plans

[18] Such self-address is most evident in 1056–8 (falling within the part of the monologue, 1056–64, whose Euripidean authorship is most open to question); but the monologue as a whole consists of alternating 'voices', predominantly that of the mother regretting the decision (1021–48, 1056–8, 1067–80, disowning the other self, esp. in 1028, 1079–80), but also that of the wife reaffirming her grounds for anger and distancing herself from the opposing arguments (1049–55, 1059–66). See further Gill (1987), 26–7.

[19] Phaedra characterises her love as folly (*anoia*), and, if acted on, as 'shameful sickness' (*noson ... dusklea*, 398, 405), but not as madness; on E. *Med.*, see n. 18 above.

[20] E.g. Jason, when looking for adequately extreme language, calls Medea a 'she-lion' or 'Scylla' (*Med.* 1342–3); Hippolytus' tirade, focusing on the ethical failings of women (*Hipp.* 616–68), does not employ the language of madness.

[21] *Hipp.* 400–2, defended further in 403–30. Despite expressing at one point the strain of maintaining this decision (503–6), there is no clear indication that she approves (akratically) of the nurse's half-disclosed initiative (507–24).

being 'mastered' by anger (1079) can be read as acknowledging (and bitterly regretting) this decision, rather than disowning it completely.[22] Thus, neither of the Greek tragic examples is quite parallel to the analogous Senecan cases. However, it would have been conceivable, even so, that Euripides' Phaedra or Medea could have disowned her state of mind with the language of madness (perhaps in some more or less extended form of 'hyperbolic' madness); the fact that they do not is striking in itself, as well as for the question of the influences on Seneca's formulation.

It is equally striking that the language of madness is absent from at least some of the Latin presentations of akratic self-surrender (apart from those in the *Aeneid*) which Seneca might well have known. Catullus' Lesbia-poems, for instance, constitute memorable expressions of conscious inability to suppress his love for his unfaithful mistress. But, although Poem 76 uses 'sickness' (*morbum*, 25) in this connection, Catullus does not describe his akratic love as a form of madness.[23] The same point applies to certain descriptions of hesitation and inner conflict in Ovid's *Metamorphoses* which may well have helped to shape the final monologue in Seneca's *Medea* and contributed to the latter's depiction of Phaedra.[24] These Ovidian passages seem especially to anticipate the style of third-personal self-description (sometimes linked with akratic self-surrender) that we find in the Senecan examples.[25] We also find, within one of these passages (in *Met.* 8), an appeal to the Furies (here, Eumenides) to support a punishment that is also a crime (a mother killing her son on behalf of her brothers) of a kind that anticipates the final stages of the monologue in Seneca's *Medea*.[26] But, in none of these passages, apart from a passing description of Medea as 'mad' (*demens*), when she is,

---

[22] See further Gill (1996c), ch. 3, sect. 5; Foley (1989); also Evans (1994), on both Medea's monologue and Phaedra's great speech. Lines 1078–80, in my translation, mean: 'I know that what I am about to do is bad, but anger is master of my plans, which is the source of human beings' greatest troubles.'

[23] See e.g. Cat. 8, 72, 75, 85; Catullus' self-description in 7.10 as 'mad' (*uesano*) in his desire for innumerable kisses is not linked with the inner conflict prominent in the poems just listed. In the epyllion 64, Catullus uses *furor* (54), *furentem* (124), *amenti caeca furore* ('with mad, blind frenzy', 197) of the grief of the abandoned Ariadne, but not in connection with akratic self-surrender. On the significance of *morbum* in 76, see Booth, Ch. 8.

[24] *Met.* 7.1–99 (on Medea), esp. 9–11, 18–21, 69–83, 93–4; also 6.619–35 and 8.451–514, on mothers (Procne, Althaea) agonising before killing their sons because of their crimes or those of their fathers.

[25] Cf. esp. *Met.* 7.20–1: 'I approve the better course, and follow the worse' with *Phaed.* 177–9; see also *Met.* 7.72–3, 92–3, 506–11; the (narrative) description and simile of 8.465–74 seem to underlie the self-description and simile in *Med.* 937–43.

[26] Cf. Ov. *Met.* 8.481–4 with Sen. *Med.* 953, 958–68, also 931–5, taken with text to nn. 9, 12

against her better judgement, erotically attracted to Jason,[27] do we find the use of the language of madness that is so well marked a feature of the Senecan passages.

I have not, of course, discussed all the material in Greek and Roman literature that might be considered as relevant to this question.[28] But the contrast between the material noted and the Senecan formulations is striking and implies the conclusion to be drawn shortly. First, however, I summarise the characteristics of the 'madness' arising from akratic self-surrender in Seneca. By contrast with the predominant type of madness in Greek tragedy, this madness emerges from within the personality of the figure as agent. Phaedra 'thinks her way into', and half-justifies, her love for Hippolytus; Medea urges herself, throughout the play and within the monologue, to live up to her self-ideal as evil and violent.[29] There thus arises the state of intense, passionate lust or anger, which is marked by the visible signs and feverish, sometimes fluctuating, behaviour that is described by other figures as 'frenzied' or 'mad'.[30] This is coupled with other features, displayed in dialogue: an obsessive focus on the object of passion, and one that leads the figure to partial miscommunication with others not so affected, or to strained, unnatural reasoning.[31] The figure herself tends to describe her own passionate state as 'mad' at those moments when she is displaying what are, to some degree, virtuous attitudes, those of motherly duty or guilt, and is thus partly detached from her passion.[32] It is true that Medea, in the final stage of her monologue, experiences a quasi-hallucination (which seems to bring her closer to Greek tragic madness, for instance, that of Orestes seeing the Furies). But this quasi-hallucination stems from the (psychologically intelligible) response that she makes to the conflict generated between

---

above. Cf. also Ov. *Met.* 8.488–90 with Sen. *Med.* 957, 964–5. Althaea in *Met.* 8 is not, however, 'seeing' the Furies, as Medea does in *Med.* 958–66.

[27] Ov. *Met.* 7.87, taken with 69–73, 92–3.

[28] Another influential representation of inner conflict is that in Apollonius of Rhodes, *Argonautica* 3, esp. 652–3, 742–3, 785–821, though again without the language of madness. The relationship between the language of madness and that of sickness in Hellenistic and Roman poetry and the question of the possible influence of Hellenistic philosophy on the development of both these kinds of language merit separate study; for some relevant observations, see Booth, Ch. 8, Sect. III, esp. text to nn. 42–3.

[29] See text to nn. 6, 8–9 above.

[30] See text to nn. 7–8, 10–11, and refs. in n. 8 above.

[31] See e.g., for the first feature, *Phaed.* 629–45; for the second, *Med.* 919–25, 932–6, 954–7.

[32] See e.g. *Phaed.* 177–9, 698–701, 710–12, 1180, 1192–3; *Med.* 930. On this feature in Virg. *A.*, see text to nn. 60, 93–4 below.

mother-duty and bitter anger and represents a complex way of resolving this. Seneca's Phaedra terminates her life in a similar state of conflict, though without any such quasi-hallucination.[33]

What is implied in the preceding summary, taken in conjunction with the negative outcome of the discussion of poetic antecedents, provides the basis, I think, for locating the primary source of Seneca's portrayal. In the absence of any evident poetic prototypes (apart from those in the *Aeneid*)[34] for the pattern outlined, it is natural to look for philosophical influence. Of the two theories of the emotions which Seneca, in his *De ira*, as well as Cicero, in the *Tusculans*, presents as the dominant candidates for serious considera- tion, the Stoic seems much more relevant than the Aristotelian.[35] Apart from other relevant factors, vice is conceived in an Aristotelian framework as the failure to hit the 'mean' (or as the failure to 'moderate' the emotions) not as (a kind of) 'madness'.[36] Indeed, given Seneca's explicit and consistent adherence to Stoicism, Stoic influence presents itself as the obvious factor, so much so that the previous consideration of poetic parallels may seem redundant. However, Marcus Wilson and Alessandro Schiesaro, in this volume, offer reasons for being cautious about assuming that Seneca's presentation of emotions, in the tragedies or, indeed, the theoretical works, can be straightforwardly or uniformly identified as Stoic.[37] The case needs to be argued; and we need also to be clear about what kind of theory of emotion we count as 'Stoic'. In addition, the discussion of possible poetic parallels has served partly to define the distinctive character of the Senecan pattern, and also to enable us to pin-point the Stoic form of the pattern.

This inheres primarily in two, seemingly opposed, features of Stoic

---

[33] *Med.* 958–71 and *Phaed.* 1176–90, taken with text to nn. 12–13 above.

[34] I have omitted this here, since I suggest in Sect. IV that the relevant features of *A.* seem also to be influenced by Stoic ideas (in conjunction with other influences).

[35] See further, on the Roman reception of these two theories, Introd., Sect. II, esp. n. 9.

[36] See Introd., Sect. II, text to nn. 12, 16, on the two kinds of 'Aristotelian' framework relevant to this point (that of the school texts, and that of the Peripatetic tradition); and on vice as 'madness' in Stoicism, see Sect. IV, text to nn. 67–73.

[37] See Ch. 3 (Wilson), esp. Sects. IV–V; Ch. 5 (Schiesaro). Schiesaro's claims, in particular, might seem in direct conflict with the approach taken here. However, what Schiesaro denies is not that Seneca's dramatic psychology is conceived in the light of Stoic ideas (the view assumed here). He claims (1) that the literary embodiment of these ideas (e.g. in Sen. *Med.*) does not fully bear out this conception (Sect. I), and (2) that Stoic aesthetic theory does not entirely match the didactic role often ascribed to Seneca's tragedies (Sect. II–IV). For the more usual view that Seneca's tragedies can plausibly be read as serving his Stoic ethical objectives, see e.g. Nussbaum (1993), esp. 137, 148; see also nn. 49, 54–5 below.

thinking on emotions, which are also reflected in the Senecan pattern. As emphasised in the Introduction to this volume, Stoics conceive emotions as, in different senses, both 'rational' and 'irrational'. They are 'rational' in the sense that they involve beliefs (typically, of the sort that x is good or bad, and that it is right to react accordingly); to this extent, they fall within human agency or rationality, and are 'up to' the person concerned. But they are 'irrational' in two related senses. The beliefs involved are false and reflect a misguided understanding of what is genuinely good and bad. Also, and relatedly, emotions (at least sometimes) involve powerful, even violent, psychophysical reactions, so much so that the person concerned feels 'taken over' by them, even though they derive, in origin, from her own agency.[38]

Both these features seem to be reflected in distinctive aspects of the Senecan pattern. On the one hand, the way that Phaedra 'thinks her way into' her passion, and, more strikingly, the way that Medea urges herself into hers, can be taken as signalling the fact that the passions derive from the person's own agency and express the value-laden judgements made about the situation.[39] On the other hand, the fact that the figures themselves, as well as others, sometimes describe their responses as 'mad' accentuates the point that their emotions are 'irrational' in the two respects just noted. This mode of presentation underlines that the emotions express (what those concerned can sometimes see as) 'false' or misguided ethical judgements, a point also conveyed by their strained reasoning and their inability to communicate properly with those who are not in the same state of mind.[40] The characterisation of these states as 'madness' (by the figures themselves as well as others) also highlights the overwhelming and (now) uncontrollable character of the emotions, despite the fact that these have originated from the figure's own judgements.[41]

This resemblance goes some way, perhaps, to providing an explanatory framework for the pattern outlined. But some questions remain. If Stoic thinking represents the key influence, why is this type of madness presented as the outcome of *akratic* self-surrender; what is

---

[38] See further Introd., Sect. II, text to nn. 21–2.

[39] See refs. in n. 29 above.

[40] See text to n. 31 above. A further feature of the presentation of Phaedra's emotional state, its fluctuating and unstable character, corresponds to the inconsistency or 'fluttering' (*ptoia*) that Stoics take to be characteristic of the non-wise: LS 65 A(2), R, T.

[41] See text to nn. 7–8 above (also refs. in n. 8). This point also applies to the special case of Medea's quasi-hallucination in *Med.* 958–71, discussed in text to nn. 12–13 above.

especially Stoic about this linkage? Also, more fundamentally, why is the passion presented as *madness*? Although human folly is standardly described as 'madness' in Stoic theory, this description is not especially associated with the kind of folly constituted by passion. Medea's madness, in particular, resembles, at least, the raving, hallucinatory madness of Greek tragedy; and it is not part of Stoic theory that the latter kind of madness can be identified with 'passion', in a Stoic sense.[42]

I defer the question of the kind of 'madness' involved until I consider Virgil (Sect. IV). I focus first on the question why it is akratic self-surrender that is presented as generating the passion of madness in these cases. On the face of it, it is unclear how Stoic psychological theory, which insists on the unity of (adult) human motivation, can accommodate *akrasia* at all, let alone stimulate a literary pattern in which *akrasia* has a key role. However, we know from Galen that the issue of how to analyse (apparent) self-division and *akrasia* was a subject of intense debate in Stoicism. Chrysippus argued that these phenomena could be explained (for instance, by unnoticed changes in belief) in a way that was compatible with his monistic psychological model. Posidonius argued that they could only be explained by modification of Chrysippus' model.[43] According to Galen, the changes he proposed were very substantial, amounting to the reintroduction of the Platonic tripartite psyche. However, Galen (who is very hostile to Chrysippus' monistic theory) may exaggerate the changes. Posidonius may only have argued that, to explain *akrasia*, we need to acknowledge the existence of 'affective motions' (*pathētikai kinēseis*), which form part of our psychological make-up from childhood onwards, and remain, in some people, incompletely matched with their belief-structure.[44] Posidonius may have combined this view with the Chrysippan principle that adult human motivation is, essentially, belief-based, and that emotions such as anger involve beliefs, or, more precisely, 'assent' to rational impressions.[45]

---

[42] See further text to nn. 67–73 below.

[43] See Gal. *PHP* 4.5.19–7.44, De Lacy (1978–84), vol. 1 263–91, esp. 4.7.1–44, De Lacy 281–91; also LS 65 G, I, M–R.

[44] On *pathētikai kinēseis*, see Gal. *PHP* 4.7.36–44, De Lacy (1978–84), vol. 1 288–91; 5.5.21, De Lacy 320–1.

[45] For the view that Posidonius' revision of Chrysippus was substantial, see e.g. I. G. Kidd (1971). For the view that it was limited, and that the introduction of *pathētikai kinēseis* was designed to supplement, rather than replace, Chrysippus' view that *pathē* are belief-based, see Fillion-Lahille (1984), part 3, chs. 1–3; Cooper (forthcoming); Gill (forthcoming*a*).

Although there is no extant discussion of this Stoic debate in Roman texts, Posidonius' philosophy was well known to Roman thinkers, including Seneca; and *De ira* 2 is sometimes taken to show the influence of Posidonius' psychological thinking. Seneca there stresses the existence of a class of 'pre-emotions' (*propatheiai*) or 'preliminary stimuli to emotions' (*principia proludentia adfectibus*), involuntary or instinctive reactions, which only become full-scale emotions (and thereby become overwhelming and 'irrational' states) when we 'assent' to the relevant 'impression' (such as, that it is right for me to seek revenge).[46] These pre-emotions seem to be based on Posidonius' 'affective motions';[47] more speculatively, Seneca's analysis of anger in *De ira* 2, and his strategy for dealing with it, can be seen as based on Posidonian ideas about how to build up character-structures that can prevent or resist affective motions.[48] If one pursued this line of thought, it would be possible to suggest that the Senecan tragic pattern studied here constitutes an extension of the Posidonian strategy in *De ira*. The stress, in these two plays, on the idea that the 'madness' of uncontrollable and perverse passion derives from akratic self-surrender might be taken to reflect the distinctively Posidonian model with its relatively greater acknowledgement of psychic complexity. Phaedra and Medea, in this reading, represent cautionary examples of the consequences of assenting to, rather than counteracting, pre-emotions; and their own acknowledgement of their 'madness', similarly, expresses the form of self-division that Posidonius' theory allows.[49]

However, given our incomplete understanding of Seneca's doctrinal position, it may be unwise to tie any explanation of this tragic pattern to a specific, and to some degree non-standard, version of

---

[46] See *De ira* 2.2.1–4.2, esp. 2.2.5 and 2.4.1–2. On this feature of Seneca's theory, compared with Epicurean thinking on emotions, see Fowler, Ch. 1, Sect. II.

[47] For this view, see e.g. Inwood (1985), 175–81; Fillion-Lahille (1984), 164–5, 167; see also the parallel texts in LS, vol. 2, pp. 417–18. Inwood (1993) offers an alternative explanation: *De ira* 2.1–4 offers a version of orthodox (Chrysippan) psychology which defines the 'rationality' of (adult) human impulses, including passions, by the criterion of conscious rational decision rather than by the combination of verbal impressions and assent (whether conscious or not); see 164–83, esp. 174–5.

[48] See e.g. *De ira* 2, on childhood training (21), and on adult self-management (22–31); for comparable themes in Posidonius, see Gal. *PHP* 5.5.32–5, De Lacy (1978–84), vol. 1 324–5; 4.7.8–11, De Lacy 282–5. See further Fillion-Lahille (1984), 180–99.

[49] Pratt (1983) suggests that Senecan tragedy reflects a modified and dualistic version of Stoicism (which he calls 'neo-Stoicism') and that this is reflected in *Med.* and *Phaed.*; see esp. 59–61, 64–5, 76, 89–93. But his view was developed before the emergence of the account of Posidonius' modifications assumed in text to nn. 43–8 above.

Stoic psychology. In any case, Chrysippus' own analysis of passion, as reported by Galen, may provide an explanatory framework that takes us closer to the specific form of the Senecan pattern. Chrysippus, despite his monistic psychological model, gave special emphasis to cases where people in a state of *pathos* acknowledge that what they are doing is wrong, but cannot now act otherwise, citing in this connection the final three lines of the famous monologue in Euripides' *Medea* (1078–80): 'I know that what I am about to do is bad, but anger is master of my plans, which is the source of human beings' greatest troubles.'[50] Chrysippus underlined in this way several key features of his conception of a *pathos*. These include the point noted earlier: that a *pathos*, while deriving from the agent's beliefs, can become so 'excessive' that (like running rather than walking legs) it passes outside the person's present control. He seems also to have taken Medea's lines, and similar poetic examples, as an expression of the fact (as Stoics regard it) that a *pathos* constitutes a 'rejection' or 'disobedience' of the rationality of which human beings are constitutively capable.[51] In so doing, such figures also display, in spite of their current unreasonable state, an acknowledgement of the fact (as Stoics take it to be) that all human beings 'have the seeds of virtue', and have, at some level, the capacity to recognise, and make progress towards, the rationality from which the *pathos* temporarily estranges them.[52]

In several respects, the Chrysippan analysis seems to provide a more illuminating background for the Senecan tragic pattern than the Posidonian thinking outlined earlier. The way that the two tragic figures play an active role in thinking their way, or urging themselves, into their passion corresponds to Chrysippus' stress on the belief-based character of the *pathos*, rather than to the Posidonian picture of people assenting to instinctive drives (or 'pre-emotions'). The dialogues in which the two figures refuse the advice of their more reasonable advisers, as they go deeper into their passions, can be taken as displaying the Chrysippan idea that a passion constitutes a (sometimes conscious) 'rejection' or 'disobedience' of a rationality whose validity they at some level recognise. The fact that Phaedra's

---

[50] See n. 22 above.

[51] See Gal. *PHP* 4.2.8–27, De Lacy (1978–84), vol. 1 240–5; 4.6.19–27, De Lacy 274–5; see further Gill (1983a), (1996c), 228–32; Gosling (1990), 56–65; Nussbaum (1994), 383–6; Price (1995), 157–61.

[52] For this idea, see e.g. Cic. *Tusc.* 3.2; D.L. 7.89; LS 61 L, taken with 65 J, esp. (1).

'madness' is punctuated by guilt (and is, on those occasions, seen as 'madness' by her), and that Medea's revenge is only acceptable to her when it also serves (bizarrely) as a means of expiating her guilt, can, similarly, be taken as showing that, in spite of everything, they possess the fundamentally human sense of virtue and rationality.[53] In these respects, which constitute the most distinctive features of the Senecan presentation of these figures,[54] the Senecan pattern makes sense as a way of exemplifying the Chrysippan conception of *pathos*, and of its understanding of akratic self-surrender.

IV

Virgil's 'Aeneid': passion as madness

In exploring the relevance of this literary pattern to Virgil's *Aeneid*, I accept, first, that the pattern appears in a less straightforward form, and, second, that it figures within a poem which is, ethically and psychologically, more complex than Seneca's tragedies.[55] None the less, I think that this pattern forms a significant strand within the *Aeneid*, and one that helps us to define the way, and the extent, to which the poem is shaped by Stoic thinking. Also, the *Aeneid* provides a rich vein of material for pursuing a question which is also relevant to Seneca: why, in these Roman poetic works, is akratic self-surrender presented as generating not just passion but also a kind of 'madness'?

The closest parallel to the Senecan pattern is the presentation of Dido in *Aeneid* 4. Her surrender to love, displayed in the dialogue with Anna, is marked as akratic (in contradiction to her vow of loyalty to her dead husband) by Dido herself and by the narrator.[56]

---

[53] See further text to nn. 6–13 above, summarised in text to nn. 29–33 above; for the two dialogues between heroine and nurse, see *Phaed.* 129–273, esp. 165–219; *Med.* 150–78. Pigeaud (1981), 398–402, also sees Sen. *Med.* as embodying Chrysippan monistic psychology.

[54] On self-exhortation to passion, and on dialogues in which the main figures 'reject' reason, as characteristic features of Senecan drama, and ones to be explained by reference to Seneca's Stoic objectives, see e.g. Herington (1966), esp. 453–6; D. and E. Henry (1985), 56–67.

[55] For readings which stress the ethical and psychological complexity of Seneca's tragedies, see e.g. Segal (1986), esp. 3–17, on *Phaed.*; Nussbaum (1994), ch. 12, on the interplay between Stoic and Aristotelian strands in *Med.* My point here is not that Senecan tragedies lack complexity but that the complexity of Virg. *A.* is more obvious and pervasive; and that this bears on my project of isolating a literary pattern which is distinctively Stoic rather than Aristotelian.

[56] See *A.* 4.15–19, esp. *culpae* ('fault', esp. sexual infidelity), 24–9, 55 ('broke down her shame', *soluitque pudorem*). The significance of this dialogue in generating her 'madness' is marked by

As soon as she has surrendered herself, her behaviour is characterised as 'mad', in the sense of being intensely emotional and uncontrolled.[57] Her 'madness' is intensified by the news of Aeneas' departure;[58] thereafter, her speeches are marked, increasingly, by a combination of intense emotions: continuing passionate love, violent anger, consciousness of guilt at breaking her vow to her former husband. The comparison at one point (465–73) of Dido's state of mind to the madness of tragic figures such as mad (*demens*) Pentheus and Orestes underlines (what is also central to Senecan tragedy) that the 'madness' involved is *not* the raving insanity of Pentheus and Orestes.[59] The fact that her responses are described as 'mad' not just by the narrator but also by Dido herself (typically, in moments of guilt)[60] implies an idea which is also implied in her final moments of rational lucidity before her suicide, when she reviews her life with 'cosmic' detachment.[61] This is that, in spite of the occurrent 'madness-passion' which is gripping her, she can still see that her state represents a negation of the virtuous rationality that is fundamental to her nature as a human being.[62]

Elsewhere in the *Aeneid*, there are a number of features that can be, at least partly, associated with this pattern. Turnus, in Books 7–12, also goes through a period of emotional violence, which is sometimes characterised as 'madness', and which is marked as distinct by its sudden onset in Book 7 and its partial replacement by rational lucidity in Book 12. The onset of Turnus' madness-passion is less clearly marked as akratic than Dido's (or that of Seneca's Phaedra), but it involves a comparable change from a (relatively) 'reasonable' to an 'unreasonable' state of mind.[63] In Aeneas' case, there are grounds for including under this heading any of the well-marked occasions on which he slips from the level of rational self-

---

Dido herself in 548–9: ' . . . you, sister, first burdened me, in my frenzy (*furentem*) with these troubles'.

[57] See esp. 68–9 ('in a frenzy', *furens*); 78–9 ('madly', *demens*); also 'frenzy' (*furorem*) in 91, 101.

[58] 'She goes wild, and loses control of her mind, and runs inflamed, like a Bacchant throughout the city' (*saeuit inops animi . . . incensa . . . bacchatur*, 300–1).

[59] The 'theatrical' character of the latter type of madness is perhaps underlined by the insertion of 'on stage' (*scaenis*, 471), in the reference to the mad Orestes seeing the Furies (I am grateful to Charles Segal for pointing this out to me). For the contrast between tragic and (the relevant type of) Senecan 'madness', see text to nn. 14–17 above.

[60] See 376, 433, 548, 595–6.

[61] 651–8; on 'cosmic' detachment in Stoicism and Virg. *A.*, see text to n. 81 below; on Turnus' analogous moment of rational detachment, see text to n. 94 below.

[62] For the comparable features in Sen. *Phaed.* and *Med.*, see text to nn. 7–8, 12–13 above.

[63] See text to nn. 87–91, and, for a partial regaining of rationality, text to nn. 93–4 below.

control that the poem seems to require of him into phases of madness-passion.[64] But I focus, for the present purpose, on the question of the extent to which the description of his state of mind, in killing Turnus, corresponds to this pattern.

As stated earlier, I think that the instances of this pattern in the *Aeneid*, and to some extent in Seneca, make sense as a synthesis of Stoic and Roman cultural patterns; and it is this synthesis I want shortly to examine. But, in doing so, I am not ignoring those features of the *Aeneid* which are sometimes taken (for instance, by M. R. Wright) to lend themselves to interpretation in terms of an ethical psychology that is, in some sense, 'Aristotelian'.[65] My general view, which I cannot develop fully here, is that the ethical complexity, even ambivalence, which is so well marked a feature of the *Aeneid*, can be analysed, in part at least, by reference to the interplay, or tension, between Stoic and Aristotelian strands in the presentation of emotion.[66] But my aim here is the more limited one of seeking to bring out the underlying logic of the passion-as-madness theme, not that of locating this in the complex fabric of the *Aeneid*.

I focus initially on the question why the Senecan and Virgilian pattern centres on 'madness' (of the type exemplified here) rather than simply passion. What underlies this mode of presentation? The paradox that all those who fall short of complete virtue (or 'wisdom') are not only 'foolish' but 'mad' was one of the most famous, or notorious, of Stoic claims. The Stoic claim is not that all the non-wise are, all the time, displaying the specific kind of 'madness' embodied in passion.[67] But they do believe that the 'madness' of non-wisdom (above all, failing to recognise that virtue is the only good and that the other so-called goods are, in comparison with

[64] See e.g. 2.314–17, 575–95; 10.513–20; 12.494–9. Notable examples of self-control are 4.437–49; 11.106–20. See further e.g. Lyne (1983), 191–9; and, on the interpretative issues raised, text to nn. 96–104 below.

[65] On the relevant senses of 'Aristotelian', see Introd., Sect. II, text to nn. 11–19; Wright's view is that Virg. *A.* embodies a 'vernacular' form of the approach of the school texts. For a broadly similar view, as regards anger, see Galinsky (1988), esp. 330–5.

[66] Another possible way of defining this complexity is in terms of the rhetorical contrast between 'ethical' and 'pathetic' modes of presentation (for this contrast, see Gill (1984), esp. 165–6, and for application of a related contrast, see Levene, Ch. 7, Sect. 1). A further possible way is in terms of a contrast between ethico-political discourse and (for instance) an 'elegiac' mode of presenting emotions, which is more characteristic of Latin love-poetry. For other ways of defining this complexity, see Lyne (1987).

[67] The Stoic claim is more general: see e.g. *SVF* 664 (= D.L. 7.124), 'All the non-wise are mad in that they are not wise but do everything in line with that madness that is the equivalent of folly.' See further *SVF* 3.657–70, and, for parody of the Stoic idea, Hor. *S.* 2.3, esp. 43–6, 208–24.

virtue, 'matters of indifference') makes one liable to fall into the specific type of 'madness' that constitutes passion.[68] Although Stoic passion-madness is differently conceived from conventional madness, Chrysippus emphasises that the symptoms of passion include some, such as being incapable of listening to reason and being 'beside oneself' or 'outside' one's normal state, which resemble those of conventional madness.[69] I suggested earlier that the distinctive features of the Senecan pattern studied here (which has partial analogues in Virgil's *Aeneid*) are best understood as an expression of the Stoic conception of *pathos*. In particular, they convey the characteristically Stoic idea that to experience passion is to 'reject' your natural rationality (a rejection or surrender which anyone is, at some level, conscious of making).[70] What we can now add is that the characterisation of this state of mind as 'madness', and not just 'passion', is also indicative of the Stoic (rather than Aristotelian) understanding of emotions.[71]

The fact that this way of understanding emotion belongs to a Stoic, rather than Aristotelian, framework of thinking is underlined by the analysis of passion offered in Cicero's *Tusculans* and Seneca's *De ira*. These Roman thinkers reject the Peripatetic view that virtue consists in setting a proper limit (*modus*) to emotion, and that 'moderate emotion' (*metriopatheia*) is ethically acceptable. Rather, they maintain that to give way to emotion at all (and thus to give up the ideal of passionless virtue-wisdom) is to throw oneself 'headlong' (*praeceps*), as though from a precipice, into a passionate state that one can no longer control.[72] They emphasise, like Chrysippus, that the

---

[68] For this linkage between Stoic thinking about values and about passions, see Introd., Sect. II, text to nn. 26–8; it is brought out well in Engberg-Pedersen (1990), 184–6; Brennan (forthcoming, 1.2).

[69] See Gal. *PHP* 4.6.24–5, De Lacy (1978–84), vol. 1 274–5, esp. 'we behave towards these persons suffering from affections (τῶν ἐμπαθῶν as we do toward persons out of their minds (ἐξεστηκότων) and ... who have taken leave of their senses (παρηλλαχότας) and are not in their right minds or in possession of their faculties (οὐ παρ' ἑαυτοῖς οὐδ' ἐν αὐτοῖς ὄντας)', trans. De Lacy. See also 4.6.35–7, 42–8, De Lacy 276–81.

[70] See Sect. III, text to nn. 29–41, 50–4, also (on V. A.), text to nn. 56–64 above.

[71] More characteristic of Aristotle's ethical writings, by contrast, is the idea that vice, as well as virtue, reflects deliberate choice and a settled (defective) character, i.e. not being 'outside oneself'; see e.g. *NE* 2.5, esp. 1105b28–1106a6, 7.8, esp. 1150b29–31. See also refs. in n. 36 above.

[72] Cic. *Tusc.* 4.41, taken as part of the advocacy of the Stoic (not Peripatetic) understanding of emotions in 4.37–46; Sen. *De ira* 1.7.4, taken with 1.7.1–3, 1.9–10; also 3.6.1–2. On the Peripatetic approach to emotions (by partial contrast with that of the Aristotelian school texts), see Introd., Sect. II, text to nn. 15–19. These passages in *Tusc.* and *De ira* develop Chrysippus' idea that *pathos*, once launched, becomes out of control like running (not

state of mind produced in this way resembles conventional madness (*furor* or *insania*) in its violent intensity and in the fact that one is 'outside oneself'.[73] Thus, the fact that the literary pattern considered here shows akratic self-surrender leading not only to passion but also to (a kind of) madness is a further reason for associating this pattern with the Stoic, rather than Aristotelian, strand in Roman thinking about emotions. In Seneca, the pattern can plausibly be seen as a deliberate means of dramatising the Stoic conception of the passions.[74] In Virgil's case, it is more plausible to see the Stoic pattern as one of a number of culturally available paradigms.[75] It was a pattern which may have suggested itself more strongly because it was reinforced by certain kinds of assimilation between Stoic and Roman thinking in this period. These kinds of assimilation tend to promote a strong polarisation between virtue-reason and passion-madness; and, taken together, they go some way towards explaining the (complex) significance that attaches to Virgil's use of this literary pattern in the *Aeneid*.

One kind of assimilation is evident in Cicero's *Stoic Paradoxes* 4.1 (27), namely that between Stoic terminology and the reason–madness polarisation as used in Roman political rhetoric. Cicero sets out to demonstrate not that 'you [Clodius] are foolish (*stultum*), as often, or wicked (*improbum*), as always, but that you are actually mad (*dementem*)'. The assimilation of the Stoic 'mad' person (or 'fool') to Roman ethico-political 'wickedness' is coupled with the assimilation of Clodius' political opponent (Cicero) to the contrasting character

---

walking) legs; see Gal. *PHP* 4.2.13–18, De Lacy (1978–84), vol. 1 240–3, 4.5.10–15, De Lacy 260–3. I am grateful to Gisela Striker for underlining the significance of these passages, as well as the point that the characterisation of passion as 'madness' (in the relevant sense) has its natural home in Greek as well as Roman Stoic thinking.

[73] See e.g. Cic. *Tusc.* 3.11; 4.52–4, 77; Sen. *De ira* 1.1.2–4; 2.36.4–6; see also n. 69 above.

[74] See Sect. III, and, on the issue of how far Senecan dramatic representation is Stoic, see nn. 37, 49, 54–5 above. The self-consciousness that is characteristic of the Senecan figures' descent into passion (see Sect. II, esp. text to nn. 6–10) may be seen as a means of articulating, through drama, the process involved (surrender to passion-madness), rather than as a (realistic) portrayal of the degree of self-consciousness involved in every instance of passion. For a related suggestion, see Gill (1983a), 144–5; and, for an alternative explanation (in terms of 'metadrama'), see Schiesaro, Ch. 5, Sect. I.

[75] My suggestion is not the implausible one that Virgil was consistently Stoic (the question of the nature of the intellectual influences on his poetry is much more open, as indicated by the current debate noted in Sect. V, text to nn. 96–104). Rather, it is that Virgil's deployment of this literary pattern is shaped by Stoic thinking (in conjunction with other cultural influences); also that the kinds of assimilation between Stoic and Roman thinking summarised in text to nn. 76–82 below are particularly relevant to *A.* because this poem, like those kinds of assimilation, is linked with Roman public life and ideology.

of the Stoic wise person.[76] Cicero's own political rhetoric illustrates the kind of contrast to which the Stoic usage is here assimilated, a contrast in which *furor* and *insania* are used to convey the combination of violent, uncontrolled emotion and misguided or criminal behaviour.[77]

Another relevant type of assimilation, and one that is more often noted, is that of the Stoic ideal of passionless virtue (*apatheia*) with a state of mind idealised in Roman ethico-political rhetoric of the period. The state of mind is that of the person whose commitment to public service is so great that ordinary emotions and desires, and attachments other than those to the state, count as nothing. Regulus, in one of Horace's Roman Odes, is a striking exemplar of this state of mind.[78] A similar ideal is implied in Cicero's idealisation of Regulus in *De officiis* 3, taken with his analysis in Book 1 of the kind of peace of mind and indifference to misfortune that derives from total commitment to public service.[79] The relevance of this point to the idea of passion as madness is this. What such passages convey is strong ideological pressure on the Roman political and intellectual élite towards a high degree of emotional commitment to ethico-political norms and identification with those figures who exemplify these. The standards of what counts as 'virtue' and 'rationality' are, in this type of discourse, pitched very high; this implies a correspondingly high threshold for failure to meet those standards. In other words, this ideological pressure promotes a sharp distinction between *ratio* and *furor*, between the normative ethico-emotional state and *any* degree of failure to meet this norm, rather than a more finely graded set of such distinctions, such as those found in an Aristotelian or Peripatetic ethical framework.[80] To put the point differently, Roman ideological

[76] ' ... will the mind of a wise man (*sapientis animus*) that is defended by the ramparts of high purpose, by endurance of the human lot, by disregard for fortune, and by all the virtues, be defeated when it cannot even be exiled from the city', trans. M. R. Wright (1991), 90–1; see also Wright, 203–6.

[77] See e.g. Cic. *Sest.* 97, 99; *Cael.* 15; *Pis.* 46–7; also [Sal.] *Cic.* 7. I am grateful to Peter Wiseman for supplying these refs.

[78] See Hor. *Carm.* 3.5, esp. 41–56; for a related ideal, see 3.3.1–8; and for the reason-madness polarisation discussed in text to nn. 76–7 above, see 1.37, esp. 7–15.

[79] See Cic. *de Off.* 3.99–111 (involving the assimilation of Stoic sage-type and Roman exemplar), taken with 1.66–7, 69, 80 (on the Book 1 passages, see Gill (1994), 4609–10). See also Cic. *Tusc.* 4.49–52 (anger not necessary for heroism, with Roman exemplars); Sen. *De ira* 3.38 (lack of anger the mark of strength of character, e.g. Cato).

[80] For such gradations between degrees and types of partial defectiveness or virtue, see e.g. *NE* 7.6, 8 (on forms of *akrasia*); see also n. 71 above, and Introd., Sect. 11, text to nn. 11–19, on

discourse in this period, which is, of course, partly shaped by Stoic philosophy, contains an analogue for the sharp wisdom–folly, reason–passion/madness contrast which is fundamental to Stoic thought.

There is one further form of assimilation between Stoic and Roman thought-forms which bears on the identification of passion with (a kind of) madness in the *Aeneid*. Although too complex to analyse fully here, it is too important and relevant not to be noted. Central to Stoic thought is the idea that the natural universe and the totality of events are permeated by providential rationality. Crucial to the rationality of the normative wise person is her capacity to recognise, as if from a 'cosmic' perspective, the providential rationality embodied in the universe, and this capacity underlies her 'passionless' character or state of mind. Relatedly, in so far as human beings achieve or fail to achieve wisdom-virtue, they are acting in line, or out of line, with this providential rationality, whether or not they recognise this themselves. It is generally supposed that this Stoic pattern informs the *Aeneid*'s way of presenting Jupiter's plan, or Fate, and the relationship of human agents to this, though some scholars have also underlined important points of divergence between these two conceptions.[81] The relevance of this theme to the idea of passion as madness is this. The threshold of what counts as 'virtue-rationality', in the *Aeneid*, is set still higher than I have suggested so far. What is required is not just passionless commitment to public service, but also commitment to *that form of* public service which is in line with the world-historical outcome of events (or 'fate'). Given, again, the strong polarisation between virtue-reason and vice-passion-madness that operates in the poem, behaviour that fails to meet this very high condition, even if it might seem reasonable or virtuous from other standpoints, tends to be presented as *furor* (passion as madness), though not usually for this reason alone.[82]

Most, and perhaps all, of the points just made about the reason–passion contrast in Roman thought may also be relevant to Seneca's

types of 'Aristotelian' ethical framework. The idea of 'progress' towards the normatively rational state is, of course, an important one in Stoicism (it pervades Sen. *Epp.*), but the progress is shaped by the objective of moving ever closer to this normative state.

[81] On providential rationality in Stoicism, see LS 54; on the 'cosmic' perspective of the wise person, Cic. *Tusc.* 4.37; D.L. 7.88; Sen. *Ep.* 95.57. See also Kerferd (1978); White (1990); and, on the cosmic perspective and *apatheia*, Gill (forthcoming*b*). On differences between the Stoic and Virgilian conception, see e.g. Lyne (1987), ch. 2.

[82] On the linkage in *A.* between this type of 'irrationality' and the others noted, see Sect. v, text to nn. 92–4.

tragedies, and could help to explain the presentation of passion as (a kind of) madness in the pattern examined there.[83] However, I focus here on the bearing of these points on the *Aeneid*, and on the versions of this literary pattern outlined earlier. The combined effect of these points is that the *Aeneid* is a poem charged with the anxiety of trying to meet (at least) three norms of virtue-rationality simultaneously. One norm is that of effective kingliness, exercising the virtues in peace and war in a way that reliably benefits one's city and its people (see Cairns (1989), chs. 2–3). Another is that of quasi-Stoic *apatheia*, passionless virtue and rationality, typically (though not always) linked with total commitment to the kingly role or the service of the city. A third is that of effective commitment to *that* city-state which the world-historical outcome of events will reveal as having the greatest capacity for survival and success. Given the almost superhuman difficulty of meeting, consistently, all these norms simultaneously, it is understandable that the slipping from (at least partial) rationality to passion-madness, as determined by one or more of these criteria, is so frequent an occurrence in the poem, affecting all the main figures, including Aeneas (text to nn. 56–64 above).

However, the theme on which I have focused is not just the slippage from reason to passion-madness, but specifically *akratic* slippage. Although the criteria, as well as the analysis, of *akrasia* are, of course, a matter of substantive philosophical debate, the most obviously problematic case is widely recognised as the 'clear-eyed' *akrasia* in which someone acts consciously against what is, at the relevant time, her better judgement.[84] This can be exemplified in Seneca's Phaedra, or, less satisfactorily, Euripides' Medea. In the *Aeneid*, it is, I think, only Dido's surrender to a love that she herself sees as wrong, by at least one criterion, that clearly meets those conditions.[85] Elsewhere in the poem, we find *akrasia* of a weaker kind, in which figures act in a way that they are capable of seeing as wrong (more precisely, as passion-madness), as is indicated by their words or actions elsewhere. However, in so far as the poem is informed by the kind of Stoic–Roman pattern of thinking about reason–passion just outlined, which reflects in turn the Chrysippan model of *akrasia* considered earlier, this kind of *akrasia* is stronger

---

[83] On some relevant features of Senecan tragedy, interpreted as poetic responses to Virg. *A.*, see Putnam (1995), ch. 11.

[84] See Gosling (1990), index s.v. '*akrasia*, clear-eyed'; Price (1995), index s.v. 'acrasia, hard'.

[85] For these three cases, see text to nn. 6–8, 22, 56–62 above.

than it might seem. In so far as anyone, qua human, is in principle capable of the highest level of virtue-rationality, anyone must, at some level, recognise that slippage from (partial) reason to passion-madness represents the negation, or 'rejection', of human rationality.[86]

V

'Aeneid': examples of this pattern

I conclude by considering passages representing Dido, Turnus and Aeneas, which go some way towards illustrating the general points made, including the last one. Although the portrayals of the slippage into passion-madness of Dido in Book 4 and Turnus in Book 7 differ in the extent to which the passion is marked as contrary to their better judgement, they share one notable common feature. The process is a two-stage one in which, first, reasons are offered (by another figure) for thinking that it is right to react with love or anger, and, second, the figure is described as 'mad' with the uncontrollable force of the passion.[87] As my description suggests, this two-stage process lends itself to analysis in terms of the Stoic *pathos*; and the version of this analysis that seems to me most relevant is the Chrysippan, discussed in connection with Seneca. The reasons given for succumbing to love or anger (like the reasons by which Phaedra thinks her way into passionate love, or Medea urges herself into anger) can be seen as corresponding to the rational (verbal) impression ('that it is right to react') in Chrysippus' model. It is the acceptance of those reasons (in Stoic terms, the 'assent' to them) that triggers the 'mad' reactions described by the narrator, which correspond, in Stoic theory, both to the intense psychophysical reactions and to the excessive, uncontrollable character of a belief-based *pathos*.[88]

The Virgilian versions, obviously, contain one feature not present in the Stoic (or Senecan) versions. Turnus' 'assent' to the reasons for intense anger offered (by Allecto–Calybe) is imposed, after initial

---

[86] For cases of weaker *akrasia* in *A.*, see text to nn. 63–4 above; on Stoic–Roman thinking on reason–madness, text to nn. 76–82 above; and on the relevance of Chrysippus' conception of *pathos* to this literary pattern, text to nn. 50–4 above.

[87] See (Dido) 4.31–53 (Anna developing Dido's own words in 10–14, 19, 22–3), and 54–5, 66–9, taken with text to nn. 56–7 above; (Turnus) 7.421–34, 458–66.

[88] See Sect. III, esp. text to nn. 38–41, 50–4.

resistance, by Allecto's divine power; and the 'breaking down' of Dido's 'shame' by Anna's reasons for love is underpinned by the prior divine 'inflaming' of her heart.[89] What role should be allocated to this element in the Stoic–Roman interpretative model being applied here? There are two principal possibilities. One is that the divine element corresponds to the idea that, in the Stoic pattern, the assent to the (rational) impression produces a state of mind that is 'unreasonable' in being excessive and uncontrollable (like running, not walking, legs) and in making the person concerned reject any reason offered for not having the emotion.[90] The other is that the divine agency (deriving from Venus or Juno, not Jupiter) encapsulates the factors that make the emotion involved, and the correlated actions, in contradiction to the fated outcome of events. From a certain standpoint (though not from a strictly Stoic, or Roman, one), the emotions concerned might seem not unreasonable. But the association with divine agents working against, or at least not with, Jupiter's plan adds an extra respect in which the emotions are 'unreasonable' ('mad' in the relevant sense) in addition to the other respects.[91]

In the narration of the passion-madness of Turnus, as of Dido, the linkage between these (and other) respects in which the person's state of mind is 'irrational' or 'contrary to reason' is sometimes implied by the structure of the action and sometimes underlined explicitly. For instance, Turnus, near the end of Book 11, abandons his attempted ambush of Aeneas at just the wrong moment. In this passage the narrator brings together the ideas of passion-misjudgement and of acting in a way that is inconsistent with the fated outcome of events, but without trying to establish a causal relationship between the two: '[Turnus] in a frenzy (*furens*) (and this is what the harsh will of Jupiter required), abandoned the hills he was occupying ...' (901–2). In

---

[89] See 7.435–57; 4.1–2, 54–5, 66–9, also 94–5, 100–1, taken with 1.657–722. On divine-human interaction in *A.*, stressing the importance of giving independent weight to (and not over-rationalising) the divine role, see Feeney (1991), 164–80.

[90] See text to nn. 51, 69 above. For an alternative Stoicising reading of divine intervention in *A.* (centred on the interplay between 'external' and 'internal' causes), see Babel (1981–2), focusing on *A.* 7.378–84.

[91] In a more Aristotelian reading (see Introd., Sect. II, text to nn. 12–14), the reasons given by Anna or Allecto–Calybe (refs. in n. 87 above) might make the emotion itself 'reasonable'. From a Stoic perspective, love (except in certain exceptional circumstances, on which see Schofield (1991), ch. 2 and App. B–C) and anger, as passions, cannot be 'reasonable'. From a Roman perspective, these emotions run counter to the world-historical sequence of events leading to the supremacy of Rome (see Sect. IV, text to nn. 81–2). On the significance of Juno as an anti-providential, 'unreasonable' force in *A.*, see e.g. Feeney (1991), 134–5.

another passage, it is suggested that Turnus' passion-madness played a key causal role in ensuring that the fated outcome (and not Turnus' misguided objective) prevailed. We are told that it was only Turnus' frenzy and insane desire for slaughter (*furor ... caedisque insana cupido*) that ensured that this day was not 'the last of the war and of the [Trojan] race' (9.759–60). Such passages underline the linkage between the 'irrationality' (or 'madness') of the state of mind involved and the fact that such states are inconsistent with the immanent rationality in the universe (though, in an apparent paradox, such states of mind serve to bring about the providentially planned outcome of events).[92]

However, the passage relating to Turnus that is most suggestive, in this connection, is a line that falls within his final moment of lucid rationality, when he stops racing round the battlefield and goes to meet his expected death at Aeneas' hands. He tells his divine sister, Juturna (who has been preventing him from encountering Aeneas): 'let me do this one mad act (*furere ... furorem*) before I die' (680). In the whole poem, there is no other line that recalls more vividly those poetic phrases cited by Chrysippus in his illustration of the (sometimes conscious) 'rejection' of (normative) reason by those in a state of passion.[93] Paradoxically, this line figures here within Turnus' *cessation* of passion, when he, in effect, recognises his *previous* state of mind as one of passion-madness. The act that he describes as 'mad' is that of going to meet his death; but it is, in the Stoic–Roman terms that Virgil seems to assume here, his key 'rational' act in that he finally meets his responsibilities to his army and people in engaging in single combat with Aeneas. The 'rationality' is signalled by his recognition of the 'cosmic' standpoint, as he resolves to follow 'where the god and my hard fortune call' (677), thus bringing his phase of passion-madness to the

---

[92] On the larger Stoic–Roman theme, see text to nn. 80–2 above; on the question how far human evil could be reconciled with a belief in divine providence, see LS 54 I(3), taken with LS vol. I, pp, 332–3. There is a striking contrast between *A.* 9.759–60 and Hom. *Il.*, where 'madness' is not linked with fatal misjudgements. Although Hector is sometimes described as 'raging' in battle (*Il.* 8.355–6; 9.237–9), this kind of language is not linked with (what turned out to be) his crucial error in rejecting Polydamas' advice in *Il.* 18.310–12. For an analogous contrast between madness in Greek tragedy and the moralised Senecan 'madness', see Sect. III, text to nn. 14–22.

[93] See text to n. 50 above. See e.g. Gal. *PHP* 4.6.27, De Lacy (1978–84), vol. I 274–5: 'we hear [people in anger say] ... that they want to gratify their anger and to let them be, whether it is better or not and to say nothing to them, and that this is to be done by all means, even if they are wrong and if it is not to their advantage'. For other examples, including E. *Med.* 1078–80, see De Lacy, ibid. 274–9.

outcome that is in line with the immanent rationality in events, or fate.[94] The paradox of the use of this line to signify the closure of Turnus' phase of passion-madness is stronger if we suppose that Virgil was aware of the way in which Chrysippus interpreted such lines as expressions of the 'rejection' of reason.[95] But the paradox remains, even if we assume that it derives simply from Virgil's own use of the language of rationality and madness, and of the cultural connotations outlined in Section IV.

Virgil's much-debated account of Aeneas' killing of Turnus (12.930–52) comes soon after Turnus' speech. To include this account here (in an exploration of a literary pattern in which akratic self-surrender generates a kind of madness) may seem to prejudge the principal issue of current scholarly debate: whether Aeneas' killing (rather than sparing) Turnus is presented as ethically justified, or as a kind of 'madness'. I see the force of the argument that the passage should be read in a broadly 'Aristotelian' way, in which the emotions attributed to Aeneas are justified by the ethical claim of avenging Turnus' brutal killing of his young ally.[96] On the other hand, I think that the literary pattern discussed in this chapter underlines the force of the contrasting (broadly Stoic) reading. In this reading, the use of the language of madness in describing Aeneas' killing ('inflamed by fury [or the Furies, *furiis*],[97] and terrible in his anger ... boiling (*feruidus*)') implies that the replacement of sparing

---

[94] On the Stoic–Roman thinking that seems to be presupposed in this passage, see Sect. IV, text to nn. 76–82. The reading offered here may be reinforced by the preceding image of Turnus now 'seeing' the results of his own actions (12.669–71, taken in the context of 631–96), following the confused mixture of passionate and virtuous reactions in 665–8. For the image of sight (of fated reality) following passionate blindness, see 2.588–625, taken with Putnam (1990), 29, 34–5; also (though stressing more the ambivalence of Turnus' state of mind and of the cosmic framework) Hershkowitz (1995a), ch. 2.

[95] The closest analogue of such lines known to me is Prop. 1.25–8: 'Allow me, whom Fortune wants to lie sick forever, to devote the end of my life to this worthlessness (*sine me, quem semper uoluit fortuna iacere, | huic animam extremam reddere nequitiae*). Many have pined away willingly in a long love-affair; may the earth cover me too along with them', trans. R. Rothaus Caston, who drew my attention to this passage. Prop. 1 is usually dated to 28 BC, Virg. *A.* to 26–19. This motif is absent from Catullus' regretful picture of his *akrasia* (see nn. 23 and 28 above).

[96] For this type of reading, see Galinsky (1988), esp. 321–7, 330–5; Cairns (1989), 78–84; also, though with more qualifications, Wright, Ch. 9, text to nn. 23–6. On complementary Epicurean readings, see n. 102 below. Key relevant passages for this view are *A.* 10.491–505; 11.176–81.

[97] On the significance of the plural *furiis*, rather than *furore*, see Thomas (1991a), responding effectively to Cairns (1989), 83–4; see also Putnam (1990), 22–3, 27–32. The usage may perhaps be associated with others which, though recalling the imagery of Greek tragic madness, underline by implication the difference of the madness involved; see n. 59 above.

by killing is unjustified.[98] In particular, the informing presence of this literary pattern may bring out the point that (for the 'Stoic' reading) Aeneas' decision-making is akratic. To formulate this idea in Stoic terms, Aeneas is about to assent to the 'reasonable' impression (based on Turnus' words in 932–8) that 'it is right to spare him', when he is distracted by the 'unreasonable' impression (one rendered 'fresh' or 'vivid' by the visual impact of Pallas' baldric)[99] that 'it is right to be angry and to kill him in justified anger'. In this reading, the colouring of the second impression with the language of passion as madness marks its content as 'unreasonable' (an idea that can be defined in Virgilian as well as strictly Stoic terms),[100] and locates the whole passage within the akratic pattern discussed here. The couching of the second impression in third-personal terms ('it is Pallas, Pallas, who sacrifices you', 948–9) can be also seen, in this reading, as implying the kind of self-distancing from an 'unreasonable' response that is found, in a more marked form, in other cases of akratic self-surrender.[101]

As suggested earlier, one way of defining the ethical and emotional complexity of the *Aeneid* is by saying that it lends itself to both (broadly) Stoic and Aristotelian readings.[102] Here, the two readings

---

[98] For this type of reading, see e.g. Lyne (1983), esp. 199–202; Putnam (1990), 14–18 (1995), ch. 8, esp. 157–60.

[99] Note esp. *apparuit* ('there appeared'), *fulserunt* ('shone'); and the linkage between 'he drank in with his eyes' and 'inflamed by fury/furies and terrible in his anger' (945–7). For Chrysippus' idea that a *pathos* consists of assent to a 'fresh' (i.e. 'vivid') impression (based on false beliefs about what is good and bad), see Gal. *PHP* 4.7.3–5, De Lacy (1978–84), vol. 1 280–1. For Posidonius' emphasis on visual impact or imagination as effective in producing *pathos*, see *PHP* 5.6.24–6, De Lacy ibid. 330–1. On ancient thinking about the emotional effect of visualisation, see Webb, Ch. 6, esp. Sect. III.

[100] The idea that the passion-as-madness language (including 'savage grief', *saeui ... doloris*, 945, as well as *furiis* and the language of 'inflammation' in 945–7, 951) reinforces the grounds for sparing rather than killing Turnus is stressed by Lyne (1983), 193–4, 200–2; Putnam (1990), 16–18, 22–32. Referring esp. to Anchises' advice in 6.852 ('spare the conquered'), they argue that these grounds are Roman as well as Stoic.

[101] For such distancing language, see text to nn. 6–8, 10–11, 60 and (with added complexity) 93–5 above. As in E. *Med.* 1053–5, the characterisation of the killing as a form of (human) sacrifice can be seen as signalling the ethically doubtful character of the response, esp. when coupled with 'furies' (*furiis*, 946; for this coupling, cf. E. *Med.* 1059). See also Putnam (1995), 160, 169; and, for the contrasting ('Aristotelian') view that 947–9 encapsulates the 'reasonable' grounds for anger, see n. 96 above.

[102] See text to n. 66 above. A further proposal has been that the Epicurean view of anger, less wholly negative than the Stoic, may provide an appropriate conceptual framework in which to place Aeneas' (arguably) justified anger in 12.941–51; see Erler (1992a); Galinsky (1988), 335–7; (1994), 193–9. For this line of thought to be convincing, a connection would have to be established between the highly qualified defence of anger, in the case of an Epicurean wise person (on which see Fowler, Ch. 1), and the ethico-political anger of Aeneas. Put bluntly, why should an *Epicurean* think it was right to kill (in anger) a political

are, clearly, in tension; but it is not obvious what criteria we could use to rule out decisively either reading. The passage may thus be taken as exemplifying the point made earlier, that the poem is charged with the anxiety of meeting simultaneously a series of standards, which may come (or at least seem to come) into conflict: those of passionless virtue, effective kingliness, and consistency with the fated world-historical outcome of events.[103] However, my own impression is that the 'Stoic' reading is the more strongly embedded in the passage, and that this chapter's exploration of the akratic literary pattern helps to underline the force of this reading. Turnus' phase of passion as madness ends with a line (12.680) that, in a paradoxical way, marks the 'rational' closure of this phase (text to nn. 93–4 above). Similarly, the poem ends with the paradox that the figure who is the principal bearer of world-historical rationality, as well as the one on whom the claims of passionless virtue are most strongly impressed, gives way to an ethical misjudgement that constitutes a kind of madness.[104]

enemy? For some complementary methodological considerations, see Fowler, Ch. 1, text to nn. 22–5; and, on the relevant question of the relationship between Epicurean and Roman ethics, see Introd., text to n. 31.

[103] See p. 235 above. I am not denying that, in the Stoic reading, Aeneas' anger in killing Turnus can be seen as unjustified on all three counts (text to nn. 99–101 above); but I do not see the grounds for wholly ruling out the Aristotelian reading, and hence the possibility of conflict between these standards. On the ethical ambiguity of the ending of *A.*, by contrast with that of Stat. *Theb.*, see Braund (forthcoming).

[104] This chapter is based on papers given at the Universities of Bristol, Brown, Exeter and Harvard. I have learnt a great deal from the many helpful responses (both critical and positive) made on these occasions; also from detailed comments made on two written versions by Susanna Morton Braund, and on the last version by Peter Wiseman. See also Gill (1996*a*), outlining the theme of this chapter in an interdisciplinary volume on the passions, K. Cameron (1996).

Bibliography

Abrams, M. H. (1958), *The Mirror and the Lamp: Romantic Theory and the Critical Tradition* (New York)

Ahl, F. M. (1986), 'Statius' *Thebaid*: A Reconsideration' in Haase and Temporini 2.36.5 (1986): 2803–912

Alles, G. D. (1990), 'Wrath and Persuasion: The *Iliad* and its Contexts', *The Journal of Religion* 70: 167–88

Anderson, W. S. (1982), *Essays on Roman Satire* (Princeton)

André, J.-M. (1991), 'Tacite et la philosophie' in Haase and Temporini 2.33.4 (1991): 3101–54

Annas, J. (1989),'Epicurean Emotions', *Greek, Roman and Byzantine Studies* 30: 145–64

  (1992), *Hellenistic Philosophy of Mind* (Berkeley)

  (1993), *The Morality of Happiness* (Oxford)

Anton, J. P., and Preus, A., edd. (1983), *Essays in Ancient Greek Philosophy*, vol. 2 (Albany, NY)

Arnold, E. V. (1911), *Roman Stoicism* (Cambridge)

Arnold, M. B. (1968), *The Nature of Emotion* (London)

  (1970), *Feelings and Emotions: The Loyola Symposium* (New York)

Asmis, E. (1990), 'Philodemus' Epicureanism' in Haase and Temporini 2.36.4 (1990): 2359–406

Averill, J. R. (1979), 'Anger', *Nebraska Symposium on Motivation* 26: 1–81

  (1982), *Anger and Aggression: An Essay on Emotion* (New York)

Axelrod, R. (1984), *The Evolution of Cooperation* (New York)

Babbitt, F. C., trans. (1960), *Plutarch's 'Moralia'* (Cambridge, Mass.)

Babel, R. J. (1981–2), 'Vergil, Tops, and the Stoic View of Fate', *Classical Journal* 77: 27–31

Bailey, C., ed. (1947), *Titi Lucreti Cari 'De Rerum Natura' Libri Sex*, 3 vols. (Oxford)

Balsdon, J. P. V. D. (1964), 'Cicero the Man' in Dorey (1964): 171–214

Barnes, J., ed. (1984), *The Complete Works of Aristotle: The Revised Oxford Translation*, 2 vols. (Princeton)

Barnes, J. (1989), 'Antiochus of Ascalon' in Griffin and Barnes (1989): 51–96

Barnes, J., Schofield, M., and Sorabji, R., edd. (1979), *Articles on Aristotle*, vol. 4, *Psychology and Aesthetics* (London)

Basore, J. W., trans. (1965), *Seneca: 'Moral Essays'* (Cambridge, Mass.)

Baxter, R. T. S. (1971), 'Virgil's Influence on Tacitus' *Histories* 3', *Classical Philology* 66: 93–107

Behr, C. A., trans. (1981), *Aelius Aristides: The Complete Works*, vol. 2 (Leiden)

Benjamin, A. (1989), *Translation and the Nature of Philosophy* (London)

Betts, J., ed. (1986), *Studies in Honour of T. B. L. Webster*, vol. 1 (Bristol)

Billerbeck, M. (1986) 'Stoizismus in der römischen Epik der neronischer und flavischer Zeit' in Haase and Temporini 2.36.5 (1986): 3116–51

Bloom, A. D. (1987), *The Closing of the American Mind* (New York)

Blundell, M. W. (1989), *Helping Friends and Harming Enemies: A Study in Sophocles and Greek Ethics* (Cambridge)

Bonner, S. F. (1977), *Education in Ancient Rome* (London)

Booth, J. (1991), *Ovid, Amores 2*, ed. with trans. and comm. (Warminster)

Borszák, I. (1973), '*Spectaculum*: ein Motiv der "tragischen Geschichtschreibung" bei Livius und Tacitus', *Acta Classica Universitatis Scientarum Debreceniensis* 9: 57–67

Bowersock, G. W., ed. (1974), *Approaches to the Second Sophistic* (University Park, Pennsylvania)

Bowie, E. L. (1982), 'The Importance of Sophists', *Yale Classical Studies* 27: 29–59

Braden, G. (1985), *Renaissance Tragedy and the Senecan Tradition* (New Haven)

Braund, S. H. (1988), *Beyond Anger: A Study of Juvenal's Third Book of Satires* (Cambridge)

Braund, S. M. (formerly S. H.) (forthcoming), 'Statius, Theseus, and Epic Endings', *Proceedings of the Cambridge Philological Society*

Brennan, T. (forthcoming), 'The Old Stoic Theory of Emotions' in Engberg-Pedersen and Sihvola (forthcoming)

Briessmann, A. (1955), *Tacitus und das flavische Geschichtbild*, Hermes Einzelschriften 10 (Wiesbaden)

Brown, P. (1981), *The Cult of the Saints: its Rise and Function in Latin Christianity* (London)

  (1992), *Power and Persuasion in Late Antiquity: Towards a Christian Empire* (Wisconsin)

Brown, R. (1987), *Lucretius on Love and Sex* (Leiden)

Brunschwig, J., and Nussbaum, M. C., edd. (1993), *Passions and Perceptions: Studies in Hellenistic Philosophy of Mind* (Cambridge)

Buresch, C. (1887), *Consolationum a Graecis Romanisque scriptarum historia critica* (Leipzig) (= *Leipziger Studien zur klassischen Philologie* 9, 1886)

Cairns, F. (1972), *Generic Composition in Greek and Roman Poetry* (Edinburgh)

  (1989), *Virgil's Augustan Epic* (Cambridge)

Cameron, A., ed. (1989), *History as Text: The Writing of Ancient History* (London)

Cameron, K., ed. (1996), *The Literary Portrayal of Passion Through the Ages: An Interdisciplinary View* (Lewiston)

Campbell, D. A. (1982), *Greek Lyric*, vol. 1 (Cambridge, Mass.)

Campbell, K. (1985), 'Self-mastery and Stoic Ethics', *Philosophy* 60: 327–40

Cancik, H. (1967), *Untersuchungen zu Senecas 'Epistulae Morales'* (Hildesheim)

Cannon, W. B. (1927), 'The James–Lange Theory of the Emotions' in Arnold (1968): 43–52

Chilton, W., ed. (1971), *Diogenes of Oenoanda: The Fragments* (London)

Colish, M. L. (1985), *The Stoic Tradition from Antiquity to the Early Middle Ages*, vol. 1, *Stoicism in Classical Latin Literature* (Leiden)

Commager, S. (1965), 'Notes on Some Poems of Catullus', *Harvard Studies in Classical Philology* 70: 83–110

Cooper, J. (forthcoming), 'Posidonius on Emotions' in Engberg-Pedersen and Sihvola (forthcoming)

Copley, F. O. (1949), 'Emotional Conflict and its Significance in the Lesbia Poems of Catullus', *American Journal of Philology* 70: 22–40

Costa, C. D. N., ed. (1974), *Seneca* (London)

Courtney, E. (1980), *A Commentary on the Satires of Juvenal* (London)

Craik, E. (1988), *Euripides: 'Phoenician Women'*, with trans. and comm. (Warminster)

Cupauiolo, G. (1975), *Introduzione al 'De Ira' di Seneca* (Naples)

Cushman, R. E. (1958), *Therapeia: Plato's Conception of Philosophy* (Chapel Hill)

Dällenbach, L. (1977), *Le récit spéculaire: essai sur le mise en abyme* (Paris), trans. as *The Mirror in the Text* (Cambridge, 1989)

Davidson, J. (1991), 'The Gaze in Polybius' *Histories*', *Journal of Roman Studies* 81: 10–24

De Lacy, P. (1948), 'Stoic Views of Poetry', *American Journal of Philology* 69: 241–71

—— (1978–84), *Galen: On the Doctrines of Hippocrates and Plato ('De Placitis Hippocratis et Platonis')*, *Corpus Medicorum Graecorum* 5 4, 1, 2, ed. with trans. and comm., 3 vols. (Berlin)

De Man, P. (1984), *The Rhetoric of Romanticism* (New York)

den Boeft, J., and Kessels, A. H. M., edd. (1982), *ACTUS: Studies in Honour of H. L. W. Nelson* (Utrecht)

Dewar, M., ed. (1991), *Statius 'Thebaid' 9* (Oxford)

Diano, C. (1974), *Scritti Epicurei* (Florence)

Dillon, J. (1983), '*Metriopatheia* and *Apatheia*: Some Reflections on a Controversy in Late Greek Ethics' in Anton and Preus (1983): 508–17

Dorey, T. A., ed. (1964), *Cicero* (London)

Dougan, T. W., and Henry, R. M., edd. (1934), *Cicero: 'Tusculan Disputations'*, 2 vols. (Cambridge)

Douglas, A. (1991), review of MacKendrick (1989), *Classical Review* 41: 66–7

Dover, K. J. (1974), *Greek Popular Morality in the Time of Plato and Aristotle* (Oxford)

Du Bois, P. (1991), *Torture and Truth* (New York)

Dudley, D. R. (1967), *A History of Cynicism*, repr. of 1st edn (London, 1937) (Hildesheim)

Earl, D. C. (1961), *The Political Thought of Sallust* (Cambridge)

Edmunds, L. (1972), 'Juvenal's Thirteenth Satire', *Rheinisches Museum* 115: 59–73

Edwards, C. (1993), *The Politics of Immorality in Ancient Rome* (Cambridge)

Elliott, R. C. (1960), *The Power of Satire: Magic, Ritual, Art* (Princeton)

Elsner, J., and Masters, J., edd. (forthcoming), *Art and Society in the Age of Nero* (London)

Engberg-Pedersen, T. (1990), *The Stoic Theory of Oikeiosis: Moral Development and Social Interaction in Early Stoic Philosophy* (Aarhus)

Engberg-Pedersen, T., and Sihvola, J., edd. (forthcoming), *The Passions in Hellenistic Philosophy*

Erler, M. (1992*a*), 'Der Zorn des Helden, Philodems "De Ira" und Vergils Konzept des Zorns in der "Aeneis"', *Gräzer Beiträge* 18: 103–26

  (1992*b*) 'Orthodoxie und Anpassung: Philodem, ein Panaitios des Kepos', *Museum Helveticum* 49: 171–200

Erskine, A. (1990), *The Hellenistic Stoa: Political Thought and Action* (London)

Esteve-Forriol, J. (1962), *Die Trauer- und Trostgedichte in der römischen Literatur* (Munich)

Evans, S. (1994), 'The Self and Moral Agency in the *Hippolytus* and *Medea* of Euripides' (Cambridge Ph.D. thesis)

Everson, S. (1991), *Psychology: Companions to Ancient Thought 2* (Cambridge)

Fantham, E. (1972) *Comparative Studies in Republican Latin Imagery* (Toronto)

  (1982), *Seneca's 'Troades': A Literary Introduction, Text and Commentary* (Princeton)

Fantham, E., ed. (1992*a*) *Lucan: 'De Bello Civili' 2* (Cambridge)

Fantham, E. (1992*b*), 'Lucan's Medusa Excursus', *Materiali e discussioni per l'analisi dei testi classici* 29: 95–119

Feeney, D. C. (1993), 'Epilogue' in Gill and Wiseman (1993): 230–44

Feeney, D. J. (1991), *The Gods in Epic* (Oxford)

Fillion-Lahille, J. (1970), 'Une méprise à propos du *de ira* de Sénèque: la polémique du livre II ne vise pas Aristote mais Epicure', *Revue des études latines* 48: 296–308

  (1984), *Le 'De Ira' de Sénèque et la philosophie stoïcienne des passions* (Paris)

Fitch, J. G., ed. (1987), *Seneca: 'Hercules Furens'* (Ithaca, NY)

Flashar, H., and Gigon, O., edd. (1986), *Aspects de la philosophie hellénistique*, Fondation Hardt, *Entretiens sur l'antiquité classique* 32 (Vandoeuvres-Geneva)

Foley, H. (1989), 'Medea's Divided Self', *Classical Antiquity* 8: 61–85

Fornara, C. W. (1983), *The Nature of History in Ancient Greece and Rome* (Berkeley)

Fortenbaugh, W. W. (1975), *Aristotle on Emotion* (London)

  (1979), 'Aristotle's Rhetoric on Emotions' in Barnes, Schofield and Sorabji (1979): 133–53

Fortenbaugh, W. W., and Mirhady, D. C., edd. (1993), *Peripatetic Rhetoric after Aristotle* (New Brunswick)

Foucault, M. (1986), *The History of Sexuality*, vol. 2, *The Use of Pleasure*, trans. R. Hurley (Harmondsworth)

(1988), *The History of Sexuality*, vol. 3, *The Care of the Self*, trans. R. Hurley (Harmondsworth)

Fowler, D. P. (1989), 'Lucretius and Politics' in Griffin and Barnes (1989): 120–50

(1989), 'First Thoughts on Closure: Problems and Prospects', *Materiali e discussioni per l'analisi dei testi classici* 22: 75–122

Frede, M. (1986), 'The Stoic Doctrine of the Affections of the Soul' in Schofield and Striker (1986): 93–110

(1987a), 'Philosophy and Medicine in Antiquity' in Frede (1987b): 225–42

(1987b), *Essays on Ancient Philosophy* (Oxford)

Fredericks, S. C. (1971), 'Calvinus in Juvenal's Thirteenth Satire', *Arethusa* 4: 219–31

Fuhrmann, M. (1960), 'Das Vierkaiserjahr bei Tacitus', *Philologus* 104: 250–78

Funke, H. (1990). 'Liebe als Krankheit in der griechischen und römischen Antike' in Stemmler (1990): 11–30

Galinsky, K. (1988), 'The Anger of Aeneas', *American Journal of Philology* 109: 321–48

(1992a), 'The Interpretation of Roman Poetry and the Contemporary Critical Scene' in Galinsky (1992b): 1–40

Galinsky K., ed., (1992b), *The Interpretation of Roman Poetry: Empiricism or Hermeneutics?* (Frankfurt)

(1994), 'How to be Philosophical about the End of the Aeneid', *Illinois Classical Studies* 19: 1–11

Giannantoni, G. (1984), 'Il piacere cinetico nell-etica epicurea', *Elenchos* 5: 25–44

Gill, C. (1983a), 'Did Chrysippus understand Medea?', *Phronesis* 28: 136–49

(1983b), 'The Question of Character-Development: Plutarch and Tacitus', *Classical Quarterly* 33: 469–87

(1984), 'The *Ethos/Pathos* Distinction in Rhetorical and Literary Criticism', *Classical Quarterly* 34: 149–66

(1985), 'Ancient Psychotherapy', *Journal of the History of Ideas* 46: 307–25

(1986), 'The Question of Character and Personality in Greek Tragedy', *Poetics Today* 7: 251–73

(1987), 'Two Monologues of Self-Division: Euripides, *Medea* 1021–80 and Seneca, *Medea* 893–977' in Whitby, Hardie and Whitby (1987): 25–37

(1988), 'Personhood and Personality: The Four-*Personae* Theory in Cicero, *De Officiis* I', *Oxford Studies in Ancient Philosophy* 6: 169–99

(1990), 'The Character–Personality Distinction' in Pelling (1990): 1–30

(1994), 'Peace of Mind and Being Yourself: Panaetius to Plutarch' in Haase and Temporini 2.36.7 (1994): 4599–640.

(1995a), *Greek Thought, Greece and Rome*, New Surveys in the Classics No. 25 (Oxford)

(1995b), review of Nussbaum (1994), *Classical Review* 40.2: 290–2

(1996a), 'Ancient Passions: Theories and Cultural Styles' in K. Cameron (1996): 1–10

(1996*b*), 'Mind and Madness in Greek Tragedy', *Apeiron* 29.3: 249–66

(1996*c*), *Personality in Greek Epic, Tragedy, and Philosophy: The Self in Dialogue* (Oxford)

(forthcoming*a*), 'Did Galen Understand Platonic and Stoic Thinking on Emotions?' in Engberg-Pedersen and Sihvola (forthcoming)

(forthcoming*b*), 'Ethical Reflection and the Shaping of Character: Plato's *Republic* and Stoicism', *Proceedings of the Boston Area Colloquium in Ancient Philosophy* 12

Gill, C., and Wiseman, T. P., edd. (1993), *Lies and Fiction in the Ancient World* (Exeter)

Gilmartin, K. (1975), 'A Rhetorical Figure in Latin Historical Style: The Imaginary Second Person Singular', *Transactions of the American Philological Association* 105: 99–121

Giuffrida, P. (1950), *Lucrezio e Catullo – L'epicurismo nella letteratura latina del I secolo a. cr.* (Turin)

Glick, R. A., and Roose, S. P. (1993), *Rage, Power, and Aggression* (New Haven)

Gomme, A. W., and Sandbach, F. H. (1973), *Menander: A Commentary* (Oxford)

Gosling, J. (1987), 'The Stoics and *akrasia*', *Apeiron* 20.2: 179–202

(1990), *Weakness of the Will* (London)

Gosling, J. C. B., and Taylor, C. C. W. (1982), *The Greeks on Pleasure* (Oxford)

Gottschalk, H. B. (1987), 'Aristotelian Philosophy in the Roman World' in Haase and Temporini 2.36.2 (1987): 1079–174

Goulet-Cazé, M.-O., and Branham, R. B., edd. (1993), *The Cynic Movement in Antiquity and its Legacy for Europe* (Cambridge, Mass.)

Griffin, J. (1985), *Latin Poets and Roman Life* (London)

Griffin, M. (1976), *Seneca, A Philosopher in Politics* (Oxford)

Griffin, M., and Atkins, E. M. (1991), *Cicero: 'On Duties'*, trans. with introd. and notes, Cambridge Texts in the History of Political Thought (Cambridge)

Griffin, M., and Barnes, J., edd. (1989), *Philosophia Togata* (Oxford)

Griffiths, J.G. (1990), 'Love as a Disease' in Israelit-Groll (1990): 349–64

Griffiths, M., and Mastronarde, D. J., edd. (1990), *Cabinet of the Muses* (Berkeley)

Gunmere, R. M., trans. (1962), *Seneca: 'ad Lucilium Epistulae Morales'* (Cambridge, Mass.)

Haase, W., and Temporini, H., edd. (1974–) *Aufstieg und Niedergang der römischen Welt* (Berlin/NewYork)

Habinek, T. (1990), 'Sacrifice, Society, and Virgil's Ox-born Bees' in Griffiths and Mastronarde (1990): 209–23

Hadot, I. (1969), *Seneca und die griechische-römische Tradition der Seelenleitung* (Berlin)

Hadot, P. (1981, 2nd edn 1987), *Exercises spirituels et philosophie antique* (Paris)

Halliwell, S. (1986), *Aristotle's Poetics* (London)

Hamon, P. (1977), 'Texte littéraire et métalangage', *Poétique* 31: 261–84

Hardie, P. R. (1986), *Virgil's 'Aeneid': Cosmos and Imperium* (Oxford)
(1993), *The Epic Successors of Vergil* (Cambridge)

Harvey, F. D. (1971), 'Sick Humour and Aristophanic Parody of a Euripidean Motif', *Mnemosyne* 24: 362–5

Heinz, W.-R. (1975), *Die Furcht als politisches Phänomenon bei Tacitus*, Heuremata 4 (Amsterdam)

Henry, D. and E. (1985), *The Mask of Power: Seneca's Tragedies and Imperial Rome* (Warminster)

Henry, E. (1989), *The Vigour of Prophecy* (Bristol)

Herington, C. J. (1966), 'Senecan Tragedy', *Arion* 5: 422–71

Hershkowitz, D. (1994), 'Sexuality and Madness in Statius' *Thebaid*', *Materiali e discussioni per l'analisi dei testi classici* 33: 123–47
(1995a), 'Madness in Greek and Latin Epic' (Oxford D.Phil. thesis)
(1995b), 'Patterns of Madness in Statius' *Thebaid*', *Journal of Roman Studies* 85: 52–64

Hillman, J. (1992), *Emotion: A Comprehensive Phenomenology of Theories and their Meaning* (Illinois)

Hinds, S. (1986), *The Metamorphosis of Persephone: Ovid and the Self-conscious Muse* (Cambridge)

Hofmann, H., ed. (1990), *Groningen Colloquia on the Novel 3* (Groningen)

Humbert, J. (1925), *Les plaidoyers écrits et les plaidoiries réelles de Cicéron* (Paris)

Hutcheon, L. (1980), *Narcissistic Narrative: The Metafictional Paradox* (Waterloo)

Indelli, G., ed. (1988), *Philodemus 'De ira'* (Naples)

Inwood, B. (1985), *Ethics and Human Action in Early Stoicism* (Oxford)
(1993), 'Seneca and Psychological Dualism' in Brunschwig and Nussbaum (1993): 150–83

Israelit-Groll, S., ed. (1990), *Studies in Egyptology presented to Miriam Lichtheim* (Jerusalem)

Izard, C. E. (1977), *Emotions* (New York)

James, L., and Webb, R. (1991), 'To Understand Ultimate Things and Enter Secret Places: Ekphrasis and Art in Byzantium', *Art History* 14: 1–17

Jensen, B. F. (1981–2), 'Crime, Vice and Retribution in Juvenal's Satires', *Classica et Mediaevalia* 33: 155–68

Jocelyn, H. D. (1967), *The Tragedies of Ennius*, ed. with comm. (Cambridge)

Jones, C. P. (1974), 'The Reliability of Philostratus' in Bowersock (1974): 11–16

Kassel, R. (1958), *Untersuchungen zur griechischen und römischen Konsolationsliteratur* (Munich)

Kearney, R. (1988) *The Wake of the Imagination: Ideas of Creativity in Western Culture* (London)

Keil, B., ed. (1898), *Aelius Aristides, Opera*, vol. 2 (Berlin)

Keitel, E. (1992), '*Foedum spectaculum* and Related Motifs in Tacitus *Histories II–III*', *Rheinisches Museum* 135: 342–51

Kennedy, D. (1993), *The Arts of Love* (Cambridge)

Kennedy, G. (1972), *The Art of Rhetoric in Ancient Rome* (Princeton)

Kenney, E. J., and Clausen, W., edd. (1982), *Cambridge History of Classical Literature*, vol. 2, *Latin Literature* (Cambridge)

Kerferd, G. B. (1978), 'What does the Wise Man Know?', in Rist (1978): 125–36

Kidd, D. A. (1963), 'The Unity of Catullus 51', *Journal of the Australasian Universities Language and Literature Association* 20: 298–308

Kidd, I. G. (1971), 'Posidonius on Emotions', in Long (1971): 200–15

Kirby, J. T. (1990), *The Rhetoric of Cicero's 'Pro Cluentio'* (Amsterdam)

Knox, B. M. W. (1968), 'Silent Reading in Antiquity', *Greek, Roman and Byzantine Studies* 9: 421–35

Kovecses, Z. (1986), *Metaphors of Anger, Pride and Love: A Lyrical Approach to the Structure of Concepts* (Amsterdam)

Kroll, W. (1929), *Catull*, ed. with comm. (2nd edn, Leipzig)

Kühner, R., and Stegmann, C. (1955), *Ausführliche Grammatik der lateinischen Sprache: Satzlehre*, vol. 2 (3rd edn rev. A. Thierfelder) (Leverkusen)

Lada, I. (1993), ' "Empathic Understanding": Emotion and Cognition in Classical Dramatic Audience-Response', *Proceedings of the Cambridge Philological Society* 39: 94–140

Lamberton, R. D., and Keaney, J. J., edd. (1992), *Homer's Ancient Readers* (Princeton)

La Penna, A. (1957), 'Note sul linguaggio erotico dell' elegia latina', *Maia* 4: 187–209

Lavery, G. B. (1980), 'Metaphors of War and Travel in Seneca's Prose Works', *Greece and Rome* 27: 147–57

Lazarus, R., Kanner, A. D., and Folkman, S. (1980), 'Emotions: a Cognitive-Phenomenological Analysis' in Plutchik and Kellerman (1980), vol. 1: 189–217

Lazarus, R., Opton, E., and Averill, J. R. (1970), 'Towards a Cognitive Theory of Emotion' in Arnold (1970): 207–32

Lear, J. (1988), 'Katharsis', *Phronesis* 33: 297–326, repr. as Rorty (1992): 315–40

Lee, A. G., trans. (1991), *The Poems of Catullus* (Oxford)

Lefkowitz, M. (1981), *Lives of Greek Poets* (Baltimore)

Levene, D. S. (1993), *Religion in Livy* (Leiden)

Lévy, C., and Pernot, L., edd. (forthcoming), *Dire l'evidence: actes du colloque international, 24–25 mars 1995* (Paris) (= *Cahiers d'histoire de la philosophie et de philosophie du langage*, numéro spécial)

Lichtheim, M. (1976), *Ancient Egyptian Literature*, vol. 2 (Berkeley)

Lloyd, A. C. (1978), 'Emotion and Decision in Stoic Psychology' in Rist (1978): 233–46

Long, A. A., ed. (1971), *Problems in Stoicism* (London)

Long, A. A. (1986a), 'Pleasure and Social Utility – the Virtues of Being Epicurean' in Flashar and Gigon (1986): 283–324

(1986*b*), '*Pro* and *Contra* Fratricide: Aeschylus' *Septem* 653–719' in Betts (1986): 179–89

(1991), 'Representation and the Self in Stoicism' in Everson (1991): 102–20

(1992), 'Stoic Readings of Homer' in Lamberton and Keaney (1992): 41–66

Long, A. A., and Sedley, D. N. (1987), *The Hellenistic Philosophers*, 2 vols. (Cambridge)

Longo Auricchio, F., and Tepedino Guerra, A. (1979), 'Chi è Timasagora?' in *Atti del convegno internazionale. La regione sotterrata dal Vesuvio: studi e prospettive* (Naples): 1–9

(1981), 'Aspetti e problemi della dissidenza epicurea', *Cronache Ercolanesi* 11: 32–8

Lucas, D. W. (1968), *Aristotle: 'Poetics'* (Oxford)

Lutz, A., and Abu-Loghod, L., edd. (1990), *Language and the Politics of Emotion* (Cambridge)

Lutz, C. E. (1947), 'Musonius Rufus "The Roman Socrates"', *Yale Classical Studies* 10: 3–147

Lynch, J. (1972), *Aristotle's School* (Berkeley)

Lyne, R. O. A. M. (1980), *The Latin Love Poets from Catullus to Horace* (Oxford)

(1983), 'Vergil and the Politics of War', *Classical Quarterly* 33: 188–203

(1987), *Further Voices in Vergil's 'Aeneid'* (Oxford)

(1994), 'Vergil's *Aeneid*: Subversion by Intertextuality. Catullus 66.39–40 and Other Examples', *Greece and Rome* 41: 187–204

McGann, M. J. (1969), *Studies in Horace's First Book of Epistles* (Brussels)

MacKendrick, P. (1989), *The Philosophical Books of Cicero* (London)

MacLeod, C. W. (1979), 'The Poetry of Ethics: Horace *Epistles* I', *Journal of Roman Studies* 69: 16–27

Madow, L. (1972), *Anger* (New York)

Maehler, H. (1990), 'Symptome der Liebe im Roman und in der griechischen Anthologie' in Hofmann (1990): 1–12

Malherbe, A. J. (1988), *Ancient Epistolary Theorists* (Atlanta)

Manning, C. E. (1973), 'Seneca and the Stoics on the Equality of the Sexes', *Mnemosyne* 26: 170–7

(1974), 'The Consolatory Tradition and Seneca's Attitude to the Emotions', *Greece and Rome* 21: 71–81

(1981), *On Seneca's 'Ad Marciam'* (Leiden)

Manuli, P. (1988), 'La passione nel *De placitis Hippocratis et Platonis*' in Manuli and Vegetti (1988): 185–214

Manuli, P., and Vegetti, M., edd. (1988), *Le opere psicologiche di Galeno* (Naples)

Martin, R. H., and Woodman, A. J., edd. (1989), *Tacitus: 'Annals' Book IV* (Cambridge)

Masters, J. (1992), *Poetry and Civil War in Lucan's 'Bellum Civile'* (Cambridge)

Maurach, G. (1970), *Der Bau von Senecas 'Epistulae Morales'* (Heidelberg)

Mazzoli, G. (1970), *Seneca e la poesia* (Milan)

(1979), 'Le *Epistulae Morales* di Seneca. Valore letterario e filosofico' in Haase and Temporini 2.36.3 (1979): 823–77

Meijering, R. (1987), *Literary and Rhetorical Theories in Greek Scholia* (Groningen)

Michel, A. (1969), 'Rhétorique, tragédie, philosophie: Sénèque et le sublime', *Giornale Italiano di Filologia* 21: 245–57

Miller, F. J., trans. (1961), *Seneca's Tragedies* (Cambridge, Mass.)

Mitchell, T. N. (1991), *Cicero, The Senior Statesman* (New Haven)

Mitsis, P. (1988), *Epicurus' Ethical Theory: The Pleasures of Invulnerability* (Ithaca)

Moles, J. L. (1986), 'Cynicism in Horace *Epistles* I', *Papers of the Liverpool Latin Seminar* 5: 33–60

(1993), 'Truth and Untruth in Herodotus and Thucydides' in Gill and Wiseman (1993): 88–121

Morford, M. P. O. (1973), 'Juvenal's Thirteenth Satire', *American Journal of Philology* 94: 26–36

Morgan, J. R. (1991), 'Reader and Audiences in the *Aithiopika* of Heliodoros', *Groningen Colloquia on the Novel* 4: 85–104

(1993), 'Make-believe and Make Believe' in Gill and Wiseman (1993): 175–229

Moritz, L. A. (1968), '*Difficile est subito longum deponere amorem*', *Greece and Rome* 15: 53–8

Most, G. W. (1989), 'Cornutus and Stoic Allegoresis' in Haase and Temporini 2.35.3 (1989): 2015–65

Most, G. W., Petersmann, H., and Ritter, A. H., edd. (1993), *Philanthropia kai Eusebeia: Festschrift A. Dihle* (Göttingen)

Myerowitz, M. (1985), *Ovid's Games of Love* (Detroit)

Nehamas, A. (1992), 'Pity and Fear in the *Rhetoric* and *Poetics*' in Rorty (1992): 291–314

Nesse, R. (1991), 'Evolutionary Explanations of Emotions', *Human Nature* 1.3: 261–83

Neubecker, A. J., ed. (1986), *Philodemus: Über die Musik IV Buch* (Naples)

Neudling, C. (1949), 'Epicureanism and the "New Poets"', *Transactions of the American Philological Association* 80: 429–30

Newman, J. K. (1990), *Roman Catullus and the Modification of the Alexandrian Sensibility* (Hildesheim)

Nisbet, R. B. M. (1992), 'The Orator and the Reader: Manipulation and Response in Cicero's Fifth *Verrine*' in Woodman and Powell (1992): 1–17

Nisbet, R. G. M., and Hubbard, M. (1970), *A Commentary on Horace 'Odes' Book 1* (Oxford)

Nussbaum, M.C. (1986a), *The Fragility of Goodness: Luck and Ethics in Greek Tragedy and Philosophy* (Cambridge)

(1986b), 'Therapeutic Arguments: Epicurus and Aristotle' in Schofield and Striker (1986): 31–74

(1987*a*), review of Bloom (1987), *New York Review of Books* 34.17: 20–6

(1987*b*), 'The Stoics on the Extirpation of Passions', *Apeiron* 15: 129–77

(1989), 'Beyond Obsession and Disgust: Lucretius' Genealogy of Love', *Apeiron* 22: 1–59

(1990*a*), ' "By Words not Arms": Lucretius on Gentleness in an Unsafe World' in Nussbaum (1990*b*): 41–90

Nussbaum, M. C., ed. (1990*b*), *The Poetics of Therapy: Hellenistic Ethics in its Rhetorical and Literary Context* (=*Apeiron* 23.4) (Edmonton)

Nussbaum, M. C. (1992), 'Tragedy and Self-Sufficiency: Plato and Aristotle on Fear and Pity', *Oxford Studies in Ancient Philosophy* 10: 107–59

(1993), 'Poetry and the Passions: Two Stoic Views' in Brunschwig and Nussbaum (1993): 97–149

(1994), *The Therapy of Desire, Theory and Practice in Hellenistic Ethics* (Princeton)

Nussbaum, M. C., and Rorty, A. O., edd. (1992), *Essays on Aristotle's 'De Anima'* (Oxford)

Ogilvie, R. M. (1965), *A Commentary on Livy Books 1–5* (Oxford)

Oltramare, A. (1926), *Les origines de la diatribe romaine* (Lausanne)

Padel, R. (1992), *In and Out of the Mind: Greek Images of the Tragic Self* (Princeton)

(1994), *Whom Gods Destroy: Elements of Greek and Tragic Madness* (Princeton)

Pantzerhielm-Thomas, S. (1936), 'The Prologues of Sallust', *Symbolae Osloenses* 15–16: 140–62

Paul, G. M. (1982), '*Urbs Capta*: Sketch of an Ancient Literary Motif', *Phoenix* 36: 144–55

Pearce, T. E. V. (1992), 'Juvenal 3.10–20', *Mnemosyne* 45: 380–3

Pears, D. F. (1978), 'Aristotle's Analysis of Courage', *Midwest Studies in Philosophy* 3: 273–85

Pedrick, V., and Rabinowitz, N. S. (1986), 'Introduction to Audience Oriented Criticism and the Classics', *Arethusa* 19: 105–14

Pelling, C. B. R., ed. (1990), *Characterization and Individuality in Greek Literature* (Oxford)

Pernot, L. (1986), 'Lieu et lieu commun dans la rhétorique antique', *Bulletin de l'Association Guillaume Budé*, 4th series: 253–84

(1993), *La rhétorique de l'éloge dans le monde greco-romain* (Paris)

Pigeaud, J. (1981), *La maladie de l'âme* (Paris)

Plutchik, R. (1980), *Emotion: A Psychoevolutionary Synthesis* (New York)

Plutchik, R., and Kellerman, H. (1980), *Emotion, Theory, Research and Experience*, vol. 1 (New York)

Powell, J. G. F. (1990), 'Two Notes on Catullus', *Classical Quarterly* 40: 189–206

Pratt, N. T. (1948), 'The Stoic Base of Senecan Drama', *Transactions of the American Philological Association* 94: 199–234

(1983), *Seneca's Drama* (Chapel Hill)

Preston, K. (1916), 'Studies in the Diction of the *sermo amatorius* in Roman Comedy' (Chicago Ph.D. thesis)

Price, A. W. (1989), *Love and Friendship in Plato and Aristotle* (Oxford)
    (1995), *Mental Conflict* (London)
Prince, G. (1977), 'Remarques sur les signes métanarratifs', *Degrés* 5: e1–e10
Procopé, J. (1993), 'Epicureans on Anger' in Most, Petersmann and Ritter
    (1993): 363–86
Pryor, A. D. (1962), 'Juvenal's False Consolation', *Journal of the Australasian
    Universities' Language and Literature Association* 18: 167–80
Putnam, M. C. J. (1990), 'Anger, Blindness and Insight in Virgil's *Aeneid*' in
    Nussbaum (1990*b*): 7–40
    (1995), *Virgil's 'Aeneid': Interpretation and Influence* (Chapel Hill)
Quinn, K. (1969), *The Catullan Revolution* (rev. edn, London)
    (1970), *Catullus, The Poems*, text and comm. (London)
Quint, D. (1993), *Epic and Empire* (Princeton)
Rabbow, P. (1914), *Antike Schriften über Seelenheilung und Seelenleitung auf ihre
    Quellen untersucht*, vol. 1, *Die Therapie des Zorns* (Leipzig)
    (1954), *Seelenführung* (Munich)
Rabe, H., ed. (1926), *Aphthonius: 'Progymnasmata'* (Leipzig)
Rabinowitz, P. J. (1986), 'Shifting Stands, Shifting Standards', *Arethusa* 19:
    115–34
Rademacher, U. (1975), *Die Bildkunst des Tacitus*, Spudasmata 29 (Hildesheim)
Rambaux, C. (1972), 'Le myth de Médée', *Latomus* 31: 1010–36
Rawson, E. (1975), *Cicero* (London)
    (1985), *Intellectual Life in the Late Roman Republic* (London)
Richlin, A. (1992), *The Garden of Priapus: Sexuality and Aggression in Roman
    Humor* (New York)
Rieks, R. (1989), *Affekte und Strukturen: Pathos als ein Form- und Wirkprinzip von
    Vergils Aeneis*, Zetemata 86 (Munich)
Rist, J. M. (1969), *Stoic Philosophy* (Cambridge)
    (1972), *Epicurus: An Introduction* (Cambridge)
Rist, J. M., ed. (1978), *The Stoics* (Berkeley)
Rist, J. M. (1989), 'Seneca and Stoic Orthodoxy' in Haase and Temporini
    2.36.3 (1989): 1993–2012
Rorty, A. O., ed. (1980), *Explaining Emotions* (Berkeley)
    (1992), *Essays on Aristotle's 'Poetics'* (Princeton)
Rosati, G. (1983), *Narciso e Pigmalione: Illusione e spettacolo nelle 'Metamorfosi' di
    Ovidio* (Florence)
Ross Jr., D. O. (1969), *Style and Tradition in Catullus* (Cambridge, Mass.)
Rudd, N. (1991), *Juvenal: The Satires* (Oxford)
Russell, D. A., ed. (1964), *Longinus: 'On the Sublime'*
Russell, D. A. (1974), 'Letters to Lucilius' in Costa (1974): 70–95
    (1983), *Greek Declamation* (Cambridge)
Russell, D. A., and Wilson, N. G., edd. and trans. (1981), *Menander Rhetor:
    'On Epideictic'* (Oxford)
Russell, D. A., and Winterbottom, M., edd. (1972), *Ancient Literary Criticism*
    (Oxford)

Sandbach, F. H. (1975), *The Stoics* (London)

(1985), *Aristotle and the Stoics, Cambridge Philological Society*, supp. vol. 10 (Cambridge)

Schetter, W. (1960), *Untersuchungen zur epischen Kunst des Statius* (Wiesbaden)

Schiesaro, A. (1992), 'Forms of Senecan Intertextuality', *Vergilius* 38: 56–63

(forthcoming), 'Seneca's *Thyestes* and the Morality of Tragic *furor*', in Elsner and Masters (forthcoming)

Schofield, M. (1979), 'Aristotle on the Imagination' in Barnes, Schofield and Sorabji (1979): 103–32

(1991), *The Stoic Idea of the City* (Cambridge)

Schofield, M., and Striker, G., edd. (1986), *The Norms of Nature: Studies in Hellenistic Ethics* (Cambridge)

Schrijvers, P. H. (1982), 'Invention, imagination et théorie des émotions chez Cicéron et Quintilian' in den Boeft and Kessels (1982): 395–408

Segal, C. P. (1986), *Language and Desire in Seneca's 'Phaedra'* (Princeton)

(1990), *Lucretius on Death and Anxiety: Poetry and Philosophy in 'De Rerum Natura'* (Princeton)

Shackleton Bailey, D. R. (1966), *Cicero's Letters to Atticus*, vol. 5 (Cambridge)

(1971), *Cicero* (London)

Shelton, J. (1978), *Seneca's 'Hercules Furens': Theme, Structure and Style* (Göttingen)

Skinner, M. (1987), 'Disease Imagery in Catullus 76.17–26', *Classical Philology* 82: 230–3

Solmsen, F. (1941), 'The Aristotelian Tradition in Ancient Rhetoric', *American Journal of Philology* 62: 32–50, 169–90

Solomon, R. C. (1976), *The Passions: The Myth and Nature of Human Emotions* (New York)

Sowards, J. K., ed. (1985), *Collected Works of Erasmus*, vol. 25 (Toronto)

Spengel, L., and Hammer, C., edd. (1894), *Rhetores Graeci*, 2 vols. (Leipzig)

Stam, R. (1992), *Reflexivity in Film and Literature: From Don Quixote to Jean-Luc Godard*, reprint of 1st edn (Ann Arbor, 1985) (New York)

Stanford, W. B., ed. (1963), *Sophocles: 'Ajax'* (London)

Stearns, F. R. (1975), *Anger: Psychology, Physiology, Pathology* (Springfield, Illinois)

Stemmler, T., ed. (1990), *Liebe als Krankheit, 3 Kolloquium der Forschungsstelle für europäische Lyrik des Mittelalters an der Universität Mannheim* (Mannheim)

Strongman, K. T. (1987), *The Psychology of Emotion*, 3rd edn (Chichester)

Strongman, K. T., ed. (1991), *International Review of Studies on Emotion* (Chichester)

Suttie, I. D. (1935), *The Origins of Love and Hate* (Harmondsworth)

Syndikus, H.-P. (1987), *Catull. Dritter Teil: Die Epigramme (69–116)* (Darmstadt)

Tavris, C. (1982), *Anger, the Misunderstood Emotion* (New York)

Thomas, J., ed. (1988), *L'imaginaire de l'espace et du temps chez les Latins* (Perpignan) (= *Cahiers de l'Université de Perpignan* 5)

Thomas, R. (1991a), '*Furor* and *Furiae* in Virgil', *American Journal of Philology* 112: 261–2

(1991*b*), 'The "Sacrifice" at the end of the *Georgics*, Aristaeus, and Virgilian Closure', *Classical Philology*: 211–8

Thornton, A. (1976), *The Living Universe* (Otago)

Tieleman, T. L. (1992), *Galen and Chrysippus: Argument and Refutation in the 'De Placitis' Books II–III* (Utrecht)

Tompkins, J. (1980*a*), 'The Reader in History' in Tompkins (1980*b*): 201–32

Tompkins, J., ed. (1980*b*), *Reader-Response Criticism from Formalism to Post-Structuralism* (Baltimore)

Toohey, P. (1992), 'Love, Lovesickness, and Melancholia', *Illinois Classical Studies* 17: 265–86

Urmson, J. O. (1988), *Aristotle's Ethics* (Oxford)

Usener, H., and Radermacher, C., edd. (1929), *Dionysius of Halicarnassus: Opuscula*, 2 vols. (Leipzig)

Vander Waerdt, P. A. (1994*a*), 'Zeno's *Republic* and the Origins of Natural Law' in Vander Waerdt (1994*b*): 272–308

Vander Waerdt, P. A., ed. (1994*b*), *The Socratic Movement* (Ithaca)

Venini, P. (1964), '*Furor* e Psicologia nella *Tebaide* di Stazio', *Athenaeum* 42: 201–13

Venini, P., ed. (1970), *P. Papinii Statii 'Thebaidos' Liber II* (Florence)

Vessey, D. (1974), *Statius and the 'Thebaid'* (Cambridge)

(1982) 'Flavian Epic' in Kenney and Clausen (1982): 558–9.

Veyne, P. (1983), *L'élégie érotique romaine: l'amour, la poésie et l'Occident* (Paris)

Viarre, S. (1988), 'Les images de l'espace et du temps chez Ovide' in J. Thomas (1988): 91–106

Ville, G. (1981), *La gladiature en occident des origines à la mort de Domitien* (Rome)

Voelke, A.-J. (1993), *La philosophie comme thérapie de l'âme: études de philosophie hellénistique* (Paris)

Walbank, F. W. (1938), 'Φίλιππος τραγῳδούμενος: A Polybian Experiment', *Journal of Hellenic Studies* 58: 55–68

(1972), *Polybius* (Berkeley)

Walsh, P. G. (1958), 'Livy and Stoicism', *American Journal of Philology* 79: 355–75

(1961), *Livy: His Historical Aims and Methods* (Cambridge)

Walz, C., ed. (1835), *Rhetores Graeci*, 8 vols. (Stuttgart)

Webb, R. (forthcoming), 'Mémoire et imagination: les limites de l' *enargeia* dans la théorie rhétorique grecque' in Lévy and Pernot (forthcoming)

Wellesley, K. (1972), *Cornelius Tacitus: The Histories Book III* (Sydney)

West, M. L. (1969), 'Near Eastern Material in Hellenistic and Roman Literature', *Harvard Studies in Classical Philology* 73: 113–34

Wheeldon, M. J. (1989), ' "True Stories": The Reception of Historiography in Antiquity' in A. Cameron (1989): 33–63

Whitby, M., Hardie, P., and Whitby, M., edd. (1987), *'Homo Viator': Classical Essays for John Bramble* (Bristol): 28–37

White, N. (1990), 'Stoic Values', *Monist* 73: 42–58

Whitman, J. (1987), *Allegory: The Dynamics of an Ancient and Medieval Technique* (Oxford)

Wilamowitz-Moellendorff, U. von (1919), *Griechische Tragödie* (Berlin)

Williams, G. (1968), *Tradition and Originality in Roman Poetry* (Oxford)

Wilson, M. J. (1987), 'Seneca's *Epistles to Lucilius*: A Revaluation', *Ramus* 16: 102–121

Winnington-Ingram, R. P. (1980), *Sophocles: An Interpretation* (Cambridge)

Wiseman, T. P. (1985), *Catullus and his World: A Reappraisal* (Cambridge)

(1993), 'Lying Historians: Seven Types of Mendacity' in Gill and Wiseman (1993): 122–46

Woodman, A. J. (1988), *Rhetoric in Classical Historiography* (London)

Woodman, T., and Powell, J., edd. (1992), *Author and Audience in Latin Literature* (Cambridge)

Wright, J. R. G. (1974), 'Form and Content in the *Moral Essays*' in Costa (1974): 39–69

Wright, M. R. (1991), *Cicero: On Stoic Good and Evil: 'De Finibus' 3 and 'Paradoxa Stoicorum'*, ed., trans. and comm. (Warminster)

Wright, W. C., trans. (1968), *Philostratus: Lives of the Sophists* (Cambridge, Mass.)

Yardley, J. C. (1987), 'Propertius 4.5, Ovid, *Amores* 1.6 and Roman Comedy', *Proceedings of the Cambridge Philological Society* 33: 179–89

Zanker, G. (1981), '*Enargeia* in the Ancient Criticism of Poetry', *Rheinisches Museum* 124: 297–311

Index of ancient passages

Histories 2.31.1: 144–5; 2.64: 142;
  3.36–86: 136–47
TERENCE, *Eunuch* 225–6: 157
THEOCRITUS, *Idylls* 2.85–90, 104–10: 156

VIRGIL, *Aeneid* 1.11, 25–8, 41: 174; 1.150:
  178–9; 1.361: 200; 2.314–17: 180;
  4.1–5, 66–7, 76: 156; 4.15–19, 24–9,
  55: 228; 4.31–53: 236; 54–5, 66–9:
  236–7; 4.194: 178; 4.465–73: 229;
  4.530–1: 176–7; 4.548–9: 228–9;
  4.641–6: 183; 5.173: 174; 5.454: 178;
  5.659: 179; 6.586: 174; 6.851: 33;
  7.327–36: 199–200; 7.421–66:
179–80, 236; 7.508: 179; 7.571:
199–200; 8.225–71: 183; 8.700–3:
205; 9.107: 174; 9.759–60: 238;
10.270–5: 180; 10.692, 853, 905:
200; 10.802, 813–16: 181; 11.452–3:
179; 11.901–2: 237; 12.19–20:
170; 12.101–2: 180; 12.107–8:
178; 12.229–37: 176; 12.332–6:
205; 12.494–9: 182–3; 12.525–8:
181–2; 12.631–96: 238, 240;
12.667–8: 181; 12.830–1: 174;
12.841: 175; 12.946–7: 30,
182–3; 12.945–51: 182–3, 213,
240; 12.930–52: 200, 239–40

General index

For conventions on abbrevations see p. x above.

Achilles, 175–6, 182, 184
adfectus (emotion, passion), 105–6, 119, 121
Aelius Aristides, 114–17
Aeneas: emotional lapses, 229–30; and Hercules 183; killing of Lausus, 181; killing of Turnus, interpretations of, 2, 30–4, 169–70, 182–4, 200, 213, 239–41; *see also* Virgil, *Aeneid*
Ajax, 176–7, 184, 186, 190–3, 219
akrasia (weakness of will): in Catullus, 163, 221; in Euripides, 220–1; in Ovid, 221–2; in Sen. *Med.*, 195, 217–18; in Sen. *Phaed.*, 215–16; in Stoicism, 161, 225–8; in Virg. *A.*, 235–41; other, 213, 222n.
Allecto, 179, 199–200, 236–7
allegory, 202, 205–6, 212n.
Anderson, W. S., 87n.
anger: in Aristotle, 6, 16, 171–3, 175–7, 182, 184, 186–7; as a cognitive response, 175–6; as desire for retaliation/revenge, 6, 10, 16, 18, 26, 70, 77–8, 84–6, 172, 174, 176–8, 193–4, 217; and disposition or temperament, 20–1, 28, 173–4, 177–8n.; in E. *Med.*, 193–5, 220–1; in Epicureanism, 19–35, 240–1nn.; an indeterminate phenomenon, 34–5; and grief, 68–9, 80–2, 84; and hatred, 186–7, 202, 204, 206, 209; in Hom. *Il.*, 175–6, 180, 184; in Juv. 13, 68–9, 76–88; in Lucretius, 20–1, 173n.; in modern theory, 16–19; in Peripatetic thought, 6–7, 182–4, 231; as a physiological reaction, 16–17, 20–1, 172, 174–5, 177, 180; in Seneca, 21–4, 26, 80, 82–6, 105–6, 188n., 202n., 231–2; as a social response, 6, 16, 18, 172–3, 175–6, 178; as a survival mechanism, 178–9; in Stat. *Theb.*, 202, 204, 209; in Stoicism, 21–4, 26, 82–6, 169–70, 182–4, 187–8, 231–2, 236–41; in Virg. *A.*, 30–4, 169, 174–84, 236–41; in Western civilisation, 17–18

'analytic' approach to emotion, 132–40, 145–6, 148–9
Annas, J., 2, 24–7, 164n.
Antigone 193
Antiochus of Ascalon, 130
apatheia (absence of passion, tranquillity) 43, 100, 233–4; translation into Latin, 60–1
Apollonius of Rhodes 156, 222n.
apotropē (steering away), 104, 110
Archilochus, 156
Aristotle: on anger, 6, 16, 171–3, 175–7, 182, 186–7; on arousal of emotion, (in *Po.*) 131, 133, 135, (in *Rh.*) 112, 131, 133, 172, 186–7n.; cognitivist approach to emotions, 133–5; contrasted with Stoicism on emotions, 5, 10–14, 43–4, 128–31, 169–70, 182–4, 186–8, 223, 230–2, 239–41; and conventional thinking on emotions, 7–8, 12–14, 130–1, 148–9, 172–3, 186; on fear, 130, on the 'mean', 130, 171, 182; on hatred, 186–7, 191–2; three types of 'Aristotelian' approach to emotions, 6–8, 129–31; *see also* Peripatetic thought
Artemisia, 38
Asmis, E., 29
assent, 8, 22, 105, 109, 236
ataraxia (absence of disturbance, tranquillity), 10, 129, 164–5
atonia (flaccidity), 160
'audience-based' approach to emotion, 132–6, 139–41, 143–6, 148–9
audience-response: based on shared ethical values, 124–7; predictable, 112–13, 121–4; produced by visualisation, 115–21; in Stoic thinking on poetry, 102–11; cannot be determined by author, 107–10; *see also* internal audience
Averill, J. R., 17–19

260

Lightning Source UK Ltd.
Milton Keynes UK
UKOW051136110612

194211UK00002B/42/A